BEHAVIORAL PUBLIC FINANCE

BEHAVIORAL PUBLIC FINANCE

EDWARD J. MCCAFFERY AND JOEL SLEMROD
EDITORS

Russell Sage Foundation · New York

The Russell Sage Foundation

Library of Congress Cataloging-in-Publication Data

Behavioral public finance / Edward J. McCaffery and Joel Slemrod, editors.
    p.   cm.
Includes bibliographical references and index.
ISBN 0-87154-597-7
    1. Finance, Public—Psychological aspects.   2. Economics—Psychological aspects.   3. Emotions and cognition.   4. Finance, Public—Decision making.
5. Human behavior—Economic aspects.   I. McCaffery, Edward J.
II. Slemrod, Joel.
HJ141.B42 2006
336'.001'9—dc22   2005044938

Text design by Suzanne Nichols.

RUSSELL SAGE FOUNDATION
112 East 64th Street, New York, New York 10021
10 9 8 7 6 5 4 3 2 1

Contents

Contributors

Edward J. McCaffery is Robert C. Packard Trustee Chair in Law and Political Science at the University of Southern California and visiting professor of law and economics at the California Institute of Technology.

Joel Slemrod is Paul W. McCracken Collegiate Professor of Business Economics and Public Policy, director of the Office of Tax Policy Research in the Stephen M. Ross School of Business, and professor of economics at the University of Michigan.

Caroline Adams teaches psychology at the University of Plymouth, England.

Jonathan Baron is professor of psychology at the University of Pennsylvania.

James J. Choi is assistant professor of finance at the Yale School of Management.

Terrence Chorvat is associate professor in the George Mason University, School of Law.

John Cullis is reader in economics in the Department of Economics and International Development at the University of Bath in England.

Henk Elffers is senior researcher at the Netherlands Institute for the Study of Crime and Law Enforcement and professor of psychology and law at Antwerp University in Belgium.

Richard A. Epstein is James Parker Hall Distinguished Service Professor of Law at the University of Chicago and Peter and Kirsten Bedford Senior Fellow at the Hoover Institution.

Hanming Fang is associate professor of economics at Yale University and faculty research fellow of the National Bureau of Economic Research.

Lee Anne Fennell is associate professor of law at the University of Illinois College of Law.

Bruno S. Frey is professor of economics at the University of Zurich and research director of CREMA (Center for Research in Economics, Management and the Arts).

Howell E. Jackson is John S. Reid, Jr., Professor of Law at Harvard University.

Philip Jones is professor of economics in the Department of Economics and International Development at the University of Bath in England.

David Laibson is professor of economics at Harvard University.

Alan Lewis is professor of economic psychology in the Department of Psychology at the University of Bath in England.

George Loewenstein is professor of economics and psychology in the Department of Social and Decision Sciences at Carnegie Mellon University.

Brigitte C. Madrian is associate professor of business and public policy and Boettner Chair in Financial Gerontology at the Wharton School of the University of Pennsylvania.

Andrew Metrick is associate professor of finance at the Wharton School of the University of Pennsylvania.

Dan Silverman is assistant professor of economics at the University of Michigan and faculty research fellow of the National Bureau of Economic Research.

Deborah A. Small is assistant professor of marketing at the Wharton School of the University of Pennsylvania.

Jeff Strnad is Charles A. Beardsley Professor of Law at Stanford Law School.

Alois Stutzer is lecturer of economics at the University of Zurich.

Paul Webley is professor of economic psychology and deputy vice-chancellor at the University of Exeter in England.

PART I

PSYCHOLOGY, ECONOMICS, AND ECONOMETRICS

Chapter 1

Toward an Agenda for Behavioral Public Finance

EDWARD J. MCCAFFERY AND JOEL SLEMROD

THIS chapter is about the intersection—or the possible intersection—between the fields of behavioral economics and public finance, which we call behavioral public finance. Public finance is a venerable field in the economics fold. Its positive and normative branches rest on two basic assumptions. One, and central to public finance's positive agenda, is that individuals are rational, maximizing agents, in the simple sense that they act consistently on the basis of a well-defined utility function.[1] We call this the rationality assumption. Two, and central to public finance's normative agenda, is that the basis for evaluating social policies should be the well-being of society's members, as they judge this well-being to be. We call this the consumer sovereignty principle.

Behavioral economics, in contrast, is a newcomer on the social science field. It rests on a series of empirical challenges to the rationality assumption that can, if taken to a certain limit, call the consumer sovereignty principle into question. Perhaps because of this perceived nihilistic possibility—or simply because it represents a challenge to received orthodoxy—skeptics continue to question both the facts and the relevance of behavioral economics to any field of study.

Given this inherent tension, can behavioral public finance be a happy marriage?

We believe—however tentatively—that it can. We are more certain that it is important to try and advance the union. To the extent that behavioral economics rests on empirically verifiable (and verified) understandings about how real people think, choose, decide, and act in real-life settings, public finance models that aim for real-world relevance ought to take behavioral insights into account. This does not mean abrogating traditional public finance wholesale, or abandoning consumer sovereignty principles. As in all marriages, there will be give and take; the whole will be different from—and at least potentially better than—the sum of the parts. The challenge—as in any marriage—is to keep the lines of communication open.

After some additional background comments on the two disciplines, we illustrate the possible relevance of behavioral public finance with three broad clusters of questions, concerning the forms of public finance mechanisms, problems of intertemporal choice, and models of taxpayer compliance. We mean these examples to be suggestive, not definitive. We invite the reader to consider more examples, some of which are provided in the other chapters in this volume.

Three Faces of Public Finance

Public finance has been a principal concern of economics at least since Adam Smith. Its subject matter is the role of the government in addressing society's economic tasks, regarding both the allocation of scarce resources and their distribution or redistribution. Indeed, as classically divided by Richard Musgrave (1959), public finance consists of two parts, a government expenditure and revenue-raising aspect or, in more colloquial terms, tax and spending dimensions. Public finance also divides naturally into descriptive or positive analysis versus prescriptive or normative analysis. Positive analysis seeks to understand the actual effects of government tax and spending programs on the behavior of individuals and businesses and on the well-being of individuals. Normative analysis seeks, by contrast, to establish guidelines for what the government should—and should not—do. Answers to fundamental normative questions inevitably depend on values to which economic analysis cannot contribute directly, but these answers also depend on the positive analysis to which public finance can speak. The discipline can lay out the costs and benefits—the welfare implications—of various alternative government actions.

On the spending or allocative side, the most fundamental question is why do anything—what the role of the public sector should be. Within the neoclassical welfare framework familiar to economists, free and private markets generally work to achieve an efficient allocation, defined as an equilibrium outcome where no one could be made better off without making someone else worse off, the Paretian condition. The case for any particular government expenditure program must therefore turn on some demonstration of a market failure, such as the presence of a public good, externality or, increasingly, an informational asymmetry. In the case of any market failure, government intervention can, at least in theory, increase social wealth and welfare, improving allocative efficiency.

Public finance also looks to the distribution or redistribution of social wealth, whether the income distribution is taken to be a public good or not (Thurow 1971), because the free market alone does not necessarily give rise to an attractive distribution of society's collective resources. In contemporary advanced democracies, public tax and transfer programs actually comprise a larger share of the economy than do more traditional tax and spending programs.

In the neoclassical framework, public finance seeks both to describe what policies maximize social welfare by alleviating market failures (as by providing public goods) in an allocatively efficient manner, and to redistribute the (greater) social wealth to achieve a more desirable distribution of resources (Mirrlees 1971; Kaplow and Shavell 2002).

Another shoe falls inevitably because government spending and transfer programs require government revenues. Public finance thus considers the appropriate structure of taxation. The ideal tax would be a lump sum or per capita one, because it would not distort behavior and thus not affect the allocation of resources. But given the infeasibility of such first-best or non-distortionary taxation, public finance economists have developed sophisticated analyses of optimal taxation (Ramsey 1927; Mirrlees 1971; Atkinson 1996). But adopting optimal tax systems in real-world settings—even bracketing the difficult social choice problems of agreeing on the appropriate welfare function in the first place—is problematic (Slemrod 1990). Public finance economists thus go beyond the pure theory of tax to consider compliance and administration, attempting to minimize the transaction costs of tax in the real world. As part of its core mission, public finance studies the behavioral response of individuals and firms to alternative tax systems. Its goal is to understand and predict both revenue effects and the deadweight costs of various alternative tax regimes and reforms—that is, to understand the inputs needed for the normative theory of optimal tax to point to best practices, for example, the labor supply elasticities needed to implement optimum income tax policies—and the tradeoffs entailed in second-best, real-world settings.

In addition to these two traditional functions of public finance—tax and spending or transfer—government now often pursues a third function through its legally sanctioned control over fiscal matters. Government today acts to modify behaviors, not as an unavoidable by-product of its usual tasks, such as taxation, but purposefully in response to a perceived need to induce people to behave more "appropriately." Under what, if any, circumstances government should engage in this sort of activity is a part of the challenging intersection between behavioral economics and traditional economics. Within the neoclassical framework, taxes have long been advocated as a tool to correct for externalities, or (equivalently) the problem of social cost diverging from private cost (Pigou 1951).[2] Today, however, the government often acts through fiscal mechanisms in one of two ways: first, to encourage what are arguably goods (charitable giving, savings) beyond what people would choose on their own; second, to discourage what are arguably bads (smoking, drinking). In either case, traditional externality-correcting grounds may or may not guide it (Gruber and Kőszegi 2002; O'Donoghue and Rabin 2003; Sunstein and Thaler 2003). This expansion of the domain of public finance raises questions under and about the consumer sovereignty principle.

The New Kid on the Block

In contrast to welfare economics, behavioral economics is a fledgling in the field of social science. It has roots in the seminal work of Herbert Simon (1955) on "bounded rationality," and grew enormously under the guidance of Daniel Kahneman and Amos Tversky (1979), who argued that there are two broad features of human judgment and decision making. One aspect involves various errors in coding mechanisms—how matters are understood, or entered into mental processes—known as heuristics and biases. These lead to violations of the laws of logic and consistency. The second aspect consists of evaluatory functions that differ from the expected utility function of the neoclassical rational choice models (von Neumann and Morgenstern 1944; Savage 1954). Other treatments (Thaler 1980, for example) differ in terminology and detail, but share the characteristic of showing that real people do not follow logically consistent choice and decision protocols. By now abundant experimental and real-world observed evidence (Camerer 2000)—buttressed by common sense—confirms that individuals do not always think and act in ways consistent with the standard, and limited, axioms of rational choice (List 2004).

With the recent Nobel Prize awarded to Kahneman, the field of behavioral economics is blossoming.[3] But it would be premature to say that it has yet reached full flower. In particular, the area self-consciously lacks a general field theory of human behavior, let alone one that would be as parsimonious as the rational agent model (Camerer 1990; Epstein 2003). Indeed, behavioral economics rests on a rejection—of the axiom of rational agency—rather than on the affirmation or acceptance of any specific alternative theory of human behavior and thought. Given this, care must be taken in extending behavioral models to new fields. But there are also compelling reasons to go forward.

The most compelling is to resolve the fundamental questions that deviations from rationality pose to normative public finance. If preferences are inconsistent, how can any lawmaker choose which one is "correct"?

What does the consumer sovereignty principle even mean in the face of consumer inconsistency? Having established that individuals sometimes make decisions that are apparently inconsistent with rational choices serving a stable objective or utility function, how does government go about substituting an alternative metric for evaluating the success or failure of policies? If, as we discuss later, the form in which public policies are presented matters for decisions, what is the appropriate form? And are we even sure that all heuristics and biases are problems, or sources of inefficiency, that ought to be corrected?

This volume does not by any means resolve these questions. It means rather to raise them, and others like them, and, in addressing the various questions from many empirical and theoretical perspectives and disciplines, to begin to construct a multidisciplinary program to make progress toward answering them.

Behavioral Public Finance: Three Views of a Possible Cathedral

Here we sketch out three broad clusters of questions raised by behavioral public finance. We mean this discussion to be illustrative, both of the range of issues within each cluster and of the field of behavioral public finance itself. It does not even purport to be a systematic survey of what is included in this volume.

Form Matters: Framing and Other Optics of Public Finance

A central descriptive component of behavioral economics is that form matters. Contrary to the dictates of ideal rationality, whereby the substance or underlying reality of various alternative states of the world ought solely to matter, the purely formal aspects of a choice or decision set often affect substantive outcomes. This leads to violations of such basic rational choice axioms as transitivity and the independence of irrelevant alternatives: preference shifts and reversals can turn on logically irrelevant matters such as how a choice set is described.[4] One cluster of questions for behavioral public finance turns on these violations of the rationality assumption: what implications do citizen heuristics and biases have for central public finance questions?

Consider, for example, the framing effect, under which individuals respond to the rhetorical characterization of a constant set of facts, such as preferring a half-full to a half-empty glass (McCaffery and Baron 2004b; Levin et al. 2002). An instance of framing relevant to public finance is the metric effect. Subjects react differently depending on the unit in which a question is posed, preferring, for example, a tax system featuring higher taxes when asked about taxes in percent rather than in dollar terms (McCaffrey and Baron 2003). Other examples include penalty aversion, wherein people prefer policies described as bonuses to their punitive converse (child bonuses versus childless penalties); the Schelling effect, wherein people want progressive bonuses (more for the poor than the rich) and progressive penalties (higher for the rich than the poor), which are inconsistent given a trivial framing manipulation; and tax aversion, wherein people prefer government surcharges described as something other than a tax, such as a payment or user fee (McCaffery and Baron 2003; Schelling 1978; Eckel, Grossman, and Johnston 2005). Real-world evidence suggests that successful politicians have at least intuited many of these heuristics and biases.

In the variously described endowment effect, loss aversion, status quo bias, or reference-dependent utilities (Kahneman, Knetsch, and Thaler 1986), subjects react differently depending on their perception of the baseline or status quo: experiencing more disutility from a loss off a high baseline than from a corresponding failure to obtain a gain from a low baseline. The baseline itself can be set arbitrarily—as a matter of framing—and still affect choice. In a classic example from Thaler, individuals will use cash to avoid a penalty for using credit cards at the gas pump, but will foreswear from using cash to obtain a bonus for doing so, on the same facts (for example, $1.90 a gallon for cash, $2.00 for credit cards). In public finance, the endowment effect may lead to a "stickiness" of public goods, such as Social Security benefits: once in place, citizens will react to their loss more harshly than to the failure to obtain an equivalent good. The endowment effect is also one reason why socially set default rules can matter (Sunstein and Thaler 2003), and why citizens might prefer fully hidden taxes to more transparent ones (McCaffery and Baron 2004a).

Individuals also employ mental accounts, fail to integrate across similar categories, or suffer from an isolation effect (Thaler 1999; McCaffery and Baron 2003). Although money is fungible in the rational model—a matter of substance—individuals often react as if different sources of wealth (a matter of form) map up with different uses: seeing lottery proceeds, for example, as windfalls that need not be devoted to ordinary wants and needs. In public finance, this effect can interact with the now well-documented flypaper effect (Hines and Thaler 1995) as well as with the endowment effect to suggest that there is path dependence to fiscal outcomes. Revenue sources flow to certain particular public uses and stick there, making reallocation of funds to higher and better public (or private) uses difficult.

In a related disaggregation effect (McCaffery and Baron 2003), individuals have a difficult time integrating parallel but separate systems to form consistent global judgments. Thus, for example, it is hard for individuals to keep in their minds the structure of the payroll tax system when making decisions about the appropriate level of progression in the income tax. This disaggregation (or isolation) effect suggests that citizens will be hard pressed to understand how changes in one tax, such as a negative rate bracket under the income tax, can compensate for the structure of other taxes, such as the absence of a zero bracket under the payroll tax system. The effect also suggests that many smaller taxes can add up to a greater total tax burden, with the same psychic discomfort, as fewer larger taxes, because people do not sum them up fully in their minds (McCaffery and Baron 2003). Consider also the possible privatization of presently publicly provided goods. The two welfare theorems of neoclassical welfare economics suggest that whether a good or service is provided publicly, and, if so, how, should be decided by standard welfare maximizing principles. Suppose, for example, that privatization of a particular good or service would be more efficient, meaning that social welfare would increase if public provision ceased. The greater social wealth generated by privatization could then be redistributed to meet the Paretian constraint. But the disaggregation effect suggests that subjects may not redistribute sufficiently in the tax system, standing alone, to counterbalance the effect of the privatization: they do not integrate tax and spending decisions, to use changes in tax to compensate for the losers from spending cuts (see chapter 4, this volume). This possibility pits efficiency against equity.

This overview suggests the stakes for behavioral public finance in terms of certain by now well-noted violations of the rationality assumption. One, as long as the form of public finance matters, politics will turn to at least some extent on formal matters or rhetoric. Politicians will invest time and money in rhetoric, and the better rhetoricians—or salespeople—will have an advantage. Two, and worse, public finance may be unstable, because different frames can elicit preference reversals, the key finding of the Kahneman and Tversky framing literature. As new actors enter the political scene and set new frames, public opinion may shift, supporting a high level of turnover, as it were, in public finance systems, with the attendant transition and transaction costs (Feldstein 1976). Three, and worst of all, real wealth can be left on the table, an homage to cognitive illusions, if the more attractively framed public finance form is not the one that maximizes social welfare. Politicians may choose to please voters with an inefficient tax or spending program; taxes have real effects, independent of their optical or cognitive properties. Here is an example of where public finance, as traditionally practiced, matters: it can tell us the welfare costs of various alternative tax and spending arrangements, laying bare, as it were, the costs of popular illusions, as in a preference for distorting but hidden taxes.

Individuals' cognitive biases may also affect their behavioral responses to tax and other public finance mechanisms, a central concern of public finance. What behavioral assumptions should lawmakers employ when modeling the effects of tax or other public finance reform? Do for example citizens react differently to something called a tax as opposed to something else? Recent experimental work on the crowding out hypothesis suggests that they do, reducing their charitable contributions when taxes go to the charity, but not when unlabeled exactions do (Eckel, Grossman, and Johnston 2005). Do the observed labor and capital supply elasticities to tax law changes reflect behavior biases? And so on. As a matter of applied public finance, we need models that are behaviorally realistic, and the insights of behavioral economics may be indispensable in such settings.

And so various actors in public finance—lawmakers, citizens, and taxpayers—can have various biases, interacting in complex and multidimensional ways. Putting it all together—that is, sketching out a full political economy model of public finance with behavioral biases in play—is beyond the scope of the present essay. Such a task is one of the great potential projects for the field of behavioral public finance. But we can say a few things about what such a project might look like. It is by now well accepted that utility-maximizing applies to politicians as much as to ordinary citizens. Gary Becker (1983) has argued for a model in which politicians reward pressure groups with favors (tax breaks, spending programs, and so on), constrained by the opposition of the residual taxpayer class. In the Becker model, equilibrium is reached when efficient interest groups are rewarded by efficient taxes. But what if some taxes produce less psychic pain, strictly on account of their formal properties, than others? Taxes, even hidden ones, have real effects on prices, regardless of their perceived burden. What if politicians are choosing suboptimal taxes, from a welfare maximizing perspective, to make citizens feel better because of the form of the tax? The celebrated social pie will shrink on account of the choice.

One reason for concern is that the lawmakers themselves may be biased. Much evidence suggests that frequent players in private markets overcome heuristics and biases (see List 2003, 2004). After all, success in private markets is measured by the objective benchmark of wealth, and turns on matters of skill. The cognitively disadvantaged is economically disadvantaged as well. In public settings, by contrast, political success turns to a considerable degree on rhetorical skill. It may be that successful policy makers are indeed subject to the same type of cognitive biases we have just catalogued. Indeed, being subject to popular biases might even help politicians to be more communicative with their fellow citizens: the lawmaker who really believes it important to "get corporations to pay their fair share" is a better salesperson than one who is conscious of the deceit involved. The subject of behavioral public choice can complement the field of public choice that James Buchanan and others have championed. If not exactly a theory of the blind leading the blind, behavioral public choice might be a theory of the cognitively biased leading the cognitively biased, without the same disciplining mechanisms of the private sector to help see us all through the maze.

Whenever distortions arise—from cognitively disadvantaged or brilliantly savvy lawmakers—a related question is, where behavioral heuristics and biases have led to suboptimal public finance structures, can some form of debiasing mechanism improve welfare, measured from a more enlightened or consistent set of preferences? Suppose, that is, that individuals prefer hidden taxes over direct ones, in part because of loss aversion: they do not notice a loss when they have failed to obtain the gain in the first place. This might, for example, explain the persistence and popularity of the corporate income tax, which diverts resources from their otherwise ultimate placement in private hands, such that its ultimate incidence is difficult to ascertain (McCaffery 1994; McCaffery and Baron 2004a). Suppose further that the corporate income tax is more distorting, in a traditional public finance, welfare economic meaning, than alternative sources of revenue—and perhaps suppose, too, that the hidden tax does not simply replace other, more transparent taxes, but leads instead to a larger government (Hines and Thaler 1995; Becker and Mulligan 2003). In such a case real wealth is being left on the table, a sacrifice to cognitive illusion and inconsistency. Should public finance help to lay bare the illusions? And, if so, how?

One way is to educate citizens to better understand public finance. Here again the fundamental things apply. Understanding that true or ultimate incidence diverges from nominal or statutory incidence, and that corporations are not real people, is not all that complex, whatever the final truth of the incidence puzzle happens to be. But widespread education in areas where the average person has little experience or political efficacy will be challenging. It is not clear who has the time and resources to take on the chore.

A second way is to rely on various arbitrage mechanisms, that is, structural devices to counterbalance the effects of irrational biases. The paradigms in private finance are the market and competition itself. Even if some—most?—agents are irrational, and tend to buy high and sell low, markets can be expected to counteract the bias and appropriately value securities, as long as there is at least one rational actor without liquidity constraints. Individual investors may still incur losses but the price system will be on net efficient, diminishing the aggregate harm to social welfare. Similarly, competition in consumer markets keeps prices at marginal cost, however much some individual agents might be able to be tricked into paying more. Arbitrage in this sense is a comforting tale in private markets, though some behavioralists doubt its accuracy or at least its breadth (Barberis and Thaler 2003). Be that as it may, there is no obvious arbitrage mechanism in public finance, where the presence of lawmakers creates a principal-agent problem at the core that we discuss further. Indeed, public finance can be defined as the study of nonmarket economic activity. Standard rational choice gives reason to fear the difference. Whereas in private markets arbitrage of the sort described is a private good, the benefits of which can inure to the individual agent, in public finance arbitrage is a public good, the benefits of which inure to the general public (McCaffery and Baron 2004a). A short seller in a financial market, for example, can capture profits from the irrational exuberance (if such it is) of others; but the political actor who aims to lay bare the illusion of hidden taxes, say, can have no assurance that he, personally—or even his political party generally—will benefit from any efficiency gains. Standard rational choice theory predicts that debiasing or arbitrage in the public sector will be undersupplied, increasing the stakes for behavioral public finance.

Finally, a third means out of the suboptimal state that the intersection of cognitive biases and politics may lead us to involves constraining the political process. There is evidence from behavioral economics that quick or hot judgments are more distorted, and less consistent, than calm and cool ones: a reason to delay and "strike while the iron is cold" sometimes (see Noll and Krier 1990). Balanced budget amendments or paygo rules that force legislators to designate new revenue sources for new spending programs, or to cut specific spending programs to offset tax cuts, may have the salutary effect of bringing all data into full view, undercutting the isolation effect and making for calmer, more consistent judgments.

Absent some cure, in education, arbitrage, or self-binding constraints on decision making, the aggregate effect of all the various heuristics and biases on the big questions of public finance is not clear. Will government be too big? Too slanted towards programs with highly salient, short-term benefits? Too dependent on hidden, excessively distorting taxes? These central questions of public finance should be reexamined in the light of what we are learning about cognitive biases. If the result of the biases is a collection of tax and expenditure program elements that resemble the packaging, price presentation, and product placement one encounters at the local supermarket, then the stakes are not necessarily high. But recall again the disciplining effect of private markets, missing at least in part from government actions. What if, in public finance, Smith's celebrated invisible hand is replaced with an invisible sleight of hand?

Time Matters Too: Time Inconsistency and Problems of Self-Control

The first cluster of questions concerned an array of heuristics and biases that call the rationality assumption into question, rewarding rhetoric among politicians, making public finance potentially volatile, and running the risk of leaving real wealth on the table. A second cluster of questions concerns a more specific set of inconsistencies, which calls into the question the very meaning of the consumer sovereignty principle.

Specifically, many people seem to have intertemporal preferences that are not only present-oriented but also time-inconsistent. People act as if they do not have the self-control to resist behavior that has short-term benefits but larger long-term costs. There is also considerable evidence that many people misforecast their own future preferences: as two future periods get closer, they give higher relative weight to consumption in the earlier period. One particular form of time inconsistency, known as hyperbolic discounting, has attracted much recent attention (Phelps and Pollak 1968; Laibson 1997; O'Donoghue and Rabin 1999). Under it, the discount factor between consecutive future periods is constant but far smaller than the discount factor between the next period and the immediately present one, leading to a rolling present-tense bias.

This phenomenon has potentially profound implications for both the positive and normative aspects of public finance. These implications for behavior depend to some extent on whether people are aware that, once the next period arrives, they will again become impatient with respect to the new current period and the new next period. If a person is sophisticated enough to realize that she will change her mind in the future, she can make decisions now accordingly. In particular, it may be advantageous to pursue self-commitment devices that limit future choices, like Ulysses did when he bound himself to the mast as his ship passed the Sirens' sweet song.

Related time-inconsistency models have important applications to saving and retirement decisions; people seem to save too little on their own, all but certain to later rue the day they failed to save more. This kind of myopia has been used as a justification for a system of compulsory saving like Social Security, and even for specific design features such as the payment of benefits only as annuities (Aaron 1999). O'Donoghue and Rabin (1999) explore how time-inconsistent people will tend to procrastinate in preparing for retirement, and suggest that default investment options and imposing deadlines on financial decisions might satisfy a criterion of cautious paternalism—valuable for people who are making errors, but with relatively small costs for people who are fully rational. Experience has shown that default rules can have a powerful influence on the saving behavior of employees (see chapter 11; see also Thaler and Benartzi 2004).

More recently, models of intertemporal choice have been applied to addictive and harmful commodities, defined as those goods for which past consumption increases the attractiveness of current consumption, and for which future costs are large relative to present benefits. Imagine that the consumers of such goods are rational and forward-looking, in the sense of Becker and Murphy (1988), but also have time-inconsistent intertemporal preferences and are unable to overcome the self-control problems these preferences imply. In this setting there is a justification for "sin taxes" that help prevent present selves from acting for their own future harms. The optimal sin tax can be calculated using the standard optimal taxation framework, assuming that the policy objective is to maximize utility based on long-term preferences rather than those that guide the actual decisions—another example of using standard public finance, welfare economics tools with a behavioral twist. Jonathan Gruber and Botond Köszegi (2002) estimate the optimal tax on cigarettes to be at least $1 per pack, and quite likely much higher.[5] Furthermore, the utility or deadweight cost of a tax on a harmful addictive good is lower than for a nonaddictive good because the consumer places a positive value on the self-control provided by the higher price. Indeed, Gruber and Köszegi argue that for a wide range of parameter values, levying a tax on an addictive commodity will on net benefit the addicted person.

The welfare analysis of optimal cigarette taxes is another illustration of a fundamental question posed by behavioral public finance. When welfare economics seeks to maximize the satisfaction of individual preferences, as it typically does, which preferences should it use? The fact that the individual is impatient when faced with a choice between today and tomorrow, but would like to become patient in the future, creates a conflict between the current self and the future self. This type of question is acute when time inconsistency is in play. If policy makers know that citizens want to spend (smoke) today, but are likely to rue their failure to save (quit smoking) tomorrow, which set of preferences—which self—should they choose to please?

Note that the structure of the paternalistic argument has moved from arguing that a judicious setting of a default rule can benefit many people while harming none, because of the option to opt out (Sunstein and Thaler 2003), to arguing that an inescapable tax on certain behaviors can benefit precisely the people who behave in the targeted way. This is a dramatic change. In traditional public finance terms, one may be concerned about high taxes on cigarettes, alcohol, or unhealthy eating habits, for example, on both vertical and horizontal equity grounds. Take cigarettes. Gruber and Köszegi (2001) present data showing that the share of income spent on cigarettes is eight times as high for the bottom income quartile compared to the top quartile, and is four times as high when the quartiles are defined by consumption, arguably a better indicator of lifetime income. But when the self-control problem joins the model, the beneficial effect of the tax on the smoker's own welfare undercuts the apparent regressivity of cigarette taxes.[6] Of course, this only makes more pressing the normative question of which self or set of preferences is to count in the analysis—today's happy smoker, or tomorrow's dying patient.

The possibility of widespread time inconsistency looms over one of the most daunting of today's public finance issues: the implications of future liabilities, as for Social Security and Medicare, on present government finances (Jackson 2004). A strictly rational choice or rational expectations perspective would suggest that citizens today account for all known future liabilities (Barro 1974). But do they? And, if they do not, are there mechanisms to make future liabilities more salient today? How should one even think about such problems under the consumer sovereignty principle, with the problems of this and the preceding cluster of behavioral issues in play? If people want to live for the moment, and let the future care for itself, running up large deficits or whatever in the meanwhile, who are we—who is any we—to tell them otherwise? As with the formal matters considered in the prior section, however, lesser and less paternalistic steps may help to lessen the problem. To the extent that time inconsistency is driven by the different salience of the present and the future, or on account of an isolation effect, then measures such as personal account statements, as discussed in chapter 10 in this volume, may lessen the problem.

Compliance Matters: Does Citizen Duty Trump Rational Self-Interest?

The first cluster of questions looked at inconsistencies and confusions in the popular perception of public finance system design; the second raised questions about how to even think about, let alone implement, welfare-improving fiscal policies in the light of behavioral inconsistencies. These are questions at least in part of high theory. The final cluster of questions concerns a more practical, but still central, subject matter for public finance: why do citizens pay taxes, and how can a government keep them doing so, and prevent them from not complying?

Once again, our intent here is to illustrate the range of issues that behavioral public finance can concern, not to weigh them. Compliance matters seem second order compared to the possible large distortions in efficiency and equity occasioned by widespread citizen cognitive errors, and different in magnitude, too, from the conceptual puzzles posed by time-inconsistent preferences. Still, the stakes in understanding tax compliance here can be high. Whatever the motivation, the fact is that the cost of raising taxes, and of running government, is lower to the extent that taxpayers "volunteer" to comply. This argument applies more broadly than to compliance with the tax system. Christopher Clague argues that "a society with very low levels of rule obedience cannot . . . have a net of institutions that is conducive to economic progress" (1993, 412).[7] Rational choice provides a simple paradigm for compliance, but is it rich enough to accommodate real world settings? Behavioral public finance may help to unify a broad and disparate set of challenges to the standard view that individuals' compliance behavior is best explained by a model of rational self-interested behavior constrained only by a deterring enforcement regime.

The rational choice story is simple. Because one's own benefit from government activity is, with some exceptions, not significantly affected by one's contribution, in the traditional model purely self-interested persons do not voluntarily contribute to a public good—that is, pay taxes—unless the threat of punishment makes it sensible. The standard public finance model of the demand for tax evasion, due to Allingham and Sandmo (1972), assumes free-riding to be ubiquitous. It models the compliance decision as a choice under uncertainty made by amoral individuals, whose decisions depend—strictly—on the chance of being caught and penalized, the penalty imposed, and one's risk aversion.

Looking at real world data, however, some have argued that the Allingham-Sandmo model is flawed: given the probability of audit and the penalties typically assessed, evasion seems to be a winning proposition for many more people than actually do evade.[8] This suggests that something is going on outside of the standard rational choice model—either in the utility functions, as in the altruistic and reciprocal altruism explanations, or in some failure of rationality, as in a misperception of the odds of detection. Although the first possibility need not venture into the field of behavioral economics (there is, after all, no disputing taste), the second might.

Although free-riding is indeed widespread, much experimental work (and anecdotal evidence) suggests that such behavior is also context specific. Ostrom (2000, 140) remarks that the finding that "the rate of contribution to a public good is affected by various contextual factors" is one of several phenomena that "have been replicated so frequently that these can be considered the core facts that theory needs to explain." What is going on? There is an active literature that seeks to determine to what extent such behavior is motivated by pure altruism, in the sense that people put positive value on the well-being of others unconditioned by their behavior, or reciprocal altruism, under which preferences over other people's well-being depend on the behavior, motivation, and intentions of those other people.[9] Either one of these behaviors would be rational, of course, although the factual bases for at least reciprocal altruism might not obtain, and any static level of compliance in a model depending on reciprocity is unlikely to be a stable equilibrium.

But it is also possible that "excessive" compliance might relate to an irrationality, a behavioral anomaly or inconsistency of some sort. Some have proposed substituting the expected-utility-maximization framework with an alternative framework, in the spirit of Kahneman and Tversky's 1979 prospect theory, that has immediate implications for the theory of tax evasion. Loss aversion relative to a reference point defined by no evasion will reduce the attractiveness of evasion, because the harm of getting caught will seem worse than the benefit from evading, even if the two are of equal magnitude. Much the same effect can be obtained by overweighting the low probabilities of detection and the penalties for evasion.[10] Dhami and al-Nowaihi (2004) argue that such a framework (and a stigma cost for discovered evasion) can more satisfactorily explain the level of observed evasion, the non-ubiquity of evasion, and the fact that tax rates negatively impact evasion.[11]

There are also indications that individuals' tax compliance behavior depends on variables that lie outside of the free-rider cost-benefit calculus. Some laboratory experiments have found that subjects respond not only to the probabilities and stakes of a tax evasion game, but also to context provided to them, though this finding is not widely documented.[12] Frey differentiates between the intrinsic and extrinsic motivation to comply with tax liabilities (1997). With intrinsic motivation, taxpayers pay because of civic virtue; with extrinsic motivation, they do so because of threat of punishment. Frey argues that increasing extrinsic motivation—say with more punitive enforcement policies—crowds out intrinsic motivation by making people feel that they pay taxes because they have to, rather than because they want to.[13]

If tax equity strengthens the social norm against evasion, then evasion becomes more costly in terms of bad conscience (if not caught) or bad reputation (if caught) in a society with a more equitable system (Falkinger 1995). An individual can also find unfairness in the wider public finance system due to the government's provision of the wrong goods—someone such as Thoreau may avoid taxes because he thinks government policy wrong. But this is not a simple matter. Expenditures on warfare might be tolerated in a patriotic period but rejected during one characterized by antimilitarism (Daunton 1998). Expenditure on welfare might at times be seen as a socially desirable pooling of risk, and at other times seen as a source of national decay. And so on.

All this behavior suggests that reciprocal altruism may be at work, but where the taxpayer's behavior depends on the behavior, motivations, and intentions not of any subset of particular individuals, but of the government itself. Some taxpayers may be willing to surrender some of their own potential advantages to effect a more fair distribution of outcomes, but only if they perceive the tax system and tax enforcement process overall to be fair. This characterization is very similar to the spirit of Levi (1998, 90), who argues that citizens are likely to trust government only to the extent that they believe that it will act in their interests, that its procedures are fair, and that their trust of the state and others is reciprocated.[14] Moreover, government trustworthiness, plus the perception that others are doing their share, can induce people to become "contingent consent-ers" who cooperate even when their short-term material self-interest would make free-riding the individual's best option. In Levi's words, "the willingness to pay taxes quasi-voluntarily or to give one's contingent consent to conscription often rests on the existence of the state's capacity and demonstrated readiness to secure the compliance of the otherwise noncompliant" (1998, 91).[15] Once again, this can be a strictly rational matter, a result of preferences, or the government's activities can make the penalties more salient, exacerbating a prospect-theory like effect.

It is notable that all of the literature about whether attitudes affect compliance applies to individual taxpayers, although in most countries the bulk of taxes are remitted (as opposed to borne, in the sense of ultimate incidence) by businesses, either because the taxes are levied on business entities or because labor income taxes are withheld by the employer. Whether a company's policy would react as an individual is a fascinating and open question, one that is related to the motivations behind corporate charitable contributions. This query applies more broadly— under what circumstances do organizations mitigate or perhaps exacerbate cognitive biases?[16]

In sum, behavioral public finance can contribute to an understanding of citizen compliance with the tax system as well as other fiscal measures to the extent that compliance decisions depend on factors beyond the rational self-interested calculus, such as nonstandard preferences and the reality and framing of what government does with the money it collects. Indeed, the idea that the behavioral response to tax and expenditure policies may hinge on how benevolently one views the purpose of those policies holds the promise of explaining a wide range of apparent behavioral anomalies discussed here.

Objections and Conclusions

We cannot conclude without at least noting that skeptics about the entire enterprise of behavioral economics are still out there. Some continue to deny that the various heuristics and biases exist, though this is getting increasingly difficult in the face of abundant experimental and real-world evidence. The most enduring critiques fall into two major (and somewhat related) camps. One holds that the biases might exist, but they are artifacts of the experimental design or other institutional settings in which they are found (Plott and Zeiler 2005). Better design, education, incentives and so on can mitigate or altogether eliminate the biases (List 2004). A second camp picks up the theme, as Barberis and Thaler (2003) and others note, of arbitrage mechanisms. Here, the reasoning goes, conceding that heuristics and biases exist and are even rampant—that individuals cannot and do not overcome them (individual-level debiasing, as through education, has its limits)—the biases do not much matter, because they do not materially affect how markets work. Systems solve individual errors. Thus, for example, behavioral economics may not pose a challenge to perhaps the most celebrated finding of the standard rational choice view, the efficient market hypothesis: even if almost all agents are irrational, markets can still work, in a fashion to do Adam Smith proud.

We find it interesting that many of the by-now standard responses to the perceived challenge of behavioral economics in private market domains depend on factors—learning, learning by doing, incentives, arbitrage mechanisms such as the market or the impersonal forces of competition—that may be altogether lacking and in any event are very different in the public setting. Inefficient structures ought not to persist long in private markets, as long as there are at least a few one-eyed persons in the land of the blind. But unless these people are also saints, public finance has a long way to go.

We thus suspect that much of the skepticism about incorporating behavioral economics into public finance is a resistance to abandoning the elegant and powerful conceptual structure currently used to evaluate economic policies. Embedded in the fundamental theorems of welfare economics, the conceptual structure implies that in the absence of market failures, an unfettered market economy will ensure efficiently, but not necessarily fairly, allocated resources. In the presence of market failures, government intervention can in principle, but not necessarily in practice, improve the efficiency of resource allocation unless the cost of government failures outweighs the benefit of alleviating the market failure. In considering behavioral public finance, we must confront the question of whether the cost of government failures will outweigh the benefits of alleviating human failure, in the sense of failure to act as the standard normative models presume. There is a fear that behavioralism would leave economics, public or otherwise, with nothing to do, certainly from a normative perspective: if preferences are inconsistent, they are inconsistent, and social science must end. We are not so pessimistic. We feel that this nihilistic approach short-sells the role of traditional public finance and what it can bring to behavioral economics. There are, it is worth noting, objectively valued goods, such as health and wealth. Inconsistent choices made under different frames can and do affect the quantity of these real goods. Thus traditional public finance can point out the welfare cost of hidden taxes, or sketch out the likely optimal savings policies for individuals. This can then lead to better debiasing mechanisms, such as accounting or cost-impact statements, or the setting of default rules in a manner likely to improve welfare, with opt-out provisions. In all these cases, we would never have seen any problem with the behavioral biases absent traditional, rational-choice-based public finance theory to show us the light.

Still, the skittishness that many economists feel about embracing behavioral perspectives is illustrated by the proliferation of terms recently applied to modify the word paternalism, the term we use to describe policies that override consumer sovereignty as the governing principle in the light of behavioral anomalies: benign, cautious, enlightened, libertarian, weak, to name a few of the more prominent modifiers (see, for example, Camerer et al. 2003; O'Donoghue and Rabin 2003; Sunstein and Thaler 2003). There are good reasons for this skittishness. In most cases, people's judgment of what is in their best interest is best. It is a safeguard against authoritarian government, as Richard Epstein reminds us. Overruling the choices that citizens—even confused, time-inconsistent, and downright irrational ones—make places tremendous responsibility on the benevolence of decision makers. For example, knowing the fact that many individuals respond to default rules can be useful in the possession of enlightened, benevolent decision makers, but history has shown that individuals' tendency to be obedient to authority can have horrible consequences. So care must be taken before pronouncing the union of behavioral and public finance economics permanent.

Yet in the end, none of this means that we as scholars should turn our heads from the reality of how real people make decisions in real situations. Instead, we more humbly suggest pursuing the research agenda that this essay outlines. The remaining chapters in this volume represent new research that addresses many of the nascent field's key issues. All save the last were presented in earlier forms at a conference at the Stephen M. Ross School of Business at the University of Michigan held on April 23 and 24, 2004, in Ann Arbor; a precursor conference had been held at the University of Southern California Law School on February 7 and 8, 2003. The topics of this research, and these chapters, are a sampler of what we feel the wider field should encompass.

The first chapters explore the idea that form and framing matter in public finance. George Loewenstein, Deborah A. Small, and Jeff Strnad draw out the implications of the well-documented identifiable victim effect in chapter 2. This is a bias whereby ordinary people show greater sympathy toward identifiable victims such as Baby Jessica or Free Willy the whale than toward statistical victims, such as the vast masses of people worldwide suffering from AIDS or malaria. This effect is relevant to fiscal policy in a large jurisdiction, when the costs and benefits of policies are spread widely. The authors stress that, though the identifiable victim effect is usually associated with an overreaction to identifiable victims, framing of public policies to capitalize on it can shift people's responses in a normatively desirable direction if people are insufficiently sympathetic toward statistical victims. In addition, the identifiable victim effect provides some conceptual underpinning for the political popularity of "hidden" taxes over those whose incidence is more easily assessed—

fully hidden taxes, like the corporate income tax, have *no* real, observable human victims at all.

Although behavioral economics has apparently identified several classes of systematic biases, not much progress has been made in providing a unifying model of behavior or general field theory that encompasses all biases. Indeed, most empirical analysis has focused on one bias at a time, though in many settings it is reasonable to suppose that multiple deviations from the standard model apply. Hanming Fang and Dan Silverman offer an exploratory treatment in chapter 3 of what is likely to be a major preoccupation of behavioral economics in the future—empirically distinguishing among biases. They illustrate the methodological problems and offer a few tentative solutions in the context of a simple model of welfare participation, an issue that is clearly important in public finance. In deciding whether to enroll for welfare benefits, potential participants may be subject to one or both of two well-documented cognitive biases: projection bias, in which people falsely project their current preferences over consumption onto their future preferences, and present bias, in which at any one point in time people excessively discount the immediate future. Although both projection and present bias may each suggest too much welfare use by some families (who value the benefits today), precisely how each of these biases affect labor supply and welfare program participation decisions has potential implications for policy design. If, for example, projection bias had an important influence on the decisions of welfare recipients, then programs that promote gradual transitions into work and thus permit low cost adaptation of preferences may be more successful in terms of attachments to the labor market than stronger pushes such as mandatory workfare or time limits. The opposite, however, may be true if present bias has a more important influence on the labor supply of the welfare-eligible: there is little reason for gradual transitions, because individuals are looking only or primarily at the present period. Fang and Silverman argue that individuals subject to both biases will exhibit different attitudes toward time limits and other welfare eligibility restrictions, both before and after such restrictions are implemented. In principle, then, one can empirically distinguish between the two and sharpen our understanding of the policy implications.

Jonathan Baron and Edward J. McCaffery pick up and continue this theme of the framing of public finance issues in chapter 4, studying tax progressivity and showing that in experimental settings ordinary subjects' preferences for bottom-line redistribution depends on the form of public finance mechanisms. They group many heuristics and biases under the common label of isolation effects. People make decisions on the basis of the information immediately before them, failing to integrate related matters in a wider data set. Most strikingly, most subjects want tax systems to reflect moderate levels of progressivity, with upper-income taxpayers contributing more in absolute and percent terms, and so on. When a government cuts goods and services in a privatization or down-sizing move, subjects continue to desire moderate progression in the re-maining, now smaller, tax system. But because cuts to goods and services provided equally to all taxpayers have a greater impact on the poor, the global tax-and-transfer system becomes less progressive. In fact, adding in reasonable replacement costs—made available to the subjects—shows that privatization can easily violate the Pareto constraint, because people will not adjust the tax system enough to offset the regressive effect of the spending cuts. This finding suggests that behavioral biases may pit eq-uity against efficiency, given the need or desire for widespread citizen support.

Bruno S. Frey and Alois Stutzer change directions in chapter 5 to look at the extent to which the political process will mitigate—or accentuate—the impact of individual biases. They focus on the systematic tendency of people to mispredict future utility by overemphasizing the lasting posi-tive effects of acquiring income and gaining status: activities featuring what the authors call extrinsic attributes. Utility from intrinsic attributes such as feelings of autonomy and communal well-being gets less weight. The consequences of mispredicting utility, such as working too hard for the wrong reasons, are not restricted to the private realm; mispredictions also affect people's behavior as citizens. This occurs in two ways. First, citizens evaluate government policy, often underestimating intrinsic at-tributes relative to extrinsic attributes. Second, in a perfectly competitive democratic system of party competition, the two parties may not be able to afford to deviate from the short-term evaluation of their program by the median voter, and have to provide a policy bundle with strong ex-trinsic attributes. However, the political process can also generate condi-tions such that citizens get a more detached view of their evaluation and become partly aware of their or others' misprediction of utility. More-over, in modern democracies, public discourse puts people's awareness of their anomalous behavior on the political agenda.

Lee Anne Fennell challenges us in chapter 6 to look beyond the pre-vailing view that the most important cognitive bias related to choice over time is hyperbolic discounting, very much related to the present bias Fang and Silverman discuss. Under hyperbolic discounting, the "dis-count rate" applied to the present and the immediate future period is always greater than the discounting among future periods, leading to under-saving and other problems, as relevant to chapter 11 on 401(k) savings plans. Fennell argues that individuals often display hyperopic behavior, wherein they choose a lower (or at least lower in present value) payoff received later, leading to over-saving (of all things). Such behav-ior is at least arguably rampant in the contexts of overwithholding for income tax liabilities, and foregoing the advance payment option under the earned income tax credit; both effectively entail making interest-free loans to the government. Fennell cautions that such behavior has many explanations that are consistent with other psychological evidence, such as a preference for improving sequences or as a precommitment device to overcome anticipated consumption self-control problems. Moreover, people often prefer to get dreaded events (paying taxes, for example) over with earlier rather than later. The chapter offers an excellent example of how a given behavior can be overdetermined by behavioral explanations, and how careful analysis, of the type suggested in the chapter by Fang and Silverman, is required to sort out what underlies the behavior.

The next three chapters—one conceptual and two empirical—turn to issues of tax compliance. Paul Webley, Caroline Adams, and Henk Elffers offer fascinating evidence in chapter 7 that the Allingham-Sandmo framework, in which individuals treat the decision to evade taxes or not as a rational choice under uncertainty, omits two concerns relevant to compliance with value added taxation in the United Kingdom. They find that both perceptions of fairness, which have no place in the standard framework, and mental accounting—the ownership of VAT liabilities— are predictive in explaining compliance among restaurant owners and other retailers. They speculate that their data suggest that because there is little flexibility in varying VAT rates, taxpayers concerned with fairness may react adversely to the lack of "horizontal equity," which may in turn undermine voluntary compliance.

Terrence Chorvat explores in chapter 8 what might explain the experimental and field findings that increases in the rate of detection and fines are often negatively correlated with compliance; another finding in tension with the standard rational choice explanation. Chorvat stresses the potential importance of intrinsic motivation (a term echoing Frey and Stutzer) that is conceptually separate from the deterrent effects of punishment for detected noncompliance, and argues that econometric and experimental economic evidence indicates that the tax system is able to take advantage of the trustworthiness one finds in society. An important point to emerge here is that, although tax system compliance is likely affected by the level of trust in society, the tax system itself also affects the trust level. If we have a relatively high trust society in which we can trust citizens to pay their taxes, then trusting the taxpayer is in fact reinforcing norms. If trustworthy behavior is not prevalent, however, and if individuals in particular are likely to cheat on their taxes, then relying on voluntary compliance mechanisms may actually decrease trustworthiness. To Chorvat, the proper question should not be so much whether higher rates of audit or fines can increase compliance, but whether they are the *best* way to increase compliance. This is particularly true if one accepts the notion that complying with tax laws may lead to greater trustworthiness in other areas of life. If compliance can increase by other ways, this is likely the optimal route to more tax revenue. However, deciding which mechanism to rely upon therefore calls for an understanding of the trustworthy behavior of the members of society.

John Cullis, Philip Jones, and Alan Lewis in chapter 9 also look beyond the Allingham-Sandmo deterrence model of tax evasion, calling into question the view of the taxpayer as an individual wealth-maximizer weighing up the costs and benefits of evasion and suggesting that, depending on the situation, taxpayers may or may not behave instrumentally. Based on a series of experiments with students, the authors conclude that, because compliance rates vary significantly depending on the audit rate, at least some respondents behave instrumentally. Instrumental reasoning and behavior are much more common among students of economics units who declare less taxable income in all scenarios than students studying psychology. Indeed the majority of psychology students declare all their income even when the probability of investigation is only 1 percent! The fact that an instruction to behave instrumentally or "to be yourself" has no statistically significant effect on compliance behavior suggests to the authors that instrumentality is not an immediately elastic choice, but rather comes almost naturally to economists who behave this way whether they are bidden to or not, whereas psychologists cannot bring themselves to do so even when explicitly asked. Moreover, the framing of taxation, as already withheld or yet to be paid, was statistically significant: when tax is yet to be paid it is perceived as a loss, thereby encouraging risk. This framing effect occurs whether one studies economics or psychology.

In chapter 10 Howell Jackson addresses a mechanism that might at first glance be seen as a partial cure for prevalent citizen cognitive errors: specifically, the statements sent out by the Social Security Administration to all eligible workers over the age of twenty-five. Although the greater information thus obtained might be thought to lead to better-informed citizens, Jackson asks instead how the contents of these statements may lead program participants to misinterpret the value of their Social Security benefits, making it difficult for participants to compare Social Security benefits to other retirement savings. In addition, the current Social Security statements obscure the extent to which additional years of labor market participation increase the value of Social Security benefits. Jackson describes how the current statements could be supplemented with estimates of the actuarial value of Social Security benefits. Although such information could mitigate the problems with the current statements, Jackson also notes the potential drawbacks of providing it, including the possibility that it might make the redistributive aspects of the system more transparent, potentially weakening support for the program among some constituencies.

James Choi, David Laibson, Brigitte Madrian, and Andrew Metrick take a step down from the world of high theory to study a pressingly practical problem in chapter 11, and offer rather precise (and simple) solutions. Specifically, they assess the impact of several different features of 401(k) plans on employee savings behavior. By examining the impact on employee plan choice when several large corporations implemented changes in their 401(k) plan design, the authors detected a persistent behavioral principle—that people often follow the path of least resistance. Almost always, the easiest thing to do is nothing whatsoever, a phenomenon the authors call passive decision. Passive decision making implies that employers have a great deal of influence over the savings outcomes of their employees. For example, and significantly, the employer choice of default savings rates and default investment funds strongly influences employee savings levels. Despite having the opportunity to opt out of defaults, many employees never do so. The authors find that, in companies without automatic enrollment, the typical employee takes over a year to enroll in their company-sponsored retirement plan. In contrast, in companies with automatic enrollment, employees overwhelmingly accept the automatic enrollment defaults, including default savings rates and default fund choice. Moreover, many plan participants allow the menu of investment funds to drive their asset allocation decisions. Finally, employees do succeed in raising their contribution rates if they are given a low-effort opportunity to sign up for an automatic schedule of increases in their contribution rate. This phenomenon has important implications for public policy because it implies that, for better or worse, plan administrators can manipulate the path of least resistance to influence the saving and portfolio choices of their employees. By implication, government regulations about plan design can affect pension—and probably saving—choices as well.

The noted libertarian Richard Epstein closes the book with an essay in which he asks some characteristically big, and skeptical, questions. He evaluates whether accepting the behavioral economics agenda makes it more plausible to favor a variety of paternalistic regulations whose main purpose is to protect individuals from their own biases and excesses. He argues that the key test for rationality is not whether individuals make mistakes, but whether they can resort to a range of personal, institutional, and market mechanisms to minimize the effects of these mistakes. For Epstein, differential susceptibility to cognitive biases, far from being a reason to reject markets, helps explain their configuration in a wide range of contexts, including employment and credit transactions; economic models of perfect competence are indispensable to indicate the steps that people must take to combat cognitive biases. He offers a cautious defense of libertarian paternalism and presents a critique of hard paternalism as against its softer rival. To illustrate his arguments, Epstein identifies the ambiguities in the use of libertarian paternalism to deal with sticky default provisions. He closes with a public choice and behavioral examination of Social Security reform, concluding that the public choice problems both dominate and exacerbate the cognitive difficulties that ordinary workers face in making their savings and consumption decisions.

These chapters reflect a wide range of scholarly methods and subject matters. But they all try to grapple with challenges at the intersection between behavioral economics, or the study of real human economic judgment and decision making, warts and all, and public finance, set in a modern era of very large government involvement in just about all aspects of our social and economic lives. As we all collectively struggle with issues about how to tax and spend, save for the future, and control our own behaviors, for better or for worse, in sickness and in health, in good times and in bad, we have little choice but to bless this marriage of disciplines, and hope for ever better answers to ancient but ever more pressing questions.

Notes

1. See Gary Becker: "Now everyone more or less agrees that rational behavior simply implies consistent maximization of a well-ordered function, such as a utility or profit function" (1962, 1).
2. This use of public finance mechanisms was harshly criticized by Ronald Coase (1960, 1988).
3. For good general surveys, see Daniel Kahneman and Amos Tversky (2000) and Jonathan Baron (2000). Matthew Rabin has been highly influential (1998).
4. That form matters in consumer decisions is well understood by marketing directors. Witness the proliferation of cereal boxes that cost $3.99 and gasoline that sells for $1.499 per gallon, and the ubiquity of discounting from "regular" prices. Aradhna Krishna and Joel Slemrod address to what extent marketers' insights can explain income tax design features (2003).
5. Ted O'Donoghue and Matthew Rabin carry out a similar exercise (2003).
6. Jonathan Gruber and Botond Köszegi conclude that, as long as the poor do not have life values and/or marginal damage from smoking very far below the rich, and as long as their discount rate is not much lower, the regressivity of cigarette taxes is reduced for sophisticated time-inconsistent smokers (2001).
7. The use of the term "obedience" will raise a red flag among those familiar with the psychology literature that addresses how people behave toward authority, because what psychologists have learned here is very unsettling. In perhaps the most controversial psychology experiment of all time, Stanley Milgram demonstrated that, if so instructed by an authority figure, most ordinary citizens would deliver apparently very painful electrical shocks to apparently innocent subjects (1974). That most people are malleable with re-

spect not only to the use of well-intentioned default rules and debiasing, but also to malevolent suggestions, raises concerns about the slippery slope of paternalistic policies. Here we just note this important issue, and leave the debate to the (behavioral) political scientists to pursue.

8. The evidence often cited for this claim—that an average audit rate for individual tax returns in the United States of less than 1 percent combined with what we know about risk aversion from other contexts suggests that compliance should be much, much lower—is flawed. A wage or salary earner whose employer submits this information electronically to the Internal Revenue Service (as on W-2 forms or 1099s), but who does not report that income on his own personal return, will be flagged for further scrutiny with a probability much closer to 100 percent than to 1 percent. Looking exclusively at areas where there is no strong system of third-party reporting—as for the self-employed, or for unregulated asset classes—the rate of compliance is far lower, getting closer to the rational choice model's predictions.

9. The theory and evidence concerning reciprocal altruism is summarized in Ernst Fehr and Klaus Schmidt (2003).

10. Michele Bernasconi and Alberto Zanardi explore the implications of reference dependence (2002). James Alm, Betty Jackson, and Michael McKee discuss experimental evidence that is consistent with the outweighing explanation (1992; see also Yaniv 1999).

11. Dhami and al-Nowaihi's numerical simulation exercises use parameters based on independent experimental evidence, but strain to explain why observed evasion is so low in light of an assumed probability of detection between 1 and 3 percent. As argued in endnote 8, however, the actual probability of detection for income subject to withholding and verifiable from third-party information returns is much higher than this, so that the expected utility model does not grossly under predict tax evasion of this kind of income, after all.

12. Michael Spicer and Lee Becker (1980) and Alm, Jackson, and McKee (1992) find support for this proposition. Frank Cowell reports on experiments that fail to find links between perceived inequities in the tax system and noncompliance (1990, 219). See also John Cullis and Alan Lewis (1997) and Robert Mason and Lyle Calvin (1984).

13. John Scholz and Mark Lubell, in an experimental setting, find that the level of cooperation in certain settings declines significantly when penalties are introduced, suggesting that the increased deterrence motivation did not compensate for the change in decision frame brought about by the penalties (2001).

14. Similarly, Lars Feld and Bruno Frey (2002) argue that to sustain citizens' commitment to the contract and therefore their morale, the tax authority must act respectfully toward citizens while at the same time protecting the honest from the free rider. It does this by giving taxpayers the benefit of the doubt when it finds a mistake, by sanctioning small violations more mildly, and by sanctioning large and basic violations (for example, the failure to file a return) more heavily.

15. Margaret Levi reminds us that military service is another important way that democratic governments are able to elicit both money and labor from

their populations in the face of tax evasion, draft evasion, and other forms of disobedience (1997).
16. Jennifer Arlen, Matthew Spitzer, and Eric Talley find some support for the idea that the endowment effect—the tendency to value goods more highly when one perceives an ownership of them—is lessened in the agency context familiar to the corporate world (2002).

References

Aaron, Henry J. 1999. "Retirement, Retirement Research, and Retirement Policy." In *Behavioral Dimensions of Retirement Economics*, edited by Henry J. Aaron. New York: Brookings Institution and Russell Sage Foundation.

Allingham, Michael G., and Agnar Sandmo. 1972. "Income Tax Evasion: A Theoretical Analysis." *Journal of Public Economics* 1(3/4): 323–38.

Alm, James, Betty R. Jackson, and Michael McKee. 1992. "Estimating the Determinants of Taxpayer Compliance with Experimental Data." *National Tax Journal* 45(1): 107–14.

Arlen, Jennifer H., Matthew L. Spitzer, and Eric Talley. 2002. "Endowment Effects Within Corporate Agency Relationships." *Journal of Legal Studies* 31(1): 1–37.

Atkinson, Anthony B. 1996. *Public Economics in Action: The Basic Income/Flat Tax Proposal.* Cambridge: Clarendon Press.

Barberis, Nicholas, and Richard Thaler. 2003. "A Survey of Behavioral Finance." In *Handbook of the Economics of Finance*, volume 1B, edited by George M. Constantinides, Milton Harris, and Rene M. Stultz. Amsterdam: Elsevier Science Publishers.

Baron, Jonathan. 2000. *Thinking and Deciding*, 3rd ed. New York: Cambridge University Press.

Barro, Robert J. 1974. "Are Government Bonds Net Wealth?" *Journal of Political Economy* 82(6): 1095–117.

Becker, Gary S. 1962. "Irrational Behavior and Economic Theory." *Journal of Political Economy* 70(1): 1–13.

———. 1983. "A Theory of Competition among Pressure Groups for Political Influence." *Quarterly Journal of Economics* 98(3): 371–400.

Becker, Gary S., and Casey B. Mulligan. 2003. "Deadweight Costs and the Size of Government." *The Journal of Law & Economics* 46(2): 293–340.

Becker, Gary S., and Kevin M. Murphy. 1988. "A Theory of Rational Addiction." *Journal of Political Economy* 96(4): 675–700.

Bernasconi, Michele, and Alberto Zanardi. 2002. "Tax Evasion, Tax Rates, and Reference Dependence." Mimeo, University of Bologna.

Camerer, Colin. 1990. "Comments on 'Some Implications of Cognitive Psychology for Risk Regulation,' by Roger Noll and James Krier." *Journal of Legal Studies* 19(2, part 2): 791–99.

———. 2000. "Prospect Theory in the Wild." In *Choices, Values, and Frames*, edited by Daniel Kahneman and Amos Tversky. Cambridge: Cambridge University Press.

Camerer, Colin, Samuel Issacharoff, George Loewenstein, Ted O'Donoghue, and Matthew Rabin. 2003. "Regulation for Conservatives: Behavioral Economics and the Case for 'Assymetric Paternalism.'" *University of Pennsylvania Law Review* 151(3): 1211–54.

Clague, Christopher. 1993. "Rule Obedience, Organizational Loyalty, and Economic Development." *Journal of Institutional and Theoretical Economics* 149(2): 393-414.

Coase, Ronald H. 1960. "The Problem of Social Cost." *The Journal of Law and Economics* 3(1): 1–44.

———. 1988. *The Firm, the Market and the Law*. Chicago: University of Chicago Press.

Cowell, Frank. 1990. *Cheating the Government*. Cambridge, Mass.: MIT Press.

Cullis, John G., and Alan Lewis. 1997. "Why People Pay Taxes: From a Conventional Economic Model to a Model of Social Convention." *Journal of Economic Psychology* 18(2/3): 305–21.

Daunton, Martin. 1998. "Trusting Leviathan: British Fiscal Administration from the Napoleonic Wars to the Second World War." In *Trust and Governance*, edited by Valerie Braithwaite and Margaret Levi. New York: Russell Sage Foundation.

Dhami, Sanjit, and Ali al-Nowaihi. 2004. "Why Do People Pay Taxes? Prospect Theory versus Expected Utility Theory." Mimeo. University of Leicester.

Eckel, Catherine C., Philip J. Grossman, and M. Rachel Johnston. 2005. "An Experimental Test of the Crowding Out Hypothesis." *Journal of Public Economics* 89(8): 1543–60.

Epstein, Richard A. 2003. *Skepticism and Freedom*. Chicago: University of Chicago Press.

Falkinger, Josef. 1995. "Tax Evasion, Consumption of Public Goods, and Fairness." *Journal of Economic Psychology* 16(1): 63–72.

Fehr, Ernst, and Klaus M. Schmidt. 2003. "Theories of Fairness and Reciprocity— Evidence and Economic Applications." In *Advances in Economics and Econometrics*, by Mathias Dewatripont, Lars Peter Hansen, and Stephen J. Turnovsky. Econometric Society Monographs, Eighth World Congress, vol. 1. Cambridge: Cambridge University Press.

Feld, Lars P., and Bruno S. Frey. 2002. "Trust Breeds Trust: How Taxpayers Are Treated." *Economics of Governance* 3(2): 87–99.

Feldstein, Martin. 1976. "On the Theory of Tax Reform." *Journal of Public Economics* 6(1/2): 77–104.

Frey, Bruno. 1997. "A Constitution for Knaves Crowds Out Civic Virtues." *Economic Journal* 107(443): 1043–53.

Gruber, Jonathan, and Botond Köszegi. 2001. "Is Addiction 'Rational'? Theory and Evidence." *Quarterly Journal of Economics* 116(4): 1261–303.

———. 2002. "A Theory of Government Regulation of Addictive Bads: Optimal Tax Levels and Tax Incidence for Cigarette Excise Taxation." NBER Working Paper No. 8777. Washington, D.C.: National Bureau of Economic Research.

Hines, James R., Jr., and Richard H. Thaler. 1995. "The Flypaper Effect." *Journal of Economic Perspectives* 9(4): 217–26.

Jackson, Howell. 2004. "Accounting for Social Security and its Reform." *Harvard Journal on Legislation* 41(1): 59–147.

Kahneman, Daniel, Jack L. Knetsch, and Richard H. Thaler. 1986. "Fairness as a Constraint on Profit Seeking: Entitlements in the Market." *American Economic Review* 76(4): 728–41.

Kahneman, Daniel, and Amos Tversky. 1979. "Prospect Theory: An Analysis of Decision under Risk." *Econometrica* 47(2): 263–91.

———, eds. 2000. *Choices, Values, Frames.* New York: Russell Sage Foundation.

Kaplow, Louis, and Steven Shavell. 2002. *Fairness versus Welfare.* Cambridge, Mass.: Harvard University Press.

Krishna, Aradhna, and Joel Slemrod. 2003. "Behavioral Public Finance: Tax Design as Price Presentation." *International Tax and Public Finance* 10(2): 189–203.

Laibson, David. 1997. "Golden Eggs and Hyperbolic Discounting." *Quarterly Journal of Economics* 112(2): 443–78.

Levi, Margaret. 1997. *Consent, Dissent, and Patriotism.* Cambridge: Cambridge University Press.

———. 1998. "A State of Trust." In *Trust and Governance,* edited by Valerie Braithwaite and Margaret Levi. New York: Russell Sage Foundation.

Levin, Irwin P., Gary P. Gaeth, Judy Schreiber, and Marco Lauriola. 2002. "A New Look at Framing Effects: Distribution of Effect Sizes, Individual Differences, and Independence of Types of Effects." *Organizational Behavior and Human Decision Processes* 88(1): 411–29.

List, John A. 2003. "Does Market Experience Eliminate Market Anomalies?" *Quarterly Journal of Economics* 118(1): 41–71.

———. 2004. "Neoclassical Theory versus Prospect Theory: Evidence from the Marketplace." *Econometrica* 72(2): 615–25.

Mason, Robert, and Lyle D. Calvin. 1984. "Public Confidence and Admitted Tax Evasion." *National Tax Journal* 37(4): 489–96.

McCaffery, Edward J. 1994. "Cognitive Theory and Tax." *UCLA Law Review* 41(7): 1861–1947.

McCaffery, Edward J., and Jonathan Baron. 2003. "The Humpty Dumpty Blues: Diasaggregation Bias in the Evaluation of Tax Systems." *Organizational Behavior and Human Decision Processes* 91(2): 230–42.

———. 2004a. "Heuristics and Biases in Thinking about Tax." In *Proceedings of the 96th Annual Conference on Taxation (2003).* Washington, D.C.: National Tax Association.

———. 2004b. "Framing and Taxation: Evaluation of Tax Policies Involving Household Composition." *Journal of Economic Psychology* 25(6): 679–705.

Milgram, Stanley. 1974. *Obedience to Authority: An Experimental View.* New York: Harper & Row.

Mirrlees, James A. 1971. "An Exploration in the Theory of Optimum Income Taxation." *Review of Economic Studies* 38(114): 175–208.

Musgrave, Richard. 1959. *The Theory of Public Finance.* New York: McGraw Hill.

Noll, Roger G., and James E. Krier. 1990. "Some Implications of Cognitive Psychology for Risk Regulation." *Journal of Legal Studies* 19(2): 747–79.

O'Donoghue, Ted, and Matthew Rabin. 1999. "Doing It Now or Later." *American Economic Review* 89(1): 103–24.

———. 2003. "Studying Optimal Paternalism, Illustrated by a Model of Sin Taxes." *American Economic Review* 93(2): 186–91.

Ostrom, Elinor. 2000. "Collective Action and the Evolution of Social Norms." *Journal of Economic Perspectives* 14(3): 137–58.

Phelps, Edmund S., and Robert A. Pollak. 1968. "On Second-Best National Saving and Game-Equilibrium Growth." *Review of Economic Studies* 35(2): 185–99.

Pigou, Arthur C. 1951. *A Study in Public Finance*, 3rd ed. London: Macmillan.

Plott, Charles R., and Kathryn Zeiler. 2005. "The Willingness to Pay—Willingness to Accept Gap, the 'Endowment Effect,' Subject Misconceptions, and Experimental Procedures for Eliciting Valuations." *American Economic Review* 95(3): 530–45.

Rabin, Matthew. 1998. "Psychology and Economics." *Journal of Economic Literature* 36(1): 11–46.

Ramsey, Frank P. 1927. "A Contribution to the Theory of Taxation." *Economic Journal* 37(145): 47–61.

Savage, Leonard J. 1954. *The Foundations of Statistics*. New York: John Wiley & Sons.

Schelling, Thomas C. 1978. "Ergonomics, or the Art of Self-Management." *American Economic Review* 68(2): 290–94.

Scholz, John T., and Mark Lubell. 2001. "Cooperation, Reciprocity, and the Collective Action Heuristic." *American Journal of Political Science* 45(1): 160–78.

Simon, Herbert A. 1955. "A Behavioral Model of Rational Choice." *Quarterly Journal of Economics* 69(1): 99–118.

Slemrod, Joel. 1990. "Optimal Tax and Optimal Tax Systems." *Journal of Economic Perspectives* 4(1): 157–78.

Spicer, Michael W., and Lee A. Becker. 1980. "Fiscal Inequity and Tax Evasion: An Experimental Approach." *National Tax Journal* 33(2): 171–75.

Sunstein, Cass M., and Richard H. Thaler. 2003. "Libertarian Paternalism Is Not an Oxymoron." *University of Chicago Law Review* 70(4): 1159–202.

Thaler, Richard H. 1980. "Toward a Positive Theory of Consumer Choice." *Journal of Economic Behavior and Organization* 1(1): 39–60.

———. 1999. "Mental Accounting Matters." *Journal of Behavioral Decisionmaking* 12(3): 183–206.

Thaler, Richard H., and Shlomo Benartzi. 2004. "Save More Tomorrow™: Using Behavioral Economics to Increase Employee Savings." *Journal of Political Economy* 112(1, part 2): S164–87.

Thurow, Lester. 1971. "The Income Distribution as a Pure Public Good." *Quarterly Journal of Economics* 85(2): 327–36.

Von Neumann, John, and Oskar Morgenstern. 1944. *The Theory of Games and Information*. Princeton, N.J.: Princeton University Press.

Yaniv, Gideon. 1999. "Tax Compliance and Advance Tax Payments: A Prospect Theory Analysis." *National Tax Journal* 52(4): 753–64.

Chapter 2

Statistical, Identifiable, and Iconic Victims

GEORGE LOEWENSTEIN, DEBORAH A. SMALL,
AND JEFF STRNAD

I N the ideal vision of public finance, each dollar of government spending is allocated to the area where it can do the most good, and taxes are
levied and revenues spent to the point where the marginal value of a
public dollar is equal to that of a private dollar. Reality falls short of this
ideal in many ways. The political system doesn't necessarily aggregate
preferences the way a market would; politicians and government workers may be corrupt or have their own personal agendas; and different
groups have different incentives and capabilities to coordinate and lobby
for their interests.

Here we focus on yet another reason for why taxation and government
spending can go awry: human psychology, and specifically the lack of
proportionality between human sympathy and the wants and needs of
those toward whom the sympathy, or lack thereof, is directed. As Adam
Smith observed in the *Theory of Moral Sentiments*, we often feel little sympathy toward people who deserve it. He illustrates the point vividly with
the hypothetical case of a European man who gets more upset over losing
his little finger than over a calamity that wipes out a large fraction of the
population of China. However, the disproportionality can also go in the
opposite direction. As Smith also points out, "we sometimes feel for another, a passion of which he himself seems to be altogether incapable," as
illustrated by the dismay of the mother of a sick child which, as he puts it,
"feels only the uneasiness of the present instant, which can never be
great" (1759/2000, 8). Smith adds dryly that "we sympathize even with
the dead, who themselves experience nothing" (1759/2000, 8).

Our main focus here is on a specific source of arbitrariness in human sympathy: the disproportionate sympathy and attention to identifiable rather than statistical victims.

Background

Several lines of research have shown that individual cases motivate people more powerfully than statistics, even when the latter are objectively more informative. Eugene Borgida and Richard Nisbett (1977), for example, found that students who were selecting courses paid much more attention to the verbally expressed opinions of a single individual who had taken a class during the previous year, than to carefully compiled statistics about levels of student satisfaction derived from a census of students. Ruth Hamill, Timothy Wilson, and Richard Nisbett (1980) found that subjects reading a vivid description of a single welfare recipient changed their view of welfare recipients (relative to a control group) more than those who received valid statistics about welfare recipients. Laurie Hendrickx, Charles Vlek, and Harmen Oppewal (1989) likewise found that public health and safety warnings changed behavior more effectively when they were linked to people and anecdotes than when they were based on statistics. Melissa Finucane, Ellen Peters, and Paul Slovic (2003) found that people reacted much more strongly to a risk presented as a relative frequency—for example, one out of a hundred—than the same risk represented as a probability—for example, a 1-percent chance. They argued that the frequency representation makes people think more about specific individuals, and hence react more strongly emotionally, than does the probabilistic representation. George Loewenstein and Jane Mather examined the relationship, over time, of public concern about different types of risks and the objective levels of those risks (1990). They found that public concern generally tracked problem severity fairly closely, but that for a number of the risks there were periods of public "panic" during which indicators of fear suddenly spiked, often with no change in the level of the underlying problem. All of the panics that they identified could be tied to specific vivid cases that captured the public's imagination—for example, news that Rock Hudson had contracted AIDS.

Identifiable Victims

One of the best developed lines of research in this area has investigated the "identifiable victim effect," a phenomenon first described by Thomas Schelling He noted that "the death of a particular person evokes anxiety and sentiment, guilt and awe, responsibility and religion, [but that] . . . most of this awesomeness disappears when we deal with statistical death" (1968, 142). Schelling might have foretold the 1987 events following the fall of eighteen-month-old Jessica McClure down a narrow well in Texas. Within hours her plight was a national sensation, her face constantly appeared on every news channel, and people reacted with tremendous sympathy, which took the material form of hundreds of thousands of dollars sent to her family to assist in the rescue effort. She was indeed rescued, and her misfortune turned into a fortune: a $700,000 trust fund to which she will gain access on her twenty-first birthday.

Although casual empiricism, such as the tale of Baby Jessica, supports Schelling's intuitions, until recently there was very little positive evidence for such an effect (see Jenni and Loewenstein 1997). Demonstrating the effect proved difficult because identifying a victim generally means providing information about him or her, and it is always possible that strong reactions to the victim are due to the information provided rather than to identifiability alone. For example, the outpouring of support for Baby Jessica may have stemmed, not from the fact that she was an identified victim per se, but because she was a cute identified victim. Deborah Small,and George Loewenstein (2003) circumvented this problem, and provided the first unconfounded empirical demonstration of the effect, by showing that simply indicating that there is a specific victim, without providing any personalizing information, increases caring.

In one study, Small and Loewenstein (2003) created "victims" by giving all subjects in a group $10 and then having half lose their money. Subjects who had retained their endowment were then given the opportunity to contribute a portion of it to the "victims" who had lost theirs. The only information available to potential donors about the particular victim who would receive the contribution was an ID number assigned to that victim by the experimenters and drawn at random by each potential donor. Victims were identified if the potential donor drew the number *before* deciding on how much to give, and unidentified if the potential donor drew the number only immediately *after* deciding how much to give. This weak form of identification had a large impact on contribution levels. Gifts to identified victims were significantly greater than gifts to unidentified victims, even though participants did not know and would not learn anything about the recipient other than his or her ID number.

In a second study, potential donors were presented with a letter requesting money for a house being built for a needy family by Habitat for Humanity (Small and Loewenstein 2003). The letter described several families on a waiting list to move into homes. Identifiability was manipulated by informing respondents that the family either had been selected or would be selected. In neither condition were respondents told which family had been or would be selected; the only difference between conditions was whether the decision had already been made or was just about to be made. Contributions to the charity were significantly greater when the respondents were informed that the recipient family had already been determined, demonstrating that the concreteness of a determined family compelled people to give more.

Identifiable Perpetrators

If people are more sympathetic toward identifiable victims, will they also be more punitive toward identifiable perpetrators? Deborah Small and George Loewenstein (2004) applied the research design from their work on the identifiable victim effect to address this question. Participants who had behaved cooperatively in a social dilemma by contributing their funds to a common pool were given the opportunity to penalize another participant who had behaved in a self-interested fashion by refusing to contribute. Contributors who chose to penalize had to pay a fraction of the penalty out of their own pockets. Much like the dictators in the studies of identifiable victims (Small and Loewenstein 2003), contributors made the decision to punish either just before or just after they had drawn the identification number of a noncontributor and had no other information about the noncontributor. Consistent with the victim studies, participants levied greater punishment, at their own expense, on identified noncontributors than on unidentified noncontributors.

Beyond generalizing the earlier work to a different target (perpetrators instead of victims), Small and Loewenstein (2004) also examined whether differences in punitiveness toward identifiable and unidentifiable perpetrators were associated with different affective reactions. Participants reacted with greater anger and blame toward an identified perpetrator than toward an unidentified perpetrator. Furthermore blame and anger mediated the relationship between identifiability and punishment: Although identification is positively related to punishment, almost all of the variation in the decision to punish is explained by blame and anger after controlling for whether the victim is identified. More specifically, in a regression of the decision to punish on an identification variable and a measure of blame and anger, the blame and anger measure is strongly significant, but the identification variable is not.

This research suggests that the identifiable victim effect is a special case of a more general identifiable other effect whereby any identifiable target evokes a stronger emotional and moral reaction than an equivalent, but unidentifiable target.

Are Identifiable Other Effects Good or Bad?

The Baby Jessica episode raises the specter of potentially large efficiency losses flowing from the disproportionate influence of identifiable others on public attitudes and sympathies. On the victim side, the danger is that available charity and government dollars will flow to particular high profile individuals while the mass of statistical victims will be short-changed. It is hard to come up with any coherent theory of allocation that would support Baby Jessica receiving $700,000 upon reaching adulthood when 16 percent of American children continue to live in poverty, unrelieved by government spending or charity. It might seem that identifiable other effects are pernicious, leading to a misallocation of social resources. However, a general conclusion along those lines may be quite wrong.

An initial question is whether those who are moved by identifiable other effects are making correct or desirable assessments. In some contexts, there is a strong argument that such effects play a critical role in guiding behavior in the proper direction. For instance, many scholars have suspected that the extreme violence of modern warfare and the mass atrocities of the past century stem, at least in part, from the lack of identifiability of the victims (Lorenz 1966; Morris 1967; Glover 1999). Suppose a soldier pushes a button to drop a bomb in an urban area that kills a group of enemy troops but also kills and maims innocent bystanders. Would the same act occur if the soldier engaged in it had to kill and maim both the troops and bystanders individually and face-to-face? Dropping a bomb in an urban area involves a degree of identifiability far weaker than in the unidentified conditions of the studies we just discussed. The soldier who pushes the button knows that innocent civilians may die or be injured but does not know the exact number or identity of such victims.

It is possible that identifiable other effects serve as an important component of what Cass Sunstein (2005) describes as "moral heuristics—moral short-cuts, or rules of thumb, that work well most of the time, but that also systematically misfire." In the case of warfare, identifiability may reduce the tendency for noncombatants to be killed or injured. Even if, consistent with the studies discussed earlier, soldiers experience an enhanced desire to kill identifiable enemy troops because they are seen as perpetrators, the soldiers will feel offsetting inhibitions if a by-product is the death or injury of civilians perceived to be innocent. The end result may be a military strategy that reduces civilian casualties. This strategy has a strong connection to explicit moralizing in the West because reducing such casualties is an important element of the just war doctrine, one of the two most widely held theological positions toward war—the other being pacifism. As Konrad Lorenz (1966) and Desmond Morris (1967) suggest, it may be that human mechanisms for making moral judgments are designed for face-to-face interactions in small groups and are not able to function well in situations, such as modern warfare, that involve anonymous and statistical lethal attacks on other human beings. In such contexts, identifiable other effects would tend to restore our true morality—that is, our morality as it tends to manifest itself in small group, face-to-face, settings. In modern societies, although identifiable other effects may result in systematic overcompensation of high-profile victims (such as Baby Jessica), it is possible that they do in fact propel behavior in a "desirable" direction most of the time.

The central problem in the Baby Jessica case is the failure to equate marginal benefits per dollar of aid expended. Shifting some of the aid dollars from Baby Jessica to other more desperate victims would improve social welfare. However, the failure to equate marginal benefits per aid dollar may be consistent with a second best optimum. Suppose, for example, that we would provide massive aid to individuals suffering from hunger if we were able to experience the condition of each victim. In this situation, highlighting the plight of individual victims would trigger identifiable other effects that would tend to reveal the correct preferences toward such victims. Consider three outcomes:

1. Charities exploit identifiable other effects to induce tax-subsidized donations. As a result, the charities are able to save 10 percent of the hunger victims. The other 90 percent die of starvation.

2. Charities apply the same fiscal resources (including the revenue cost of the tax subsidy) used to save 10 percent in the first situation in the most efficient manner. As a result, 20 percent are saved instead of 10 percent.

3. All the victims die because no aid is given.

Although situation two is better than situation one, the real (second best) choice may be between one and three. Exploitation of identifiable other effects in situation one resulted in 10 percent being saved. The same money resources could save more statistical lives in theory, but there is no impetus to do so in the absence of the identifiable other effects. Small, Loewenstein, and Slovic (2004) demonstrate that this dilemma may be quite common. They elicited donations for a cause—Save the Children's battle against hunger in Africa—using either a pitch that emphasized statistics about the problem or that showed a picture of a single charismatic victim—a Malawian girl. Crossed with this experimental treatment, they instructed half of the subjects about the identifiable victim effect in generic terms that did not take a position (about whether identifiable victims elicit too much sympathy or statistical victims too little) before they elicited a contribution. Providing this information had a negative impact on donations in the identifiable (photograph) condition, driving donations down to the level obtained with statistics.[1] Although Save the Children may be somewhat hamstrung when they raise money for specific victims, it is likely that the money they raise aids many more people than those featured on the Save the Children Web site. Thus, even if raising money for specific victims distorts aid allocation somewhat, it may very well provide a better outcome than soliciting aid purely on the basis of statistics.

Furthermore, the government might not be able to do any better than charities. The political impetus to provide aid may depend on parading high-profile victims before the public, thus exploiting identifiable other effects in exactly the same way as a charity campaign would. This approach, however, might then constrain the government to favor the same more limited set of victims with the same result—saving 10 percent instead of 20 percent from starvation. It also might be true that charities are much better than the government at identifiable other campaigns. The government alternative might result in a higher death rate. It also is worth noting that charities and donations to charities receive very large tax subsidies in the United States and in some other developed countries. In addition, the associated tax rules condition eligibility for such subsidies both on the nature of the charitable activities and on the mode of operation of the charities. The extent, content, and operational methods of charitable activities are thus shaped substantially by tax policy, and the charitable sector is very much part of the scheme of public finance in these countries.

In sum, the normative implications of identifiable other effects are subtle and depend on context. Despite the Baby Jessica case, these effects are not necessarily pernicious. In some situations, outcomes will deviate sharply from deep and noble human desires absent the prompts that arise from identification. With these considerations in mind, we examine more closely the role of identifiable other effects in public finance.

Identifiable and Iconic Victims and Perpetrators in Public Finance

So far, we have discussed cases that would fall on the spending side of the public finance equation: allocation of aid among victims of hunger or poverty. But identifiable other effects can have a strong influence on the tax side also, even in areas that are technical and not familiar to the public.

Hidden Taxes

Ultimately, all money raised by taxes, or by any other means, has to come out of someone's pocket. The incidence of any particular tax may not be obvious because price changes induced by the tax may shift the burden from the nominal payor (the entity or individual who remits money to the government) to someone else. Economists traditionally have studied the actual incidence of different taxes and have not attached much importance to the identity of the nominal payor. However, the psychology and thus the politics of taxation may turn on who appears to pay the tax rather than who actually bears the burden. The public tends to ascribe the burden to the nominal payor and to ignore taxes that they do not explicitly pay. For example, to most consumers, the VAT tax is simply part of the purchase price of an item. The nominal payors are businesses. One argument against adopting a VAT tax in the United States has been the worry that there would be too little resistance to raising taxes exactly because it is hidden.

Similarly, it is well known that wage withholding increases the palatability of an individual income tax. Because individuals do not make direct payments to the government equal to the withheld amounts, they tend to think of the withheld portion as not being theirs in the first place. McCaffery (1994a) points out that corporate income taxes are a classic example of a hidden tax. The short-run incidence of these taxes is unclear, but corporations are the nominal payor. For most of the public, it may seem obvious that corporations (that is, shareholders) pay the taxes, but many economists believe that the long-run incidence falls largely or entirely on labor, and even the short-run incidence may fall partly on labor and consumers as well as on shareholders. Russell Long, one of the most powerful and influential tax legislators in his long reign as chairman of the Senate Finance Committee, summed up the psychological appeal of hidden taxes in his very famous and often-quoted aphorism: "Don't tax him, don't tax me, tax the man behind the tree."

It is important to note that the concept of a hidden tax hinges on psychology and appearance. Consider the classic example, the corporate income tax. This may fall on consumers, on various factors of production (such as labor or raw goods suppliers), or on shareholders. In one perceptual state of the world, each of these groups might believe that it bears the entire burden of the tax. In this situation, the tax certainly is not hidden. The polar opposite case, where each individual believes that the tax falls on some other individual or group is the paradigmatic case of a hidden tax. Thus, the defining characteristic of a hidden tax in its pure form is that all of the possible ultimate payors believe that someone else (or some other group) is paying the tax. Similarly, we might say that a tax is hidden with respect to a particular group if that group believes, perhaps counterfactually, that some other group bears the entire burden. It is obvious from these definitions that whether a tax is hidden is an empirical issue. Psychology and perception play a critical role. A VAT may be hidden with respect to consumers, despite being enumerated on their sales receipts, if consciously or unconsciously they believe that it is in fact being paid in its entirety by other groups such as the owners of the businesses that sold them the goods or services.

Estate Taxes

If one followed the usual tenets of political economy, the estate tax should be wildly popular among the American electorate. Historically, the tax has been levied on only a tiny fraction of the population, and it certainly appears to be a source of several billion dollars of revenue, thus apparently reducing the tax burden on everyone else.[2] The reason for its lack of popularity has been the topic of considerable speculation and debate.

One explanation is that many people expect to become wealthy, and that, as a result, far more people think they will be negatively affected by the estate tax than will be. Nonetheless, it is hard to imagine that this delusion affects a large enough proportion of the population to create the existing and historical level of discomfort with the estate tax. An at least equally salient explanation involves clever marketing by individuals whose heirs really stand to lose from the estate tax. Michael Graetz (1983, 284), attempting to explain the mysterious unpopularity of the tax, observes that "it is often said that opponents of tax increases hide behind selected widows" and that "when one considers estate taxation, both widows and orphans are readily at hand." He also notes that "the objections of owners of small businesses and farms" are an "important political obstacle to estate taxation" despite the fact that the assets of these individuals comprise a very small portion of the base for the tax. The specter of individual small business owners or farmers being forced to sell out what their parents built up solely to pay estate taxes created a politically compelling victim scenario entirely separate from the political power of these groups as such.

Even more perversely, as Adam Smith pointed out in the *Theory of Moral Sentiments*, there seems to be a natural tendency to reserve some of our most profound sympathy for the high and mighty rather than for the poor and unfortunate who so much more deserve it:

> When we consider the condition of the great, in those delusive colours in which the imagination is apt to paint it, it seems to be almost the abstract idea of a perfect and happy state. It is the very state which, in all our waking dreams and idle reveries, we had sketched out to ourselves as the final object of all our desires. We feel, therefore, a peculiar sympathy with the satisfaction of those who are in it. We favour all their inclinations, and forward all their wishes. What pity, we think, that any thing should spoil and corrupt so agreeable a situation! It is the misfortunes of kings only which afford the proper subjects for tragedy. (1759/2000, 72)

Smith's description brings another, more recent Briton, Princess Diana, to mind.

Taxpayer Compliance Measurement Program (TCMP)

For many years, the federal government engaged in annual comprehensive TCMP audits of 50,000 lucky taxpayers chosen quasi-randomly. The word comprehensive was taken seriously. The audit covered all items on the tax return and included requests for taxpayer documentation for all such items. For example, the auditor asked for cancelled checks or other evidence for every charitable contribution. Although TCMP audits were very painful for the taxpayer, TCMP audit data was invaluable for the government. Using the data, it was possible to adjust the government's audit strategy (via DIF scores) to be much more precise in collecting missing revenue and policing noncompliance.

It appears that the program met its demise largely because "victim" concerns became salient. The experiences of various audited individuals became public, exposing the comprehensive (and painful) nature of the audit and emphasizing that it fell at random. As a result, the audit picked up the descriptor "audit from hell" and was an early and prominent casualty of the taxpayer rights movement. The IRS halted the program in 1995. From a policy perspective, this result—given the obvious benefits of the program—is curious. Part of the problem seems to have been a strong reluctance on the part of the IRS to compensate the "victims" of the audits with monetary payments or otherwise in the face of a public belief that those audited richly deserved such compensation.

This pattern and the subsequent history of the TCMP suggest that identifiable other effects may have been decisive. For several years after the demise of the TCMP, the IRS did not run any programs to generate data. Finally, in 2002, it implemented the National Research Program, which involves examining about the same number of returns as under the TCMP audit scheme, but with a less uniform approach. There is no standard NRP audit. Some returns are examined by information check, some by correspondence, some by a sit-down but not line-by-line audit, and some (but only very few) by line-by-line audits. This nonuniform approach makes the victim designation much less applicable. Instead of fifty thousand identifiable instances, each of which is a standardized "audit from hell," the whole situation is quite murky, with many taxpayers receiving quite lenient and "polite" treatment. Iconic victims are lacking. If an individual does go public with what might seem like mistreatment, the IRS can argue that the instance, though perhaps unjustified and mistaken, is exceptional rather than representative of the process.

The Political Origins of Alternative Minimum Tax

Potential examples of psychological phenomena from real life lack the clarity of experimental results. It often is easy to posit alternative explanations. We conclude this section with an example that is particularly hard to explain without resorting to identifiable other effects. In addition, at the normative level, the example raises the general set of issues concerning the beneficial or detrimental nature of the effects in a very clear manner.

The Alternative Minimum Tax (AMT) ensures that high-income taxpayers pay a certain minimum amount of tax on income that excludes many of the preferences and deductions available under the normal tax rules. To the extent that these preferences and deductions create incentives for socially valuable activities, the AMT is harmful because it blunts these incentives. On the other hand, it ensures that high-income taxpayers cannot abuse the preferences and deductions to pay little or no tax.

Much of the economic debate about the AMT turns on the degree to which tax preferences are capitalized. For example, if the highest tax bracket is 40 percent and tax-exempt state and local bonds yield 5 percent along with taxable alternatives such as Treasury bonds or corporate bonds, then high-income individuals who invest in the tax-exempts receive a 2-percentage-point subsidy. At the same time, the state and local government issuers, who are the intended beneficiaries of the exemption, do not receive preferential lending rates compared to corporate and federal issuers. On the other hand, if competition among high-income individuals to hold tax-exempt bonds drives the yield on those bonds down to 3 percent (versus 5 percent for Treasury and corporate bonds), then high-income taxpayers receive no after-tax benefit. In that case, the entire subsidy (in the form of the national government's revenue loss) flows to state and local government issuers. The tax benefit is fully capitalized and therefore it is not a matter of concern if a high-income individual reduces his or her taxes to zero by earning income solely from tax-exempt sources. That individual's pre-tax income will be lower by an amount equal to what the tax would have been. In effect, the individual is subject to an implicit tax at the full statutory rate. Depending on individual perceptions, this implicit tax may be at least partially hidden from both the victim payors and members of the public who might have sympathy for those payors.

The precursor of today's AMT passed in 1969, but serious AMT-like proposals had been floated much earlier. Russell Long, the powerful chairman of the Senate Finance Committee quoted above, proposed and was pushing just such a proposal in the mid-1960s, but it did not catch on. An incredibly powerful identifiable other event in early 1969 almost certainly triggered enactment. Michael Graetz and Deborach Schenk (2002) describe this event and its aftermath in detail.

In the last few weeks of the Johnson administration, Joseph Barr was serving temporarily as secretary of the Treasury. In January 1969, only days before the Nixon administration took the reins at Treasury, Barr made a public statement that 154 taxpayers had adjusted gross incomes of $200,000 or more (approximately $800,000 in 2004 dollars) but taxable incomes of zero. This announcement generated more letters to Congress during 1969 than the Vietnam War, the principal and most passionate political issue of the day. Before the end of that year, Congress passed a 10 percent add-on tax applicable to certain preferences, the precursor of the current AMT. It is hard to avoid the conclusion that Barr's identification of the 154 taxpayers was critical in ensuring passage. Before 1969, it was clear and public that several generous deductions and preferences in the tax code permitted high-income taxpayers to reduce their tax burdens substantially. Nonetheless, the earlier AMT-like proposals, such as the one championed by Russell Long, did not pass or even achieve much political salience despite strong support from key politicians and policy makers. Furthermore, passage of AMT in 1969 occurred in the face of a new Republican president, an individual much less likely to support such measures than his populist Democratic predecessor.

Assuming, as seems to be the case, that identifiability effects were critical in bringing the AMT into the tax code, the question arises as to whether this influence was beneficial or pernicious. Not surprisingly, the answer depends heavily on one's view of the AMT, and radically different characterizations of Barr's political act are conceivable.

On the negative side, the AMT may be viewed as blunting the impact of deductions and preferences that make policy sense and adding considerable unnecessary complexity to the tax code. This view is particularly salient if the deductions and preferences are largely capitalized into asset prices. If they are, the high-income recipients actually receive little or no benefit but are subject to implicit taxes in the form of lower pre-tax returns. The hidden nature of the implicit taxes may have provided necessary political support for the system—a beneficial application of the identifiable other effect. Under this scenario, Barr's public statement appears pernicious, severely hampering a smoothly functioning political and economic arrangement by exploiting a detrimental version of the identifiable other effect in a demagogic and McCarthy-esque way during the dying days of a defeated administration.

On the positive side, the AMT may be viewed as offsetting the unintended distributional consequences of preferences and deductions. This view is enhanced if some of the deductions and preferences themselves are of questionable efficacy as public policies or are not offset by lower pre-tax returns, or both. This perspective leads to a very different characterization of the Barr episode: Barr's heroic and politically brilliant application of the identifiable other effect allowed the general public to see what was really happening in a concrete way. True human aspirations, so apparent in small group interactions but often lost in the anonymous and ponderous operation of modern societies, triumphed as a motivated populace galvanized politicians to undertake curative political action.

Conclusions

Strong identifiable other effects, involving both victims and perpetrators, emerge unmistakably from experimental research. This research shows that only a very weak degree of identifiability results in significant effects. Individuals, drawing from their own resources, will be substantially more beneficent toward victims and more punitive toward perpetrators if they know that a particular victim or perpetrator is involved, even if they know nothing about that victim's or perpetrator's identity or history.

Identifiable other effects play a potentially important role in diverse domains, and public finance is no exception.[3] We have detailed some important tax and spending phenomena that are difficult to explain without invoking such effects. These instances arise from masking identifiable targets through hidden taxes as well as from making them more salient in various ways to the public and the political process.

Although it seems clear that identifiable other effects are important for public finance, our discussion leaves unresolved whether such effects are (in the net) beneficial or detrimental to the functioning and structure of public finance systems. Due to the intellectual association of such effects with the psychological literature concerning behavioral and cognitive errors, it is easy to presume that the net effects are detrimental. However, though they sometimes may lead to deficient outcomes, a case can be made that identifiable other effects function as an important component of moral intuition. This role may be particularly significant in the modern world, allowing human beings designed to function in small-group and face-to-face situations to attach appropriate salience to the statistical or anonymous processes generated by governments and other large organizations. Not surprisingly, answering the question of detriment in particular instances turns out to depend on the factual and political context.

The paper was presented at the University of Michigan Business School, Conference on "Behavioral Public Finance: Toward a New Agenda," April 23 to 24, 2004. We thank Ed McCaffery, Joel Slemrod, and attendees at the conferences (particularly Bill Gale, who proposed the term iconic victim) for helpful comments.

Notes

1. They obtained a similar result when, rather than explicitly teaching subjects about the effect, they accentuated the difference between the two appeals by presenting both types of appeals—statistics and the photograph—together.
2. McCaffery (1994b) discusses evidence that the tax actually may lose revenue when certain subtle interactions with the rest of the tax system are taken into account.
3. There are a myriad of examples from contexts other than public finance. For instance, Guido Calabresi and Philip Bobbitt (1978, 138) discuss the significant role of Franklin Delano Roosevelt as high profile victim in prompting the relatively high (almost entirely private rather than government) expenditures on eradicating poliomyelitis that are hard to explain in terms of risk of equivalent harm.

References

Borgida, Eugene, and Richard E. Nisbett. 1977. "The Differential Impact of Abstract vs. Concrete Information on Decisions." *Journal of Applied Social Psychology* 7(3): 258–71.
Calabresi, Guido, and Philip Bobbitt. 1978. *Tragic Choices.* New York: W. W. Norton.
Finucane, Melissa L., Ellen Peters, and Paul Slovic. 2003. "Judgment and Decision Making: The Dance of Affect and Reason." In *Emerging Perspectives on Judgment and Decision Research,* edited by Sandra L. Schneider, James Shanteau, and Lola Lopes. Cambridge: Cambridge University Press.
Glover, Jonathan. 1999. *Humanity: A Moral History of the Twentieth Century.* New Haven: Yale University Press.
Graetz, Michael. 1983. "To Praise the Estate Tax, Not to Bury It." *Yale Law Journal* 93(2): 259–86.
Graetz, Michael, and Deborah Schenk. 2002. *Federal Income Taxation: Principles and Policies.* New York: Foundation Press.
Hamill, Ruth, Timothy D. Wilson, and Richard E. Nisbett. 1980. "Insensitivity to Sample Bias: Generalizing from Atypical Cases." *Journal of Personality and Social Psychology* 39: 578–89.
Hendrickx, Laurie, Charles Vlek, and Harmen Oppewal. 1989. "Relative Importance of Scenario Information and Frequency Information in the Judgment of Risk." *Acta Psychologica* 72(1): 41–63.
Jenni, Karen, and George Loewenstein. 1997. "Explaining the Identifiable Victim Effect." *Journal of Risk and Uncertainty* 14(3): 235–57.
Loewenstein, George, and Jane Mather. 1990. "Dynamic Processes in Risk Perception." *Journal of Risk and Uncertainty* 3(2): 155–75.
Lorenz, Konrad. 1966. *On Aggression.* New York: Bantam Books.
McCaffery, Edward J. 1994a. "Cognitive Theory and Tax." *U.C.L.A. Law Review* 41(7): 1861–947.
———. 1994b. "The Uneasy Case for Wealth Transfer Taxation." *Yale Law Journal* 104(2): 283–365.
Morris, Desmond. 1967. *The Naked Ape.* New York: Crown Publishers.

Schelling, Thomas C. 1968. "The Life You Save May Be Your Own." In *Problems in Public Expenditure Analysis*, edited by Samuel B. Chase. Washington, D.C.: The Brookings Institution.

Small, Deborah A., and George Loewenstein. 2003. "Helping *a* Victim or Helping *the* Victim: Altruism and Identifiabilty." *Journal of Risk and Uncertainty* 26(1): 5–16.

———. 2004. "The Devil You Know: The Effect of Identifiability on Punitiveness." Unpublished manuscript. University of Pennsylvania, Philadelphia.

Small, Deborah A., George Loewenstein, and Paul Slovic. 2004. "Inconsistent Valuation of Life Saving Efforts for Statistical vs. Identifiable Victims: Can Education Change This?" Unpublished manuscript. University of Pennsylvania, Philadelphia.

Smith, Adam. 1759/2000. *The Theory of Moral Sentiments*. London: A. Millar.

Sunstein, Cass. 2005. "Moral Heuristics." *Behavioral and Brain Sciences* 28: 531–73.

Chapter 3

Distinguishing Between Cognitive Biases

HANMING FANG AND DAN SILVERMAN

ECONOMISTS have recently taken increased interest in a number of cognitive biases and heuristics first documented by psychologists.[1] In theoretical studies, economists typically introduce such biases and heuristics into stylized models with a goal of understanding how small, but psychologically relevant, deviations from the standard economic framework can influence decisions such as saving and consumption (Harris and Laibson 2001), investment (Barberis and Huang 2001), and labor supply (Fang and Silverman 2004a). In empirical studies, economists have followed two basic strategies. The first is to derive distinctive empirical implications from a model of a particular bias or heuristic and then check if the data are qualitatively consistent with the bias model's predictions but inconsistent with the standard model's (see, for example, Babcock et al. 1997; Genesove and Mayer 2001; Della Vigna and Malmandier 2004). The second involves estimating structural models that allow a particular bias and attempt to measure the degree of that bias and its implications (Fang and Silverman 2004b; Paserman 2004). It, unlike the first strategy, assumes an explicit model that permits simulations of the behavioral and welfare consequences of counterfactual policy experiments.

An important motivation for incorporating cognitive biases and heuristics in economic analyses is public policy. When a public economist evaluates a policy, the typical first step is to consult the formalization of Adam Smith's invisible hand in the first fundamental theorem of welfare. According to this theorem, when competitive markets exist and their participants share information commonly, the allocations of those markets are efficient. That is, no other feasible allocation could make one person better off without making someone else worse off. It follows that if markets are missing, or imperfectly competitive, or if economic agents are acting with incomplete information, policy interventions may be justified on efficiency grounds.

The implications of cognitive biases and heuristics for decision making form the basis of another rationale for policy interventions into economic activity. Biases and heuristics may drive a wedge between normative or long-term preferences and revealed preferences. That is, biases and heuristics can make what an individual actually chooses to do different from what it would be if bias did not color perception, if choices were made from a temporal distance, or if careful attention to decisions might be paid at zero cost. If biases or heuristics lead economic agents to decisions at odds with their normative or long-term preferences, then public policy interventions could in principle make some better off yet none worse off. Thus, even in cases where perfect markets exist, the influence of cognitive biases and heuristics may justify public policy interventions on efficiency grounds.

Although investigations into the relevance of cognitive biases and heuristics for economic decision making may have profound policy implications, those with such a research agenda face a fundamental difficulty: given the large number of deviations from strict rationality that psychologists have documented, how should we determine which ones apply to which economic settings?

So far, both the theoretical and the empirical studies in economics have tended to investigate the implications of cognitive biases and heuristics one bias at a time (Barberis and Huang 2001 is an exception). The strategy of limiting attention to one potential bias may, in some cases, be justified by a priori indications of the primacy of that bias in determining behavior. Even when there is no such logic, an incremental approach offers some clear advantages. For theory, isolating the influence of a minimal deviation from the standard framework has intrinsic interest and provides greater potential for clarity and tractability. An additional advantage derives from a concern for distinguishing among the effects of various biases. In some quite standard settings it is impossible to empirically distinguish between a model of even a single bias and a traditional model (see, for example, Barro 1999). Distinguishing among multiple models of bias at once may present substantial challenges.

Nevertheless, in many cases several biases might plausibly explain behavior. The obvious question for empirical research is whether we can distinguish these various biases from each other, and from a traditional model, using readily available data. If such data are not sufficient, it then becomes important to investigate what additional data should be collected. Distinguishing among biases is important because, as we will demonstrate, different biases may lead to very different policy recommendations.

Here our primary task is to determine whether certain biases can be distinguished using data on labor supply and welfare program participation. In the context of a simple model of work and welfare program participation, we investigate whether it is possible to distinguish between two psychological biases: time inconsistent discounting in the form of present-biased (hyperbolic) time preferences and nonrational beliefs in the form of projection bias. We show formally that indeed these can be distinguished from each other, and from a conventional model using standard data. In addition, we highlight a novel distinction between the two biases and argue that individuals under the two biases may exhibit different attitudes and changes in attitude toward welfare eligibility restrictions such as time limits. To the extent that such data may be collected, these differences in attitudes provide an unexplored channel that researchers may exploit to distinguish biases in belief and time discounting.

Cognitive Biases and Public Policy

As noted, cognitive biases and heuristics create the potential for important efficiency gains from public policy interventions—even in settings where, if agents were strictly rational, the first fundamental theorem of welfare would hold. The behavioral economics literature on present-biased preferences provides a set of concrete examples of both the potential for these efficiency gains, and the potential importance of multiple biases.

Present-Biased Preferences and Public Policy

The recent literature studying the influence of present-biased time preferences on economic decision making is a prominent example of how economists have introduced cognitive biases into their analyses. By way of background, present-biased time preferences are a simple way of modeling the intuitive notion of a taste for immediate gratification and the resulting problems of self-control. Following the lead of David Laibson (1997), who built on earlier work by Robert Strotz (1956) and Robert Pollak (1968), economists have used quasi-hyperbolic time discounting models to study a variety of economic questions.

An important feature of present-biased time preferences is that they provide a simple way for economists to explain choice reversals commonly observed in experimental and survey research: subjects choose the larger and later of two prizes when both are distant in time, but prefer the smaller and earlier one as both prizes draw nearer to the present.[2]

The essence of such choice reversals is conveyed by two simple examples. In the first example, imagine that subjects are asked on February 1 to choose between spending seven hours on the tax return (an unpleasant task) on April 1 versus spending eight hours on April 15. Almost everyone would prefer to spend seven hours on April 1; but when April 1 arrives, most subjects, facing the same two alternatives, would put the work off until April 15. That is, individuals have a tendency to procrastinate on unpleasant tasks. In the second example, imagine that subjects are asked to choose whether to receive a prize of a $100 certified check available immediately or to have a $200 certified check that could not be cashed for two years. A majority of the subjects choose to receive the $100 certified check that can be cashed immediately. However, the same people do not prefer a $100 certified check that could be cashed in six years to a $200 certified check that could be cashed in eight years (see Ainslie and Haslam 1992). That is, when faced with a pleasant reward, individuals show a short-run desire for instantaneous gratification.

An important implication of present-biased preferences is that revealed rates of time discount tend to decline with time and thus introduce the potential for both problems of self-control and utility gains from restricting choice sets. These gains from fewer choices contrast starkly with the implications of the time-consistent, exponential time discounting that economists conventionally assume; with time-consistent discounting, the restriction of an individual's choice set can never make her better off in a single-agent decision problem.

Efficiency Gains from Policy

Present-biased preferences have been used to explain a variety of otherwise anomalous economic behaviors. Of primary importance here, however, are the implications this bias has for public policy. We examine these implications in the context of three examples from the behavioral economics literature.

Example 1: The Design of Cigarette Taxes   In a recent paper, Jonathan Gruber and Botond Köszegi (2001) consider the influence of present-biased preferences on cigarette smoking decisions and optimal tax policy. They combine a theoretical investigation with a quantitative evaluation of the impact of intentional smoking choices on the well-being of smokers. Cigarette taxation is, of course, an example in the standard public economics literature of the taxation of activities with externalities. By definition, such activity by one individual has spillover effects on others that are not reflected in the price of the activity. When the spillovers are positive, the activity is overpriced and will be underconsumed from a social standpoint; theory argues it should be subsidized. If the spillover effects are negative, the activity is underpriced and will be overconsumed, and should thus be taxed.

The standard analyses of smoking externalities focus on the health costs of smoking that are not included in the price of cigarettes but are borne by both smokers and non-smokers. Gruber and Köszegi's startling finding is that, if consumers have present-biased preferences consistent with experimental psychology, the costs of smoking's standard externalities may be dwarfed by what the authors call aggregate internalities— that is, the health costs *to the smoker* from oversmoking due to self-control problems. The key point is that present-biased preferences may harm smokers by causing them to oversmoke with respect to their own normative or long-term preferences if they were to see their world without bias and make decisions from a temporal distance. The policy implications of such internalities are profound. Gruber and Köszegi's calculations suggest that an optimal tax response to smoking internalities would indicate cigarette taxes many times larger than current levels.

Example 2: The Design of 401(k) Savings Plans   Chapter 11 in this volume presents compelling evidence that, when making decisions about contributions to 401(k) retirement savings accounts, individuals often follow the path of least resistance, and end up saving less than they had planned. More specifically, the evidence collected indicates that individuals often choose to do nothing when it comes to retirement savings decisions and simply adopt the default options set by their employers. These default saving options (including both saving rates and portfolio choices) can therefore have a profound influence on saving outcomes.

One interpretation of the tendency to do nothing about important life decisions is that it is a form of procrastination. Self-control problems may lead individuals continually to postpone the research and thinking required to make an important saving choice. Again, time-inconsistent preferences can account for this counterproductive urge even, perhaps especially, when the decisions are highly consequential.[3] Thus present-biased preferences may once more justify policy interventions that facilitate self-regulation or, as in setting positive default saving rates, exploit tendencies to procrastinate to achieve superior saving outcomes.[4]

Example 3: The Design of Welfare Policy   In "On the Compassion of Time-Limited Welfare Programs," we investigated the implications of present-biased preferences for the labor supply and welfare program participation decision of single mothers with children (Fang and Silverman 2004a). Our analysis was motivated by the common claim that long-term dependence on welfare is suboptimal, not just for taxpayers but also for the recipients. That claim has, in turn, led some policy makers to argue that policies such as time limits, which restrict an individual's cumulative benefits to a certain number of years, and workfare, which provides benefits only to those who satisfy work requirements, may actually benefit welfare recipients. This claim runs counter to a fundamental property of single-agent economic decision problems with standard time preferences: the restriction of an individual's choices can, at best, leave one's well-being unchanged, but it can never make one better off.

Our paper showed that, when single mothers have present-biased time preferences, time limits could benefit the welfare-eligible by providing them with a commitment to work—one that alleviates problems of self-control. We explained why some, who according to their long-term preferences would have preferred to work (and eventually consume) more, instead choose welfare. Thus if preferences are present biased, welfare policy interventions could in some cases generate efficiency gains, even if markets were perfect. In fact, when we examined data on labor supply and welfare program participation among single women with children, and estimated a model that allowed but did not assume a simple form of present-biased time preferences (Fang and Silverman 2004b), we found evidence of present bias among single mothers with children. More specifically, our estimates of the time-discount function indicated significantly higher rate of time discount for the near versus the more distant future. We also found, however, that when we used the estimated model to simulate the effects of policy changes, the imposition of time limits and work requirements failed to make most single mothers better off despite the present-biased preferences. In this context, it appeared that though some single mothers sometimes could benefit from an exogenously imposed commitment to work, time limits and workfare were too crude instruments to realize this benefit. Too often time limits and workfare forced women to work when their best option was in fact welfare.

The Implications of Alternative Biases

Present-biased time preferences are just one of many deviations from a strictly rational model of decision making documented by psychologists. We now consider how the presence of other cognitive biases, perhaps in addition to present-biased time preferences, might influence behavior and thus the evaluation of public policies. Let us begin with a bit of background on two well-documented belief biases: optimism and projection bias.

Optimism Bias

Considerable evidence indicates that individuals consistently exhibit a bias toward optimism (overconfidence) in beliefs. Psychological evidence of overconfidence is reflected in the "above median effect," whereby well over half of survey respondents typically judge themselves as having more desirable attributes than 50 percent of others in the relevant group. In Ola Svenson (1981), eighty-one American and eighty Swedish students were asked to judge their skill in driving and how safe they were as drivers. Findings indicated that 92.8 percent of American and 68.7 percent of Swedish subjects rated their safe driving as being in the top 50 percent. In Larwood and Whittaker (1977), seventy-two undergraduate management students and forty-eight presidents of New York state manufacturing firms are asked to rate themselves relative to their classmates or fellow presidents in IQ, likelihood of success, predicted growth in a hypothetical marketing problem, and so forth. The results indicate an astonishing level of overconfidence: of the seventy-two students, only ten felt that they had merely average intelligence relative to their classmates and only two thought themselves below average; and only eighteen of the seventy-two predicted that their hypothetical firm's sales would be below the industry average. The executive sample also predicted inordinate success, even though more moderate than the students.

Psychological evidence of overconfidence is also reflected in the "fundamental attribution error" (Aronson 1994); that is, people tend to attribute their successes to ability and skill, but their failure to bad luck or to factors beyond their control. Such self-serving biases are bound to reinforce overconfidence. Psychologists have gathered a great deal of evidence indicating that we take credit for the good and deny the bad. For example, students who do well on an exam attribute their performance to ability and effort, whereas those who do poorly attribute it to a poor exam or bad luck (Arkin and Maruyama 1979); gamblers perceive their success as based on skill and their failure as a fluke (Gilovich 1983). When married couples estimate how much of the housework each routinely did, their combined total of housework performed amounts to more than 100 percent—in other words, each one thinks he or she did more work than the other thinks he or she did (Ross and Sicoly 1979). Two-person teams performing a skilled task accept credit for the good scores but assign most of the blame for the poor scores to their partner (Johnston 1967). When asked to explain why someone else dislikes them, college students take little responsibility for themselves (that is, there must be something wrong with this other person), but when told that someone else likes them, the students attributed it to their own personality (Cunningham, Starr, and Kanouse 1979).

Projection Bias

Another particularly relevant and well-documented bias is the deviation from rational beliefs known as projection bias. Projection bias refers to a tendency to mispredict future utilities. Specifically, experimental evi-

Table 3.1   Subjects Making an Advance Choice of an Unhealthy Snack

		Future State	
		Hungry	Satiated
Current	Hungry	78%	56%
State	Satiated	42%	26%

Source: Data reprinted from Read and van Leeuwen (1998, 198) with permission from Elsevier.

dence indicates that, in many contexts, individuals understand qualitatively how their tastes will change with time or circumstances, but systematically underestimate the magnitudes of these changes. In particular, people tend to exaggerate the degree to which their future tastes will resemble their present ones.

An example of a projection-bias experiment illuminates the nature of the bias. In Daniel Read and Barbara van Leeuwen (1998), two hundred workers were asked to choose between a healthy snack (fruit) and an unhealthy snack (candy, nuts, chips) that they would receive, free of charge, a week later (cited in Loewenstein, O'Donoghue, and Rabin 2003). The workers were told that their snack would be delivered either in the late afternoon, when they should be hungry, or just after lunch, when satiated. Some workers were asked to make this advance choice in the afternoon, when they were hungry, and the remainder were asked just after lunch. Table 3.1 describes the workers' choices based on their current and anticipated future states of hunger.

Those who anticipated being hungry when the snacks were to be delivered were more likely to choose the unhealthy snack if they were hungry when the question was asked. The same is true of those who anticipated being satiated. The current state of hunger, then, appears to influence predictions about future preferences. Those who are currently hungry, and who presumably have a greater taste for the unhealthy snack, appear to project their current tastes onto their future ones.[5] The respondents are aware that their preferences depend on their current state. For example, the currently hungry choose the healthy snack more often when they anticipate being satiated. They seem, however, judging by the choices of the currently satiated, to seriously underestimate the change in their preferences.

Alternative Biases and Public Policy

Returning to our three examples from the behavioral economics literature, we now consider how optimism and projection biases might influence behavior and therefore public policy design.

Example 1: The Design of Cigarette Taxes It seems natural that the smoking decision would be strongly influenced by time discounting. The rewards of smoking—the flavor, relief of cravings, feeling of relaxation—are immediate, whereas the health costs are usually borne in a distant future. Thus a bias toward immediate gratification might profoundly influence behavior. However, optimism and projection biases might also influence the smoking decision in important ways, and lead to either over- or undersmoking with respect to normative or long-run preferences.

Consider optimism bias. If, knowing the distribution of health risks from smoking, the typical consumer thinks herself less likely than average to suffer these costs, then optimism bias would lead to oversmoking for a reason other than self-control problems. Specifically, if the consumer could view her environment without optimism bias, her preference would be to smoke less. If policy makers give priority to this unbiased preference, optimal cigarette tax designs that ignored the influence of optimism could, therefore, result in too much smoking.

Alternatively, projection bias might also significantly influence smoking decisions. Recall that projection bias leads consumers to exaggerate the extent to which their future tastes will resemble their current ones. Suppose that young people overestimate the degree to which their current tastes for vigorous physical activities and energy will apply at older ages; and suppose older people place a lower value on physical vigor. To the extent that poor health curtails physical activities, young people making decisions about whether to smoke may put too much weight on the disutility of related future health costs, and may smoke "too little." Optimal cigarette tax policies that ignored this form of projection bias would result in overtaxation and socially suboptimal levels of smoking.

Example 2: The Design of 401(k) Saving Plans Similarly, it is natural to think that saving choices would be influenced to a large degree by the nature of time discounting. Analogous to the effort required not to smoke, the costs of foregone consumption and planning for retirement are immediate, but the rewards are considerably delayed. Thus, in particular, a taste for immediate gratification could generate costly deviations from the choices that are optimal with respect to long-term preferences. Several studies have found, however, that variation in time discount rates explains relatively little of the variation in wealth (see, for example, Barsky et al. 1997; Bernheim, Skinner, and Weinberg 2001; Ameriks, Caplin, and Leahy 2003). Moreover, there is reason to think that some of the other well-documented cognitive biases could influence saving decisions and therefore optimal public policy design.

For example, the optimism bias could, as in the case of smoking, lead to suboptimal saving decisions. For instance, the average person who believes that income will grow at an above average rate will tend to save too little for retirement. Certain forms of projection bias, on the other hand, would seem to generate too much saving. One such scenario is related to the finding that, according to a variety of estimates, the average household reduces its consumption by 10 to 30 percent at retirement (see, for example, Banks, Blundell, and Tanner 1998; Bernheim, Skinner, and Weinberg 2001). If this decline reflects intentional behavior, and if working-age families with children overestimate the extent to which their tastes for consumption in retirement will resemble their current tastes, these families will tend to oversave with respect to their normative preferences.

The potential influence of these other cognitive biases on saving choices may prove important for policy design especially if, as seems natural, policy makers use surveys to elicit the saving preferences of individuals, and then use these preferences to determine default saving rates. If, indeed, time-inconsistent preferences lead to procrastination on saving choices, then eliciting preferences about relatively distant saving choices and setting defaults accordingly could generate important utility gains. This strategy for setting defaults has important potential because a distinguishing characteristic of time-inconsistent discounting is that normative preferences over choices are little affected if those choices occur in the relatively distant future. Other cognitive biases, such as optimism and projection bias, do not have this feature. If they apply, even (and perhaps especially) stated preferences over choices far in the future may differ from what an individual would prefer with an unbiased view of the world. It follows that a better understanding of the influence of various cognitive biases on saving preferences may be important for policy design.

Example 3: The Design of Welfare Policy   It is natural to think that time discounting—like smoking and saving—may play an important role in labor supply and welfare program participation decisions. Again, the costs of leaving welfare for work—that is, trading home production, leisure, and welfare benefits for a low wage—are immediate, but the benefits, if they exist, are delayed until human capital accumulates and delivers higher wages. Nevertheless, the logic behind investigating the influence of present-biased time preferences on labor supply and welfare program participation decisions would seem to apply to projection bias as well. If individuals tend to project their current tastes onto their future tastes, those currently on welfare may mispredict their future utility from work versus staying home. More specifically, suppose that nonworking welfare recipients anticipate that leaving children with a baby-sitter, or commuting long distances, or behaving respectfully to a boss will be more distasteful than it in fact will be. In that case, even if preferences were time consistent, there may be utility gains from policy interventions that, effectively, create incentives for would-be recipients to enter the paid labor force.

Although both projection and present bias may each suggest too much welfare use by some families, precisely how each of these biases affect labor supply and welfare program participation decisions has potential implications for policy design. If, for example, projection bias had an important influence on the decisions of welfare recipients, then programs that promote gradual transitions into work and thus permit low cost adaptation of preferences may be more successful in terms of attachments to the labor market than stronger pushes such as workfare or time limits. The opposite may be true if present bias has had an important influence on the labor supply of the welfare-eligible. In that case, if future changes in the return to welfare versus work are not abrupt or large, these changes may provide insufficient incentive to overcome the tendency to delay entry into the labor force driven by present bias.

Distinguishing Among Biases

Each of these examples from behavioral economics literature suggests that cognitive biases may have important policy implications, and that optimal policy design may depend on precisely which biases play the most significant roles in decision making. The policy implications of multiple biases motivates the question: how can we determine which biases are most important in which contexts?

As noted, in some contexts there may be strong a priori reasons to think that one bias would play a more important role than another. For example, decisions under uncertainty when costs and rewards are nearly simultaneous, such as the decision to wear a seat belt or to undertake some medical options, are more likely to be influenced by optimism or confirmatory biases than by projection or present biases. In such cases, researchers could more confidently exclude certain biases from consideration.

Calibration exercises are another method for ranking the relative importance of various cognitive biases. Calibration involves developing a model of behavior and choosing parameters of the model, including degrees of bias, so that the behavior it predicts fits summary statistics of relevant data. If there are many combinations of parameters that fit the same data, the researcher can experiment with different levels of biases and simulate their effects on decision making. With these simulations, one can evaluate whether the degree of bias necessary to have an economically substantial impact is plausible. The plausibility of the relevant bias calibrations may in turn be evaluated in terms of their implications for other decisions. For example, one may consider whether the degree of projection bias necessary to have an important influence on smoking decisions is compatible with decisions about saving levels.

A third option is to use field and experimental data to perform direct assessments of the preferences and beliefs that in principle guide decision making.[6] If, for example, both present bias and optimism bias are logically important contributors to the decision to smoke, survey research could collect data on the beliefs and rates of time discount of both smokers and nonsmokers and then assess the ability of these measures to predict behavior. If those with steeper time discount functions are no more likely to smoke, then present-biased preferences are less likely to be important determinants of behavior. Alternatively, if smokers have no more sanguine beliefs about their expected costs of smoking, then optimism is less likely to be a driving force behind the decision to smoke.

Yet another approach to identifying the importance of various biases and heuristics uses economic theory to inform inference based on data about choices. More precisely, economic theory may provide enough structure to allow us to distinguish the effects of various biases from each other, and from a traditional model, using readily available data. We now summarize our investigation into whether, in fact, theory provides a structure sufficient to distinguish the effects of present bias versus projection bias in the context of the labor supply welfare program participation choices we studied in Fang and Silverman (2004a, 2004b). We begin with an informal description of our model of labor supply and welfare-program participation.

The Model

Appendix A presents a formal model of the work-welfare decision faced by a single parent with children. That model incorporates both the present-bias and the projection-bias models as special cases. Here we discuss the basic ingredients of the model and outline its relevant predictions.

The model considers the labor supply and welfare program participation choices of a single parent with children. In each period,[7] the parent chooses whether to stay at home and receive welfare, work in the labor market, or stay at home and receive no welfare. These choices are mutually exclusive and exhaustive.[8] We normalize the value of staying home without welfare to zero. If the parent instead chooses welfare, she receives a constant real benefit in addition to the value of her leisure and home production (for example, caregiving and homemaking). The benefit includes both cash payments and in-kind assistance such as health insurance, food stamps, and housing subsidies. This is a model without welfare stigma or welfare start-up costs; thus, in the absence of welfare time limits or work requirement, the parent would never stay home without receiving welfare because doing so would mean foregoing the benefit. If she chooses to enter the labor force, and receives a job offer, her expected wage will depend on how many years she has worked. This wage captures both money and in kind forms of compensation for work. The relationship between the wage and past work experience reflects the accumulation of human capital, and represents the most important intertemporal link in the model. The opportunity cost of not working now includes the value of future higher wages, which itself depends on how much future market work will be done.

Going to work also involves a utility cost beyond the lost benefits of foregone welfare payments. This cost of work may have many interpretations: it may include, for example, the opportunity cost of forgone leisure and time with children, the monetary and time cost of child care arrangements, the difficulties of a strict schedule, or the challenge of familiarizing oneself with public transportation. We assume that this cost of work represents, to some extent, a start-up cost. Specifically, the cost of work is lower if the parent worked last period than if she chose either welfare or home last period. The start-up costs may include arranging transportation, developing routines to ensure timely arrival to work, and securing child care services. Such costs will understandably be lower once a routine and support systems have been established. This assumption also reflects the notion that tastes for work will adapt. Agents will simply get used to certain distasteful aspects of labor market work, such as keeping to a strict time schedule, respecting a boss, and dealing with the unreasonable demands of coworkers. We also want to emphasize that the preceding discussion refers to the cost of work that will actually be experienced. We will allow the perception of the future cost of work to be biased.

To allow for present-biased preferences, our model follows Laibson (1997) and O'Donoghue and Rabin (1999), who each adopted a relatively simple form of possibly time-inconsistent discounting, so-called (β, δ)-preferences. This is a now standard way of modeling the taste for immediate gratification; details are provided in appendix A.

Next we describe how the parent forms her expectations for the future that are critical for her current decision making. As described, there is considerable evidence that decision makers are subject to projection bias when forecasting future tastes. There is little evidence, however, that this bias extends to expectations for the future size of budget sets. We therefore focus in this model on the bias in predicting the disutility of being away from children, or having to keep a strict time schedule, or having to behave respectfully to a boss. That is, we allow projection bias to affect only predictions of the future cost of working. Following George Loewenstein, Ted O'Donoghue, and Matthew Rabin's lead (2003), we model the projection bias concerning the future cost of working as follows.

When an agent makes predictions about the cost of working in the future, we assume that to some degree she projects her current tastes onto her future ones. More precisely, we assume there is no misprediction when the agent is contemplating the cost of working in a future state that, in terms of the previous period's decision, is the same as her current situation. But if her current state differs from the one she is contemplating, she predicts her future cost of working will resemble her current cost. Because the costs of work are to some extent start-up costs, this latter assumption implies that, when staying at home and receiving welfare, the parent will perceive her cost of working as higher than it will be. The greater her projection bias, the greater her overestimate of the cost of working. Thus our formulation captures in a simple way the idea that an individual called on to predict taste for work in the future overestimates the similarity of future taste to current taste.[9]

Why This Form of Projection Bias?

As explained, we have assumed a particular form of projection bias. We now provide additional justifications for modeling projection bias as a tendency to overestimate the future utility costs of work.

That many welfare recipients lack significant experience in the labor force makes the notion that they mispredict their utility from working more plausible. Just as those who have never lived in a cold climate, and who know few who have, may mispredict their ability to adapt to the winter, so welfare recipients who have never worked, and know few who have, may mispredict their ability to adapt to being away from children, or to commuting, or to showing respect for a boss.

It is not immediately clear, however, that if welfare recipients mispredict their taste for work, they mispredict it with a negative bias; they might also overestimate the utility of time spent away from children or the pride in earning a wage. If such positive projection bias were the sole bias influencing welfare decisions then there would be, in some sense, too few welfare recipients and restrictions aimed at moving women from welfare to work would certainly make the former recipients worse off. We are not aware of direct empirical evidence regarding the accuracy of the predictions of welfare recipients about their utility of work.[10] However, an Urban Institute study of mothers in 1997 found that, conditional on demographic and economic characteristics, welfare recipients were less likely than other mothers to agree with the statement that a working mother can establish just as warm a relationship with her children as a mother who does not work (Wertheimer, Long, and Vandivere 2001). These differences in attitudes about work and parenting represent the opinions of different women in different work-welfare situations, and not the opinions of the same women at different times and in different situations. Thus the findings are consistent with a simple model of selection into work based on preferences for work. These finding are also consistent, however, with welfare recipients being subject to negative projection bias about their tastes for work.

More generally, suppose we take a traditional approach and think of time spent away from work as a desirable good. In that case assuming that parents underestimate their ability to adjust to less of that good is consistent with evidence from a large literature on hedonic adaptation. That literature shows, quite robustly and across a wide range of domains, that individuals overestimate the disutility that unpleasant circumstances will give them over the long term (see, for example, Sackett and Torrance 1978; Gilbert et al. 1998; Riis et al. 2005). We view this evidence of individuals' systematic underestimation of their ability to adapt to negative circumstances, along with the conventional treatment of leisure as a good, as favoring the modeling choice of a negative projection bias regarding predictions of the future taste for work.

Projection-Bias Model Versus Present-Bias Model

Our most general model allows any combination of projection bias and hyperbolic discounting models. However, our formal analysis limits attention to two classes of models that are nested as special cases of the general model just outlined:

> Projection-Bias Model: If the general model is restricted to have time-consistent preferences, but continues to allow projection bias, we will call it the projection-bias model.

> Present-Bias Model: If the above model is restricted to allow no projection bias, but continues to permit present bias, we will call it the present-bias model.

Distinguishing Biases Using Data on Choices, Outcomes, and Attitudes

We now summarize our analysis of whether the projection-bias and present-bias models can be distinguished using data on choices, outcomes, and attitudes toward welfare policies.

Choice and Outcome Data

To establish that one can empirically distinguish the projection-bias models and present-bias models using only data on choices and possible outcomes (for example, wages), one has to show formally that the observed data is consistent with one model but not the other. In appendix B, we conduct such an exercise and show that, indeed, standard data can be used to distinguish a present-biased individual from a decision maker with projection bias, and each from a time-consistent, rational decision maker. More precisely, in the context of our models, there is no set of parameters such that the behavior of a present-biased agent could be replicated by that of an agent with projection bias. Similarly, the behavior of a time-consistent agent cannot be replicated by an agent with either bias.

Why can't the optimal behavior and outcomes of a population of present-biased parents be replicated by the optimal behavior of either time-consistent or projection-biased parents, and vice versa? The analysis in appendix B shows that such replication is impossible because the optimizing choices and outcomes of present- and projection-biased agents must, at some point, be inconsistent. In particular, data on the welfare benefit level and the lowest wages ever accepted at the very end of the planning horizon allow us to pin down the common costs of working across all three models. Similarly, the probabilities of various choices—choices that depend on work experience, wages accepted, and welfare benefits—pin down the values derived from different choices, regardless of the underlying model driving the behavior. With the same costs, values, and outcomes (and in particular the same wages), the equations describing optimizing behavior in various states of the world cannot be simultaneously satisfied for both present-biased and projection-biased populations. In this setting, the data can support one interpretation or the other, but not both. A similar argument distinguishes an unbiased population from either a present-biased or a projection-biased population.

These results are useful to the extent that they inform us about the driving forces for identification. However, such identification results rely on the structures the models impose; as such they should be interpreted with care. Specifically, we show that if the true data generating process is a present-bias model in the form of (quasi-) hyperbolic discounting, then such data cannot be rationalized by a projection-bias model in the simple form found in Loewenstein, O'Donoghue, and Rabin (2003). That is, we are able to distinguish the quasi-hyperbolic discounting from a particular model of simple projection bias. To the extent that these two are specifications designed for analytic convenience and do not capture present- and projection-bias models more generally, the applications of our results are limited. It may, for example, be impossible to distinguish between projection bias and a more general form of present-biased time preferences. Caution in interpreting these results is also justified because we do not know yet, assuming that the true data generating process combines present and projection biases, whether we will be able to disentangle the degree of these biases from the standard data.

Attitude Data

In part because the technical argument for distinguishing between biases relies on specific formulations of them, we also considered a reduced-form method of distinguishing based on the idea that agents with projection bias will often have different attitudes than those with present biases toward changes in welfare policy such as time limits or work requirements. In particular, the change in attitude toward a policy once the policy is implemented may differ. These differences in changes in attitude can in principle be measured and thus distinguish behavior.

Appendix C presents the details of the formal analysis. That analysis shows an empirically plausible set of circumstances under which the attitudes of the welfare-eligible to time limit policies could be used to distinguish among unbiased, present-biased, and projection-biased parents. A critical ingredient is that net wages must at some point decline with experience and then increase. Under these circumstances, prolonged welfare program participation for women with present-biased preferences is driven, in Fang and Silverman's terms, by a "lack of commitment" to work through the difficult times (2004a). By this we mean that an individual would prefer to work now if she could commit herself to continue working in the future; however, she knows that in the absence of an external commitment device she would not in fact work in the future, even if she did work today. The insight is that would-be welfare recipients with projection bias do not want time limits or workfare beforehand, but may prefer it afterward, when they realize that the costs of working are not as high as they had thought. Welfare recipients with present bias may want time limits or workfare beforehand, but will at some later point prefer to relax it, as they fall victim to the desire for immediate gratification. We summarize these results as two hypotheses:

> Hypothesis 1: If the early selves of present-biased agents choose welfare as a result of lack of commitment, then such agents will exhibit favorable attitudes toward time limits before time limits are imposed; however, once these are implemented, they will prefer that the limits be relaxed.

> Hypothesis 2: If agents have projection bias about the cost of working, they will exhibit negative attitudes toward time limits before time limits are imposed, but once these are implemented, they will prefer that the limits remain in place.

These two hypotheses form the basis of an empirical strategy. They suggest that, if we have accurate measures of the attitudes toward time limits before and after the limits are implemented, we can distinguish the present bias from the projection bias. An important question is, to what extent can we rely on attitudinal data from surveys? In contrast to researchers in other social sciences, economists have traditionally shied away from subjective attitudinal data, and instead relied on behavioral data to make statistical inferences. Common complaints about subjective attitudinal data include:[11]

- survey respondents do not have incentive to think hard about the question;

- their responses are very sensitive to the wording of the question;

- people simply do not have opinions about many things and if you force them to form an opinion, their answers will be uninformative.

The first complaint is applicable to any retrospective survey data, including commonly used behavioral data such as Current Population Survey. The second and third are more relevant. Indeed, researchers have found that slight changes in the framing of the questionnaire can have big effects on how respondents answer these questions. These valid concerns, however, should not be the reason for not using attitudinal data; they call instead for designing questionnaires carefully and adopting attitude elicitation techniques from cognitive psychology (see Manski 2004).[12]

Conclusion

Recent research that incorporates cognitive biases into economic models of decision making typically studies the implications of these deviations from the standard model one bias at a time. This strategy of limiting attention to one potential bias may, in some cases, be justified by a priori indications of the primacy of that bias in determining behavior. If, however, several biases might plausibly explain behavior, the obvious question is whether data allow these various biases to be distinguished from each other and from a traditional model. Distinguishing between biases is particularly important when the policy implications of the underlying explanations for behavior differ substantially. Here we take up this question in the context of labor supply and welfare program participation.

The ideas we present here are exploratory, and are a small step in an important direction of examining how the increasing number of cognitive biases that economists are introducing into economic models can be potentially distinguished.

Appendix A: Formal Model

Here we present a formal model of labor supply and welfare program participation decisions that incorporates both present and projection biases.[13] Consider a discrete time, finite horizon model with periods $t \in \{1,$

..., T}. In each period, an agent chooses either to receive welfare (option 0), or work in the labor market (option 1), or stay at home without work or welfare (option 2). An agent's choice set is denoted by $D \equiv \{0, 1, 2\}$. Her period-t choice is denoted by $d_t \in D$.

If the agent chooses welfare, she receives a benefit $b > 0$. If the agent receives a job offer and chooses work, her expected wage depends on the cumulative number of periods she has ever worked, denoted by τ. The average wage as a function of experience is denoted by $\omega(\tau)$. The wage offer in period t, w_t, for an agent with experience τ is:

$$w_t = \omega(\tau) + \eta_t$$

where η_t is a mean zero residual drawn from a continuous CDF $G_\tau(\cdot)$ that may depend on τ.

An individual who chooses work incurs a direct utility cost, c_t. This actual period-t cost of working depends on the period-$(t-1)$ choice, d_{t-1}, and satisfies:

$$c_t = c(\tau, d_{t-1}) = \begin{cases} c_l(\tau) & \text{if} \quad d_{t-1} = 1 \\ c_h(\tau) & \text{if} \quad d_{t-1} \in \{0, 2\} \end{cases} \tag{A1}$$

where $0 < c_l(\tau) < c_h(\tau)$. Thus we assume the cost of continued work is lower than the cost upon transitioning into work from either home or welfare. We emphasize that c_t is the experienced cost of work. We allow the perception of future cost of work to be biased.

In period t an agent's job offer probability, ρ_t, depends on both work experience and period-$(t-1)$ choice, d_{t-1}, as follows:

$$\rho_t = \rho(\tau, d_{t-1}) = \begin{cases} \rho_h(\tau) & \text{if} \quad d_{t-1} = 1 \\ \rho_l(\tau) & \text{if} \quad d_{t-1} \in \{0, 2\} \end{cases}$$

where $\rho_h(\tau) \in (0, 1)$, $\rho_l(\tau) \in (0, 1)$, $\rho_h(\tau) \geq \rho_l(\tau)$ and $\rho_h(\cdot)$ and $\rho_l(\cdot)$ are increasing in τ. These assumptions capture the idea that offers are easier to get when working, and with more experience.

Home

We normalize the payoff from staying home without welfare to zero and assume all agents begin the decision process at home without welfare. In the absence of time limits or work requirements, the choice of home without welfare is dominated by welfare.

State Variable and Strategies

When an agent makes a choice in period t, the relevant state variable is $h_t \equiv (t, \tau, d_{t-1}, \chi_t, \eta_t)$, indicating that the period is t; the agent has worked

τ periods and the decision last period was $d_{-1} \in D$. The variable $\chi_t \in \{0, 1\}$ indicates whether the agent receives the offer $\omega(\tau) + \eta_t$ in period t. We will often refer to the second element of h_t as τ_t.

We restrict attention to Markovian strategies; a feasible strategy in period t, σ_t, is a mapping from the set of all possible period t states into the choice set D. Given h_t and σ_t, the state variable in period $t + 1$ is denoted $\vec{h}_{t+1}(h_t, \sigma_t)$. A strategy profile is a vector of mappings $\sigma \equiv (\sigma_t)_{t=1}^T$, specifying for each period the agent's action in all possible states. For any period $s > t$, we denote the period-s state that will be reached from h_t if the strategy profile σ is followed by $\vec{h}_s(h_t, \sigma)$.

Actual Instantaneous Utility Function

We assume that the agent cannot borrow or save. Thus the period-t instantaneous utility is given by:

$$u_t = u(d_t, h_t) = \begin{cases} b & \text{if } d_t = 0 \\ w_t - c(\tau, d_{t-1}) & \text{if } d_t = 1 \\ 0 & \text{if } d_t = 2. \end{cases}$$

Modeling Projection Bias

We assume projection bias affects only predictions of the future cost of working. Borrowing from Loewenstein, O'Donoghue, and Rabin (2003), we model this projection bias as follows. In period t, the agent's predicted cost of working in period $s \geq t + 1$, with experience τ_s, denoted $\tilde{c}_s$, satisfies:

$$\tilde{c}_s = \tilde{c}_s (\tau_s, d_{s-1} \mid d_{t-1})$$
$$= (1 - \alpha)c(\tau_s, d_{s-1}) + \alpha c(\tau_s, d_{t-1}) \tag{A2}$$

where $\alpha \in [0, 1]$. Note that, if $d_{s-1} = d_{t-1}$, then $\tilde{c}_s = c_s$. That is, there is no misprediction when the agent is contemplating the cost working in a future state that, in terms of previous period's decision, is the same as her current situation. The parameter $\alpha \in [0, 1]$ reflects the degree of projection bias. When $\alpha = 0$, the agent accurately predicts her cost of working; when $\alpha = 1$, the agent perceives that future cost of working will be what her current cost of working would be with experience τ_s. When $\alpha \in (0, 1)$, the agent has an intermediate level of projection bias.

Projected Future Utilities

Reflecting this potentially biased perception of future utility, the instantaneous period-s utility, projected by the agent in period $t \leq s$ is:

$$\tilde{u}_s = (d_s, h_s \mid d_{t-1}) = \begin{cases} b & \text{if } d_s = 0 \\ w_s - \tilde{c}(\tau_s, d_{s-1} \mid d_{t-1}) & \text{if } d_s = 1 \\ 0 & \text{if } d_s = 2. \end{cases}$$

Intertemporal Preferences and Present Biased Discounting

We represent an agent's possibly time-inconsistent preferences with so-called (β, δ)-preferences. For all t, if an agent predicts a stream of utilities from period t onward $(\tilde{u}_t, \ldots, \tilde{u}_T)$, then the agent will evaluate that stream according to:

$$(\tilde{u}_t, \ldots, \tilde{u}_T \mid d_{t-1}) \equiv \delta^t \tilde{u}_t + \beta \sum_{s=t+1}^{T} \delta^s \tilde{u}_s, \text{ where } \beta \in (0, 1], \delta \in (0, 1] \quad (A3)$$

The parameter δ reflects long-run, time-consistent discounting and is called the discount factor. The parameter β captures short-term impatience, and is called the present-bias factor. When $\beta = 1$, (β, δ)-preferences are time-consistent. When $\beta \in (0, 1)$, preferences are present-biased and time inconsistent.

Following a standard approach, we analyze the behavior of an agent by thinking of the decision-maker in each period as a separate self. Each period-t self makes the choice that maximizes current preferences $V^t (\tilde{u}_t, \ldots, \tilde{u}_T \mid d_{t-1})$, knowing that future selves control their own behavior.

Sophistication and Equilibrium

The literature on time-inconsistent preferences distinguishes between sophistication and naivete (Strotz 1956; Pollak 1968; O'Donoghue and Rabin 1999). An agent is sophisticated if each period-t self knows the future selves' preferences and anticipates their behavior when making a choice. The individual is naive if each period-t self believes that the future selves' preferences are identical to those of the present. We assume agents are sophisticated with respect to both their present and projection biases.

Our equilibrium concept is an analog of subgame perfection for the intrapersonal game and generalizes perception-perfection from O'Donoghue and Rabin (1999). Given a strategy profile σ, denote by $\tilde{W}_s(\sigma, h_s \mid d_{t-1})$ the expected continuation long-run utility from period s $(s \geq t + 1)$ onward perceived by the period-t self. This value is defined recursively from period T as follows:

$$\tilde{W}_T(\sigma, h_T \mid d_{t-1}) = \tilde{u}_T(\sigma_T(h_T), h_T \mid d_{t-1}), \quad (A4)$$

and for $s = T - 1, \ldots, t + 1$,

$$\tilde{W}_s(\boldsymbol{\sigma}, h_s \mid d_{t-1}) = \tilde{u}_s(\sigma_s(h_s), h_s \mid d_{t-1}) = \delta \mathbb{E} \tilde{W}_{S+1}(\boldsymbol{\sigma}, \vec{h}_{s+1}(\sigma_s(h_s), \boldsymbol{\sigma}) \mid d_{t-1}).$$

In words, this value represents the period-t self's intertemporal preferences from some prior perspective where her own present bias is irrelevant, but accounting for her projection bias.

Definition 1

A perception-perfect equilibrium for an agent with potentially both present and projection biases is a strategy profile $\boldsymbol{\sigma}^* \equiv \{\sigma^*_t\}^T_{t=1}$ that satisfies, for all h_t, and for all t,

$$\sigma^*_t(h_t) = \arg \max_{d_t \in D}\{u_t(d_t, h_t) + \beta \delta \mathbb{E}\tilde{W}_{t+1}(\boldsymbol{\sigma}^*, \vec{h}_{t+1}(h_t, d_t) \mid d_{t-1})\}.$$

If an agent has no projection bias, our equilibrium concept reduced to that used in O'Donoghue and Rabin (1999). The analysis that follows restricts attention to two classes of models that are nested as special cases of our general model. If the general model is restricted to $\beta = 1$, we call it the projection-bias model. When we assume $\alpha = 0$, we call it the present-bias model.

Appendix B: Distinguishing Projection and Present Bias in Standard Data

Here we show that the present-bias and projection-bias models can be distinguished in standard data, and that each can be distinguished from a traditional model with no biases.

First we make precise what it means to say two models can be distinguished, or that a model is (partially) identified. Model A can be *distinguished* from model B if there exists no parameterization of model B that is consistent with a large sample of data if those data were actually generated by model A, and vice versa. We say that a model is (*partially*) *identified* if we can uniquely recover from the data all (some) of the primitives of the true data-generating model.[14]

Standard Data

In what follows, we assume access to a data set consisting of an infinite number of individuals with observations on:

[DA] experience level and choices for all individuals i at each period t: $\{t^i_t, d^i_t\}^{i \in I}_{t=1, \ldots, T}$;

[DB] welfare benefit level b;

[DC] accepted wages of those who work $\{w_t^i\}_{t=1,...,T}^{i \in I}$, if $\chi_t^i = 1$ and $d_t^i = 1$.

To determine whether we can distinguish the projection- and present-bias models, we begin by assuming the data were generated by a present-bias model with unknown primitives (denoted with a superscript *). We then ask whether there exists a projection-bias model ($\beta' = 1, \delta', \alpha' \in (0,1)$) that could have generated the data that was actually generated by the present-bias model ($\beta^*, \delta^*, \alpha^* = 0$).

Our first result shows that we can recover the working cost functions from the standard data:

Lemma B1

We can recover $c_l(\tau)$ and $c_h(\tau)$ from [DB] and [DC].

Proof

In period T, given any state h_T, the decision rule is simple: the agent works if and only if:

$$\omega(\tau) + \eta_T \geq c(\tau, d_{T-1}) + b.$$

With infinite data, [DC] gives the lowest acceptable wage for an agent with experience τ_T, whose prior choice was d_{T-1}. Let $\widehat{w_T}(\tau, d_{T-1})$ denote the lowest wage among those who chose d_{T-1} in the previous period. Consistent estimates of $c_l(\tau)$ and $c_h(\tau)$ are then given by:

$$\widehat{c_l(\tau)} = \underline{w}_T(\tau, 1) - b, \quad \widehat{c_h(\tau)} = \underline{w}_T(\tau, 0) - b. \tag{B5}$$

Proposition 1

If $T \geq 3$, then projection-bias and present-biased models are nonparametrically distinguishable in standard data.

Proof

From [DA], we can consistently estimate the conditional choice probabilities at date t, denoted by $\Delta_t(d_t | \tau, d_{t-1})$, from their sample analogues. For example,

$$\widehat{\Delta_t(1 | \tau, d)} = \frac{\#\{i : d_t^i = 1, \tau_t^i = \tau, d_{t-1}^i = d\}}{\#\{i : \tau_t^i = \tau, d_{t-1}^i = d\}}. \tag{B6}$$

Similarly, we can estimate the average wages for working agents in period t conditional on experience τ and d_{t-1}. They are denoted by $\bar{I}_t(\tau, d_{T-1})$, and estimated consistently by:

$$\widehat{\bar{I}_t(\tau, d)} = \frac{\displaystyle\sum_{\{i:d_t^i=1,\,\tau_t^i=\tau,\,d_{t-1}^i=d\}} w_t^i}{\#\{i:d_t^i=1,\tau_t^i=\tau,d_{t-1}^i=d\}}.$$

With these estimated conditional choice probabilities and average earnings, we can use Joseph Hotz and Robert Miller's approach (1993) to estimate expected continuation value functions. Consider the terminal period T. Denote the expected continuation value of an agent with experience τ who made period-(T − 1) choice d_{T-1} by $Q_T(\tau, d_{T-1})$. Consistent estimates of those expected continuation values are given by:

$$\widehat{Q_T(\tau, d)} = \widehat{\Delta_T(1 | \tau, d)}[\widehat{\bar{I}_T(\tau, d)} - \widehat{c_h(\tau)}] + [1 - \widehat{\Delta_T(1 | \tau, d)}]b.$$

Now suppose that a projection-bias model could also generate the data generated from this present-bias model. In the present-bias model (β^*, δ^*), the choice of an agent with experience τ in period-(T − 1) is determined as follows. If $d_{T-2} = 0$, then she works only if:

$$w(\tau) + \eta_{T-1} - c_h(\tau) + \beta^*\delta^* Q_T(\tau+1, 1) \geq b + \beta^*\delta^* Q_T(\tau, 0).$$

Thus the lowest accepted wage in period-(T − 1) for agents with experience τ and $d_{T-2} = 0$ is:

$$\underline{w}^*_{T-1}(\tau, 0) = b + c_h(\tau) + \beta^*\delta^*[Q_T(\tau, 0) - Q_T(\tau+1, 1)]. \tag{B7}$$

Similarly, the lowest accepted wage in period-(T − 1) for agents with experience τ and $d_{T-2} = 1$ must satisfy:

$$\underline{w}^*_{T-1}(\tau, 1) = b + c_l(\tau) + \beta^*\delta^*[Q_T(\tau, 0) - Q_T(\tau+1, 1)]. \tag{B8}$$

Under a projection-bias model (δ', α'), an agent with experience τ and $d_{T-2} = 0$ will work in period-(T − 1) only if:

$$\omega(\tau) + \eta_{T-1} - c_h(\tau) + \delta'\tilde{Q}_T(\tau+1, 1 | d_{T-2} = 0) \geq b + \delta'\tilde{Q}_T(\tau, 0 | d_{T-2} = 0)$$

where $\tilde{Q}_T$ is the net continuation value at period T perceived by the period-(T − 1) agent. Note that $\tilde{Q}_T(\tau, 0 | d_{T-2} = 0) = Q_T(\tau, 0)$, and,

$$\tilde{Q}_T(\tau+1, 1 | d_{T-2} = 0) = \Delta_T(1 | \tau+1, 1)\{\bar{I}_T(\tau+1, 1) - [(1-\alpha')c_l(\tau+1) +$$
$$\alpha'c_h(\tau+1)]\}$$

$$+ [1 - \Delta_T (1 \mid \tau + 1, 1)] \, b$$
$$= Q_T(\tau + 1, 1) - \alpha' \Delta_T (1 \mid \tau + 1, 1) [c_h(\tau + 1) - c_l(\tau + 1)].$$

Thus the lowest accepted wage in period-$(T - 1)$ for agent with experience τ and $d_{T-2} = 0$ is:

$$\underline{w}'_{T-1} (\tau, 0) = b + c_h(\tau) + \delta'[Q_T(\tau, 0) - Q_T(\tau + 1, 1)]$$
$$+ \alpha' \delta' \Delta_T (1 \mid \tau + 1, 1) [c_h(\tau + 1) - c_l(\tau + 1)]. \tag{B9}$$

An analogous argument for agents with experience τ and $d_{T-2} = 1$ shows that their lowest accepted wage in period $(T - 1)$ must satisfy:

$$\underline{w}'_{T-1} (\tau, 1) = b + c_l(\tau) + \delta' [Q_T(\tau, 0) - Q_T(\tau + 1, 1)]$$
$$+ \alpha' \delta' \Delta_T (1 \mid \tau, 0) [c_h(\tau) - c_l(\tau)]. \tag{B10}$$

If the two models are indistinguishable, it must be that:

$$\underline{w}'_{T-1} (\tau, 0) = \underline{w}^*_{T-1} (\tau, 0).$$
$$\underline{w}'_{T-1} (\tau, 1) = \underline{w}^*_{T-1} (\tau, 1).$$

The costs of work, $c_h(\tau)$ and $c_l(\tau)$, are identified from Lemma 1; they cannot be chosen differently for different models. Thus the two preceding wage equalities are satisfied only if:

$$\beta^*\delta^*[Q_T(\tau, 0) - Q_T(\tau + 1, 1)] = \delta'[Q_T(\tau, 0) - Q_T(\tau + 1, 1)]$$
$$+ \alpha' \delta' \Delta_T (1 \mid \tau + 1, 1) [c_h(\tau + 1) - c_l(\tau + 1)]$$
$$\beta^*\delta^*[Q_T(\tau, 0) - Q_T(\tau + 1, 1)] = \delta'[Q_T(\tau, 0) - Q_T(\tau + 1, 1)]$$
$$+ \alpha' \delta' \Delta_T (1 \mid \tau, 0) [c_h(\tau) - c_l(\tau)].$$

These two equalities can be simultaneously satisfied only if $\delta' = \beta^*\delta^*$ and $\alpha' = 0$. Proposition 2 goes on to show that if $T \geq 3$, then the present-bias model (β^*, δ^*) can also be distinguished from an exponential discounting model. Thus the projection- and present-bias models can be distinguished both from each other and from a standard model.

Proposition 2

If $T \geq 3$, then a present-bias model with $\beta^* \in (0, 1)$, $\delta^* \in (0, 1)$ can be distinguished from an exponential discounting model with $\beta' = 1$ and $\delta' \in (0, 1)$ using standard data.

Proof

Following the proof of the previous proposition, an unbiased model rationalizes the minimum accepted wage at period-$(T-1)$ only if $\delta' = \beta^*\delta$.

We can estimate the period-$(T-1)$ expected continuation value of an agent with experience τ and period-$(T-2)$ choice d_{T-2} as $Q_{T-1}(\tau, d_{T-2})$. Consistent estimates of these expected continuation values for a (β^*,δ^*) agent are given by:

$$\widehat{Q_{T-1}(\tau, d)} = \widehat{\Delta_{T-1}(1 \mid \tau, d)}[\widehat{I_{T-1}(\tau, d)} - \widehat{c_h(\tau)} + \delta * \widehat{Q_T(\tau + 1, 1)}]$$
$$+ [1 - \widehat{\Delta_{T-1}(1 \mid \tau, d)}][b + \delta * \widehat{Q_T(\tau, 0)}]$$

Now consider an agent with (β^*,δ^*) in period-$(T-2)$. Analogous to the argument in the proof of Proposition 1, the lowest accepted wage in period-$(T-2)$ for agents with experience τ and $d_{T-3} = 0$ must be:

$$\underline{w}^*_{T-2}(\tau, 0) = b + c_h(\tau) + \beta^*\delta^*[Q_{T-1}(\tau, 0) - Q_{T-1}(\tau + 1, 1)].$$

An analogous argument for exponential discounting agents with $\delta' = \beta^*\delta^*$ shows that their lowest accepted wage in period-$(T-2)$ for agents with experience τ and $d_{T-3} = 0$ is:

$$\underline{w}'_{T-2}(\tau, 0) = b + c_h(\tau) + \delta'[Q'_{T-1}(\tau, 0) - Q'_{T-1}(\tau + 1, 1)].$$

Note $\underline{w}^*_{T-2}(\tau, 0)$ and $\underline{w}'_{T-2}(\tau, 0)$ weigh $\widehat{Q_T(\tau + 1, 1)}$ and $\widehat{Q_T(\tau, 0)}$ differently unless $\beta^* = 1$.

So far, we have shown that, in standard data, we can distinguish projection-bias and present-bias models; and distinguish a present-bias model ($\beta^* < 1$) from a standard model. These results do not imply, however, that we can identify all the primitives of these models from standard data. Under some distributional restrictions, however, we can guarantee at least partial identification.

Proposition 3

We can recover $\omega(\tau)$ for all $\tau > 0$ up to a constant from standard data if the following two conditions are satisfied:

1 $G_\tau(\cdot) = G(\cdot)$;
2. $g'(\eta) \equiv \partial^2 G(\eta)/\partial\eta^2 \neq 0$ almost everywhere.

Proof

For this proof, we will only use data from period T. Write the period-T cumulative accepted wage distribution of agents with experience τ and

$d_{T-1} = 0$ as $F_T^\tau(w)$. From such agents' period-T optimal decision rule (see the expression in the proof of Lemma B1), we have that, if $w \geq c_h(\tau) + b$,

$$
\begin{aligned}
F_T^\tau(w) &= \Pr[\omega(\tau) + \eta \leq w \mid \omega(\tau) + \eta - c_h(\tau) \geq b, \chi_T = 1] \\
&= \Pr[\eta \leq w - \omega(\tau) \mid \eta \geq c_h(\tau) + b - \omega(\tau), \chi_T = 1] \\
&= \frac{G(w - \omega(\tau)) - G(c_h(\tau) + b - \omega(\tau))}{[1 - G(c_h(\tau) + b - \omega(\tau))]p_1(\tau)} \\
&= \frac{G(w - \omega(\tau)) - G(c_h(\tau) + b - \omega(\tau))}{\Delta_T(1 \mid \tau, \ 0)}
\end{aligned}
$$

and $F_T^\tau(w) = 0$ otherwise. The last equality holds because $[1 - G(c_h + b - \omega(\tau))] \, p_1(\tau)$ is simply the period-T probability of working for agents with experience τ and $d_{T-1} = 0$, which is observable in the data [see formula (B6) for its empirical analogue]. Thus the period-T accepted wage density of agents with experience τ and $d_{T-1} = 0$ is:

$$
f_T^\tau(w) = \begin{cases} \dfrac{g(w - \omega(\tau))}{\Delta_T(1 \mid \tau, \ 0)} & \text{if } w \geq c_h(\tau) + b \\ 0 & \text{otherwise.} \end{cases} \tag{B11}
$$

From [DC], we could observe the empirical analogue of $f_T^\tau(w)$ for all $\tau \geq 0$. Denote these empirical counterparts by $\widehat{f_T^\tau}(w)$. Together with $\widehat{\Delta_T}(1 \mid \tau, 0)$ from formula (B6), we write:

$$
\widehat{h_T^\tau}(w) = \widehat{f_T^\tau}(w)\widehat{\Delta_T}(1 \mid \tau, 0) \text{ if } w \geq c_h(\tau) + b.
$$

Now using (B11), we can construct estimates of the upper tails of $g(\eta)$. For example, from agents with experience $\tau = 0$ and $d_{T-1} = 1$, we have:

$$
\widehat{g(\eta)} = h_T^0(\widehat{\eta + \omega}(0)) \text{ if } \eta \geq c_h(0) + b - \omega(0). \tag{B12}
$$

From agents with experience $\tau = 1$ and $d_{T-1} = 1$, we have:

$$
\widehat{g(\eta)} = h_T^1(\widehat{\eta + \omega}(1)) \text{ if } \eta \geq c_h(1) + b - \omega(1). \tag{B13}
$$

Assumption 2 ensures that the upper tail of $g(\eta)$ can be identified. Thus we know (B12) and (B13) have to coincide for $\eta \geq \max\{c_h(0) + b - \omega(0), c_h(1) + b - \omega(1)\}$. That is, if we shift $\widehat{h_T^1}(w)$ or $\widehat{h_T^0}(w)$, their right tails have to exactly overlap because each estimates the upper tail of $g(\eta)$. The shift required for the right tails of $\widehat{h_T^1}(w)$ or $\widehat{h_T^0}(w)$ to overlap is exactly the difference between $\omega(0)$ and $\omega(1)$. Thus $\omega(1) - \omega(0)$ is identified. Similarly, $\omega(\tau) - \omega(0)$ is identified for all $\tau > 1$.

Proposition 3 shows that $\omega(\tau)$ can be identified up to a constant under some (non-parametric and testable) distributional restrictions on G_τ $(\cdot)$; still $G(\cdot)$ itself is not identified. In fact, since we only observe data with information about the upper tails of G_τ, standard data would never allow us to identify the whole distributions of G_τ in the absence of parametric assumptions. If G_τ is not identified, then $\rho_h(\tau)$ and $\rho_l(\tau)$ are not identified. Finally note that for the purpose of distinguishing projection- and present-bias models, it is not necessary to know $\rho_h(\tau)$ and $\rho_l(\tau)$.

Cautionary Note: The identification results we have just derived apply to a model in which present-biased preferences take the form of quasi-hyperbolic discounting and the projection bias takes the simple form from Loewenstein and his colleagues (2003). To the extent that these specifications are adopted for analytic convenience and do not capture present and projection biases more generally, the applications of our result are limited. Moreover, we do not know yet, if the true data generating process is a model with a combination of present and projection biases, whether we will be able to disentangle the magnitude of these biases from standard data.

Appendix C: Changing Attitudes

Here we demonstrate bias-dependent changes in attitude about welfare policies in simple three period examples that are special cases of the general model presented earlier.

Suppose the wage-experience profile is deterministic ($\eta_t \equiv 0$), and is given by the following:

τ	0	1	2
$w(\tau)$	0	−9	23.5

The important feature of this wage profile is that net wages get worse with experience before they get better. See Fang and Silverman (2004a) for a more detailed discussion of such a profile. In addition, presume, for simplicity, five conditions:

- Welfare benefit level is constant at $b = 1$;
- Job offers are always available ($\rho_h = \rho_l = 1$);
- The costs of working are $c_h = 4$, $c_l = 1$;
- For a present-biased agent, $\alpha = 0$, $\beta = 1/2$, and $\delta = 1$; and
- For a projection-biased agent, $\alpha = 1$, $\beta = 1$, and $\delta = 1$.

Suppose that in period 0 agents find themselves out of work. We will analyze their attitudes toward a proposed one-period welfare eligibility time limit and show that these attitudes are different for a present-biased versus a projection-biased agent.

Attitudes of a Present-Biased Agent Toward a Time Limit

Consider first the optimal decisions of a present-biased agent in the absence of a time limit. In period 3, if $\tau_3 = 2$, she must have worked in period 2. In this case, the agent chooses work because:

$$w(2) - c_1 = 23.5 - 1 > b = 1.$$

If, instead, period two was her first time in the labor market then the agent does not work because:

$$w(1) - c_1 = -9 - 1 < b = 1.$$

Similarly, if $\tau_3 = 1$ and $d_2 = 0$, the agent does not work, and if the agent has not yet worked she will not work in the third period. Thus, in period 3, an agent works if and only if $\tau_3 = 2$.

Working backwards, consider her optimal plan in period two. Even if she worked in period 1, $\tau_2 = 1$, she does not work in period 2 because:

$$w(1) - c_1 + \beta[w(2) - c_1] = -9 - 1 + \frac{1}{2}[23.5 - 1] = 1.25 < b + \frac{1}{2}b = 1.5.$$

Similarly, if $\tau_2 = 0$ the agent does not work because $w(0) - c_h < b$ and she would not work in the third period. In short, this second period self will not work no matter what.

In period 1, the agent chooses not to work. Starting a career is fruitless because her future selves would not stay in the labor force. The first period self cannot commit her future selves to work, and for this reason decides not to work herself. If, however, she could commit her future selves to work, she would have preferred a life of work to a life on welfare because:

$$w(0) - c_h + \beta[w(1) - c_1 + w(2) - c_1] = 2.25 > b + \frac{1}{2}[b + b] = 2.$$

Next we consider the agent's attitude toward a one-period time limit, and how that attitude changes depending on when she is asked.

First Attitude

If asked at the beginning of period 1 (or at any time prior to the decision making modeled here) whether she would support the implementation of a one-period time limit, the agent would answer, "Yes, I would like such a limit." She prefers the time limit because it commits her future selves to work. Consider the agent in period 2. If the agent has worked in period 1, that is, if $\tau_2 = 1$, $d_1 = 1$, the period 2 self's payoff from working would be

$$w(1) - c_1 + \beta[w(2) - c_1] = -9 - 1 + \frac{1}{2}[23.5 - 1] = 1.25.$$

If instead she stays on welfare in period 2, the third period self would stay at home (because of the time limit), thus her expected payoff from participating in welfare in period 2 is given by:

$$1 + \beta[0] = 1.$$

The second period self works if the period 1 self worked. Anticipating this, the period one self would work and, as we showed earlier, achieve a higher discounted payoff than that from a life on welfare. She thus strictly prefers that the time limit be implemented.[15]

Later Attitudes

After the policy is implemented, however, the agent's attitude changes. If asked then whether she would prefer the time limit remain in place, she would either say, "No, I prefer that the limit be relaxed," or she would say she is indifferent. In period 2, having worked in the previous period she would strictly prefer to relax the welfare time limit, choose welfare today and anticipate a payoff of:

$$1 + \beta[1] = 1.5,$$

which strictly exceeds her payoff under the time limit. In period 3 if we ask the agent the same question she will say she is indifferent, she will work no matter what.

Attitudes of a Projection-Biased Agent Toward Time Limit

Now we analyze a projection-biased agent's preferences for policy. We again first consider behavior in the absence of a time limit. In period 3, optimal choice is like that of a present-biased agent; the agent works only if she worked in the previous two periods. In period 2, if $\tau_2 = 1$, then $d_1 = 1$ and the payoff from working is given by:

$$w(1) - c_1 + w(2) - c_1 = -9 - 1 + 23.5 - 1 > 2$$

so she works. If $\tau_2 = 0$, then $d_1 = 0$, and the expected payoff from working is $w(0) - c_h + b < 2b$ so she will not work. Thus, in period 2 the agent works only if she worked the previous period.

In period 1, the agent foresees that if she chooses work, she will work for the rest of her career. However, projection bias leads her to perceive the utility from working as:

$$[w(0) - c_h] + [w(1) - c_h] + [w(2) - c_h]$$
$$= 0 - 4 + [-9 - 4] + [23.5 - 4] = 2.5 < 3b = 3.$$

Thus in period 1, the agent chooses welfare because she over-predicts the future cost of work.

First Attitude

Now consider the agent's attitudes toward a one-period time limit. In period 1 (or at any time she is unemployed prior to the decision making modeled here) she opposes the idea. She opposes the limit, her choices are now choose work and anticipate payoffs:

$$[w(0) - c_h] + [w(1) - c_h] + [w(2) - c_h] = 2.5$$

or choose welfare and anticipate:

$$b + 0 + 0 = 1.$$

Each is strictly dominated, from her perspective, by a lifetime on welfare.

Later Attitudes

Sometime later, however, after the policy has been implemented, the agent's attitude changes. If asked then whether she would prefer that the time limit remain in place, she would say "I am indifferent." In period 2 or 3, having worked in the previous period she would strictly prefer to work regardless of the limit on welfare. If the horizon were longer and, more realistically, ρ_h, $\rho_l < 1$ then a working agent could strictly prefer that the time limit remain in place. In this case, if the agent fears losing her job, she would properly be concerned that once unemployed she would come to view the costs of working as too high and remain stuck on welfare.

An earlier draft of the paper was presented in the conference "Behavioral Public Finance: Toward a New Agenda" at the University of Michigan on

April 23 to 24, 2004. We are grateful to George Loewenstein, Edward Mc-Caffery, Joel Slemrod, and other conference participants for helpful comments. All remaining errors are our own.

Notes

1. The biases studied by economists include present-biased discounting (Strotz 1956; Laibson 1997; O'Donoghue and Rabin 1999), confirmatory bias (Rabin and Schrag 1999), loss aversion (Genesove and Mayer 2001), mental accounting (Barberis and Huang 2001), and projection bias (Loewenstein, O'Donoghue, and Rabin 2003).
2. See George Ainslie and Nick Haslam (1992) and several papers in Loewenstein and Elster (1992) for reviews of these experiments. Shane Frederick, George Loewenstein, and Ted O'Donoghue (2002) provide a comprehensive critical survey of time discounting and time preferences. Ariel Rubinstein (2003) provides alternative explanations of the choice reversal phenomenon, and presents a set of experiments contradicting the implications from hyperbolic discounting formulation.
3. Ted O'Donoghue and Matthew Rabin (2001) show how consumers with time-inconsistent preferences may procrastinate more when pursuing important goals than unimportant ones.
4. An example of one such successful policy is described in Richard Thaler and Shlomo Benartzi (2004).
5. A week later, the experimenters arrived at the promised times and allowed the subjects to make an immediate choice of snack, regardless of the choice they had made in advance. Those who were currently hungry chose the unhealthy snack more often than those who were satiated. However, both the hungry and the satiated opted for the unhealthy snack much more often than they had when the same choice was offered a week in advance.
6. Given the difficulties of identifying any model of behavior from choices alone, Charles Manski (2004) also argues for the direct measurement of expectations or beliefs to enrich empirical analysis.
7. We think of a period as six months to a year.
8. In practice, a single mother can work and be on welfare at the same time, as long as the income is lower than the break-even income to retain welfare eligibility. For simplicity, we abstract from this possibility.
9. At a more technical level, our model also assumes the parent is "sophisticated" about her projection bias. In this context, sophistication amounts to the agent having the ability to recognize her future tendency to place too much weight on present state preferences, but does not recognize that tendency in her current self. We adopt this assumption of sophistication, in part, to emphasize that the observable differences in present-versus projection-biased decision makers do not depend on having different levels of sophistication about these biases.
10. We emphasize the mispredictions considered here are limited to biased beliefs about future tastes. We do not, for example, consider mispredictions about the size of future budget sets. There is relatively little evidence that

individuals systematically mispredict how changes in circumstance will affect their budgets for consumption or time.

11. Marainne Bertrand and Sendhil Mullainathan (2001) offer an interesting
discussion about the reliability of subjective survey data.

12. More and more economists are now using subjective data to answer important policy questions. For example, Matthew Shapiro and Joel Slemrod
(2003) used consumer surveys to study the extent to which households
spent the tax rebate in 2001; Gruber and Mullainathan (2002) use self-reported happiness to measure the welfare consequence of cigarette tax hike.

13. This model is an extension of Fang and Silverman (2004a).

14. Questions of distinguishing or identifying a model are different from questions of estimation. A study of distinction or identification assumes an infi-
nitely large sample and abstracts from the difficulties posed by finite sample estimation.

15. An unbiased agent would, of course, never strictly prefer a time limit.

References

Ainslie, George, and Nick Haslam. 1992. "Hyperbolic Discounting." In *Choice
Over Time*, edited by George Loewenstein and Jon Elster. New York: Russell
Sage Foundation.

Ameriks, John, Andrew Caplin, and John Leahy. 2003. "Wealth Accumulation and the Propensity to Plan." *Quarterly Journal of Economics* 118(3): 1007–
47.

Arkin, Robert M., and Geoffrey M. Maruyama. 1979. "Attribution, Affect and
College Exam Performance." *Journal of Educational Psychology* 71(1): 85–93.

Aronson, Elliot. 1994. *The Social Animal*, 7th ed. New York: W. H. Freeman.

Babcock, Linda, Collin Camerer, George Loewenstein, and Richard Thaler. 1997.
"Labor Supply of New York City Cab Drivers: One Day at a Time." *Quarterly
Journal of Economics*, 112(2): 407–41.

Banks, James, Richard Blundell, and Sarah Tanner. 1998. "Is There a Retirement
Savings Puzzle?" *American Economic Review* 88(4): 769–88.

Barberis, Nicholas, and Ming Huang. 2001. "Mental Accounting, Loss Aversion,
and Individual Stock Returns." *Journal of Finance* 56(4): 1247–92.

Barro, Robert. 1999. "Ramsey Meets Laibson in the Neoclassical Growth Model."
Quarterly Journal of Economics 114(4): 1125–52.

Barsky, Robert, F. Thomas Juster, Miles Kimball, and Mathew Shapiro. 1997.
"Preference Parameters and Behavioral Heterogeneity: An Experimental Approach in the Health and Retirement Study." *Quarterly Journal of Economics*
112(2): 537–79.

Bernheim, B. Douglas, Jonathan Skinner, and Steven Weinberg. 2001. "What Accounts for the Variation in Retirement Wealth Among U.S. Households?"
American Economic Review 91(4): 832–57.

Bertrand, Marianne, and Sendhil Mullainathan. 2001. "Do People Mean What
They Say? Implications for Subjective Survey Data." *American Economic Review*
91(2): 67–72.

Cunningham, John D., Philip A. Starr, and David E. Kanouse. 1979. "Self as Actor, Active Observer, and Passive Observer: Implications for Causal Attribution." *Journal of Personality & Social Psychology* 37(7): 1146–52.

Della Vigna, Stefano, and Ulrike Malmendier. 2004. "Overestimating Self-Control: Evidence from the Health Club Industry." Mimeo, University of California, Berkeley.

Fang, Hanming, and Dan Silverman. 2004a. "On the Compassion of Time-limited Welfare Programs." *Journal of Public Economics* 88(7–8): 1445–70.

———. 2004b. "Time-inconsistency and Welfare Program Participation: Evidence from the NLSY." Cowles Foundation Discussion Paper 1465. New Haven, Conn.: Yale University.

Frederick, Shane, George Loewenstein, and Ted O'Donoghue. 2002. "Time Discounting and Time Preference: A Critical Review." *Journal of Economic Literature* 40(2): 351–401.

Genesove, David, and Christopher Mayer. 2001. "Loss Aversion and Seller Behavior: Evidence from the Housing Market." *Quarterly Journal of Economics* 116(4): 1233–260.

Gilbert, Daniel T., Timothy D. Wilson, Elizabeth C. Pinel, Stephen J. Blumberg, and Thalia P. Wheatley. 1998. "Immune Neglect: A Source of Durability Bias in Affective Forecasting." *Journal of Personality & Social Psychology* 75(3): 617–38.

Gilovich, Thomas. 1983. "Biased Evaluation and Persistence in Gambling." *Journal of Personality & Social Psychology* 44(6): 1110–126.

Gruber, Jonathan, and Botond Köszegi. 2001. "Is Addiction 'Rational'? Theory and Evidence." *Quarterly Journal of Economics* 116(4): 1261–1305.

Gruber, Jonathan, and Sendhil Mullainathan. 2002. "Do Cigarette Taxes Make Smokers Happier?" Mimeo, MIT, Cambridge, Mass.

Harris, Christopher, and David Laibson. 2001. "Dynamic Choices of Hyperbolic Consumers." *Econometrica* 69(3): 397–421.

Hotz, Joseph, and Robert Miller. 1993. "Conditional Choice Probabilities and the Estimation of Dynamic Models." *Review of Economic Studies* 60(3): 497–530.

Johnston, William A. 1967. "Individual Performance and Self-Evaluation in a Simulated Team." *Organizational Behavior and Human Performance* 2(3): 309–28.

Laibson, David. 1997. "Golden Eggs and Hyperbolic Discounting." *Quarterly Journal of Economics* 112(2): 443–77.

Larwood, Lauri, and William Whittaker. 1977. "Managerial Myopia: Self-serving Biases in Organizational Planning." *Journal of Applied Psychology* 62(2): 194–98.

Loewenstein, George, and Jon Elster, eds. 1992. *Choice Over Time*. New York: Russell Sage Foundation.

Loewenstein, George, Ted O'Donoghue, and Matthew Rabin. 2003. "Projection Bias in Predicting Future Utility." *Quarterly Journal of Economics* 118(4): 1209–248.

Manski, Charles F. 2004. "Measuring Expectations." *Econometrica* 72(5): 1329–346.

O'Donoghue, Ted, and Matthew Rabin. 1999. "Doing It Now or Later." *American Economic Review* 89(1): 103–24.

———. 2001. "Choice and Procrastination." *Quarterly Journal of Economics* 166(1): 121–60.

Paserman, M. Daniele. 2004. "Job Search and Hyperbolic Discounting: Structural Estimation and Policy Evaluation." IZA Discussion Paper No. 997. Bonn, Germany: IZA.

Pollak, Robert A. 1968. "Consistent Planning." *Review of Economic Studies* 35(2): 201–8.

Rabin, Matthew, and Joel Schrag. 1999. "First Impressions Matter: A Model of Confirmatory Bias." *Quarterly Journal of Economics* 114(1): 37–82.

Read, Daniel, and Barbara van Leeuwen. 1998. "Predicting Hunger: The Effects of Appetite and Delay on Choice." *Organizational Behavior and Human Decision Processes* 76(2): 189–205.

Riis, Jason, George Loewenstein, Jonathan Baron, Christopher Jepson, Angela Fagerlin, and Peter Ubel. 2005. "Ignorance of Hedonic Adaptation to Hemodialysis: A Study Using Ecological Momentary Assessment." *Journal of Experimental Psychology: General* 134(1): 3–9.

Ross, Michael, and Fiore Sicoly. 1979. "Egocentric Biases in Availability and Attribution." *Journal of Personality & Social Psychology* 37(3): 322–36.

Rubinstein, Ariel. 2003. "Economics and Psychology? The Case of Hyperbolic Discounting." *International Economic Review* 44(4): 1207–16.

Sackett, David L., and George W. Torrance. 1978. "The Utility of Different Health States as Perceived by the General Public." *Journal of Chronic Diseases* 31(11): 697–704.

Shapiro, Matthew, and Joel Slemrod. 2003. "Consumer Response to Tax Rebates." *American Economic Review* 93(1): 381–96.

Strotz, Robert H. 1956. "Myopia and Inconsistency in Dynamic Utility Maximization." *Review of Economic Studies* 23(3): 165–80.

Svenson, Ola. 1981. "Are We All Less Risky and More Skillful Than Our Fellow Drivers?" *Acta Psychologica* 47(2): 143–48.

Thaler, Richard, and Shlomo Benartzi. 2004. "Save More Tomorrow™: Using Behavioral Economics to Increase Employee Saving." *Journal of Political Economy* 112(1, part 2): S164–87.

Wertheimer, Richard, Melissa Long, and Sharon Vandivere. 2001. "Welfare Recipients' Attitudes toward Welfare, Nonmarital Childbearing, and Work: Implications for Reform?" New Federalism: National Survey of America's Families Report #310300. Washington, D.C.: Urban Institute Press.

PART II

BEHAVIOR AND POLICY

Chapter 4

Masking Redistribution (or Its Absence)

JONATHAN BARON AND EDWARD J. MCCAFFERY

B EHAVIORAL economics considers the ways that actual people make economic decisions and take economic actions (Thaler 1980; Kahneman and Tversky 2000; Sunstein 2000). In a nutshell, people make mistakes, showing inconsistent judgment in the face of framing and other formal manipulations of the presentation of choice problems. Most everyone, it seems, likes the glass half full; few like it half empty.

Behavioral public finance, we believe, ought to consider how ordinary people think about specifically governmental actions, paradigmatically tax and spending programs. Our experiments have shown that, in general, people suffer from much the same heuristics and biases in thinking about public as private finance. And their decisions about public finance are typically less subject to the discipline that feedback, as through private market mechanisms, provides.

In our thinking about people's thinking about public finance, we group a cluster of biases as specific instances of a more general isolation effect, whereby people make decisions about complex subjects quickly, responding to the most salient aspects of a choice or decision set, ignoring or underusing logically relevant information not immediately before them. Although we follow some in calling this an isolation effect (Camerer 2000; Kahneman and Lovallo 1993; McCaffery and Baron 2003; Read, Loewenstein, and Rabin 1999), others have called the phenomenon a focusing effect (Idson et al. 2004; Jones et al. 1998; Legrenzi, Girotto, and Johnson-Laird 1993). The idea of the focusing effect came from the theory of mental models in reasoning, as Legrenzi and his colleagues explained: people reason from mental models, and when possible they use a single, simple model that represents just the information they are given. Other factors are ignored or underused.

Whatever it is called, this tendency to make decisions while considering only part of a global whole, as if with blinders on, can have dramatic consequences for how people think about government tax and spending programs. This matters, because we assume that public opinion matters—it helps shape and constrain what public officials do (Steinmo 1993). And public opinion may be out of step with a better informed public policy, on account of the heuristics and biases. As Kahneman (2000) has demonstrated in the private context, the utility weights people use in deciding on matters of relevance to them differ from those they later experience as a result of their choices. In the cases we explore here, we find that the amount and extent of redistribution that subjects support varies with the form of public finance policy. The reason is that people are not considering the total effects of a particular policy change—such as using deductions to help subsidize private choices, or privatizing government services—on global patterns of distribution. Preference shifts and reversals occur based on the framing of public finance issues. The people can wake up with a tax and transfer system that they have chosen but do not want.

Consider, for example, an instance of an isolation effect we termed disaggregation bias (McCaffery and Baron 2003). We asked subjects what they thought would be a fair distribution of tax burdens across different households at different income levels. In a series of screens presented on a Web site, we listed one tax system, identified as either payroll or income, and asked the subjects either to set only the other tax system or to set the entire, aggregated tax system. We thereby replicated the effects of income tax reform given a payroll tax system in place—offstage, as it were. Rational choice theory suggests that the distributive characteristics of any one tax system, such as the payroll tax, should not matter, as long as a policy maker could adjust another tax, such as the income tax, to effect her desired bottom line. We found that most subjects desired at least a moderately progressive tax system when asked to design a whole. But when half of the revenue was collected by one tax, subjects underadjusted when choosing a tax system for the other half, though they were transparently able to achieve the same overall level of redistribution (progressiveness) as when they were choosing an entire system. In sum, subjects focused in only on what they were being asked to choose, making it moderately progressive—just as they wanted the system as a whole to be—though the global tax system then varied dramatically, depending on the properties of the so-called offstage tax.

These and related cognitive limitations raise troubling issues for the traditional practice of public finance. The two welfare theorems of neoclassical welfare economics suggest a two-part agenda for public finance, and for economic regulation more generally (Kaplow and Shavell 2000). First, policy makers should choose socioeconomic policies that maximize social welfare, for which wealth-maximization typically serves as a suitable proxy. Second, policy makers should redistribute the greater social wealth, through a tax and transfer system, to achieve a desired location on the Pareto frontier. In public finance, this means that decisions about the proper role for the government, and the structure of that role—what public goods ought to be provided, to what extent, and how financed—should be made in a strict welfare maximizing fashion, minimizing the deadweight losses or excess burdens of the fiscal intervention (Musgrave 1959; Rosen 2001). Logically, in other words, the welfarist view of public finance entails separating the allocative and distributive dimensions of public finance to achieve an optimal merger of efficiency and equity concerns, in the spirit, say, of Rawls's difference principle (1971), or of the utilitarian argument that the declining marginal utility of money justifies some redistribution. If a current government program is inefficiently designed, social welfare can be enhanced—and all individuals in society can stay at the same or a higher level of personal welfare—by moving to a more efficient government (or private) provision, coupled with a redistribution of the greater wealth within the Pareto constraint.

So it is in logic. But cognitive biases may get in the way of ordinary people understanding matters once two or more aspects of government action are separated. The experiments we detail here explore ways in which the extent of redistribution that people are willing to support depends on the form of government provision of goods and services. We ask whether people take into account the distributional effects of two kinds of policy changes: the use of tax deductions as a way of funding services, and the effect of privatization or elimination of government services and programs. Our main hypothesis is that, by failing to take distributional effects fully into account, people end up supporting policies that undercut their own values. These decisional biases can lead to violations of the two welfare theorems by generating a conflict between equity and efficiency—between total social wealth and the well-being of society's members—that does not exist in pure, rational theory.

General Experimental Method

We followed the same general procedure in each of the studies reported here.

Subjects completed an online questionnaire and were paid $3 or $4 each for doing so. Subjects came to the studies through postings on various websites or Usenet news groups, or through prior participation in other studies. They were paid by check (after some minimum amount was accumulated), and had to register their address and (for U.S. residents) their Social Security number to be paid. After this registration, however, they identified themselves only with their email address, and this was stored separately from the registration data, to ensure privacy and anonymity.

Our subject pool is roughly representative of the adult U.S. population in terms of income, age, and education (Babcock et al. 2003), but not in terms of sex, because (for unknown reasons) women predominate in our respondent pool.

The studies were programmed in JavaScript so that one case was presented on each page, and subjects were required to answer all questions on the page before proceeding. We recorded the time spent on each response, and usually eliminated subjects who went noticeably faster than everyone else (outliers, typically 2 to 3 percent). Many of our experiments have had internal checks to ensure that subjects understand the questions and answer in the appropriate range; the first and third experiments reported below, for example, had such checks on understanding, the results of which we report. It bears stressing that though the subject matters we are testing are undeniably complex, they are realistic, and our screen-by-screen presentation allowed subjects to focus on one case at a time.

Our experimental designs were all within subject (Baron 2000). Subjects have the option of trying to be consistent between the cases we present, but we present so many that the memory load would be excessive if anyone tried. Thus, we suspect that most subjects respond to each case on its own, much of the time, as they would in a between-subject design.

Hypotheses

Public finance actions typically have multiple effects, on both the allocation and distribution of resources. For example, government redistribution often comes bundled with other fiscal actions, such as the public provision of goods and services. Although research has long shown that subjects on average prefer at least moderately progressive tax rates (Lewis 1978; Hite and Roberts 1991; McCaffery and Baron 2003), we wondered how subjects would react to programs that affected distribution in an indirect or nonsalient way. For example, the use of tax deductions to (partially) fund some program—the intended, direct, and salient effect—has a regressive effect on distribution, compared to other alternatives, given a tax system featuring progressive marginal rates. On account of the isolation effect, we surmised that subjects would not be consistently attentive to the redistributive aspects of a fiscal program.

In these experiments, we expected that subjects would ignore or underadjust to the distributional effects of policies when those effects were not made salient. For example, subjects might favor tax deductions from a progressive marginal rate tax, unless the question reminds them of the regressive nature of subtractions under such a tax system (cf. the Schelling effect, discussed in McCaffery and Baron, forthcoming).[1] We explored this in the first experiment, on deductions. Subjects might also ignore the distributional effects of government provision, or privatization, of goods and services. They may fail to take into account these effects in choosing a level of redistribution through a progressive tax. We explore this failure in the final two experiments, on privatization.

In sum, just as taxes can be hidden—and different systems can evolve on account of this cognitive fact (McCaffery 1994; McCaffery and Baron, forthcoming)—so too can progressiveness. We hypothesized that these optics, as it were, would affect evaluation, leading to preference reversals and other inconsistencies.

Experiment 1: Tax Deductions

When the government chooses to subsidize private economic choices, in whole or in part, it has several options. It can provide subsidies in kind, make direct payments or transfers, or allow deductions (subtractions) from a tax. In a system featuring progressive marginal rates, in which those with higher incomes pay more, in percentage as well as in absolute terms, than those with lower incomes, the effects of deductions or subtractions from income are, compared to the alternative methods of payment, regressive: they benefit the upper-income bracket more than the lower. A $1,000 deduction saves a taxpayer in the 30-percent bracket $300, for example, and a taxpayer in the 15-percent bracket $150.

The main purpose of the first experiment was to ask whether people favor tax deductions in part because they do not know, or do not adequately consider, that deductions benefit the rich to some degree when marginal tax rates are progressive, where under a direct payment mechanism they do not. We asked this by looking at attitudes toward deductions before and after a de-biasing or prompting manipulation, in which we explained the effect of deductions on rich versus poor and then tested understanding. Thus this experiment also gives a quick look at the possibilities of education in the public finance context (see Larrick 2004, for a general review of de-biasing).

A second goal was to examine some of the determinants of favoring government provision of a good. We examined attitudes toward progressiveness and perceived self-interest.

Method

The questionnaire was completed by 104 subjects, ages seventeen to seventy (median thirty-four), of whom 72 percent were female. An additional sixty-seven subjects were tested on some questions, as described at the end of this section. For the total sample of 174, the ages ranged from seventeen to seventy (median thirty-seven), and 79 percent were female.

All subjects first saw an introductory screen, which began:

Paying for goods and services

Goods and services can be provided in different ways. Here are the ways we ask about:

- Government pays, and the money comes from income taxes. The rich pay a higher rate of income tax than the poor.
- Users pay, and government reimburses them.
- Users pay from their own funds.
- Users pay, but the cost is adjusted (by law) based on users' different abilities to pay.

We then presented a list of ten goods and services we would ask about, with parenthetical descriptions given to subjects to help explain some of the items:

Primary education: Grades 1–8;

Secondary education: Grades 9–12;

Theft insurance/compensation: Insurance or compensation for replacement cost of stolen or vandalized items;

Basic telephone service;

Mail delivery;

Health insurance: Including what basic health-policies now cover;

Social security: Basic income after retirement;

Disability insurance: Replaces some income if you have to stop working because of disability;

Unemployment insurance: Provides time-limited salary after job loss;

Natural disaster insurance: Replacement costs after damage by wind, flood, or earthquake.

We explained to the subjects that we were interested in their views about how these goods should be provided and paid for. In the "first cycle," the ten items were presented on separate screens in an order randomized for each subject. We then repeated the items, in the same order but with different questions following each one, in a "second cycle," for a total of twenty screens.

In the first cycle, the questions asked for a rating of each method of provision, and then asked about the status quo for the subject, how the good or service was paid for in the subject's home jurisdiction. Here is an example of the rating scale, using health insurance:

The good or service in question is HEALTH INSURANCE

Rate each of the following ways of providing this good or service. (Remember that government funds come from income tax revenues.)

[Each item answered on a 9-point scale from Awful to Excellent]

- Government pays.
- Users pay, and government reimburses them.
- Users pay, but they can deduct the cost from their income taxes.
- Users pay. No tax deduction.
- Users pay, but the cost is adjusted (by law) based on ability to pay.

Where you live now, how is this good or service provided?

[Not at all   Partially   Fully]

- Government pays.
- Users pay, and government reimburses them.
- Users pay, but they can deduct the cost from their income taxes.
- Users pay. No tax deduction.
- Users pay, but the cost is adjusted (by law) based on ability to pay.

Each screen in the second cycle began with a de-biasing or prompting manipulation meant to explain how deductions work, with a test for understanding. So, in the example of health insurance, subjects were told:

A tax deduction saves more money for those with high incomes than for those with low incomes. The lowest earners pay no tax and thus save nothing from a deduction. Their tax cannot be reduced because there isn't any. But a person who pays 30% in tax will save 30% of the cost of anything that is tax deductible.

Assume that the rich pay a higher percent tax than the poor on their income. What will happen if the government allows people to deduct the cost of health insurance from their taxable income?

The rich will save more money than the poor, from the deduction.

The explanation says that the poor will save as much money as the rich, or more money.

The explanation says that the rich will save more, but that won't happen in this case.

I don't know.

After this explanation and question, we once again asked subjects to evaluate the alternative policies, and then asked about attitudes toward the distribution of payment, their beliefs about the distribution of benefits, and the effect of method of payment and distribution of payment on their perceived self-interest:

Rate each of the following ways of providing this good or service. (You may change the ratings you made before.)

- Government pays.
- Users pay, and government reimburses them.
- Users pay, but they can deduct the cost from their income taxes.
- Users pay. No tax deduction.
- Users pay, but the cost is adjusted (by law) based on ability to pay.

How should the cost of health insurance be distributed between those with high income (the rich) and those with low income (the poor)?

- The rich should pay more and the poor should pay less.
- The rich and poor should contribute equally.
- The poor should pay more and the rich should pay less.

Who benefits more from health insurance?

The rich   The poor   Both equally

How are you and those you care about affected by whether users pay for health insurance or whether the government pays?

- Better off if users pay.
- Better off if the government pays, even if taxes were raised to cover the extra cost.
- It doesn't matter.

How are you and those you care about affected by the relative cost of health insurance for the rich and the poor?

- Better off if the rich paid more and the poor paid less.
- Better off if the cost were the same for everyone.
- Better off if the poor paid more and the rich paid less.
- It doesn't matter.

The original 104 subjects were informed in the introduction to the questionnaire: "Note that when the government pays for something, the money must come from somewhere. Please assume that, in these cases, taxes increase to cover the cost, by some percent of the tax, for everyone." If subjects had taken this information into account, they should have regarded deductions as roughly equivalent to no deductions, because the benefit of the deduction would be canceled by an equivalent tax increase. Results from our other studies (for example, McCaffery and Baron, forthcoming) indicate that most people do not spontaneously (that is, without prompting) think ahead about secondary effects in this way. However, to check our results, we tested sixty-seven new subjects without this statement, and without the questions about status quo and perceived self-interest (to save time). Because the results were qualitatively and statistically the same as the original results, we report the results of the combined sample of 174 when possible.

Results

We were most interested in how subjects perceived the effects of using deductions on the global level graduation in the tax and transfer system. Thus we calculated a response starting with the score (on the 9-point scale) of the deduction option—"users pay, but they can deduct the cost from their income taxes"—and subtracting the mean rating of the reimbursement—"users pay, and government reimburses them"—and ability-to-pay items—"users pay, but the cost is adjusted (by law) based on ability to pay." This ensured that the attitude toward deductions would be measured in comparison to alternatives (thus removing the effects of tendency to rate all items highly), and without contamination by the basic attitude toward government payment, because all three options included some government payment.

We considered only trials on which the test question in the second cycle—"what will happen if the government allows people to deduct?"—was answered correctly—"rich will save more"—and on which the subject said that the rich should pay more; that is, we considered only subjects who both understood the instruction and could be expected to have it move them in a less favorable direction. The mean adjusted deduction score was .38 on the first pass (where one unit is a step on the 9-point scale where 9 is Excellent) and −.04 on the second (where $t_{127} = 3.66$, $p = 0.0004$, across subjects, for the change). Each of the ten items showed movement in the expected direction, that is, against deductions after the de-biasing manipulation.

In sum, the subjects seemed unfamiliar with the idea that deductions help the rich more than the poor. Many of them could understand this after a simple explanation. When they understood, they liked deductions less, especially if they were already inclined to support redistribution. But the movement against deductions was slight,

Table 4.1   Mean Ratings on One to Nine Scale of Payment Mechanisms, Experiment 1

Method	Cycle 1	Cycle 2
Government pays	4.70	4.87
Reimburse	3.58	3.69
Deduction	4.07	3.79
No deduction	2.51	2.51
Ability to pay	3.80	3.98

Source: Authors' compilation.

and 29 percent of the responses to the test questions indicated continued misunderstanding.

For the same set of selected cases (test question correct and subject says that the rich should pay more), the mean ratings (averaged first within each subject and then across subjects) on the 9-point response scale are shown in table 4.1. Notice that support for deductions declines after de-biasing, but support for all other methods increases. Most of these changes were not significant by themselves, though the change in deduction was significantly less, because it was negative, than the positive changes in each other method, at $p < .05$, except for "No deduction." However, the mean rating for deductions even in Cycle 2 was higher than that for no deductions ($t_{127} = 7.09$, $p = 0.0000$).

A secondary question in this experiment concerned the determinants of attitudes toward different payment mechanisms. We examined this in two ways. First, as shown in table 4.2, we computed each subject's mean response to each question across the ten items in the second cycle (that is, after de-biasing), and then we computed correlations of these means

Table 4.2   Correlations of Subject Means Across the 104 Subjects

	Payment Mechanisms				
	Government Pays	Reimburse	Deduction	No Deduction	Ability to Pay
Should be graduated	0.18	−0.05	−0.10	−0.27	0.34
Rich benefit more	−0.11	−0.12	−0.14	−0.02	−0.02
Better for me if government pays	0.41	0.06	−0.23	−0.29	0.12
Better for me if rich pay more	0.01	0.09	0.05	−0.11	0.11

Source: Authors' compilation.
$r > .16$ is "significant" at $p < .05$ one tailed, for $N = 104$

Table 4.3   Correlations Across the Ten Items, Computed for Each Subject and Then Averaged Across Subjects

	Payment Mechanisms				
	Government Pays	Reimburse	Deduction	No Deduction	Ability to Pay
Should be graduated	0.59	0.75	0.85	−0.78	0.85
Rich benefit more	−0.14	0.21	0.45	−0.23	0.40
Better for me if government pays	0.97	0.77	0.64	−0.91	0.59
Better for me if rich pay more	0.46	0.72	0.75	−0.69	0.88

Source: Authors' compilation.
r > .55 is "significant" at p < .05 one tailed, for N = 10

across subjects. These correlations tell us about individual differences among subjects. Second, as shown in table 4.3, we computed correlations across the ten items in the second cycle for each subject, and we averaged the correlations across subjects. These correlations tell us about differences among goods. These analyses used the original 104 subjects.

In general, in both analyses, differences in attitudes toward payment mechanisms were predicted by the relevant questions about perceived self-interest (whether graduation is better for the subjects and "those they care about," and whether it is better, again for subjects "and those they care about" if the government pays), by preferences about whether the rich should pay more, and by perception of whether the rich benefit more. The results for perceived self-interest contrast somewhat with other results showing that self-interest plays little role in actual political behavior (for example, Sears and Funk 1991; Tyran 2004; Tyran and Sausgruber, forthcoming), though our subjects may have interpreted self-interest broadly, given the wording of the questions.

We found the result in table 4.3, when subjects favored deductions on those items for which they felt that payment should be graduated, as indicated by the correlation of .85, of greatest interest. The corresponding correlation across subjects of .34 in table 4.2 was also significant. The same positive attitude toward graduation correlated with the other items that, in fact, helped the poor more than the rich—government pays, reimburse, and ability to pay—and it correlated negatively with the most obviously regressive proposal, namely no deduction. Subjects seemed to understand that, with no deductions, the cost (in percentage and hence arguably disutility terms) would fall more heavily on those least able to pay. But subjects apparently did not realize that this was also true for deductions, despite our informative manipulation (the effect of which was, as noted, small). In sum, when subjects think that a particular good should be funded in a more progressive way, they are more likely to favor deductions, even though the use of deductions in a progressive marginal rate system is regressive.

Experiment 2: Cutting Government Services

Experiment 1 drew attention to the fact that government fiscal systems both provide goods—that is, spend money—and pay for them, that is, raise money. All actions have benefits and burdens. There is no reason why the distributional effects of the two sides have to match. Experiments 2 and 3 generalize this idea to the setting of the privatization of previously public goods.

When governments raise taxes by a progressive tax scheme and then pay for services that cost the same to rich and poor alike, the net effect is to redistribute income, a "cross-subsidy" through the provision of the good. Government provision in such a case also saves money for the poor, assuming that the poor would buy the services if the government did not provide them, and the government provides them with reasonable efficiency. This is a paradigm example of the "bundling" of two distinct government actions, allocative (providing the good or service in the first place) and redistributive. Were government simply to privatize or otherwise cut government services, without continuing the redistribution effected through the tax and spend program, a greater burden would fall on those who are relatively poor. Logically, however, in the spirit of the two welfare theorems, the government can continue to redistribute resources through the tax system with or without the provision of the good or service. But will subjects support a consistent level of redistribution, independent of government provision of goods?

To examine the effects of cutting services on support for the overall progressiveness of the public finance system, we asked subjects to imagine that their national government could provide five basic services, spending equal amounts on each: defense, education, health care, social security, and everything else. We presented sixteen cases in which government provided all possible combinations of the first four. In each case, we asked the subjects to choose the fairest level of progressiveness, including the possible use of negative taxes. Consistent with our prior research on the disaggregation bias and isolation effects (McCaffery and Baron 2003), we anticipated that subjects would not maintain the same level of redistribution—would not fully take into account or integrate the effects of the service cuts on household welfare—choosing less overall redistribution with fewer services.

Method

Seventy-eight subjects completed the questionnaire. Their ages ranged from nineteen to sixty-four (median forty), and 18 percent were male. The questionnaire began as shown in figure 4.1:

Figure 4.1 Statistics of the Three Groups

Tax and spend: We are interested in how you think government expenditures should affect the distribution of income taxes. All governments spend money enforcing their own laws and regulations. Many other expenses are optional. We are concerned here with five categories of spending: national defense; basic health care; basic education; social security; and "all other functions" (law enforcement, etc.). For purposes of these questions, assume:

- The government spends the same amount on each of the five categories.

- The national government pays for all of these services, if any government does.

- The government contributes to a regional defense force (in the "other functions" category), so it does not absolutely need national defense.

- Otherwise, the country is like your own country in standard of living.

- The government pays $2,000 each year for each good or service for each household.

- If the government does not provide health care, education, or social security, people must pay at least that much on their own.

Each screen shows several possible distributions of income tax among three groups of households: low, middle, and high pre-tax household income. (We exclude a small proportion of households that have little or no income, pay no tax, and receive some sort of assistance.) The three groups have the same proportion of all the pre-tax income. You see the average tax for each group. Here are some statistics for the three groups (approximately correct for the United States):

	Low	Middle	High
Percentage of all income	33.3%	33.3%	33.3%
Percentage of households in group	60%	30%	10%
Average annual household income	$20,000	$50,000	$130,000

Government can redistribute money from those with high incomes to those with low incomes. It can have a negative tax, in which it gives money to some people in order to accomplish this redistribution. Negative taxes are shown as bars to the left.

Source: Authors' compilation.

A typical screen is shown in figure 4.2:

Figure 4.2   Fairest Distribution of Income Taxes

In this case, suppose the government provides:

- NATIONAL DEFENSE
- BASIC EDUCATION
- ALL OTHER FUNCTIONS OF GOVERNMENT

But the government does not provide:

- BASIC HEALTH CARE
- SOCIAL SECURITY

When the government does not provide a service that people must pay for themselves, the extra annual household cost is $2,000, regardless of income. How much extra will each household have to pay per year, on the average, because of what the government does not provide in this case? (Pick the closest.) $0 $2,000 $4,000 $6,000

Which of the following is the fairest distribution of income taxes among the three income groups, in this case? [A button was provided next to each of the six distributions.]

Top	15%	
Middle	15%	
Bottom	15%	
Top	20%	
Middle	15%	
Bottom	10%	
Top	25%	
Middle	15%	
Bottom	5%	
Top	30%	
Middle	15%	
Bottom	0%	
Top	35%	
Middle	15%	
Bottom	−5%	
Top	40%	
Middle	15%	
Bottom	−10%	

Source: Authors' compilation.
Note. The average annual pre-tax incomes of the three groups are, respectively, $130,000, $50,000, and $20,000.

The first question, about the extra cost per household, was designed to encourage attention to this cost, but it could also serve as a check on understanding. The right answer was $2,000 times the number of nondefense cuts.

The basic case—with no cuts, such that all five sets of services were provided by the government—had a 25 percent tax for each group in the least progressive (top) distribution. When cuts were made, the tax for each group was reduced by 5 percent of income for each cut. Thus the same response would represent the same degree of progressiveness, regardless of the cuts, if each taxpayer would have to pay 5 percent of income for the missing service. But the cost in dollars of the services described is independent of income, so the poor would have to pay more, and the rich less, than implied by this assumption.

In the case of defense, a cut leads to an increase in income as a result of tax reduction with no additional costs. The average increase in income is 20 percent of the baseline tax paid, or 5 percent of income. We thus assume, for example, that taxes of 25 percent, 15 percent and 5 percent for three brackets, respectively, is just as progressive as taxes of 20 percent, 10 percent, and 0 percent, if the difference is a result of a cut in defense.

The order of the sixteen conditions (which differed according to what the government provided) was randomized for each subject.

Results

Six subjects always chose the least progressive distribution, which was equal percentage rates for all three groups, and two subjects always chose the most progressive. The mean choice was 3.42, on a 6-point scale with 6 the most progressive. This amounts to a difference (in absolute dollars) of 24.2 percent between the high- and low-income groups.

We calculated, for each subject, the mean effect of each cut on progressiveness, first ignoring the effect of cuts on out-of-pocket cost. The mean effects (in the change in percent difference between high and low groups) were, respectively, 1.1 percent for defense ($t_{77} = 1.70$, $p = 0.0931$), −0.1 percent for health care (n.s.), 0.4 percent for education (n.s.), and −0.4 percent for social security (n.s.), where a positive effect indicates less progressiveness with the cut than without it. The mean of these effects was not significantly positive, and the four services were not significantly different. Thus subjects maintained the same degree of progressiveness without taking into account the effect of the cuts on out-of-pocket cost. This is a clear example of the isolation effect.

But cuts do affect out-of-pocket costs, at least for three of the goods of interest: health care, education, and Social Security, both in the experiment and in the real world. A more relevant analysis of the data therefore includes the effects of these cuts in public services on net—after public tax and spending—household welfare. Do subjects use the tax system to compensate for the effects of public spending cuts? If so, they would increase the progressiveness of taxes for these three goods. An attempt to make such compensation may account for the difference between the three goods and defense. But do subjects compensate enough? Or do they show an isolation effect or disaggregation bias: maintaining a constant level of redistribution or progressiveness in the tax system alone, but supporting less global redistribution on account of their failures to take into account (or take fully into account) changes on the expenditure side of the government ledger?

The information we provided allows us to estimate the effects of cuts on out-of-pocket costs as a percent of income. The $2,000 figure we gave for the effect of each cut is, respectively, 10 percent, 4 percent, and 1.5 percent of the three income levels ($20,000, $50,000, $130,000). To achieve a redistribution between the high and low groups of 10 percent vs. 1.5 percent would require almost two steps on our graduation scale. Thus, to be conservative, we assumed one step for inferential statistics. Of course, we could not expect subjects to make these precise calculations, but we do think that the numbers we explicitly provided were plausible, so that subjects might have made some attempt to compensate for cost effects even without calculating, and evidently some did so, given the difference with national defense.

All three of the cost-yielding cuts (health care, education, social security) yielded corrections far less than the one step we conservatively assumed would be the required (minimum $t_{77} = 12.45$, $p = .0000$). Hence, it seems clear that, although some subjects attempted to offset the cost-increasing effects of cuts, on average the attempt falls far short of what is needed. (Note, however, that the response options we provided did not always allow the subjects to fully compensate for cuts. Still, only twelve subjects favored the maximum graduation response when all three cuts were made.)

Looking at the bottom line, table 4.4 shows the mean response of subjects, using the same type of graph they saw, both in the absence of any cuts and in the presence of three. The lowest panel represents the results of including out-of-pocket costs. Table 4.4 provides an excellent look at the isolation effect or disagreggation bias, playing out in a unified tax and spending system. Subjects preferred at least moderate progressivity in the baseline, global condition, with government provision of all five sets of goods and services. With three major private-cost items removed from the mix of public goods, subjects continued to choose a tax system reflecting moderate progressivity, even accepting a negative tax bracket for the poor, as the second panel shows. But when realistic private replacement costs were built back in, showing a global tax and out-of-pocket effect, the overall system now looks regressive, in the bottom panel. Compared to the subjects' own chosen baseline, the bottom line

Table 4.4   Mean Responses and Inferred Responses for Presence and
Absence of Health Care, Education, and Social Security,
Experiment 2

	No Cuts	
Top	33.6%	████████████████████████████
Middle	22.5%	██████████████████
Bottom	11.4%	████████

	Three Cuts, Raw Responses	
Top	18.9%	████████████████
Middle	7.5%	██████
Bottom	−3.9	██

	Three Cuts, Responses Plus Out-of-Pocket Cost	
Top	23.4%	██████████████████
Middle	19.5%	████████████████
Bottom	26.1%	████████████████████

Source: Authors' compilation.

reflects a steep cut in costs (taxes plus out-of-pocket) for the upper income level, a slight drop for the middle income level, and a dramatic (230 percent) rise in effective burdens on the lowest income level. By focusing on the "optics" of taxes alone, or disproportionately, a preference reversal in the bottom-line effects—what really matters—followed.

Aversion to progressivity cannot explain the results, given that subjects (on average) consistently chose progressive taxes. Nor can ignorance of the financial effects of public spending cuts explain the results. Subjects made many errors on the test question about the extra cost per household caused by cuts. But the most common error seemed to be to simply count the number of cuts, including defense cuts, which (by specification) should have had no effect on household spending. Yet 95 percent of the subjects gave the correct answer or higher for the effects of cuts on household finances. Moreover, the mean answer to the test question was 2.53 on a 4-point scale, where the mean correct answer is 2.5. Subjects did not underestimate the effects of public spending cuts on net household costs. The results were essentially unchanged when we examined only the subjects who estimated cost correctly or overestimated it, on the average.

What can explain the results is the disaggregation bias or isolation effect. Subjects looked only (or primarily) at the tax system when adjusting it. They did not adequately factor in the effect of public spending cuts. The result is that effective progressivity decreased as the number of cuts increased—disappearing altogether with enough government downsizing.

Experiment 3: More Cuts

The final study extended Experiment 2, to which we made several changes. One, we eliminated defense, using only the three cuts that would require increased spending. This meant that we could present all possible combination in eight items. We presented these cases four times each, in a random order chosen for each subject, for a total of thirty-two items.

Two, in half of the items, we presented taxes and incomes as dollars rather than percent. This allowed us to replicate, though with a different method, our finding that preferred graduation is higher when taxes are in percentages (McCaffery and Baron 2003).

Three, in half of the items, we presented a display indicating the extra costs required, in the same format as that used to display taxes. We thought that this might serve as a de-biasing method. (It did not.)

Finally, we extended the list of response options but asked only the fairness question for each item. We gave options in which the lowest tax was zero, to test the possibility that some people resist negative taxes. We included two flat tax options (constant percent, constant dollars). Subjects in Experiment 2 and other studies we have undertaken often commented afterward that they favor what they called a flat tax, but we have been unsure what they meant. We also included options that would look more evenly graduated when presented in dollars. We did this so that subjects would not reject a graduated option just because it did not look evenly spaced. We made other minor changes, mostly to make our calculations easier.

Method

Seventy-nine subjects completed the questionnaire. Their ages ranged from twenty-four to fifty-eight (median thirty-nine), and 24 percent were male.

The instructions and questions were modified somewhat from Experiment 2. Most important, the introduction explained: "Taxes can be 'flat,' so that everyone pays the same percent, or the same dollars. Taxes can be 'graduated,' so that those with low incomes pay less and those with high incomes pay more." It also stated, "If the government does not provide health care, education, or social security, each taxpayer must pay an average of $2,500 per year to replace the service that government provided." The mean incomes of the three groups were given as $20,000, $50,000, and $125,000, so that they would differ by multiplicative constant.

We provided explanations of the response options and grouped them, so that a typical example (for the dollars version, with two cuts) is shown in figure 4.3:

Figure 4.3   Response Options for Experiment 3

Here is the extra cost that each of the three income groups must pay as a result of what the government does not provide.

Top	$5,000
Middle	$5,000
Bottom	$5,000

Which of the following is the fairest distribution of income taxes among the three income groups, in this case? (All raise the same total amount.)
Flat tax in dollars (everyone pays the same number of dollars):

Top	$5,769
Middle	$5,769
Bottom	$5,769

Flat tax in percent (everyone pays the same percent):

Top	$18,750
Middle	$7,500
Bottom	$3,000

Graduated, varying in amount of graduation and position of middle group:

Top	$25,000
Middle	$7,500
Bottom	$2,000

Top	$31,250
Middle	$7,500
Bottom	$1,000

Top	$27,500
Middle	$10,500
Bottom	$4,000

Top	$37,500
Middle	$7,500
Bottom	$0

Top	$33,750
Middle	$10,500
Bottom	–$600

Top	$43,750
Middle	$7,500
Bottom	–$1,000

Top	$40,000
Middle	$10,500
Bottom	–$1,600

Figure 4.3 *Continued*

Graduated, lowest group pays zero. (Note: These may be identical to
distributions listed earlier. If so, they are equivalent answers.)

Top	$37,500	████████████████████████
Middle	$7,500	████████
Bottom	$0	
Top	$31,875	███████████████████████
Middle	$9,750	█████████
Bottom	$0	

Source: Authors' compilation.

When the display of amounts was not presented, subjects were simply
reminded of the three average income levels. In the percent condition,
the amounts were identical but expressed as a percent of income.

Results

We first discuss the results concerning graduation. Then we examine the
strategies that subjects used.

Graduation: Sensitivity to Units and Cuts   First consider the results concerning graduation, which replicated and extended the results of Experiment 2. We measured graduation as the difference in percent between
the high and low income groups for the chosen option. Graduation was
higher when the units were percent (21.9 percent) than when they were
dollars (18.2 percent; $t_{78} = 4.42$, $p = 0.0000$); we confirmed the metric effect that we had found earlier (McCaffery and Baron 2003, forthcoming).
The display of costs had no effect on graduation and did not interact
with dollars versus percentage.

As the number of cuts increased, graduation decreased ($t_{78} = 3.47$, $p =
0.0009$, for the slope of the function relating graduation to number of
cuts). The means of graduation were 21.2 percent, 21.2 percent, 19.0 percent, and 16.0 percent, respectively, for no, one, two, or three cuts. This
effect resulted from the fact that graduation of the last two options (those
with the low group getting exactly zero tax) is lower when the number of
cuts is greater. Subjects who chose those options apparently caused this
effect. (We discuss this later.) When these options (and the first option, a
flat dollar tax, which would have the reverse effect) were assigned a constant graduation level, graduation showed a small and nonsignificant increase with more cuts.

In sum, the results were consistent with those of Experiment 2, in
which subjects essentially ignored the distributional effects of the cuts.

Table 4.5   Mean Responses and Inferred Responses for Presence and Absence of Health Care, Education, and Social Security, Experiment 3

	No Cuts	
Top	36.7%	████████████████████████
Middle	25.0%	█████████████████
Bottom	13.3%	█████████

	Three Cuts, Raw Responses	
Top	18.5%	█████████████
Middle	10%	████████
Bottom	1.5%	■

	Three Cuts, Responses Plus Out-of-Pocket Cost	
Top	24.5%	███████████████████
Middle	25.0%	███████████████████
Bottom	39.0%	██████████████████████████

Source: Authors' compilation.

Table 4.5 shows the mean responses for the conditions shown in table 4.4, that is, the percent conditions. Once again, the implied or bottom-line tax and transfer rate is much more regressive with greater cuts, and the effect is just as great with taxes expressed in dollars.

For three pairs of response options, subjects could choose between distributions that were evenly spaced by percentage and distributions in which the tax rate was higher for the middle income group (and lower for the other two groups), giving an impression closer to equal spacing in the dollar-units condition. On the whole, subjects preferred the lower rate for the middle group, choosing it in 29 percent of all items, versus 13 percent for the higher rate ($t_{78} = 4.78$, p = 0.0000, across subjects). This result suggests a "soak the rich" (or a "help the middle"?) attitude, rather than a "help the poor" (at the expense of the middle) attitude. However, preference for the higher rate was greater in the dollar-units condition, where it appeared to be more equidistant from the rate for the other two groups: in dollar units, low middle-group rate, 21 percent and high rate 17 percent; in percent units, low 36 percent and high 9 percent ($t_{78} = 5.59$, p = 0.0000, for the effect of units). This is another appearance of the metric effect.

Strategies: Flat Tax, Graduation, Zero   We can examine the extent to which subjects followed various consistent strategies: flat percentage; flat dollars; graduation without adjustment for costs; graduation with compensation; the maximum possible graduation; negative taxes; and zero for

Table 4.6   Strategy Use, Experiment 3

Strategy	Percentage Who Never Choose	Percentage Who Always Choose	Mean Percentage for the Rest
Flat tax	39.0	12.7	30.0
Zero for low income	26.6	7.6	30.0
Negative tax	51.9	0	14.2
Maximum graduation	31.6	2.5	26.7
Maximum graduation, no negative	26.6	2.5	24.7
Graduation with adjustment	N.A.	N.A.	30.4
Graduation, no adjustment	N.A.	N.A.	69.6

Source: Authors' compilation.

the lowest bracket. The flat dollar option was chosen in 3.6 percent of the cases, and the flat percent option was chosen in 26.9 percent. It appears that subjects who favor flat taxes favor a flat percentage tax. The 3.6 percent could result from errors, though a few people might actually favor this. Henceforth we combine these two categories.

The last two options, which fix the lowest bracket at 0 percent, allow us to assess opposition to negative taxes. Subjects who generally favor graduation but oppose negative taxation will choose the zero option over one of the more graduated ones. When there were no cuts, the zero option was the most graduated.

Table 4.6 shows the use of each strategy, including those who use it consistently and avoid it consistently, and the mean percent use for those who use it sometimes. (The negative tax is based on the seven of eight cases in which it was possible.) The category "Maximum grad., no negative" is the most graduated option other than any option that involves a negative tax. The last two strategies were simply the proportion of subjects who increased graduation with more cuts and those who did not do so; this classification overlaps with the others, as it is not based on individual responses but on the overall pattern.

To determine whether subjects try to avoid negative taxes, we calculated for each subject the mean graduation for cases with no cuts, one cut, two cuts, and three cuts. We could thus examine graduation as a function of the number of cuts. Then we selected for further examination those subjects with a maximum graduation (across these four categories) exceeding 30 percent. These thirty-four subjects are the ones who favor graduation the most. They are also the ones most likely to choose negative taxes with more than one cut, since a graduation rate of 30 percent would imply negative taxes in this case. If they tried to avoid negative taxes, however, their choices would become less graduated as the number of cuts increased. Specifically, the maximum graduation possible without negative taxes with no, one, two, or three cuts, respectively, is 50 percent, 40 percent, 30 percent, and 20 percent. If the subject does not try to avoid negative taxes, the maximum possible graduation is 50 percent, 40 percent, 40 percent, and 40 percent.

For each of the subjects with maximum graduation over thirty, we fit a straight line to the graduation rate as a function of number of cuts. The slopes of these lines fell into three clear groups, as verified by a cluster analysis. Figure 4.4 shows the results for the two extreme groups, the eleven subjects with the lowest slopes (left) and the seven with the highest (right). Each subject is one line (with the line types varied to help distinguish them). The circles represent the maximum graduation rates without negative taxes. By contrast, the diamonds show the maximum possible graduation rate among the response options. For two or three cuts, negative taxes are required in order to achieve the maximum possible graduation, so the diamonds are above the circles.

For the subjects with the lowest slopes (left), graduation decreased sharply as the number of cuts increased. Because they never wanted more graduation than indicated by the circles, it appears that they were explicitly avoiding negative taxes. The group of solid lines that fall near the circles are from subjects who approximated the strategy of maximizing graduation while avoiding negative taxes.

Subjects with the highest slopes (right) had almost the opposite pattern, increasing graduation as the number of cuts increased (to the left), thus tending to compensate for the effect of the cuts. They accepted negative taxes, and these resulted in graduation rates higher than the circles. These subjects apparently had some understanding of the need to compensate for privatization with increased progressivity. The isolation effect is not universal.

To test for an overall effect of avoiding negative taxes, we fit lines to all subjects (graduation as a function of number of cuts), and we correlated the slopes of the lines with each the maximum graduation, across all subjects (excluding the data from zero cuts, because the maximum possible graduation was higher than the other three points). Subjects with higher maximum graduation rates had a more negative slope (that is, high on the left, low on the right, in figure 4.1); the correlation was $-.48$ ($p = .0000$). This is the opposite from what we would expect if subjects compensated for the effect of the cuts. In sum, part of the reason that people do not compensate for the effects of cuts is that they want to avoid negative taxes.

Conclusion

How much one supports redistribution through public finance mechanisms turns on the mere form of those mechanisms, contrary to the straightforward logic of traditional public finance theory. For example,

Figure 4.4   Subjects with a Maximum Graduation Greater than 30 Percent

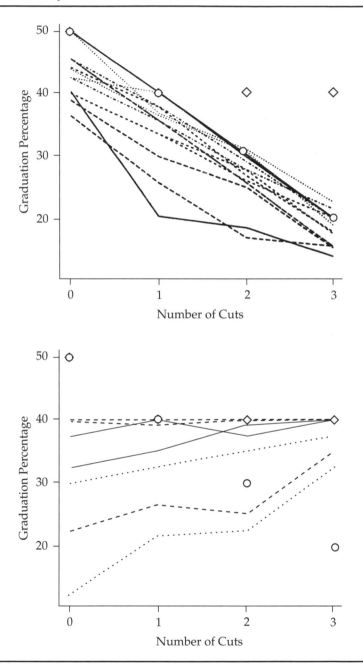

subjects who favor at least moderate progressivity in the allocation of public benefits and burdens—which seems to be the norm across time and cultures (Lewis 1978; Hite and Roberts 1991; McCaffery and Baron 2003)—can be easily fooled by the form of public finance mechanisms into supporting little or no redistribution, or even redistribution from poor to rich.

The isolation effect, common to our thinking about a wide range of issues, in private as well as public finance (as we discussed earlier) seems to explain this tendency toward preference shifts and reversals based on formal framing manipulations. We found for example in our first experiment that subjects think too little about the effects of tax deductions on progressiveness. When they are shown these effects, they are less likely to support the use of tax deductions, but only moderately so. Worse, they seem to prefer a program of private provision with tax deductions to a system of private provision without tax deductions, even when the fact of a progressive marginal rate tax system means that the deduction reduces the redistributive effect of government provision.

In the last two experiments, we found that people are also insufficiently aware of the effects of privatization or (in the case of defense) abandonment of government services on progressiveness. Most people want some progressiveness in the tax system: even those who favor a flat tax (in comments after Experiment 2) seem to mean a flat percentage rather than a flat dollar amount. Yet their failure to think through the effects of changes on progressiveness leads them to support proposals that undercut their own values.

The same mechanisms could of course work in the other direction. People who do not favor progressive taxation could fail to see the effect of changes that increase progressiveness, such as increased government funding of health care. In all cases, however, the puzzle is the same: that the form of the provision affects preference reversals in attitudes about the substance of government fiscal actions.

We have focused here on the conflict between subjects' judgments and their apparent values. But distributional effects are also real. Optimal taxation models typically take into account the declining marginal utility of money as well as the incentive effects of taxation (Mirrlees 1971). Under most welfarist models, some redistribution is beneficial, and policy makers are increasingly looking to public finance mechanisms to provide it (Kaplow and Shavell 2000). The kind of reasoning we have found here can pit equity (or redistributive) effects against efficiency (or allocative) ones, and can lead to truly harmful effects on the poor, beyond the conflict with attitudes.

The common psychological mechanism is one we have explored elsewhere (McCaffery and Baron 2003, forthcoming): a disaggregation bias or isolation effect. In a nutshell, people do not think ahead, they do not integrate logically connected matters to form consistent judgments as to bottom-line effects and realities. In studies of the effects of marriage, for example, we have found that people focus on the question they are answering, without thinking of effects of their answer on other things they care about, such as the interactive effects of marriage bonuses, penalties, and tax graduation. Likewise, people prefer hidden taxes such as business taxes in large part because they do not think enough about the money having to come from somewhere, and about where it will come from. Here we found that people underaccount for the effects of government cuts on household finances when making judgments about the appropriate remaining tax system.

The problem of failing to think more than one step ahead—failing to put two and two together—is not of course limited to taxes and public policy. But especially given the absence of any natural corrective to these tendencies in the nonmarket sectors of public finance, they are likely, if left unchecked, to wreck considerable havoc there.

What to do? Although democratic self-government is surely better than the alternatives, it can, and does, yield policies that are not optimal, in part because citizens and legislators alike fail to think through the effects of the policies they favor. To some extent, policies that are really terrible will be weeded out by a kind of evolutionary process in which states and governments that have these policies decline, lose support, and are replaced. Competition may help somewhat.

But the processes of interest here seem to occur in some of the most successful democratic states, and they are thus unlikely to be reduced by the nonsurvival of the unfit. Further improvements may come in two other ways. First, enhanced education in economics at all levels of the educational system may help people learn about effects that they now do not consider. Second, governments could turn over more control over the details of design of tax and spending systems to expert agencies (as suggested in other contexts by Breyer 1993 and by Sunstein 2002). Increased public education will still be required if these agencies are to maintain public support, which they will need.

The research was supported by NSF grant SES 02-13409. The authors thank participants at a Behavioral Public Finance Conference held at the University of Michigan in April 2004, especially Alan Lewis for his detailed commentary.

Note

1. Schelling (1981) reported a classroom observation. He asked his students, given that a tax system would have child bonuses added to it, whether these bonuses should be higher for the rich or the poor. Students overwhelmingly

answered for the poor. Schelling then pointed out that child bonuses presume a childless default rule; given a baseline of having children, the economically equivalent policy would be to institute childless penalties. Should such penalties be higher for rich or poor? Students quickly reversed their preferences, choosing higher childless penalties for the rich. We confirmed what we call the Schelling effect experimentally, a combination of penalty aversion and what we call a progressivity illusion (McCaffery and Baron 2004).

References

Babcock, Linda, Michele Gelfand, Deborah Small, and Hiedi Stayn. 2003. "The Propensity to Initiate Negotiations: Toward a Broader Understanding of Negotiation Behavior." Unpublished manuscript, Carnegie Mellon University, Pittsburgh.

Baron, Jonathan. 2000. *Thinking and Deciding*, 3d ed. New York: Cambridge University Press.

Breyer, Stephen. 1993. *Breaking the Vicious Circle: Toward Effective Risk Regulation.* Cambridge, Mass.: Harvard University Press.

Camerer, Colin F. 2000. "Prospect Theory in the Wild: Evidence from the Field." In *Choices, Values, and Frames*, edited by Daniel Kahneman and Amos Tversky. New York: Cambridge University Press and Russell Sage Foundation.

Hite, Peggy A., and Michael L. Roberts. 1991. "An Experimental Investigation of Taxpayer Judgments on Rate Structure in the Individual Income Tax System." *Journal of the American Taxation Association* 13(2): 47–63.

Idson, Lorrain C., Dolly Chugh, Yoella Bereby-Meyer, Simone Moran, Brit Grosskopf, and Max Bazerman. 2004. "Overcoming Focusing Failures in Competitive Environments." *Journal of Behavioral Decision Making* 17(3): 159–72.

Jones, Steven K., Deborah Frisch, Tricia J. Yurak, and Eric Kim. 1998. "Choices and Opportunities: Another Effect of Framing on Decisions." *Journal of Behavioral Decision Making* 11(3): 211–26.

Kahneman, Daniel. 2000. "Experienced Utility and Objective Happiness: A Moment-based Approach." In *Choices, Values, and Frames*, edited by Daniel Kahneman and Amos Tversky. New York: Cambridge University Press and Russell Sage Foundation.

Kahneman, Daniel, and Dan Lovallo. 1993. "Timid Choices and Bold Forecasts: A Cognitive Perspective on Risk Taking." *Management Science* 39(1): 17–31.

Kahneman, Daniel, and Amos Tversky. 2000. *Choices, Values, and Frames.* New York: Cambridge University Press and Russell Sage Foundation.

Kaplow, Louis, and Steven Shavell. 2000. *Fairness v. Welfare.* Cambridge, Mass.: Harvard University Press.

Larrick, Richard P. 2004. "Debiasing." In *Blackwell Handbook of Judgment and Decision Making*, edited by Derek J. Koehler and Nigel Harvey. London: Blackwell.

Lewis, Alan. 1978. "Perceptions of Tax Rates." *British Tax Review* 6: 358–66.

Legrenzi, Paolo, Vittorro Girotto, and Philip Johnson-Laird. 1993. "Focusing in Reasoning and Decision Making." *Cognition* 49(1–2): 37–66.

McCaffery, Edward J. 1994. "Cognitive Theory and Tax." *UCLA Law Review* 41(7): 1861–947.

McCaffery, Edward J., and Jonathan Baron. 2003. "The Humpty-Dumpty Blues: Disaggregation Bias in the Evaluation of Tax Systems." *Organizational Behavior and Human Decision Processes* 91(2): 230–42.

———. 2004. "Framing the Family: Evaluation of Tax Policies Involving Household Composition." *Journal of Economic Psychology* 25(6): 679–705.

———. Forthcoming. "Thinking about Tax." *Psychology, Public Policy and Law.*

Mirrlees, James A. 1971. "An Exploration in the Theory of Optimum Income Taxation." *Review of Economic Studies* 38(114): 175–208.

Musgrave, Richard. 1959. *The Theory of Public Finance.* New York: McGraw-Hill.

Rawls, John. 1971. *A Theory of Justice.* Cambridge, Mass.: Harvard University Press.

Read, Daniel, George Loewenstein, and Matthew Rabin. 1999. "Choice Bracketing." *Journal of Risk and Uncertainty* 19(1–3): 171–97.

Rosen, Harvey. 2001. *Public Finance*, 6th ed. Chicago: McGraw-Hill/Irwin.

Schelling, Thomas C. 1981. "Economic Reasoning and the Ethics of Policy." *Public Interest* 63(Spring): 37–61.

Sears, David O., and Carolyn L. Funk. 1991. "The Role of Self-interest in Social and Political Attitudes." In *Advances in Experimental Social Psychology*, vol. 24, edited by Mark Zanna. New York: Academic Press.

Steinmo, Sven. 1993. *Taxation and Democracy: Swedish, British and American Approaches to Financing the Modern State.* New Haven, Conn.: Yale University Press.

Sunstein, Cass, ed. 2000. *Behavioral Law and Economics.* Cambridge: Cambridge University Press.

Sunstein, Cass R. 2002. *Risk and Reason: Safety, Law, and the Environment.* New York: Cambridge University Press.

Thaler, Richard H. 1980. "Toward a Positive Theory of Consumer Choice." *Journal of Economic Behavior and Organization* 1(1): 39–60.

Tyran, Jean-Robert. 2004. "Voting When Money and Morals Conflict: An Experimental Test of Expressive Voting." *Journal of Public Economics* 88(7/8): 1645–64.

Tyran, Jean-Robert, and Rupert Sausgruber. Forthcoming. "A Little Fairness May Induce a Lot of Redistribution in Democracy." *European Economic Review.*

Chapter 5

Mispredicting Utility and the Political Process

BRUNO S. FREY AND ALOIS STUTZER

INDIVIDUAL decisions involve difficult trade-offs between pursuing material wealth, status, and fame on the one hand and, on the other, investing in social relationships and choosing activities that provide autonomy and the experience of competence. There is an increasing belief that people systematically err in these decisions and spend too much time, effort, and money on goods, services, and activities with strong extrinsic attributes (Scitovsky 1976; Frank 1999; Easterlin 2003; Layard 2005).

We argue that this tendency is attributable to systematic misprediction of utility. When people make decisions, they mainly take salient extrinsic attributes of choice options into account. They thus overvalue characteristics relating to extrinsic desires such as income and status and underestimate those relating to intrinsic needs such as time spent with family and friends and on hobbies. It follows that they tend to underconsume goods and activities with strong intrinsic attributes. According to their own evaluations, people make distorted decisions when they choose between different options and obtain a lower utility level than they otherwise would. They find comparisons between attributes whose salience shifts over time difficult to make, so that learning is severely hampered.

People are, however, to some extent aware of their tendency to mispredict. They complain, for example, about their work-life imbalance and that they cannot manage it in their day-to-day decisions.

In this chapter, we analyze whether the political process helps people mitigate biased decisions attributable to misprediction or accentuates them. Scholars dealing with biases in decision making related to the mis-prediction of utility usually disregard this aspect.

We distinguish among four types of government to study government reactions to people mispredicting utility. We then identify public discourse as the key to people's learning in the political process and to adopting precautionary policies. Possible policy interventions that reduce biases attributable to misprediction are discussed as an input to the political discourse process. We then pose two sets of empirically testable propositions.

Individual Decision Making when Utility Is Mispredicted

Standard economic theory assumes that individuals are able to compare future utilities provided by goods and activities consumed. They maximize the utility in a rational consumption decision. In certain cases, it has proved useful to distinguish between the various characteristics of goods and activities (Lancaster 1966; Becker 1965) or the attributes of options (for example, Keeney and Raiffa 1976). This differentiation is not, however, taken to affect the evaluation of future utility. The utility of a chosen combination is simply the sum of the weighted value of each characteristic

Options with Changing Salience of Attributes

The standard economic model of consumer decisions is appropriate for most goods and activities, and for most situations. It is still appropriate when individuals make random prediction errors, or when the extent of misprediction is the same for all goods and all activities. Here we depart from these assumptions to argue that there are systematic differences in mispredictions between two types of attributes characterizing different options.[1]

Attributes of the first type relate to intrinsic needs. Edward Deci and Richard Ryan's self-determination theory provides a comprehensive view of three main needs (2000). First, there is a need for relatedness, to feel connected to others by love and affection—that is, having a family and friends and being in a social setting. Second, there is a need for competence, to control the environment and experience oneself as capable and effective. Third, there is a desire for autonomy, the experience of being in charge of one's actions or being causal.[2] Intrinsic attributes are also characterized by providing "flow experience" (Csikszentmihalyi 1990), that is, when one is completely immersed in an activity, often a hobby.

The second type of attributes relates to extrinsic desires and serves people's goals for material possessions, fame, status, or prestige. Income thus becomes one of the critical attributes of options in the choice set.

Each option, activity, and even good is multidimensional; in general, a particular choice alternative has both intrinsic and extrinsic attributes. But some goods and activities have a stronger intrinsic component (for example, time spent with friends),[3] others a stronger extrinsic component (such as most consumer articles, which go beyond basic material needs). Work is particularly interesting. Having work gives people a strong sense of self-determination, and being active at work provides flow experiences. Income from paid work, however, also serves extrinsic wants as it allows buying consumer items.

Systematic mistakes occur because, when individuals make decisions, the extrinsic attributes are more salient than the intrinsic attributes of different options. Therefore, individuals tend to undervalue intrinsic attributes when they decide and allocate their resources. When they experience the hedonic consequences of their choices, the intrinsic attributes get relatively more important and their ex ante negligence is reflected in lower utility. The distortion thus leads to a systematic inconsistency between predicted and experienced utility.[4]

Why Intrinsic Attributes Are Undervalued When Predicting Utility

Certain major sources for underestimating future utility from intrinsic attributes, compared to extrinsic attributes of goods and activities, may be distinguished.

Underestimating Adaptation

There is convincing empirical evidence that individuals are not good at foreseeing how much utility they will derive from their future consumption (for example, Loewenstein and Adler 1995; for an extensive survey, see Wilson and Gilbert 2003).[5] Research on affective forecasting shows, for example, that people overestimate their reactions to specific events (because they are embedded within other daily life events that they are not actively aware of) or underestimate their ability to successfully cope with negative events.[6] The general insight is that people usually have biased expectations about the intensity and duration of emotions: the impact is less than predicted largely because people are more adaptive than they think they are.

We argue that adaptation is underestimated more for extrinsic than for intrinsic aspects. People adapt less to goods and activities with strong intrinsic components because the (positive) experience tends to be renewed with every consumption. Getting together with a good friend is always rewarding, and one does not "get used to it" in the sense of valuing this experience progessively less. Similarly, many scholars have a flow experience when they immerse themselves in writing a paper or book they have always wanted to write. The corresponding utility does not wear off.

The differential effect on the intrinsic and extrinsic attributes of goods and activities is consistent with recent empirical evidence (for a survey, see Frederick and Loewenstein 1999). It has been found that individuals do not adapt their utility evaluation in the case of undesirable experiences that inhibit intrinsic need satisfaction. In particular, severe health problems—such as chronic illness or one that progressively worsens—reduce autonomy and lead to lasting reductions in reported subjective well-being (for example, Easterlin 2003). Widowers suffer, on average, for years (for example Stroebe, Stroebe, and Hansson 1993). Having a job is related to many aspects that provide flow experiences and satisfy intrinsic needs, such as being in the company of workmates and experiencing expertise and autonomy. Accordingly, being unemployed is repeatedly found to have high negative nonpecuniary effects on subjective well-being with little habituation (Clark 2002). By contrast, having a job with high autonomy, as is the case of self-employed people, is related to high job satisfaction. Frey and Benz (2002), for example, show that the self-employed derive more utility from their work than people employed by an organization regardless of income earned or hours worked. Moreover, they explain this difference with people's evaluation of initiative at the work place and satisfaction with the work itself (25). Intrinsic attributes also characterize the work of volunteers: those involved in volunteer work are more satisfied with their lives, even when the possibility of reverse causality is taken into account (Meier and Stutzer 2004).

In the case of goods and activities in which extrinsic aspects are dominant, empirical evidence indicates that individuals adapt to a considerable extent. This has been demonstrated, in particular, for income (van Praag 1993; Easterlin 2001; Stutzer 2004). After individuals experience a raise in income, their utility level initially rises as well. After a year or so, however, most of this beneficial effect has evaporated. It has been estimated (van Herwaarden, Kapteyn, and van Praag 1977) that around 60 percent of the utility increase due to an increase in household income disappears over time.

The evidence of little or no adaptation for goods and activities characterized by intrinsic aspects, and strong adaptation for those characterized by extrinsic aspects, suggests that individuals who underestimate adaptation, or even disregard it altogether, make a bigger mistake when predicting future utility from extrinsic than from intrinsic attributes.

Distorted Memory of Past Experiences

When individuals make decisions about future consumption or allocation of time, and when information from current experience is inaccessible, they resort to experience in the past, whether specific or general (for a discussion, see Robinson and Clore 2002). If specific information is available, it has priority in people's judgment. Thereby, the more memorable moments of an experience disproportionately affect retrospective assessments of feelings (Kahneman 1999). What counts as "more memorable" tends to be the most intense moment (peak) and the most recent moment (end) of an emotional occurrence. This peak-end rule or duration neglect has been established in numerous studies (Kahneman 2003).

We propose that intrinsic attributes relate to long-term experiences of moderate but enduring positive feelings and that extrinsic attributes, by contrast, are related to short-term experiences, in particular peak emotions. Consequently, we argue that when people predict utility based in retrospect, they underestimate the intrinsic aspects of goods and activities related to duration (compared to their estimates on the extrinsic aspects related to peaks).

Rationalizing Decisions

Individuals have a strong urge to justify their decisions, both to themselves and to others (for pre-decision justification, see Shafir, Simonson, and Tversky 1993). It is not only predicted consumption utility that affects the decision to buy something, for example, but also whether people think that they are getting a bargain (Thaler 1999). Findings reveal a general tendency to resist affective influences and to take rationalistic attributes into account when making decisions. Christopher Hsee and colleagues (2003) call this reason-based choice lay rationalism, finding in their experiments that people focus their decisions on absolute economic payoffs and play down noneconomic concerns. This implies, however, that they do not optimally consider various attributes of different options to maximize predicted utility.

We argue that for extrinsic and intrinsic attributes a similar inconsistency applies to decision making. It is much easier to provide rationalistic justifications for extrinsic than for intrinsic characteristics. Consider, for example, a job offer providing more income but less leisure time. Most people find it easier to justify why they should accept the job offer because the extrinsic monetary dimension is salient. It is difficult, however, to justify why the intrinsic characteristics provided by more leisure time (even when its hedonic utility might be correctly predicted) might be important enough to refuse the increase in money. As a result, goods and activities characterized by strong intrinsic attributes tend to have too little weight in decision-making compared to extrinsic components.

Intuitive Theories About the Sources of Future Utility

People, of course, have diverse intuitive theories about what makes them happy (for a discussion, see Loewenstein and Schkade 1999). Such beliefs in turn directly influence how people predict future utility and can cause them to make mistakes. Moreover, the beliefs play a significant role because they guide the reconstruction of past emotions and make them consistent with current self-conceptions (Ross 1989). Intuitive theories thus interact with the three discussed sources of misprediction.

An important belief refers to acquisition and possession as central goals on the path to happiness, that is, to materialism (see Tatzel 2002). It has been found that those with material (extrinsic) goals report lower self-esteem and satisfaction than those with intrinsic ones (for example, Kasser 2002; Sirgy 1997). This correlation is probably due in part to confounding unobserved personality traits such as neuroticism (McCrae 1990) and reversed causality, and in part to a compensatory reaction on the part of people with low subjective well-being. However, it might also indicate that people who believe intuitively in extrinsic attributes are prone to mispredict future utility. By contrast, those with intrinsic goals for personal growth, relationships, and community spirit apply intuitive theories emphasizing intrinsic attributes that in turn lead to few mispredictions in future utility. Our argument thus includes heterogeneity among individuals, which leads to additional testable predictions when combined with the three noted reasons for misprediction—underestimating adaptation, memory distortions, and rationalizing.

Commercialization

The differential effect of misprediction between intrinsic and extrinsic aspects also depends on the extent to which the market is a factor. The monetarization of a good or activity induces individuals to focus more on extrinsic attributes than they otherwise would. This applies both to work and consumption. It has been argued that introducing pay for performance leads employees to regard those performance aspects, which are relevant for the compensation they receive, as dominant. By contrast, aspects of performance irrelevant for payment are crowded out (see Frey 1997 and, for a survey of empirical evidence, Frey and Jegen 2001). In the area of consumption, advertising is often directed to extrinsic aspects of the goods to be sold. By comparison, lobbies for intrinsic values tend to be weak and sometimes do not exist. To the extent to which commercialization occurs (see, for example, Lane 1991; Kuttner 1996; Bowles 1998), individuals are induced to make mispredictions of the future utility of goods. They are led to believe that the extrinsic characteristics will make them happier than intrinsic ones.

Mispredicting Utility and Individual Learning

Systematically mispredicting future utilities, even if they differed between goods and activities, would be of little consequence for economics if individuals learned quickly in repetitive choices.[7] Mispredicting would then be a disequilibrium phenomenon basically not affecting the notion of rational decision makers maximizing individual utility.

A large literature suggests, however, that learning is a complex process that does not necessarily lead to overcoming mispredictions. It is likely to be effective with regard to predictions only if multidimensional goods and activities are reduced to one dimension expressed in monetary terms. In that case, the individual can be assumed able to rectify mistakes to a greater degree within a short period. Standard economic models then fully apply, at least in equilibrium.

In the cases considered here, where the importance of various attributes differ between the time a decision is taken and consumption time, learning is much more difficult. Learning, when decisions about future consumption are concerned, must often be based on reconstructions of feelings. They are therefore subject to the same misperceptions as remembering the utility of past experiences (see earlier discussion on distorted memory). Learning is particularly hampered when episodic memories become too few and people rely to a large extent on intuitive theories (Robinson and Clore 2002). In consequence, remembered and predicted utility become similar and relatively independent of experienced utility. Terence Mitchell and colleagues (1997), for example, document this phenomenon in three survey studies about enjoyment predicted before, experienced during, and recollected after a trip to Europe, a Thanksgiving vacation, and a bicycle trip in California. Although participants enjoyed the actual trip less than predicted, they report enjoyment levels similar to those predicted after the trip when they recall the experience.

Learning is easier when people can access their feelings directly, that is, while experiencing a particular situation. It might even inspire them to adopt institutional preconditions to sustain optimal decisions after the event. Most readers will be familiar with the experience of not getting together with friends as much as one would like when reflecting about it immediately after the meeting. What inhibits most of us is that we often cannot recall the intensity of how enjoyable the experience was once we return to our daily routine. One of us experimented with trying to overcome this problem by fixing a date while still in the company of the friends and aware of that pleasure. The result was more frequent and equally enjoyable meetings. There are also moments of bliss and traumatic experiences that can abruptly change people's intuitive theories about what constitutes happiness.

In general, however, a more elaborate learning process is required. The individual must step back from actual decision making, where the extrinsic dominate the intrinsic characteristics. He or she should attempt to make an overall evaluation, including critical self-examination, or should resort to what has been called double-loop learning (see Argyris and Schön 1978). Because such elaborate learning is more costly, and is in itself subject to error, individuals are not able to fully correct their mispredictions within a reasonably short time. In many cases, they are incapable of correcting to any degree, meaning that the misprediction of future utilities persists over time.[8]

Limited learning can well coexist with people's partial awareness of their or others' mispredicting utility.[9] Many people refer, for example, to difficulties and mistakes in balancing work and life. Yet still, on a case-by-case basis, they make decisions underestimating intrinsic relative to extrinsic attributes.[10]

Consequences

The mispredictions of future utility from goods and activities, depending on their intrinsic and extrinsic attributes, have two immediate consequences. The first is that goods and activities with pronounced intrinsic attributes are underconsumed relative to those with pronounced extrinsic attributes. The second is that the systematic distortions in allocation due to utility misprediction reduce individuals' experienced utility according to their own best interests. These consequences and the discussed sources link up to various strands of literature where similar phenomena have been identified:

- The aspect of underestimated adaptation to new situations is neatly introduced in theoretical models of intertemporal decision making with habit formation (Loewenstein, O'Donoghue, and Rabin 2003). Based on their model of projection bias, various phenomena can be modeled, like the misguided purchase of durable goods or consumption profiles with too much consumption early in life. Misprediction of utility thus provides an alternative to seemingly irrational saving behavior that is usually addressed in a framework of individuals with self-control problems.[11] Interesting implications follow when people mispredict adaptation in situations where the endowment effect applies. The endowment effect is commonly understood as the result of people adapting to owning or not owning an object and people feeling higher utility losses in absolute terms when they give up the object than when they obtain it. Underestimating adaptation then leads to accentuated feelings of loss aversion and a much stronger endowment effect (Loewenstein, O'Donoghue, and Rabin 2003).

- It has been argued that the work-life balance of individuals today is distorted. People are induced to work too much, and to disregard other aspects of life. This proposition has been forcefully put forward for the United States, where individuals are said to be overworked (Schor 1991). This is consistent with our hypothesis that individuals tend to focus too much on options characterized by strong extrinsic attributes, in particular income, compared to intrinsic attributes.[12]

- Competing for status involves negative externalities, and therefore too much effort is invested in gaining status and acquiring what are called positional goods (Frank 1985, 1999). Such goods are characterized by strong extrinsic attributes. The saying "keeping up with the Joneses" reveals that consumption is externally oriented. Thus misprediction of utility is likely to magnify the distortions of status competition in consumption.

- Procedural utility—that is, the satisfaction derived from the process rather than from its outcome—relates to innate needs. The utility derived from a particular process contributes to competence, relatedness, and autonomy, and is therefore closely related to the intrinsic attributes of goods and activities (see survey by Frey, Benz, and Stutzer 2004). Our propositions anticipate that typical decision making will underestimate sources of procedural utility. Consistent with this idea, it has been empirically shown (Tyler, Huo, and Lind 1999) that, when making decisions, individuals tend to prefer institutions promising favorable outcomes. But afterward they state that they would have preferred an institution putting more emphasis on (just) procedures.

- There is a long tradition in economics arguing that individuals tend to focus too much on material goods and disregard goods providing nonmaterial benefits (see Lebergott 1993; Lane 1991). Most important, Scitovsky (1976) claimed that comfort goods, compared to those providing stimulation, are overconsumed. The former have a strong extrinsic component, and the latter correspond closely to the intrinsic aspect, as stimulation renews the satisfaction denied.[13]

- An empirical test of people mispredicting utility analyzes people's decisions for commuting longer or shorter hours (Frey and Stutzer 2003). The decision involves the trade-off between the salary or the quality of housing on the one hand and commuting time on the other. Rational utility maximizers commute only when they are compensated. However, when people overestimate utility from goods serving extrinsic wants, they are expected to opt for too much commuting and suffer lower utility. Findings indicate that commuting is by far not fully compensated and, on average, people who commute one hour one way would need an additional 40 percent of their monthly wage to be as satisfied as those who do not commute. There is, however, significant variation between people. Incomplete compensation is much stronger for those with strong extrinsic life goals.

Mispredicting Utility and the Political Process

We speculate in our analysis how politics affects the utility losses incurred by individuals due to their misprediction of utility. In particular, does political intervention (that is the supply of public goods, services, and regulations) mitigate or accentuate the utility loss due to individual misprediction?

Government Reactions: Four Models

We proceed by considering two ideal types of government implied by the classical welfare theoretic approach and by the (dominant) public choice approach. We then consider two more realistic models of government, one dictatorial and one democratic.

Omniscient Benevolent Dictator

The traditional social welfare approach implicitly and often explicitly assumes an omniscient benevolent dictator (see Brennan and Buchanan 1986; Buchanan 1991). The dictator has the power to put all political ideas into action. He is completely informed and has the best of intentions. He wants to help individuals to reach the highest utility possible according to their own evaluations.

The dictator offers many public goods with strong intrinsic attributes, despite the fact that the individuals do not value them highly when they learn about the dictator's decision. But the dictator knows that the individuals will value them more highly in the future. Because the dictator also knows individuals' discount rate, he is able to provide those public goods, producing maximum accumulated experienced utility over time. The public goods and services supplied promote personal interaction in a number of ways: by providing communal meeting places, by granting paid maternity leave, by regulating shopping hours or the maximum work week, by supporting the arts and sports, and so on. The applied policies foster people's self-determination by giving them a say in economic democracy and by providing full employment.

In contrast, the dictator offers few public goods with strong extrinsic attributes. He correctly foresees that the individuals get used to them and that they will reap lower utility in the future. These are public goods, services, and regulations, spurring growth in consumption such as subsidized mobility or the abandonment of employee protection.

An omniscient benevolent dictator thus does not mispredict the utility people get from public goods in the future and may to some extent even correct people's mispredictions of their future utility derived from the consumption of goods and services in the private realm.

This approach is faced with fundamental problems (Buchanan and Tullock 1962; for a survey, see Frey 1983; Brennan and Buchanan 1986). No dictator has full discretionary power to undertake the benevolent policies. He is to some extent restricted by other actors, in particular by competing elites such as the military and other politicians. He has little incentive to become informed about the preferences of the people, and no incentives to correct their mispredictions about their future utility. Rather, a dictator pursues his own interests, consisting in creating a good life for himself, his family and his cronies, and securing his position.

The omniscient benevolent dictator, however, is indeed no more than an ideal.

Perfectly Competitive Parties in a Democracy

The dominant approach in the economic theory of politics, or public choice, is what is called the median voter model, resulting from "perfectly competitive parties in a democracy" (Downs 1957; for a survey, see Mueller 2003). In this model, two parties exist with continuous elections and complete voter participation. Under these conditions, the policies undertaken converge to the preferences of the median voter. Because nothing is known about the distribution of preferences with regard to goods with different intensities of extrinsic and intrinsic attributes, a normal preference distribution can be assumed, so that the median voter is the average voter and citizen.

The party leaders are not fully informed, but seek to collect enough information to take care of the average voters' preferences. Neither of the parties have any discretionary leeway, but must aim at fulfilling the median voter's preference. At election time, the parties must offer policy bundles that please the voters. They offer public goods with strong extrinsic attributes, but whose future utility is overestimated. They cannot afford to supply public goods with strong intrinsic attributes, because the voters do not predict their higher future utility and vote strictly instrumentally. Income transfers, tax reductions, material goods, and policies spurring growth are thus preferred, and public goods with strong intrinsic attributes and policies favoring interaction and "good" processes are disregarded.

In a "perfectly competitive democratic system of party competition," individuals' mispredictions are carried forward in the provision of public goods and services, and individual biases might even be accentuated rather than corrected.[14]

This standard public choice model can be criticized from several perspectives. For a start, the situation of perfect political competition with strictly two parties exists nowhere. In every country there are more than two parties competing or potentially competing with each other, and with more than two parties, there is either no equilibrium (for three parties) or different or several equilibria (Selten 1971; Mueller 2003). Furthermore, the demand and supply side of the democratic process is full of imperfections. In particular, the incumbent party has great advantages over its contenders. Information about individuals' preferences is seriously limited. Moreover, people decide about candidates and issues after election and voting campaigns with widespread political debates, which partly form people's preferences.

The model of perfect party competition, like the benevolent dictator, is again an ideal. We will now discuss two more realistic types of government, one a paternalist government in an authoritarian system, the other a majority government in a democracy.

Paternalist Government in an Authoritarian System

The government has the discretionary power to undertake those policies it sees fit to implement, but is limited by other actors. The people's preferences, however, play only a small role because the probability of what is basically an authoritarian government being toppled by a popular uprising is small (see Tullock 1987). Nevertheless, the ruler pacifies the people, especially in the capital, by offering panem et circenses—that is, public goods with strongly extrinsic attributes and with low future utility. The authoritarian ruler needs to be concerned about a possible takeover by the military or police, or perhaps by the political or social elite. He therefore makes an effort to check such aspirations by providing both material benefits (such as a good income and easily exploitable monopolistic positions) and immaterial rewards such as titles and orders. At the same time, he threatens hard sanctions if anyone opposes him. The ruler's information is incomplete, though he makes a great effort to know what people think and what is going on in the country. The information he receives, however, is typically distorted. His underlings have learned that they do best when providing information that favors the ruler.

A paternalistic ruler tends to accentuate individual utility losses due to misprediction because he offers public goods with strong extrinsic attributes. But this effect is somewhat mitigated by the fact that the ruler may have a long-term view. The authoritarian German Democratic Republic, although economically inefficient, may have had one good side, namely fostering conditions that enabled community interactions such as volunteering (see Meier and Stutzer 2004).

Majority Government in a Democracy

To stay in power, a party in a democracy must be re-elected. The government has little discretionary room at election time if its re-election chances are low. In that case, it has an interest to cater to voters' short-term preferences. It supplies and promises public goods with marked extrinsic attributes expressly to please the voters. These are the well-known election presents consisting mainly of monetary transfers, and such policy aggravates individuals' utility losses due to misprediction. A majority government thus tends to discontinually accentuate individuals' losses due to misprediction. This is the best strategy, even if voters experience and realize after elections that the policies are suboptimal.

Many government parties, however, are reasonably confident of winning the next elections and are not forced to undertake policies aimed at producing short-term benefits. Moreover, once the elections are over, the party in power has considerable leeway to pursue a policy following its own ideological preferences (see the econometric models of government behavior and of the political business cycle in Frey and Schneider 1978a; 1978b). Depending on its ideology, public goods will be offered, which may accentuate or reduce individuals' utility losses due to misprediction. Before the fact, it is not known whether a move in the direction of extrinsic or intrinsic attributes will prevail.

Extending Models of Politics: Learning by Individuals

Political discourse is a critical factor of the political process in a democracy: "The definition of democracy as 'government by discussion' implies that individual values can and do change in the process of decision-making" (Buchanan 1954, 120). In addition, people's behavior in the political realm is strongly influenced by their motivation to express their values and views (Brennan and Lomasky 1993; for empirical evidence, see, for example, Copeland and Laband 2002). Both aspects potentially allow for political decisions not biased by misprediction of utility from publicly provided goods, services and regulation. It might even be possible to overcome some of the negative effects that misprediction produces in individual decision making in the private realm. Public discourse not only enables learning for individuals, it also creates an incentive for governments to respond to citizens' needs.[15]

The four psychological sources of misprediction analyzed earlier can be transformed in the process of political discourse and expressive voting. In political discussions, people bring in their ideas of what would be good for them in general. They are thus partly aware of their misprediction in day-to-day decisions. Examples are the debates about working-time restrictions. At least some arguments hold that spending time with family and friends brings renewed pleasure, and that it is futile to accumulate more and more material goods.[16] That there are differences in the degree of adaptation thus realized. Individual decisions often have to rely on experience. Discussions, however, open the door for exchange with those experiencing a particular situation, such as being unemployed. Biases due to distorted memory or missing experiences are thus attenuated. As voters make a decision, which affects their fellow citizens as well, other reasons for rationalizing and justifying decisions are taken into account. Moreover, secret ballots make it not necessary to choose extrinsic attributes to facilitate justification toward other people. In the act of voting in favor of an issue, or voting for a candidate, the awareness of the problem can thus be expected to be expressed. The most fundamental contribution of political discussion is about changing intuitive theories of happiness. It can be expected that the more the discussion fulfills the normative criteria of a discourse free of constraints (in the sense of discourse ethics see, for example, Habermas 1993), the more likely existing beliefs about the sources of happiness are challenged and reconsidered.

Substantial evidence indicates that people base many of their opinions on what they discuss with others (see, for example, Huckfeldt and Sprague 1995; Walsh 2004). To learn about the ideas of other persons, the composition of the discussion group is relevant. To gain greater awareness of rationales for alternative perspectives, the extent to which the group includes people with opposing views is important (for example, Mutz 2002). Beyond its effect on political tolerance, discussion also affects behavior. In many laboratory experiments, the role of discussion in affecting individuals' decisions about contributing to public goods is clearly demonstrated (see, for example, Bohnet and Frey 1999).

The intensity and quality of political discussion depends, of course, on the type of democratic political institutions existing and the organization (or property structure) of the media. In a democratic system with proportional representation, a broader range of arguments is put forward than in a majoritarian system with what are often mainly two parties (see, for example, Karp and Banducci 2002; for New Zealand, a country that switched to proportional representation). In a democracy allowing for direct democratic participation in important policy areas, issues not discussed in an election campaign focusing on a limited range of topics are taken up and put to the vote. In an empirical study for Switzerland and the European Union, citizens' information about politics is related to the degree of direct democracy in Swiss cantons and whether national referendums about EU treaties were held (Benz and Stutzer 2004). Findings indicate that citizens know more and feel subjectively better informed when they have a say in politics. This result is argued to be due to the public debates preceding and following referendums. Political discussion in public is more likely to involve and affect politicians when they are organized in relatively democratic party structures than in strict party hierarchies that can easily enforce faction discipline (Teorell 1999). Arguments discussed in the media, and free from political influence, are more likely to challenge individuals' beliefs about the sources of happiness than those put forward in the media and captured by special interests or monopolistic media moguls.[17] Media ownership structures vary widely across countries (Djankov et al. 2003). In many instances, strong goverment influence is related to less freedom of the press, fewer political rights for citizens, and inferior governance and health outcomes. Having free media does not necessarily mean that people are exposed to alternative perspectives and are prompted to reflect on the reasons for their beliefs. First, people might simply choose media content that reflects their beliefs. Second, exposure to contrary information can also strengthen existing attitudes, depending on how people cognitively respond to opposing views (Sieck and Yates 1997). All these aspects can potentially serve as empirically testable hypotheses about the extent to which misprediction is carried forward in decisions in the democratic process, or the extent to which political decisions can help to prevent wrong decisions on the individual level.

Inputs into the Discourse Process to Counteract Individuals' Misprediction of Utility

Quite a number of proposals can be put forward in the discourse process to reduce individuals' misguided pursuit of status and material possessions and to make choices with strong intrinsic attributes, such as spending time with family and friends, relatively more attractive. Most straightforward from an economic perspective are proposals to tax consumption more heavily, whether by a consumption tax (Frank 1999) or by a high income tax (Layard 2005). Other proposals involve subsidies of goods that are underconsumed rather than taxation of goods that are overconsumed. Most prominent is Scitovsky (1976), who argues for government support of the arts, architecture, and education to bring about more stimulation than comfort in people's lives.

Another variety of government intervention is regulation, or setting defaults. Many specific areas allow for rules that make leisure time more attractive. This is addressed most directly by working-time regulation. Mandatory maximum working hours may help to coordinate on earning less money that can be spent for positional goods. Such regulations can, of course, be partly circumvented by holding a second job or working in the shadow economy. However, they may have a strong expressive component. It becomes salient that working less, given the income level reached, would be good. The respective rule might help to justify working fewer hours and spending more time socializing. Policies for maternity and parental leave fall along the same lines (for an overview, see OECD 1998). These are promoted as family-friendly policies to help create a better balance between work and family life. Regulation of shopping hours is another regulation that might help coordinate leisure time and free people from negotiating a trade-off between time shopping and time working on the one hand, and meeting friends or pursuing a hobby on the other hand.

When people overestimate utility from consumption and form consumption habits, they might end up spending too much early in life and saving too little for retirement (Loewenstein, O'Donoghue, and Rabin 2003) or even accumulate debts from consumer credits. One possible reaction from the regulator is to restrict consumer credits (for example, by maximum interest rates) and, in the case of saving for retirement, to introduce mandatory pension schemes. However, these interventions might entail high costs for those less prone to misprediction because they cannot escape the regulations. An alternative is provided by regulations that apply what is known as asymmetric paternalism (Camerer et al. 2003), which permit opting out of contracts designed to help overcome biases in decision making. A pertinent example is savings plans that provide self-binding mechanisms. One possibility are plans for which employees are automatically enrolled (default option) when they start a job and need to actively opt out of when they no longer want to follow the savings plan. In another program, employees are asked to commit in advance that they contribute a fraction of their future salary increases into a savings account (Thaler and Benartzi 2004).

Misprediction is argued to have particularly marked effects when it coincides with the endowment effect. Many policy arrangements can be illustrated to mitigate mistakes in decision making. For example, when books and newspapers are sent to consumers without having been requested, the perception of succumbing to the endowment effect may be raised by facilitating comparison. For this purpose, comparative advertising by competing suppliers (which would, for example, point out the higher price charged) or by consumer agencies, may be encouraged or mandated. For striking a deal, the consent of both adult members of a household might be required by law. Self-commitment could be facilitated if people have the right to have all unsolicited goods and services automatically returned to the sender (at the sender's expense). In some cases, one could have the right to exclude oneself from being able to do business.[18] A further possibility is to make the right to withdraw from contracts mandatory for consumers.

Examples of Existing Policies

Some of the policy proposals are in place in various countries. Whether the democratic systems in these countries are in fact characterized by institutions that facilitate an effective political discourse, however, needs to be left to future research. (We will formulate corresponding testable propositions shortly.)

Table 5.1 shows the adoption of policies affecting individuals' allocation of time for a range of developed countries with democratic governments. Column 1 reports on the provision of maternity leave. The indicator is the product of the number of weeks of maternity leave and the rate of pay during those weeks (OECD 2001, 144). Although there is no mandatory maternity leave provision in the United States, Australia, and New Zealand, the Scandinavian countries of Denmark, Finland, and Sweden have extended programs. All three guarantee an equivalent of thirty or more weeks of fully paid maternity leave. There are, of course, many differences in the national provisions not accounted for in the rough summary indicator.

The second policy brought into perspective is the legal maximum number of working hours per week (OECD 1998, 168). Despite many country specific rules, an overview is possible about whether working hours are a policy issue. Six developed countries portrayed in table 5.1 do not restrict the number of maximum working hours per week—namely, Canada, the United States, Japan, the United Kingdom, Australia, and New Zealand. The most restrictive arrangement is in Finland, setting a maximum of forty-five hours per week.

Data quality is worst for the regulation of shopping hours. In many countries, opening hours are at least partly regulated at the sub-federal level. As an indicator for opening policies, the maximum weekly opening hours between 8 a.m. and 12 p.m. are reported (Pilat 1997). Many countries do not restrict opening during this time frame, indicated by a number of 112 hours. At the other end of the range is The Netherlands, setting the maximum opening hours at fifty-five hours.

A Reconsideration of the "Enlightened" Policies

The free public debate is not the only factor influencing government policy making. Besides the individual interests of the professional politicians, special interests come into play. These seek to influence the political process to get regulations that generate or maintain rents for them. Well-organized producer interests may well oppose many of the mentioned policies because they might reduce the returns on their invested capital (see, for example, the opposition against legislation that protects a woman's job during maternity leave). Producers of consumer items

Table 5.1   Legal Policies Affecting Work-Life Balance

	Maternity Leave Provision 1999 to 2001	Legal Maximum Weekly Working Hours 1990s	Legal Maximum Weekly Opening Hours (8 to 24 hours) 1990s
North America			
Canada	8.25	none	—
Mexico	12	57	—
United States	0	none	112
Asia			
Japan	8.4	none	—
South Korea	8.5	56	—
Europe			
Austria	16	50	—
Belgium	11.55	50	73
Czech Republic	19.32	51	—
Denmark	30	48	63.5
Finland	36.4	45	80
France	16	48	112
Germany	14	60	66.5
Greece	8	48	112
Hungary	24	52	—
Ireland	9.8	60	112
Italy	17.2	60	66
Luxembourg	16	48	—
Netherlands	16	60 (maximum average over 13 weeks is 48)	55
Norway	42	50	80
Poland	18	—	—
Portugal	24.3	54	112
Slovak Republic	25.2	—	—
Spain	16	47	112
Sweden	40.32	48 or 52	112
Switzerland	—	61 or 66	—
Turkey	7.92	—	—
United Kingdom	7.92	none	102
Oceania			
Australia	0	none	—
New Zealand	0	none	—

Sources: The index of national maternity leave provision is the product of the number of weeks of maternity leave and the rate of pay during those weeks. Data is from OECD *Employment Outlook 2001*, table 4.7, columns 4 and 5. Legal maximum weekly working hours data is from OECD *Employment Outlook 1998*, table 5.10, column 3. Data for legal maximum weekly opening hours of shops is from Pilat (1997).
Note: — = data not available.

might even oppose the regulations mentioned because they benefit from people spending too much on their goods due to misprediction. Alternatively, well-intended policies are often influenced by special interests and misused for their rent seeking purposes (see the extensive debate about insider protection at the workplace at the expense of unemployed people, or the regulation of the retail sector to protect traditional suppliers from large new entrants).

Empirically Testable Propositions

It is in the nature of the addressed anomaly that tests based on behavioral traces are difficult. Mispredicting utility involves behavioral consequences that seem optimal for predicted utility but lead to a lower level of experienced utility. Therefore, we propose tests that involve reported life satisfaction, happiness or other measures of subjective well-being as proxies for people's utility (for an introduction to happiness research in economics see Frey and Stutzer 2002a, 2002b). Happiness research is increasingly used in economics to test behavioral theories (for a discussion, see Frey and Stutzer 2005). Moreover, research on subjective well-being contributes significant insights into the sources of people mispredicting utility.

There are two sets of testable propositions that follow from the analysis. The first refers to the different predictions following from the four models of government. The second takes up the refined modeling of the political process, including political discourse and learning. These propositions are preliminary.

- Democracies typically show less bias in consumption. People therefore enjoy higher utility than in authoritarian and dictatorial countries because in democracies governments have less need to please the opposition with goods and services providing immediate gratification. This is consistent with first evidence in Inglehart and Klingemann (2000): "New evidence from the World Value Survey supports the hypothesis that a society's level of subjective well-being is closely linked with the flourishing of democratic institutions" (177). However, the prediction of the first proposition is difficult to disentangle from the positive incentives in democratic competition to heed citizen preferences.

- Benevolent authoritarian systems provide a less distorted set of public goods and therefore more happiness than nonbenevolent systems because they try to mitigate individual biases attributable to misprediction rather than exploit them. What is benevolent must be determined after the fact.

- Incumbent governments in a tight race for re-election produce a higher consumption bias and therefore lower happiness than majoritarian democracy governments with strong chances for re-election, because the former offer or promise goods for which citizens predict high utility.

- Re-election probabilities can be determined after the fact. Thus, reported subjective well-being is lower after a close election than after one with a clear confirmation of the incument party.

- Precautionary policies are more likely in countries characterized by institutions that foster public discourse (such as free media, proportional representation, referendums, democratic party structures). Proxy measures for involving people in discussions about politics are often included in public surveys. These measures can serve as intermediary variables. People in countries applying precautionary regulations are expected to be more satisfied with their lives.

Conclusion

This chapter has pursued two goals. First, it introduces a decision framework with people mispredicting utility that leads to systematically suboptimal behavior. Second, the consequences of this anomaly are studied for different characterizations of the political process.

Individuals are argued to systematically mispredict the future utility of goods consumed and activities undertaken. Goods and activities characterized by stronger intrinsic aspects (such as spending time with family and friends and pursuing hobbies) are undervalued compared to those characterized by stronger extrinsic aspects (such as income). Although people are partly aware of this anomaly, they err when making decisions on a case-by-case basis. Learning is slow and imperfect, meaning that the distorted decisions are preserved over time. Because of this, individuals obtain a lower utility level than if they were not subject to this systematic bias of misprediction.

The result that the individuals are worse off according to their own best interests distinguishes us from the more traditional consumption critique, according to which individuals are not able to choose what is best for them—but what is "best" is evaluated according to outside preferences.

Consequences of mispredicting utility are not restricted to the private realm, but also affect people's behavior as citizens. Two modes can be differentiated. First, on a case-by-case basis in the current political process, citizens evaluate government policy, underestimating intrinsic attributes relative to extrinsic attributes. Second, however, the political process can also generate conditions such that citizens get a more detached view of their evaluation and become partly aware of their or others' misprediction of utility.

In the first mode, the effects of mispredicting utility are carried forward or even accentuated in the political process. This mode might accurately describe government decision making in a perfectly competitive democratic system of party competition. The two parties cannot afford to deviate from the short-term evaluation of their program by the median voter and have to provide a policy bundle with strong extrinsic attributes. The model of perfect party competition is, however, an ideal type that doesn't exist. The analysis might, however, also hold in situations when the re-election chances of the incumbent government are low, and it starts giving presents to cater to voters' short-term preferences.

The first mode with immediate gratification is also characterizing the policy that has to be pursued by an authoritarian ruler. Offering panem et circenses is necessary to pacify the people, mainly in the capital, and providing material benefits to the elite is necessary to prevent a military or police takeover.

The second mode with citizens being at least partly aware of their anomalous day-to-day behavior is a more accurate description of modern democracies. There, the political discourse is the crucial mechanism that allows learning in the political process and provides incentives to the government to be responsive to citizens' long-term preferences. Although some institutional conditions are known that facilitate public debate, there are many other institutions for which only untested propositions are put forward.

Many policies can be put forward to mitigate the consequences of people mispredicting utility, but we are only beginning to understand whether they are also effective in correcting people's biases and thus increasing individuals' well-being, or whether they are mainly the result of rent-seeking activities.

We are grateful for helpful remarks from Matthias Benz, William Gale, Simon Luechinger, Stephan Meier, Dina Pomeranz and participants of the conference on Behavioral Public Finance, University of Michigan Business School, April 23 to 24, 2004.

Notes

1. We borrow these categories from a large literature in humanistic or value psychology (for example Maslow 1968, Rogers 1961).
2. The underlying theories are manifold, and comprise, for instance, people's urge to master their environment for its own sake (White 1959), of being an origin (DeCharms 1968), people's resistance to loss of control (Brehm 1966) and the reflection of perceived control in more effective behavior and higher positive affects (Bandura 1977; Seligman 1992).

3. When people spend time with friends because they are famous and important, the extrinsic dimension becomes more prevalent.

4. Both utility measures—predicted and experienced utility—diverge from traditional decision utility derived from individual behavior. Utility is rather understood as a hedonic experience (see Kahneman, Wakker, and Sarin 1997).

5. Standard research designs are prospective longitudinal studies on self-reported emotions. People are asked how happy they expect themselves to be after some event has happened or some option has been chosen. These predictions are then compared with reported subjective well-being after experiencing the new situation. There are several limits to this design. First, usually only predictions for changes in the near future are assessed. Second, the way in which scales of measurement are interpreted can change over time, due to maturation or a change in the anchor, for example. Third, predictions might also affect actual feelings or might even become self-fulfilling prophecies. Some of these problems can be eliminated by conducting studies between subjects, where one group's predictions are contrasted with a different group's actual reports.

6. Young academics might be particularly worried about life after a negative tenure decision. Daniel Gilbert and his colleagues (1998) asked assistant professors how happy they would be after a positive tenure decision and after a negative one. The answers were compared with reported subjective well-being of academics affected by a tenure decision made five or less years before. Although assistants predicted they would be less happy during the first five years after being turned down, there was no statistically significant difference between those who had and had not gotten tenure. Similarly, assistants also overestimated the positive impact of receiving tenure on their well-being.

7. In contrast, for choices made once-in-a-lifetime, learning is no option. Biased decisions can then well affect the life path. We believe that misprediction of utility matters a lot in such life decisions (like career choice) but we do not study them here.

8. A more fundamental reason for people's limited learning might lie in some advantage misprediction provides in the evolutionary process. Luis Rayo and Gary Becker (2003) model how humans' utility functions formed in order to maximize success in genetic replication. Their model rationalizes that people neglect adaptation (described as self-inflicted externality). In today's world, this utility function with an inbuilt misprediction, however, is no longer helpful to guarantee an optimal mix between experienced utility and motivation for success in society.

9. Systematic differences between self-evaluation and the assessment of others' decisions is likely due to overoptimism (Weinstein 1981). Thus people are overly confident about their own ability to make the right decisions, yet at the same time being aware that the average person mispredicts utility.

10. This argument is similar to the ones about sophisticated and naive people who are fully or not at all aware of their future self-control problem (for a discussion of self awareness, see O'Donoghue and Rabin 2003).

11. In Loewenstein, O'Donoghue, and Rabin (2003), however, there is no ex-

plicit modeling of differences in adaptation across goods, attributes of different options or people.

12. There is an apparent paradox that working provides intrinsic benefits but that there can nevertheless be too much working due to mispredicting utility. The paradox vanishes when the two natures of work are taken into consideration. Although intrinsic work enjoyment and flow might in fact be undervalued in job choice decisions, people focus on the monetary compensation when trading off additional working time and time for leisure activities. For given intrinsic and extrinsic job attributes, this is hypothesized to lead to too long working days.

13. One might argue that the over-consumption of comfort goods and related biased decisions are rather explained by agents having self-control problems (see, for example, Laibson 2005 on intertemporal decision making). These agents choose goods and activities providing short run gains and incurring long run costs. However, mispredicting utility rather portrays the other extreme of people. Individuals mispredicting utility may choose to work extra hours over a long period of time in order to buy some prestigious car in the end from which long lasting satisfaction is expected.

14. We are aware that the median voter model has been further developed. Recent accounts include, for example, the problem of mobilizing voters, fundraising, party organization, and ideological capture by special interests. Future elaboration should take these extensions into account when analyzing how the misprediction of utility is transformed into policies.

15. There is strong evidence that information through the mass media encourages political competition and increases government responsiveness to citizens' preferences (Besley and Burgess 2002; Stromberg 2004).

16. In a national referendum held in Switzerland in 2002, people voted on a drastic reduction in the maximum number of legal working hours, as proposed in a popular initiative. One of the main arguments in favor, advanced by the initiative committee, emphasized an improved work-life balance: "Long working weeks and stress become a health risk for more and more people. Too much work makes people ill and work on demand is poison for family life. There is less and less time for social contacts, education, culture, sports or voluntary work. The initiative of the SGB stops this and brings working hours in line with health and allows for a better balance between family, job and leisure" (Federal Chancellery 2002, 19, our translation).

17. For the role of the media in exposing citizens to cross-cutting political viewpoints, see, for example, Mutz and Martin (2001).

18. In some casinos in Germany and gambling halls in the Canton of Zurich, Switzerland, one can officially request that one be denied access to these places.

References

Argyris, Chris, and Donald A. Schön. 1978. *Organizational Learning: A Theory of Action Perspective.* Reading, Mass.: Addison Wesley.

Bandura, Albert. 1977. "Self-Efficacy: Toward a Unifying Theory of Behavior Change." *Psychological Review* 84(2): 191–215.

Becker, Gary S. 1965. "A Theory in the Allocation of Time." *Economic Journal* 75(299): 493–517.

Benz, Matthias, and Alois Stutzer. 2004. "Are Voters Better Informed When They Have a Larger Say in Politics? Evidence for the European Union and Switzerland." *Public Choice* 119(1–2): 31–59.

Besley, Timothy, and Robin Burgess. 2002. "The Political Economy of Government Responsiveness: Theory and Evidence from India." *Quarterly Journal of Economics* 117(4): 1415–51.

Bohnet, Iris, and Bruno S. Frey. 1999. "The Sound of Silence in Prisoner's Dilemma and Dictator Games." *Journal of Economic Behavior and Organization* 38(1): 43–57.

Bowles, Samuel. 1998. "Endogenous Preferences: The Cultural Consequences of Markets and Other Economic Institutions." *Journal of Economic Literature* 36(1): 75–111.

Brehm, Jack W. 1966. *A Theory of Psychological Reactance.* New York: Academic Press.

Brennan, Geoffrey, and James M. Buchanan. 1986. *The Reason of Rules: Constitutional Political Economy.* Cambridge: Cambridge University Press.

Brennan, Geoffrey, and Loren E. Lomasky. 1993. *Democracy and Decision.* Cambridge: Cambridge University Press.

Buchanan, James M. 1954. "Social Choice, Democracy, and Free Markets." *Journal of Political Economy* 62(2): 114–23.

———. 1991. *Constitutional Economics.* Oxford: Basil Blackwell.

Buchanan, James M., and Gordon Tullock. 1962. *The Calculus of Consent: Logical Foundations of Constitutional Democracy.* Ann Arbor: University of Michigan Press.

Camerer, Colin F., Samuel Issacharoff, George Loewenstein, Ted O'Donoghue, and Matthew Rabin. 2003. "Regulation for Conservatives: Behavioral Economics and the Case for 'Asymmetric Paternalism.'" *University of Pennsylvania Law Review* 151(3): 1211–254.

Clark, Andrew E. 2002. "A Note on Unhappiness and Unemployment Duration." Mimeo, DELTA, Paris.

Copeland, Cassandra, and David N. Laband. 2002. "Expressiveness and Voting." *Public Choice* 110(3/4): 351–63.

Csikszentmihalyi, Mihaly. 1990. *Flow: The Psychology of Optimal Experience.* New York: Harper Perennial.

DeCharms, Richard. 1968. *Personal Causation.* New York: Academic Press.

Deci, Edward L., and Richard M. Ryan. 2000. "The 'What' and 'Why' of Goal Pursuits: Human Needs and the Self-determination of Behavior." *Psychological Inquiry* 11(4): 227–68.

Djankov, Simeon, Caralee McLiesh, Tatiana Nenova, and Andrei Shleifer. 2003. "Who Owns the Media?" *Journal of Law and Economics* 46(2): 341–81.

Downs, Anthony. 1957. *An Economic Theory of Democracy.* New York: Harper and Row.

Easterlin, Richard A. 2001. "Income and Happiness: Towards a Unified Theory." *Economic Journal* 111(473): 465–84.

————. 2003. "Building a Better Theory of Well-Being." Paper presented at the Conference on the Paradoxes of Happiness in Economics. University of Milano-Bicocca (March 21, 2003).

Federal Chancellery. 2002. Volksabstimmung vom 3. März 2002: Erläuterungen des Bundesrates. Bern: Federal Chancellery.

Frank, Robert H. 1985. *Choosing the Right Pond.* New York: Oxford University Press.

————. 1999. *Luxury Fever: Why Money Fails to Satisfy in an Era of Excess.* New York: Free Press.

Frederick, Shane, and George Loewenstein. 1999. "Hedonic Adaptation." In *Well-Being: The Foundations of Hedonic Psychology,* edited by Daniel Kahneman, Ed Diener, and Norbert Schwarz. New York: Russell Sage Foundation.

Frey, Bruno S. 1983. *Democratic Economic Policy: A Theoretical Introduction.* Oxford: Robertson.

————. 1997. *Not Just for The Money. An Economic Theory of Personal Motivation.* Cheltenham and Brookfield: Edward Elgar.

Frey, Bruno S., and Matthias Benz. 2002. "Being Independent Is a Great Thing: Subjective Evaluations of Self-Employment and Hierarchy." IEW Working Paper No. 135. Zurich, Switzerland: University of Zurich.

Frey, Bruno S., Matthias Benz, and Alois Stutzer. 2004. "Introducing Procedural Utility: Not Only What but Also How Matters." *Journal of Institutional and Theoretical Economics* 160(3): 377–401.

Frey, Bruno S., and Reto Jegen. 2001. "Motivation Crowding Theory: A Survey of Empirical Evidence." *Journal of Economic Surveys* 15(5): 589–611.

Frey, Bruno S., and Friedrich Schneider. 1978a. "An Empirical Study of Politico-Economic Interaction in the United States." *Review of Economics and Statistics* 60(2): 174–83.

————. 1978b. "A Political-Economic Model of the United Kingdom." *Economic Journal* 88(350): 243–53.

Frey, Bruno S., and Alois Stutzer. 2002a. *Happiness and Economics: How the Economy and Institutions Affect Well-Being.* Princeton, N.J., and Oxford: Princeton University Press.

————. 2002b. "What Can Economists Learn from Happiness Research?" *Journal of Economic Literature* 40(2): 402–35.

————. 2003. "Economic Consequences of Mispredicting Utility." Mimeo, University of Zurich.

————. 2005. "Testing Theories of Happiness." In *Economics and Happiness. Framing the Analysis,* edited by Luigino Bruni and Pierluigi Porta. Oxford: Oxford University Press.

Gilbert, Daniel T., Elizabeth C. Pinel, Timothy D. Wilson, Stephen J. Blumberg, and Thalia P. Wheatley. 1998. "Immune Neglect: A Source of Durability Bias in Affective Forecasting." *Journal of Personality and Social Psychology* 75(3): 617–38.

Habermas, Jürgen. 1993. *Justification and Application: Remarks on Discourse Ethics.* Cambridge, Mass.: MIT Press.

Hsee, Christopher K., Jiao Zhang, Fang Yu, and Yiheng H. Xi. 2003. "Lay Rationalism and Inconsistency between Predicted Experience and Decision." *Journal of Behavioral Decision Making* 16(4): 257–72.

Huckfeldt, Robert, and John Sprague. 1995. *Citizens, Politics, and Social Communication.* New York: Cambridge University Press.

Inglehart, Ronald F., and Hans-Dieter Klingemann. 2000. "Genes, Culture, Democracy, and Happiness." In *Culture and Subjective Well-Being*, edited by Ed Diener and Eunkook M. Suh. Cambridge, Mass.: MIT Press.

Kahneman, Daniel. 1999. "Objective Happiness." In *Well-Being: The Foundations of Hedonic Psychology*, edited by Daniel Kahneman, Ed Diener, and Norbert Schwarz. New York: Russell Sage Foundation.

———. 2003. "Experienced Utility and Objective Happiness: A Moment-Based Approach." In *The Psychology of Economic Decisions*, Volume 1: *Rationality and Well-Being*, edited by Isabelle Brocas, and Juan D. Carrillo. Oxford: Oxford University Press.

Kahneman, Daniel, Peter P. Wakker, and Rakesh Sarin. 1997. "Back to Bentham? Explorations of Experienced Utility." *Quarterly Journal of Economics* 112(2): 375–405.

Karp, Jeffrey A., and Susan A. Banducci. 2002. "Issues and Party Competition under Alternative Electoral Systems." *Party Politics* 8(1): 123–41.

Kasser, Tim. 2002. *The High Price of Materialism*. Cambridge, Mass.: MIT Press.

Keeney, John S., and Ralph L. Raiffa. 1976. *Decisions with Multiple Objectives*. New York: John Wiley & Sons.

Kuttner, Robert. 1996. *Everything for Sale: The Virtues and Limits of Markets*. New York: Alfred A. Knopf.

Laibson, David. 2005. "Intertemporal Decision Making." In *Encyclopedia of Cognitive Science*. Indianapolis: Wiley.

Lancaster, Kelvin J. 1966. "A New Approach to Consumer Theory." *Journal of Political Economy* 74(2): 132–57.

Lane, Robert E. 1991. *The Market Experience*. Cambridge: Cambridge University Press.

Layard, Richard. 2005. *Happiness: Lessons from a New Science*. New York: Penguin.

Lebergott, Stanley. 1993. *Pursuing Happiness: American Consumers in the Twentieth Century*. Princeton, N.J.: Princeton University Press.

Loewenstein, George, and Daniel Adler. 1995. "A Bias in the Prediction of Tastes." *Economic Journal* 105(431): 929–37.

Loewenstein, George, and David Schkade. 1999. "Wouldn't It Be Nice? Predicting Future Feelings." In *Well-Being: The Foundations of Hedonic Psychology*, edited by Daniel Kahneman, Ed Diener, and Norbert Schwarz. New York: Russell Sage Foundation.

Loewenstein, George, Ted O'Donoghue, and Matthew Rabin. 2003. "Projection Bias in Predicting Future Utility." *Quarterly Journal of Economics* 118(4): 1209–248.

Maslow, Abraham. 1968. *Toward a Psychology of Being*, 2nd ed. New York: Van Nostrand.

McCrae, Robert R. 1990. "Controlling Neuroticism in the Measurement of Stress." *Stress Medicine* 6: 237–41.

Meier, Stephan, and Alois Stutzer. 2004. "Is Volunteering Rewarding in Itself?" IEW Working Paper No. 180. Zurich, Switzerland: University of Zurich.

Mitchell, Terence R., Leigh Thompson, Erika Peterson, and Randy Cronk. 1997. "Temporal Adjustments in the Evaluation of Events: The 'Rosy View.'" *Journal of Experimental Social Psychology* 33(4): 421–48.

Mueller, Dennis C. 2003. *Public Choice III*. New York: Cambridge University Press.

Mutz, Diana C. 2002. "Cross-Cutting Social Networks: Testing Democratic Theory in Practice." *American Political Science Review* 96(1): 111–26.

Mutz, Diana C., and Paul S. Martin. 2001. "Facilitating Communication across Lines of Political Difference: The Role of Mass Media." *American Political Science Review* 95(1): 97–114.

O'Donoghue, Ted, and Matthew Rabin. 2003. "Self Awareness and Self Control." In *Time and Decision: Economic and Psychological Perspectives on Intertemporal Choice*, edited by Roy Baumeister, George Loewenstein, and Daniel Read. New York: Russell Sage Foundation.

Organization for Economic Cooperation and Development [OECD]. 1998. *Employment Outlook 1998*. Paris: OECD.

———. 2001. *Employment Outlook 2001*. Paris: OECD.

Pilat, Dirk. 1997. "Regulation and Performance in the Distribution Sector." Working Paper No. 145. Paris: OECD.

Rayo, Luis, and Gary S. Becker. 2003. "On the Foundations of Happiness." Mimeo, University of Chicago.

Robinson, Michael D., and Gerald L. Clore. 2002. "Belief and Feeling: Evidence for an Accessibility Model of Emotional Self-Report." *Psychological Bulletin* 128(6): 934–60.

Rogers, Carl. 1961. *On Becoming a Person*. Boston, Mass.: Houghton Mifflin.

Ross, Michael. 1989. "Relation of Implicit Theories to the Construction of Personal Histories." *Psychological Review* 96(2): 341–57.

Schor, Juliet B. 1991. *The Overworked American: The Unexpected Decline of Leisure*. New York: Basic Books.

Scitovsky, Tibor. 1976. *The Joyless Economy: An Inquiry into Human Satisfaction and Consumer Dissatisfaction*. New York: Oxford University Press.

Seligman, Martin E. P. 1992. *Helplessness: On Depression, Development, and Death*. New York: Freeman.

Selten, Reinhard. 1971. "Anwendungen der Spieltheorie auf die Politische Wissenschaft. In *Politik und Wissenschaft*, edited by H. Maier. München: Beck.

Shafir, Eldar, Itamar Simonson, and Amos Tversky. 1993. "Reason-based Choice." *Cognition* 49(1–2): 11–36.

Sieck, Winston, and J. Frank Yates. 1997. "Exposition Effects on Decision Making: Choice and Confidence in Choice." *Organizational Behavior and Human Decision Processes* 70(3): 207–19.

Sirgy, M. Joseph. 1997. "Materialism and Quality of Life." *Social Indicators Research* 43(3): 227–60.

Stroebe, Margaret S., Wolfgang Stroebe, and Robert O. Hansson, eds. 1993. *Handbook of Bereavement: Theory, Research, and Intervention*. Cambridge: Cambridge University Press.

Stromberg, Daniel. 2004. "Radio's Impact on Public Spending." *Quarterly Journal of Economics* 119(1): 189–221.

Stutzer, Alois. 2004. "The Role of Income Aspirations in Individual Happiness." *Journal of Economic Behavior and Organization* 54(1): 89–109.

Tatzel, Miriam. 2002. "'Money Worlds' and Well-Being: An Integration of Money Dispositions, Materialism and Price-Related Behavior." *Journal of Economic Psychology* 23(1): 103–26.

Teorell, Jan. 1999. "A Deliberative Defence of Intra-Party Democracy." *Party Politics* 5(3): 363–82.

Thaler, Richard H. 1999. "Mental Accounting Matters." In *Choices, Values and Frames,* edited by Daniel Kahneman, and Amos Tversky. Cambridge: Cambridge University Press.

Thaler, Richard H., and Shlomo Benartzi. 2004. "Save More Tomorrow™: Using Behavioral Economics to Increase Employee Saving." *Journal of Political Economy* 112(1, part 2): S164–87.

Tullock, Gordon. 1987. *Autocracy.* Dordrecht: M. Nijhoff.

Tyler, Tom R., Yuen J. Huo, and E. Allan Lind. 1999. "The Two Psychologies of Conflict Resolution: Differing Antecedents of Pre-Experience Choices and Post-Experience Evaluations." *Group Processes and Intergroup Relations* 2(2): 99–118

van Herwaarden, Floor, Arie Kapteyn, and Bernard M. S. van Praag. 1977. "Twelve Thousand Individual Welfare Functions: A Comparison of Six Samples in Belgium and The Netherlands." *European Economic Review* 9(3): 283–300.

van Praag, Bernard M. S. 1993. "The Relativity of the Welfare Concept." In *The Quality of Life,* edited by Martha Nussbaum and Amarthya K. Sen. Oxford: Clarendon.

Walsh, Katherine Cramer. 2004. *Talking About Politics: Informal Groups and Social Identity in American Life.* Chicago: University of Chicago Press.

Weinstein, Neil D. 1981. "Unrealistic Optimism about Future Life Events." *Journal of Personality and Social Psychology* 39(5): 806–20.

White, R. Winthrop. 1959. "Motivation Reconsidered: The Concept of Competence." *Psychological Review* 66(5): 297–333.

Wilson, Timothy D., and Daniel T. Gilbert. 2003. "Affective Forecasting." In *Advances in Experimental Social Psychology,* vol. 35, edited by Mark P. Zanna. New York: Elsevier.

Chapter 6

Hyperopia in Public Finance

LEE ANNE FENNELL

UMAN time preferences are complicated. People often seem to behave myopically, placing a heavy premium on present consumption over future consumption (see, for example, Baron 2000, 470). However, at other times, people appear to do just the opposite, weighting future payoffs more heavily than present ones (Loewenstein 1987; Loewenstein and Prelec 1991). This latter category of behavior has been termed "far-sighted" (Loewenstein 1987) and "hyperopic" (Kivetz and Simonson 2002, 201, 214).[1] Although myopia has received much greater attention in the cognitive literature, behaviors consistent with hyperopia have been identified as well (see, for example, Prelec and Loewenstein 1998, 19). Here I examine the relevance of hyperopic time preferences to public finance.

Hyperopic Choices

Before beginning, it is helpful to define how I will be using the terms hyperopia, hyperopic preferences, and hyperopic choices. Hyperopia itself might be narrowly understood as a perceptual rendering of temporally offset options that sharpens or enhances more distant payoffs relative to nearer ones. Likewise, we might say that someone has hyperopic preferences when she prefers the more distant of two payoffs, other things equal. This will typically be manifested by a willingness to accept a later payoff of lower present value.

However, we can observe neither perceptual renderings nor underlying preferences; we can only observe behavior. Hence it is often more accurate and useful to speak of hyperopic conduct or hyperopic choices, which can be defined as follows: choosing a later payoff that is smaller in present value (monetary) terms than an earlier available payoff. Notice that this definition focuses only on objective, observable conduct and not on the reasons for it. Therefore, a choice that we would classify as hyperopic based on the present value payoffs could well be caused by factors that have little to do with time preferences as such. It will not always be possible to infer from hyperopic choices that hyperopic preferences are responsible for generating the conduct. Consider, for example, the hyperopic choices people often make in situations where sequences of money or lump sums are at stake.

Sequences and Lumps

It has been well documented in a variety of contexts that people prefer improving sequences rather than flat or declining ones (see Frederick, Loewenstein, and O'Donoghue 2003, 28–29 (reviewing literature); Ariely and Carmon 2003, 372 (reviewing literature); Loewenstein and Sicherman 1991; Loewenstein and Prelec 1993). George Loewenstein and Drazen Prelec conclude that "for sequences of outcomes, negative time preference is the rule rather than the exception" (1993, 105). This cuts against the usual assumption of positive time discounting, which would call for moving the most favorable outcomes to as early in the sequence as possible (91).

Adaptation offers an explanation for improving-sequence preferences. People adapt quickly to changes, incorporating them into a new baseline (see Kahneman and Varey 1991). If this is so, then any drop from a previous level of consumption may be experienced as a painful loss. Because losses hurt more than failures to achieve gains (Shafir and Tversky 1995), falling from a previously high level of consumption will be more aversive than deferring gains until later in the sequence (Loewenstein and Prelec 1993, 92). By engineering improving sequences for themselves, individuals not only avoid painful downward shifts from new levels of adaptation, but also provide themselves with a continuing stream of favorable contrasts with past experiences (92–93). In addition, saving the best episodes of consumption until later in the sequence allows people to derive value from anticipation (see Loewenstein 1987).

The fact that one prefers an improving sequence of consumption should not necessarily lead one to prefer an increasing sequence of income, however, given the ability to carry money forward in time (Loewenstein and Sicherman 1991; Neumark 1995; see Frederick, Loewenstein, and O'Donoghue 2003, 31). In some of the sequence studies, the sequences in question involved in-kind consumption goods, such as fancy dinners (Loewenstein and Prelec 1991). Because these items must be consumed at a given moment and cannot be carried forward for later consumption, it is impossible to draw a distinction between the time these items are "credited" to the individual and the time they are experienced or consumed. If improving-sequence preferences were limited to such situations, the implications for public finance would be rather thin.

However, similar sequence preferences were observed in studies involving payments of money, such as wages (Loewenstein and Sicherman 1991). Of course, there might be independent reasons for wanting wages to increase, apart from consumption preferences. For example, perhaps an increasing wage profile acts as a proxy for recognition of increasing skill at one's chosen occupation (69–70). George Loewenstein and Nachum Sicherman compared reactions to sequences of wages and sequences of other payments unrelated to personal merit or skill (rental income from an inherited building) to test this possibility (69–70). They found that although a larger majority rejected present-value maximization in favor of upward-sloping sequences where wages were involved, a majority also preferred such sequences for the non–merit-based payments (75). In addition, people at a given salary level will often choose nonmaximizing payment options such as spreading a nine-month salary over twelve months (Loewenstein and Sicherman, 81; Kahneman and Varey 1991, 147). These salary distribution preferences cannot be explained by the proficiency-recognition hypothesis.

Next, consider preferences for lump sums. Because people attach value to income received in the form of a lump sum, they are willing to forgo some increment of present value to obtain income configured in this manner. At times, this can generate hyperopic choices.[2] An individual might opt for a lower present value lump sum bonus at the end of the year, for example, over an incremental increase in each paycheck (Kahneman and Varey 1991, 147). The past use of Christmas clubs also illustrates that people are sometimes willing to give up an increment of present value in order to obtain a lump sum at a later date (Thaler and Loewenstein 1992, 98).

It is easy to understand why people would want to consume in lumps. Many desirable consumer goods (cars, vacations, down payments on homes) require a significant outlay of cash. In many cases, it is possible to finance these large expenditures and to make small payments over time. However, not all individuals have the ability to borrow, not all expenditures lend themselves to financing, and some consumption experiences (such as vacations) appear to be more valuable when they are entirely prepaid (Prelec and Loewenstein 1998). In these cases, enjoyment of the consumption experience requires spending, all at once, a large sum of cash. A preference for lumpy consumption does not require that the money be received in a lump, however; it could instead be received in dribs and drabs and saved up until it is sufficient to finance the consumption item in question.

Because people could choose the higher present value option and generate for themselves a larger lump sum or engineer for themselves an increasing sequence of higher dollar value, these hyperopic choices require some explanation. Standard economic analysis assumes that individuals can spread their lifetime earnings over the life cycle to accomplish any consumption timing pattern they desire (see, for example, Souleles 1999; Wertenbroch 2003; Ando and Modigliani 1963). On this account, we would not expect preferences for a particular kind of consumption pattern to have any impact on preferences for income patterns. Instead, people would simply seek to maximize the present value total of lifetime earnings. Because moving money backward in time (from the future) is costly in present value terms, and moving money forward in time (to the future) generates income (interest), we would expect people to always want money sooner rather than later, regardless of how and when they planned to spend it.

Reality diverges from the life cycle model significantly. In fact, income and expenditure patterns do affect consumption patterns (Shefrin and Thaler 1991). For example, Nicholas Souleles (1999) found that income tax refunds—a source of income that is "both predictable and transitory"—had a positive impact on consumption. Other work has identified changes in consumption associated with fluctuations in income (see Shefrin and Thaler 1991). The marginal propensity to consume out of income also seems to depend on how the income is framed, with bonuses and windfalls triggering different levels of consumption than ordinary income (see 115–18).

There are at least two explanations for hyperopic choices involving lumps and sequences of money. The first relates to self-control problems, and the second to mental accounting and personal financial rules.

Self-Control and Intrapersonal Tragedies of the Commons

To examine the connections between liquidity, self-control, and precommitment, we might think of the life cycle not as a flat surface across which lifetime earnings can be effortlessly spread like jam on bread, but rather as a series of discrete rooms through which one moves temporally.[3] One has an interest, let us assume, in having each of these temporal rooms furnished in a suitably comfortable fashion and in enjoying certain consumption goods while in each of the rooms. Cash flows into only some of the rooms, and the amount varies from room to room; likewise, cash is demanded in varying amounts in each room. Mechanisms for reaching into future rooms to drag cash backward into the room one presently occupies are imperfect, expensive, and sometimes absent. Even when such mechanisms work reasonably well, some of the money captured from the future is dissipated in the process. Carrying cash forward does not usually involve payments to third parties, but it is cognitively cumbersome for many people. Such people can only carry cash into the future in a leaky bucket (see Okun 1975, 91–92; using leaky bucket metaphor in the context of redistribution). The leaks of relevance here involve unplanned consumption during the periods in which the money is available.

The problem can be posed as an intrapersonal tragedy of the commons (see Ainslie 1992, 161–62), featuring incentives both to underinvest in the commonly held resource and to overuse it (cf. Ostrom, Gardner, and Walker 1994, 14–15). Consider again an indivisible lump of consumption that an individual might rationally view as more valuable than the sum of the many separate consumption opportunities that could be funded by an equivalent amount of cash (see McCaffery 1994b). To obtain the more valuable lump sum consumption opportunity, various short-run consumption opportunities held by different temporal selves must be relinquished. This presents a strategic dilemma for an individual's successive selves (Ainslie 1992, 160–64). Consider an individual, Adam, who wishes to fund a lump sum of consumption from bits of cash that arrive in each paycheck. Adam is made up of temporal selves: Adam at Payday 1, Adam at Payday 2, and so on, some significant number of whom must cooperate in assembling the lump sum. For the lump sum to become available on a future date, intervening selves must not only faithfully set aside some portion of "their" paychecks, but also must refrain from raiding the store of funds already set aside by other selves.

Here, the lumpy consumption experience might be thought of as a "step good" (see Erev and Rapoport 1990) that requires the cooperation, through savings behaviors, of a series of selves. Without the participation of a sufficient number of these selves, the savings will fall short of the goal, and the desired indivisible lump of consumption will become unavailable. Suppose a desirable lump of consumption can be funded by some subset of the temporal Adams over the course of a given year, so that some of the Adams need not contribute at all. Each Adam will be tempted to believe that he should be exempt from the contribution requirement, on the grounds that the other Adams are better-positioned to make the contribution; of course, the other Adams will reason the same way (see Ainslie 1992, 160–61). Each Adam may also fear that his own contribution is likely to be either futile or superfluous, rather than pivotal in achieving the goal (cf. similar dynamic in the context of multiparty decision making about the provision of step-level public goods in Dawes et al. 1986, 1178).

Savings accounts from which withdrawals are not permitted until a specified date, such as Christmas clubs, attempt to overcome this dilemma by offering a period of illiquidity followed by a window of complete liquidity (Thaler and Loewenstein 1992, 98–99; Fetherston-haugh and Ross 1999, 194–95). Successive selves still must place money into such an account rather than spend it immediately, however, or the desired lump of cash will not be available during the window of liquidity. A system of automatic paycheck deductions can help in this regard (Fetherstonhaugh and Ross 1999, 195). Such a system requires effort to opt out of the contribution plan, rather than requiring each self to opt in by making a contribution (cf. Thaler and Benartzi 2004). Once the money is in place, the external control on liquidity keeps it from being raided on an impulse.

Similar challenges confront those who would engineer an upward-sloping consumption profile in situations where real income is not rising over time, or where future large expenditures are anticipated. A series of short-run sacrifices would be necessary to amass the resources to maintain an upward-tending consumption profile in the face of flat or declining real income or shocks to liquidity in the form of large expenditures. The problem contains elements of "scale mismatch" (see Prelec and Bodner 2003, 278; Prelec 1991). Each successive self may fail to see a connection between the small consumption choice in front of her at a given moment and any later impact on the overall shape of her consumption profile. The cost, in consumption profile terms, of deferring a plan of austerity until after one has enjoyed any given short-run consumption opportunity is likely to be minuscule (Prelec and Bodner 2003; Prelec 1991; see also Herrnstein and Prelec 1992). As in other contexts, the mismatch between the immediate pain of undertaking an unpleasant program now and the trivial impact of waiting a little longer makes procrastination attractive (O'Donoghue and Rabin 1999b). Of course, in the aggregate, the enjoyment of short-run consumption opportunities will erase any possibility of an upward-sloping consumption profile unless one's income profile already takes that shape. Unsurprisingly, savings difficulties are a common explanation for the observed robust preference for increasing wage profiles (see Neumark 1995).

In sum, do-it-yourself cash-assembly and sequence-building efforts are costly and often do not work out well. We should not be surprised to see people attaching positive value to pre-assembled lumps or upward-tending sequences. The value added by external cash-assembly services and upward-sequencing plans could make such options preferable to streams of payments with a higher present value, resulting in hyperopic choices.

Mental Accounting and Personal Rules

People do not view all money as fungible, but rather engage in mental accounting that codes money in particular ways based on factors such as when and how it was received (Thaler 1992). People often use these mental designations to construct personal rules for dealing with financial matters (Shefrin and Thaler 1991, 95–103; Thaler 1992, 109; see also, for personal rules generally, Ainslie 1992, 142–73). Mental accounting thus affects the way in which different kinds of receipts will be spent (Shefrin and Thaler 1991; Thaler 1992), and may even affect the enjoyment one can obtain from consumption that is funded in various ways (Prelec and Loewenstein 1998).

The transformation of small increments of income into a large lump of consumption ordinarily requires turning income into savings. People who operate according to the rule of "spend what you make" (Thaler 1992) may never accomplish this transformation due to self-control problems. But even those without self-control problems who are excellent savers can still lack good stopping rules for their savings behaviors. This can impede their ability to engage in desired types of consumption (see Kivetz and Simonson 2002). Once money is coded as savings, personal rules may step in to limit the uses that may be made of it (Thaler 1992, 109). Making exceptions to one's own rules is a tricky business, even when doing so would truly be in one's interest; there is a risk that any loophole will expand to swallow the rule (Ainslie 1992, 164). Hinted-for gifts from someone with whom one shares a bank account provide one way to circumvent personal rules about money (Baron 2000, 480–81; Thaler 1985, 199, 212–13). Likewise, unusual receipts such as windfalls, refunds, and bonuses are likely be coded differently than ordinary income (Souleles 1999; Shefrin and Thaler 1991, 115–18; Thaler 1992, 112–14). They may, therefore, represent useful solutions to the loophole problem by offering a bounded opportunity to depart from ordinary financial habits.

Here, notice that the temporal positioning of these special receipts is important because it marks them as out of the ordinary—distinct from merely routine, recurrent forms of income that must be treated according to the usual financial rules. If an individual must interpose a sufficient temporal buffer between lumpy receipts to mentally code them for special treatment, the results might appear hyperopic. Similar to the self-control rationale, such an explanation suggests that the operative preference is not necessarily for later consumption, but rather for a particular sort of consumption. Given mental accounting constraints, pushing the receipts forward in time is a necessary adjunct to funding that consumption.

A closely related consideration has to do with adaptation to changes in consumption levels—one of the factors that explains sequence preferences. There is significant evidence that people can enjoy special increases in consumption without suffering from an adaptation effect, if they can manage to mentally segregate the special consumption episodes (Kahneman and Varey 1991). This is one explanation for the popularity of bonuses (147). Here, the ability to code particular receipts as unique and nonrecurring prevents people from readjusting their consumption baselines in a way that would result in a painful drop in the next period.

An analogous body of empirical work examines the impact of the degree of mental "coupling" of consumption with payments: in general, consumption appears to be more enjoyable the more it is decoupled from payment (Prelec and Loewenstein 1998). Consumption-enhancing decoupling can be accomplished in a variety of ways, including interposing temporal distance between consuming and paying (whether through prepayment or delayed billing), using tokens to mask the link between marginal consumption and payment, purchasing an all-inclusive plan so that marginal consumption does not come with a price tag, or delegating payment to another individual (see 19–24; Baron 2000, 480–81; Thaler 1985, 199, 212–13). Likewise, shifting income forward in time might have the effect of decoupling it from the sacrifices that made it possible, making the consumption it can fund more enjoyable. A year-end bonus might therefore be preferred over a salary increase if it feels more like a gift of "found money" than like a quid pro quo for work performed.

Introducing a Public Finance Application: Overwithholding

Armed with a definition of hyperopic choices and some idea of the preferences that may underlie such choices, we can now make an initial foray into public finance. At first blush, the notion of hyperopia seems to offer a wealth of transferable insights. Spotting hyperopic choices (defined above simply as choices featuring a later payoff of lower present value) is relatively easy, and there are a wide variety of policy design issues that would be importantly impacted by hyperopia. To work through some of the issues associated with adapting lessons about negative time preferences to public finance settings, I begin by introducing just one example here—the familiar puzzle of income tax overwithholding. This example is somewhat trivial,[4] yet it nicely illustrates both the potential relevance of cognitive literature on hyperopia to public finance and some of the dangers associated with too-facile incorporation of psychological insights into positive and normative accounts. Later, I will discuss a variety of other public finance applications.

About three-fourths of U.S. taxpayers have more income tax than necessary withheld from their paychecks, or make excess estimated payments (Ayres, Kachelmeier, and Robinson 1999). Likewise, low-income people who qualify for the Earned Income Tax Credit rarely take advantage of the opportunity to receive advances on that credit during the year; most opt instead for a single lump-sum payment at the end of the tax year (for example, Hotz and Scholz 2003; less than 1.1 percent of eligible EITC recipients took the advance payment option in 1998). Through these behaviors, substantial segments of society—including some of its most liquidity-constrained members—make interest-free loans to the government (for example, Ayers, Kachelmeier, and Robinson 1999; Carroll 1992, 517). These individuals appear willing to accept a larger overall tax burden (or smaller tax credit) in present value terms for the dubious privilege of receiving money later. Rational taxpayers should remit to the IRS only the minimum interim amounts necessary to avoid a penalty, pay the balance at tax time, and pocket the interest. On its face, the overwithholding choice is hyperopic.

But, as you no doubt have perceived already, overwithholding and similar conduct is overdetermined, with myriad plausible explanations. Because some of these explanations relate in some measure to hyperopic preferences and others do not, overwithholding offers a useful case study for highlighting and sharpening some of the criticisms that we will explore later in the chapter. Indeed, some of the most obvious explanations for overwithholding and related conduct have nothing to do with time preferences. A considerable proportion of observed overwithholding behavior can be explained by a lack of familiarity with the applicable withholding rules, the complexity of the required paperwork, and the stickiness of default selections (Ayres, Kachelmeier, and Robinson 1999 citing Schmedel 1997; see Choi et al., chapter 11, this volume).[5] Overwithholding may also be produced by the fear of underpaying taxes and having to suffer a penalty (or, in the case of the EITC, having to repay amounts erroneously dispensed)—outcomes that may be perceived as particularly onerous given aversion to losses and penalties (see, for example, McCaffery 1994a, 1905–6).

However, recent empirical work found that many well-informed subjects (MBA students screened for their understanding of the operative rules) actually preferred making excess interim tax payments, even when given full control over the amounts that would be withheld or remitted in the form of estimated payments (Ayres, Kachelmeier, and Robinson 1999). Such preferences might seem to suggest a negative discount rate, or hyperopia (for example, Korobkin and Ulen 2000, 1119 n.274). A standard explanation for such preferences relates to the difficulty people often face in saving money rather than spending it. On this account, interim payments to the government represent precommitments designed to overcome anticipated self-control problems. The precommitment in question might be designed merely to overcome the difficulty individuals might have in saving to pay the outstanding tax liability (Ayres, Kachelmeier, and Robinson 1999, 59), or it might be designed to facilitate especially desirable consumption patterns (see Souleles 1999, 948–49 and n.9).

Consider the preference for improving sequences. If a large tax payment is required all at once, and if previous consumption has not been carefully orchestrated to compensate for the expenditure, the outlay will produce a painful downward notch in the consumption profile. Efforts to save the money on one's own may give rise to unplanned consumption that will thwart efforts to build an upward-tending sequence. Likewise, self-control problems may make it difficult for an individual to realize the theoretical possibility of translating small amounts of money into a lump sum. The withholding system provides an easy way to generate a lump sum in the form of a tax refund at the end of the year.

Income tax withholding incorporates two features that can help to co-ordinate temporal selves. First, the automatic payroll deduction system harnesses inertia by making the default option that of contributing in each period (see, for example, Thaler and Benartzi 2004, S185; cf. Korobkin 1998; and Choi et al., chapter 11, this volume). Second, the system augments that inertia with a bureaucratic delay that limits momentary temptations to change the default selection. A requested change in withholding arrangements may not be reflected in one's paycheck for nearly two months.[6] Even very modest delays before the availability of an earlier payoff can lead to more patient choices (Solnick et al. 1980).

One need not believe that people have difficulty coordinating their temporal selves in order to arrive at a plausible explanation for over-withholding, however. An alternative set of explanations relates to the anesthetic and consumption-enhancing properties of the withholding system. It appears that "withholding is important in cutting the pain of paying [taxes]" (Carroll 1992, 517). Framing effects and loss aversion provide an explanation. People dislike costs framed as losses more than they dislike forgoing gains of an equal amount. Whether a cost is perceived as a loss or a gain depends on the implicit baselines in use, and on whether the specific cost is bundled with other losses or gains (Tversky and Kahneman 1981). In the case of income tax withholding, individual withholding amounts are bundled with much larger gains (paychecks) and may not be perceived as losses. Having to write a large check to the government in April, by contrast, is very likely to be coded as a loss (see Carroll 1992).

Another pain relief argument relates to the dread associated with tax-paying (Ayres, Kachelmeier, and Robinson 1999, 58–59). Consistent with preferences for improving sequences, studies have shown that people of-ten prefer to get dreaded events out of the way earlier rather than later (Loewenstein 1987). Taxpaying seems to be a painful experience for most Americans, and getting it over with early through withholding might help to diminish the pain (Ayres, Kachelmeier, and Robinson 1999, 58–59). Pain relief can also explain overwithholding that generates re-funds, if we consider the paperwork burden of filling out tax returns as a painful event in its own right. About two-thirds of those interviewed in a recent Gallup Poll survey indicated that they either "dislike" or "hate" doing their income taxes (see Newport 2001, 44). Significant refunds effectively bundle the costs of completing tax paperwork with a larger reward (the refund), and hence could significantly reduce the pain associated with the task.[7] People probably do not have this notion consciously in mind when they overwithhold, but the positive reinforcement associated with having a large, attractive reward paired with an unavoidable and distasteful task could play a role in perpetuating overwithholding behaviors.

Another intriguing possibility is that people are using the withholding system to enhance their other consumption experiences. Overwithholding accomplishes a temporal and contextual "decoupling" of the enjoyment of consumption financed by the refund from the pain of the series of payments which made it possible (see Prelec and Loewenstein 1998). The mild element of surprise involved in later receiving a refund arguably contributes to the decoupling. Decoupling usually comes at a high price: payments that are not attached to any benefits tend to be perceived as especially painful (23 and n.14). But in the overwithholding context, the fact that payments are bundled with paychecks may help to buffer the pain. Payroll withholding also distracts people from the fact that they are deferring gratification by keeping the money entirely out of reach (Weiss 1991, 1313) while allowing them to enjoy the anticipation of future consumption.

An annually delivered refund check may also offer a nicely bounded exception to personal rules about the use of money. Withholding effectively transforms part of one's ordinary income into something that mental accounting renders markedly distinct from ordinary savings (see Thaler 1992). A refund might be used to fund different kinds of consumption than those associated with ordinary income or savings, or to heighten the enjoyment associated with such consumption. This might help to explain the uptick in durables purchases following tax refunds among households that are not liquidity constrained (Souleles 1999).[8] Significantly, refund checks may be sufficiently distinguishable from ordinary income to avoid adaptation effects. A tax refund provides one way of effectively delivering to oneself a bonus—a lump of money distinct from one's regular salary that does not alter one's overall expectations about consumption.

Finally, if people experience "tax aversion"—additional disutility associated with the fact that the payment one is making is a tax[9]—a converse phenomenon might accompany getting money back from the government. One might feel freer to spend "the government's" money than one's own and an additional element of enjoyment might therefore accompany the expenditures. Although everyone recognizes that the money is really one's own and that one could have held on to it all along, the withholding-and-refund process likely works some important trans-formations from the standpoint of mental accounting.

All these explanations provide minimally plausible accounts of a type of behavior that involves receiving what is in economic terms a smaller reward at a later time. Some of the explanations, however, seem more tenuously linked to time preferences than others. Even to the extent it seems plausible to say that time preferences drive these behaviors, there are different factors driving those time preferences. This example high-lights the need to take a step back and consider in more general terms the appropriate role of the study of time preferences in legal theory and in public finance scholarship.

Thinking About Time Preferences

The notion of hyperopia offers a window onto two sets of difficulties that confront scholars interested in incorporating time preferences into pub-lic finance work. The first concerns the accuracy of the positive account generated by a focus on time preferences. When we turn to real-world phenomena rather than controlled experiments, alternative explanations typically exist for observed choices between earlier and later payoffs, and competing time preferences may also be in play. Simply labeling such conduct hyperopic or myopic may be at best meaningless, and at worst misleading. It may also be unhelpful for making predictions in other contexts, given that people's time preferences seem to vary, both interpersonally and intrapersonally, in intensely context-sensitive ways.

The second difficulty stems from heterogeneity in the root causes of time preferences, which often generates mixed policy signals. Looking behind temporal choices to underlying preferences often means con-fronting a tangle of divergent behavioral determinants. Because these un-derlying determinants may point in different normative directions, knowing a lot about time-related behavior may still tell us little about pol-icy. For example, it may be impossible to tell whether a particular hyper-opic choice represents a mistake that should be corrected by the govern-ment through policy, or merely a preference that should be vindicated.

When Is Choice Over Time About Time?

As the discussion of overwithholding illustrates, it is not always possible to infer from a choice between temporally offset options that a time pref-erence is truly responsible for generating the result. When a lump sum is chosen over a larger payoff that must be accumulated over time, it may be chosen in spite of, without regard for, or (in whole or in part) because of its temporal position. Upward-tending consumption experiences, un-like lump-sum consumption experiences, always depend on the relative temporal positioning of different episodes. But this observation does not clarify the role of time in preferences for cashflow sequences. These difficulties with developing meaningful positive accounts for time-situated behavior raise questions about the usefulness of efforts to pin down a model of intertemporal behavior.

As George Loewenstein (1992) explains, the discounted utility (DU) model that Paul Samuelson developed in 1937 is elegant and highly tractable, but at odds with a great deal of readily observable human behavior. For example, a person who prefers a larger reward in two years over a smaller reward in one year will often change her mind after the first year has elapsed, when she is faced with a choice between an immediately available smaller reward, and a larger reward one year hence (see, for example, Camerer 1990, 793 n. 7). The hyperbolic discount function shows how preference reversals of the sort just described could occur as a set of rewards grows closer in time. As a result, it has attracted significant attention and enthusiasm.[10] However, it has some shortcomings. For example, it cannot explain why some kinds of goods produce preference reversals and others do not (Loewenstein 1988; Read 2001). Moreover, it does not explain why people sometimes exhibit negative time preferences. It is possible to posit that hyperopic choices represent precommitments made by sophisticated agents aware of their own hyperbolic discount functions, but this is only one of several positive accounts that would fit observed behavior.

The hyperbolic discount function remains prominent, but scholars continue to tweak and critique it (Loewenstein 2003). Alternative explanations continue to be explored for the time-inconsistent behavior that prompted the search for, and seemed to be so cleanly explained by, the hyperbolic discount function. For example, Daniel Read has recently suggested that subadditive time preferences may account for time-inconsistent behavior that we have been interpreting as stemming from hyperbolic discounting (2001). Likewise, Ariel Rubinstein has suggested focusing on whether options situated in time are viewed as similar or dissimilar (2003). Moreover, interpersonal and intrapersonal variations, as well as contextual factors, caution against generalizations about time preferences (see, for example, Loewenstein 1987, 680).

How, then, are we to think about time preferences? By developing increasingly nuanced models that account for more and more sorts of interpersonal and intrapersonal heterogeneity in time preferences, have we sacrificed generality and tractability? As John Harsanyi observed in a related context, "If we make our motivational assumptions complicated enough then we can always explain every conceivable form of social behavior in terms of these assumptions, which means that we are actually explaining nothing" (1968, 316). Loewenstein and Sicherman (1991) offer the following perspective on time preferences:

> Given the wide range of discounting behavior observed in even a single
> individual's behavior . . . perhaps the question of whether people dis-
> count the future positively or negatively is moot. As a research agenda, it
> may be more fruitful to address the more nuanced question of why in-
> tertemporal choice behavior is so variable and to attempt to uncover the
> situational determinants of time preference. (81–82)

Making our inquiries more context-specific offers promise, but it also
calls into question the usefulness of temporal distortions as an explanatory category. If we assemble a large enough catalogue of possible distortions, it becomes both easy and meaningless to formulate a post hoc reason for any behaviors that we actually observe. Hence, relying on time
preferences as an all-purpose explanation risks substituting apparatus
for substance and reverse-engineered conclusions for real explanations.
Focusing on time preferences might even be positively harmful if it distracts us from more important features of the choice situation that are actually responsible for behavior.

Yet even though time preferences may work poorly as final explanations, they can still provide helpful clues for working through the causes
of puzzling behaviors. Indeed, there may be cognitive reasons why recognizing a category of time preferences is useful, even if it serves mostly
as a placeholder that reminds us to dig deeper for explanations. It is impossible for human beings to notice everything, and categories like inco-
herent time preferences offer simple and salient entries on a public policy checklist.

Attitudes toward risk offer a useful analog. Although the basic presumption of risk aversion remains robust in many settings, behavioral
work continues to demonstrate instances in which individuals will act in
risk-preferring ways. Manipulation of contextual factors, such as perceived baselines, can cause individuals to flip from risk-averse to risk-
preferring, and vice versa (Tversky and Kahneman 1981). All of these
complications make risk attitudes difficult to pin down. However, they
do not in any way detract from the utility of recognizing a conceptual
category "attitudes toward risk" that stands as a placeholder for all of
the ways in which risk preferences may influence behavior. Likewise, the
fact that time preferences are enormously complicated and driven by a
host of contextual factors does not alter the utility of using the notion as
a shorthand term.

When Should We Worry About Intertemporal Choice?

The question of whether time-related behavior is "mistaken" has sur-
faced repeatedly in the literature. The use of terms like myopia and hyperopia in the time-preference context suggests that choosers suffer from

distortions in perceiving the relative size or attractiveness of rewards that are situated at different temporal distances. There are some difficulties with this analogy. George Ainslie points out that people can readily compensate for known distortions in the perception of other inputs, such as light and distance; why cannot they do the same for time? (1992, 82). Another problem inheres in defining the baseline of perfect vision. On one view, discounting future consumption at all is irrational, except to the extent that the risk of death or other uncertainties make the more distant option less likely to be enjoyed (Pigou 1920, 24–29). The interest rate offers a possible benchmark for rational discounting, though the nature of the relationship between interest rates and time preferences is not necessarily straightforward (see Baron 2000, 470–75; Kelman 1983). Some would maintain that any method of discounting the future can be rationally adopted, as long as it does not produce internal inconsistencies. For example, Derek Parfit has suggested that a discount rate can rationally take into account lesser degrees of "connectedness" to one's future selves (1984, 314–15).

Perhaps easiest to categorize as mistakes are decisions that are internally inconsistent with an individual's earlier and later preferences, or decisions that even the actor regards as mistaken. When discounting generates time-inconsistent choices (as when it follows a hyperbolic pattern) it might be deemed to violate some principle of well-ordered preferences (see Baron 2000, 473). In addition, if the individual making the choice views it as a mistake after being confronted with information on the anomaly or inconsistency in question (see Loewenstein and Sicherman 1991), this is a clue that the choice is not functional in achieving the individual's longer-range interests. But this analysis raises the question of which temporal versions of the individual we should view as having the final word about what is and is not a mistake (see Strotz 1955, 179). The earlier self might take the position that a choice inconsistent with its plans represents a mistake, but a later self might argue that the earlier self was wrong to make such plans in the first place.

Two observations seem apt. The first is that we cannot label a choice as a mistake without looking at the reasons behind it and considering its context. Choices that look mistaken in isolation may in fact be functional in counterbalancing other unfortunate behavioral tendencies. The second is that identifying behavior as mistaken does not resolve debate about the appropriate policy intervention (see Sunstein and Thaler 2003; Camerer et al. 2003). Some corrections may be unduly costly or intrusive, or, when causes of behaviors are heterogeneous, may disadvantage those for whom the behavior is not a mistake.

Consider again the case of overwithholding. If people are effectively making mistakes in the government's favor (as they arguably are when they offer the government interest-free loans) how should government respond? Here we might usefully distinguish between departures from a maximizing model that have the effect of correcting for other biases that are not in the individual's interest, and those that represent harmful errors without any compensating benefits. In this first category, we might readily include conscious precommitment activities which represent sophisticated responses by an individual to her own known cognitive shortcomings (see, for example, the distinction between sophisticated and naïve actors in O'Donoghue and Rabin 1999a).

But what of the anesthetic effect of overwithholding? It seems clear that certain kinds of government-initiated, government-administered "painkillers" (hiding taxes or tricking taxpayers) would be problematic and could interfere with the responsiveness of the democratic process (McCaffery and Baron 2003, 22; see also Lane 2000, 230). We might therefore view with skepticism any tendency for the tax system to "gravitate towards taxes that impose the minimal psychic pain" (McCaffery and Baron 2003). However, there is certainly no obligation on the part of government to make taxpaying maximally painful. Moreover, if taxpaying is already coded as particularly aversive, then easing the pain a bit might merely counteract an existing distortion. Notably, compliance levels are much higher when no positive amounts are due at tax time (see sources collected in Ayres, Kachelmeier, and Robinson 1999, 56). Because all taxpayers benefit when administrative and enforcement costs are minimized, we might imagine that taxpayers would consent to a system of limited, mutually administered painkillers to reduce the costs of providing tax-funded services.[11]

Consider next the possibility that overwithholding generates more carefree consumption at refund time. Prelec and Loewenstein discuss the tension between "outcome or decision efficiency" that requires paying attention to the costs of consumption and the "hedonic efficiency" of decoupling (1998, 25–26). This echoes in some regards the tension between anesthetized taxpaying and political optimality (see, for example, McCaffery and Baron 2003). People aware of their own longer-term interests might still decouple to some extent because it makes consumption more enjoyable (or payments less painful) but they will not do so to such a degree that they lose the ability to monitor what consumption patterns are in their best interests. It may also be useful to think of the withholding system as a decoupler that competes with other popular forms of decoupling, such as credit card usage (see Prelec and Loewenstein 1998). If people are choosing this method of enhancing consumption over some much less desirable method, then any mistake involved might still be regarded as corrective or preventative.

Another normative concern relates to the willingness of some people expecting refunds to pay high interest rates in order to receive those lump sums a few days or weeks early (Barr 2004, 166–77). In 1999, 39 percent of EITC recipients and 4 percent of non-EITC recipients purchased refund anticipation loans (Berube et al. 2002, 11). We might be tempted to assume that these individuals are hyperbolic discounters—patient as long as the lump sum is far away, but extremely myopic as soon as it comes within reach. But the discussion above should make us cautious in drawing such inferences. An individual's preferences might, in fact, be stably fixed on a particularly desirable consumption configuration that requires lump sum funding. A person who desires lumpy consumption as soon as possible, but cannot manage to assemble a lump sum for herself, might quite consistently first make choices that look hyperopic (to assemble the lump sum), and then switch to choices that look myopic (to obtain the now-assembled lump sum). We cannot be certain that either choice is a mistake.

Of particular interest here are mechanisms that would allow people to make advance judgments about the desirability of refund anticipation loans. For example, the IRS might add a "refund guard" option to the W-4 that would allow people to code their tax refunds or credits in advance so that they cannot later be used as collateral for a loan. Tax preparation services offering refund anticipation loans could then be required to check the taxpayer's Social Security number against an IRS database of guarded credits and refunds before making a loan, on pain of losing recourse against the taxpayer for the loan. If presented with this precommitment option when the lump sum is not in immediate view, people might choose to take advantage of it.

Finally, it is sometimes suggested that the government ought to correct taxpayer overwithholding by paying interest on overwithheld amounts (Carroll 1992). The IRS routinely corrects other sorts of mistakes that taxpayers make in the government's favor, and it is not immediately obvious why this mistake should be treated any differently. The fact that overwithholding helps the government minimize collection and enforcement costs seems to strengthen this case (Carroll 1992). But paying interest on overwithholding is not costless; it necessarily means taking money from someone else. Given that most people overwithhold without any inducement, we might question whether interest payments would generate a sufficient marginal improvement in compliance to justify the costs involved. Nor is it clear that the government's failure to shift money from other taxpayers to provide interest payments to overwithholders is unfair as a distributive matter. By analogy, people who choose to put money in non–interest-bearing bank accounts are not generally believed to have claims against other citizens for the interest that their money would have earned if it were better invested.

Other Public Finance Applications

I have hinted at some of the positive and normative difficulties that attend efforts to translate lessons about time preferences into policy. With these cautions in mind, an examination of hyperopic choices yields some interesting and fresh perspectives on public finance policy.

Engineering Patience

As discussed, preferences for improving sequences can drive hyperopic choices (Loewenstein and Prelec 1991, 351). Policies that encourage people to view a series of events as part of a sequence could, therefore, lead people to accept smaller payoffs in exchange for an upward sloping payoff profile. For example, distaste for downward-sloping profiles arguably helps to explain the endurance of Social Security, despite redistributive features that make it an actuarially poor bargain for many people.

The desire to turn one's life into an upward-tending narrative may also elucidate some aspects of health care policy. For example, Medicare provides health coverage for nearly all people over sixty-five in the United States, helping to safeguard in some ways the quality of the final life stages. However, Medicare does not cover most long-term care (Kaplan 2001, 66). When people learn they must exhaust nearly all of their personal resources on long-term care before they can qualify for government assistance under the means-tested health insurance program, Medicaid, they are often astonished that a lifetime of work and taxpaying could end in such a way (see 67–73). Of course, someone must pay for the long-term care, and arguably the person needing the care is in the best position to do so if she has remaining assets. But perhaps the psychic pain associated with an extremely negative and costly final episode has not been fully appreciated by policy makers. To put it in a more positive light, the fact that people are willing to pay extra to fund upward-tending sequences (or to avoid downward-tending sequences) arguably offers some unexploited policy space for improving outcomes.

Likewise, we know that lump sums can be attractive enough to induce hyperopic choices. Substituting lump sums for streams of payments could, therefore, offer a powerful and inexpensive way of leveraging patience and inducing desirable behavioral shifts. For example, Fetherstonhaugh and Ross (1999) conducted a survey that asked respondents whether a lump sum or a stream of higher retirement payments would be more likely to induce them to retire at age sixty-eight rather than age sixty-five (203).[12] Although the lump sum had a lower present value, it was overwhelmingly chosen—by some 76 percent of respondents (203). To be sure, the researchers posed the lump sum as an alternative to increases in a later stream of payments that would continue throughout retirement; hence the lump sum was presented as the earlier of the two alternatives open to subjects. However, the respondents were asked to assess their willingness to give up an earlier stream of payments (retirement payments from age sixty-five to sixty-eight) in order to obtain that lump sum. The research design asked only whether the later stream of increased payments or the lump sum would be more likely to induce later retirement, without asking whether subjects would actually be willing to exchange the stream of payments available through the earlier retirement date for either of the options presented. The latter question, which would more directly address whether parties were likely to make hyperopic choices, would be well worth asking in a follow-up study.

The observation that lump sums can motivate patient as well as impatient choices also helps to dispel the assumption, commonplace in the literature, that the choice of an earlier lump sum over a later stream of payments necessarily reflects a myopic time preference. It may instead be the case, as suggested above, that lump sums add value that will induce deviations from present-value maximization, regardless of the relative temporal orientation of the stream and lump options. The study of hyperopic choices thus helps to underscore a broader point: If behavioral economics can identify particularly valuable configurations of present-value-equivalent monetary payments (by isolating, through experimental work, attractive features such as lumpiness, timing, frequency, source, frame, and mental coding), these configurations could represent nearly costless incentive mechanisms for moving behavior in socially desirable directions. People might be cheaply induced to retire later, save more, pay taxes more promptly, and so on. In sum, policy makers should focus on exploiting the full policy potential of particular payment configurations, rather than mistakenly chalk up behavior involving those configurations to myopic tendencies on the part of citizens.

Buying a Dream: Lottery Play and Tax Cuts

The preceding discussion has focused on rather rosy possibilities for inducing patient choices through policy design. Of course, the fact that a policy induces patience does not, on its own, tell us anything definitive about the policy's normative valence. For example, it would be problematic for people to couch distributive events in their lives as early parts of an upward-sloping narrative if the latter part of the imagined story is not realistic. In short, patience is not always a virtue.

Suppose a segment of the population chooses to accept higher distributive burdens on the basis of illusory beliefs that they will be compensated later in the sequence. People will often accept arrangements or outcomes that are not in their immediate interest if they believe that their future selves have received adequate compensation. This willingness of people to accept future rewards as substitutes for present rewards offers great policy flexibility. But it also raises difficult normative questions if people systematically misgauge probabilities or overweight future pay-offs. The degree of objective risk or uncertainty associated with a given set of future payoffs seems relevant to this normative question. We might be unambiguously content to have people accept valid promissory notes that shift receipts into the future, but more uneasy when people accept lottery tickets with negative expected value.

Concerns about people taking bad gambles are not new, but an under-standing of hyperopia adds a fresh dimension to the story. Part of what might make people accept unfavorable bets is not just overoptimism about the likelihood of future payoffs (that is, a misgauging of the prob-ability term in the expected value calculation), but also an overweighting of certain kinds of future consumption—that which is part of an up-ward-tending sequence, or that which comes in a large, indivisible lump. Two public finance contexts involving significant uncertainty about fu-ture payoffs help to flesh out these worries: state-run lotteries and tax changes that reduce the degree of overall progressivity in the tax system.

Lotteries

The lottery is both a familiar public finance instrument and an object of academic curiosity. Here we see governments raising money by offering citizens deals that are, in expected value terms, losing propositions. Whether we should be troubled by this as a normative matter depends in part on what we believe is happening as a positive matter. One way of thinking about the problem is to recognize that people are effectively purchasing a two-part product when they buy a lottery ticket (see McCaffery 1994b, 90). Because the expected value of the ticket is too low to induce the purchase on its own, it must be bundled together with a second component that makes the purchase worthwhile. The difficulty is defining the content of that second component.

On one view, the extra component is merely a recreational consump-tion good that we might term lottery fun (see, for example, Cohen 2001, 707; but see, contesting this view, McCaffery 1994b, 89–93). But perhaps the second component is instead a cognitive factor that magnifies the first, expected value component in some fashion. There are two or three ways it could do so. First, people could be subject to a cognitive bias that artificially inflates the probability term in the expected value calculation. This could be due to overoptimism or magical thinking or some other cognitive factor that makes people believe that their odds of winning ex-ceed the statistical odds (see McCaffery 1994b, 86–88; Cohen 2001, 733). Second, people might be subject to a cognitive bias that artificially in-flates the payoff term of the expected value calculation. For example, the payoff might be cognitively inflated because it would represent the large, indivisible good of great wealth (McCaffery 1994b).

A third explanation would posit that people accurately gauge both the probability term and the payoff term, but that they add a factor that relates to a preference for risk. It is worth considering carefully, however, whether this is really an additional explanation or just another way of getting to the second explanation. A lottery player's goal might be to achieve a particular absolute level of wealth, perhaps understood in functional terms (for example, enough money to never have to work again) (McCaffery 1994b, 102–5). If we assume a person starts with a fixed amount of money to invest, we can reverse engineer the amount of risk she would have to take on in order to have any possibility of attaining that absolute wealth level. The fact that she takes the risk may not, then, manifest an inherent "love of the gamble" but rather a desire for something that, given her budget constraints, can only be achieved through a gamble. Another setting in which we see positive risk preferences involves recovery from an earlier loss position—the "trying to break even" phenomenon (Thaler and Johnson 1990). Here again, the continuing series of gambles represents a means for achieving the goal of "not losing money tonight" that is unachievable through less risky endeavors. The exhibited risk-taking behavior may therefore say less about a desire for risk than about the strength of the desire for an underlying goal achievable only through risk-taking.

Our ability to observe only behavior and not its underlying determinants makes us unable to know the mix of factors that drive real-world lottery play—or to say whether such play should be regarded as a mistake—without further empirical study. Perhaps a better way of approaching the lottery question is to consider what features of lotteries might be transplanted into other public finance contexts to achieve desirable ends. For example, James Alm, Betty Jackson, and Michael McKee found that adding a lottery feature to the audit environment in their tax compliance study increased tax compliance more than did a fixed reward for compliance (1992, 323–24). Subjects in the study whose tax payments were checked and who were found to be compliant were entered in a lottery with a one in twenty-five chance of winning a prize that was the rough equivalent of an entire session's earnings (319). This result offers one tentative illustration of how the extra value associated with particular payment configurations might yield policy advances that would leave no one worse off.

Progressivity-Reducing Tax Cuts

There have been many recent changes to the tax system that, if made permanent, will involve moving the system in the direction of reduced progressivity (see, for example, Gale and Orszag 2004). One high-profile change of this sort was the temporary phase-out of the estate tax—subject to a sunset provision that will bring back the tax in 2011 in the absence of further congressional action. Because a lighter tax burden for the wealthy means either a heavier tax burden for the less well-off or a society that provides fewer services, it is difficult to understand why rational individuals occupying the great bulk of the income scale would not oppose tax benefits for the rich, and especially for the very rich (see, for example, Fennell 2003, 593–95). Although a variety of explanations have been offered, to my knowledge none has yet considered the possibility that temporal elements might play a role. Including time preferences in the analysis might lead to new insights.

Two caveats are in order. First, I readily acknowledge that some proportion of the apparent lack of opposition to the favorable tax treatment of the wealthy could be illusory—the product of the dominance of wealthy interests and of opinion survey manipulations (see, for example, Alstott 1996, 396–97; Lewis 1982). Second, I acknowledge that people's political behavior in the public finance realm may not be driven by financial self-interest. Perhaps broad-based support for less progressive tax policies stems from deeply held beliefs that it is just unfair for wealthy people to have to pay high taxes, or from particular understandings about the meaning of property and of pre-tax earnings (see Murphy and Nagel 2002, 175). However, some of the standard explanations for acquiescence in tax breaks for the well-off have focused on the possibility that the less well-off mistakenly believe that these tax changes will benefit them financially. To the extent such explanations are in play, it makes sense to consider all of the cognitive factors that might contribute to such a misperception, rather than focusing on a subset of them.

Consider one simple explanation for widespread support of progressivity-reducing tax policies—that people simply do not appreciate the fact that such policies could harm their interests. The failure to connect decreased tax burdens for the well-off with increased burdens (or decreased services) for the less well-off might be understood in terms of the federal tax system's extraordinary temporal and conceptual decoupling of payments from benefits (see, for example, Rosenberg 1996, 179–83). We might imagine that this decoupling helps to make tax payments feel more painful and less justifiable, because the payment is not cognitively linked to any benefit (Prelec and Loewenstein 1998, 23 and n. 14). It is also possible that this same decoupling makes other people's tax payments look less necessary or justifiable as well. Decoupling may even have the surprising effect of conceptually turning the IRS into a common enemy of both the well-off and the less well-off, and suppressing the fact that the well-off and less well-off are actually engaged in a distributive game that simply happens to be administered through the tax system.

Another common explanation is that the less well-off are overly optimistic about their prospects for future wealth. On this account, a less well-off individual making an expected value calculation associated with a proposed tax change correctly evaluates the size of the payoff that she would receive were she later to become wealthy, but greatly overestimates the probability of becoming wealthy enough to benefit from that change. But, as in the lottery case, it is also possible that a distortion enters into the expected value calculation when the individual considers the magnitude of the payoff. Wealth for a poor person is necessarily in the future. If time preferences cause future receipts to be overvalued relative to present-day receipts, perhaps the payoff in question is magnified by virtue of its temporal positioning. The earlier discussion suggests some reasons why that might be so, including a strong preference for an upward-sloping income profile.

Although direct analogies between the tax attitudes of the lower and middle classes and their lottery play seem farfetched, similar cognitive features may be present in both cases. Just as a lottery player may enjoy a higher-stakes game more than a lower-stakes one because of the higher-quality fantasizing that it allows (notwithstanding the correspondingly lower probability of winning), the less well-off may enjoy participating in a system in which rich people are left free to enjoy their riches largely untroubled by tax burdens. To put it another way, heavy tax burdens on wealth might tarnish the dreams that many people hold for future riches, and turn the top prizes that society offers into something decidedly less fabulous. People might prefer to pay somewhat heavier taxes now to keep open a shot at what may be perceived as an indivisible package—big wealth without big taxes. If this is so, we might say that less well-off people who uncomplainingly accept (or affirmatively support) tax breaks for the wealthy are in some sense "buying a dream."

More study is necessary to disaggregate the various possible explanations for current tax attitudes—and, indeed, to pin down the content of those attitudes. At the same time, looking at the factors that drive hyperopic choices in other contexts could lead to fresh insights about the popular perception of tax reform. These insights should take their place in the developing literature about the impact of cognitive factors on tax perceptions (see, for example, McCaffery and Baron 2003).

Tax Timing Preferences

It is helpful at this point to distinguish policy preferences driven by unrealistic expectations about future wealth from those that simply grow out of preferences about the allocation of tax payments over the life cycle. For analytic purposes, consider a worker who can predict with perfect accuracy the rate at which her earnings profile will grow over her working life. That worker, who by hypothesis harbors no illusions about her future wealth, might still have time preferences that relate to the allocation of her lifetime tax burden between her younger and poorer selves and her older and wealthier selves. A progressive income tax operates to flatten somewhat the upward-tending slope of increases in earnings. Given preferences for improving sequences, it is possible that some individuals would wish to preserve or enhance the slope associated with earnings increases by moving heavier tax burdens into earlier portions of the life cycle. One way to do this is through less progressive tax policies.

If the desire to preserve the upward slope in an expected wage profile is driving support for progressivity-reducing tax policies, it would be possible to formulate policies that would respond to that desire in a more tailored fashion. For example, taxes might be customized based on age or number of years as a taxpaying wage-earner. If coupled with additional liquidity-enhancing measures to allow people to make appropriate investments in education and family in the earlier parts of the life cycle, such customization need not have distributive effects that are as severe as those that accompany blanket tax cuts for the very-well-off.

As a first step, we should further explore preferences for lifetime tax patterns—for example, whether people might prefer to pay a lower (or flat) percentage in taxes as their lives progress and as their fortunes presumably rise. An examination of investments in the Roth IRA, which permits prepayment of taxes on retirement savings, might shed light on these preferences. I do not mean to suggest that Roth investors are necessarily acting hyperopically. For a person who rationally expects her future marginal tax rate to be higher than her present rate, investing in a Roth constitutes a maximizing choice (see, for example, Poterba 2004, 7). Nevertheless, the Roth versus traditional IRA choice may generate useful data that can shed light on tax timing preferences. For example, we would expect someone who anticipates no change in tax rates to be indifferent about whether to invest in a Roth or a regular IRA. Preferences about tax timing could break the tie.

Tax code provisions that allow penalty-free withdrawals from IRA accounts for certain kinds of pre-retirement expenditures, such as first home purchases and certain higher education expenses, add an interesting wrinkle (see discussion of I.R.C. § 72(t)(2) in Kaplan 1999). The fact that taxes must be paid immediately when money is withdrawn from a regular IRA could discourage pre-retirement withdrawals even when no penalty applies—especially in the case where the pre-retirement marginal tax rate is higher than the expected marginal tax rate at retirement (see 296–97). Penalty-free withdrawals from Roth IRAs, in contrast, require no accompanying payment to the government, because the taxes were paid at the outset. Richard Kaplan has argued that, as a result, "the temptations and pressures jeopardizing the retiree's long-term retirement security in that situation are even greater than for a regular IRA" (295). If withdrawals from the two kinds of accounts are indeed viewed differently based on whether tax has already been paid or is still due, we might see choices between these two kinds of accounts turning not only on tax timing preferences, but also on grounds relating to factors like precommitment and self-control.

Conclusion

I have considered here the relevance of negative time preferences or "hyperopia" for public finance. The cognitive literature on such preferences has been relatively neglected in public finance discussions. Incorporating it can enrich our understanding of financial behavior over time. However, it must be adapted with care. Examination of hyperopia opens up important questions about the extent to which time preferences can offer a useful theoretical construct or basis for policy. Time preferences should, I conclude, be included on a public policy checklist, along with other complex preferences. Rather than providing final explanations of behavior, apparent temporal anomalies hold diagnostic potential. Only by examining the heterogeneous determinants of temporal choices can we make meaningful headway in enriching positive accounts or informing normative policy judgments.

I thank Steven Bank, Victor Fleischer, William Gale, Tom Ginsburg, Richard Kaplan, Leandra Lederman, Edward McCaffery, Michael Moore, Stephen Ross, Joel Slemrod, Kirk Stark, Lawrence Zelenak, reviewers at Russell Sage, and participants in the Behavioral Public Finance conference held at the University of Michigan in April 2004, the 2004 University of Illinois College of Law Faculty Retreat, and the spring 2005 Tax Policy and Public Finance Colloquium at UCLA School of Law for very useful comments on earlier drafts.

Notes

1. Paul Caron (1996) paired the optical terms "myopia" and "hyperopia" in a tax context when critiquing another scholar's work, although his focus was the appropriate frame of scholarly inquiry rather than systemic distortions in human decision making.
2. In other instances, it can lead to apparently myopic choices—as where one chooses an immediately available lump sum over a stream of future payments representing a higher present value total. The possibility that the lumpiness of a payment rather than its timing may determine behavior suggests one difficulty with attributing choices situated in time to time preferences.

3. The idea suggested by this metaphor—that time "passes" or that we "pass through time"—is not uncontroversial (see Parfit 1984, 178–79).

4. To be sure, the aggregate amount refunded in a given tax year is quite substantial—about $206 billion in tax year 2002 (IRS 2002). However, the overwithholding phenomenon looks insignificant when considered at the individual level. If the average individual refund of just over $2000 in 2002 equates to an approximate average overpayment throughout the year of $1000, applying current savings account interest rates of 2 percent yields just $20 in forgone interest. I thank Larry Zelenak for emphasizing this point and providing this numeric example, and Richard Kaplan for adding that the interest would also have to be taxed, making the amount forgone even lower. Interest rates have not always been this low, of course, and an interesting further investigation would be to see whether real interest rates are negatively correlated with overwithholding behavior.

5. The IRS (2004b) now offers an "online withholding calculator" that is supposed to make calculating withholding easier and more accurate. Although the online calculator requires the user to input significant amounts of information, it likely provides a more appealing interface than the W-4 worksheet.

6. To change withholding arrangements, one must file a replacement W-4 form with one's employer. According to the IRS (2004a, 6), "[i]f the change is for the current year, your employer must put your new Form W-4 into effect no later than the start of the first payroll period ending on or after the 30th day after the day on which you give your employer your revised Form W-4." For example, if an employee who is paid on the last day of each month filed a new W-4 on June 2, her employer would be required to withhold based on the replacement W-4 starting with the July pay period. The employee would receive her first paycheck reflecting the new withholding arrangement on July 31.

7. The refund can also reduce the paperwork burden by providing a ready funding source for professional tax preparation services. I thank Leandra Lederman for this point.

8. Some insight into what people who presently overwithhold might otherwise be doing with the extra take-home pay can be gleaned from Shapiro and Slemrod's (1995) study of consumers' plans for the extra paycheck money they received following changes in the withholding rules. Their findings suggested "that a substantial fraction of consumers simply spend their current paychecks," perhaps based on some personal "rule of thumb" (281–82). The fact that few taxpayers reported responding to the change in default withholding rules by making compensating adjustments to hold the amounts withheld constant also suggests a significant role for inertia (see 276: thirty-six of 381 households "claimed to have adjusted their withholding to offset the mandated change").

9. For a discussion of tax aversion, see Fennell and Fennell 2003; see also McCaffery 1994b (using the term "tax aversion"). McCaffery and Baron (2003) examined whether labeling the funding source for particular benefits a "tax" or a "payment" made a difference in how favorably it was viewed. They found that the preferred label differed depending on the service under

consideration and also differed among individuals (13–14). The phenomenon of tax aversion might be more broadly conceived to encompass negative attitudes toward any compulsory payment collected by the government, rather than just reactions to items that are labeled as taxes.

10. Six out of fifteen chapters of a 1992 edited volume on time preferences (Loewenstein and Elster) focused on hyperbolic discounting (Loewenstein 2003, 3).

11. Individuals could also derive benefits from their own increased tendency to comply. Indeed, individuals might choose to withhold at least the full liability amount as a kind of moral or ethical precommitment, recognizing their own tendency to be tempted to evade taxes in circumstances where positive sums are due at tax time.

12. The survey data were drawn from airport and ballgame "convenience samples." The authors caution that "because the samples are not representative of the U.S. population, especially with respect to income, broad generalizations are hazardous" (Fetherstonhaugh and Ross 1999, 196).

References

Ainslie, George. 1992. *Picoeconomics: The Strategic Interaction of Successive Motivational States within the Person.* Cambridge: Cambridge University Press.

Alm, James, Betty Jackson, and Michael McKee. 1992. "Deterrence and Beyond: Toward a Kinder, Gentler IRS." In *Why People Pay Taxes*, edited by Joel Slemrod. Ann Arbor: University of Michigan Press.

Alstott, Anne L. 1996. "The Uneasy Liberal Case Against Income and Wealth Transfer Taxation: A Response to Professor McCaffery." *Tax Law Review* 51(3): 363–402.

Ando, Albert, and Franco Modigliani. 1963. "The 'Life Cycle' Hypothesis of Saving: Aggregate Implications and Tests." *American Economic Review* 53(1): 55–84.

Ariely, Dan, and Ziv Carmon. 2003. "Summary Assessment of Experiences: The Whole Is Different from the Sum of Its Parts." In *Time and Decision: Economic and Psychological Perspectives on Intertemporal Choice*, edited by George Loewenstein, Daniel Read, and Roy F. Baumeister. New York: Russell Sage Foundation.

Ayers, Benjamin C., Steven J. Kachelmeier, and John R. Robinson. 1999. "Why Do People Give Interest-Free Loans to the Government? An Experimental Study of Interim Tax Payments." *Journal of the American Taxation Association* 21(2): 55–74.

Baron, Jonathan. 2000. *Thinking and Deciding,* 3rd ed. Cambridge: Cambridge University Press.

Barr, Michael S. 2004. "Banking the Poor." *Yale Journal on Regulation* 21(1): 121–237.

Berube, Alan, Anne Kim, Benjamin Forman, and Megan Burns. 2002. *The Price of Paying Taxes: How Tax Preparation and Refund Loan Fees Erode the Benefits of the EITC.* Policy Report. Washington, D.C.: Progressive Policy Institute and Brookings Institution Press.

Camerer, Colin. 1990. "Comments on 'Some Implications of Cognitive Psychology for Risk Regulation,' by Roger Noll and James Krier." *Journal of Legal Studies* 19(2, part 2): 791–99.

Camerer, Colin, Samuel Issacharoff, George Loewenstein, Ted O'Donoghue, and Matthew Rabin. 2003. "Regulation for Conservatives: Behavioral Economics and the Case for 'Asymmetric Paternalism.'" *University of Pennsylvania Law Review* 151(3): 1211–254.

Caron, Paul. 1996. "Tax Myopia Meets Tax Hyperopia: The Unproven Case of Increased Judicial Deference to Revenue Rulings." *Ohio State Law Journal* 57(2): 637–70.

Carroll, John S. 1992. "Taxation: Compliance with Federal Personal Income Tax Laws." In *Handbook of Psychology and Law*, edited by Dorothy K. Kagehiro and William S. Laufer. New York: Springer-Verlag.

Cohen, Lloyd R. 2001. "The Lure of the Lottery." *Wake Forest Law Review* 36(3): 705–45.

Dawes, Robyn, John Orbell, Randy Simmons, and Alphons van de Kragt. 1986. "Organizing Groups for Collective Action." *American Political Science Review* 80(4): 1171–185.

Erev, Ido, and Amnon Rapoport. 1990. "Provision of Step-Level Public Goods: The Sequential Contribution Mechanism." *Journal of Conflict Resolution* 34(3): 401–25.

Fennell, Christopher C., and Lee Anne Fennell. 2003. "Fear and Greed in Tax Policy: A Qualitative Research Agenda." *Washington University Journal of Law and Policy* 13: 75–138.

Fennell, Lee Anne. 2003. "Death, Taxes, and Cognition." *North Carolina Law Review* 81(2): 567–652.

Fetherstonhaugh, David, and Lee Ross. 1999. "Framing Effects and Income Flow Preferences in Decisions About Social Security." In *Behavioral Dimensions of Retirement Economics*, edited by Henry J. Aaron. Washington, D.C.: Brookings Institution Press.

Frederick, Shane, George Loewenstein, and Ted O'Donoghue. 2003. "Time Discounting and Time Preference: A Critical Review." In *Time and Decision: Economic and Psychological Perspectives on Intertemporal Choice*, edited by George Loewenstein, Daniel Read, and Roy F. Baumeister. New York: Russell Sage Foundation.

Gale, William G., and Peter R. Orszag. 2004. "Should the President's Tax Cuts Be Made Permanent?" *Tax Notes* 102(10): 1277–291.

Harsanyi, John C. 1968. "Individualistic and Functionalistic Explanations in the Light of Game Theory: The Example of Social Status." In *Problems in the Philosophy of Science*, edited by Imre Lakotos and Alan Musgrave. Amsterdam: North Holland Publishing.

Herrnstein, Richard J., and Drazen Prelec. 1992. "Melioration." In *Choice Over Time*, edited by George Loewenstein and Jon Elster. New York: Russell Sage Foundation.

Hotz, V. Joseph, and John Karl Scholz. 2003. "The Earned Income Tax Credit." In *Means-Tested Transfer Programs in the United States*, edited by Robert A. Moffitt. Chicago: University of Chicago Press.

Kahneman, Daniel, and Carol Varey. 1991. "Notes on the Psychology of Utility."

In *Interpersonal Comparisons of Well-Being*, edited by Jon Elster and John E. Roemer. Cambridge: Cambridge University Press.

Kaplan, Richard L. 1999. "Retirement Funding and the Curious Evolution of Individual Retirement Accounts." *Elder Law Journal* 7(2): 283–311.

———. 2001. "Financing Long-Term Care in the United States: Who Should Pay for Mom and Dad?" In *Aging: Caring for Our Elders*, edited by David N. Weisstub, David C. Thomasma, Serge Gauthier, and George F. Tomossy. Dordrecht: Kluwer Academic Publishers.

Kelman, Mark. 1983. "Time Preferences and Tax Equity." *Stanford Law Review* 35(4): 649–80.

Kivetz, Ran, and Itamar Simonson. 2002. "Self-Control for the Righteous: Toward a Theory of Precommitment to Indulgence." *Journal of Consumer Research* 29(2): 199–215.

Korobkin, Russell. 1998. "Inertia and Preference in Contract Negotiation: The Psychological Power of Default Rules and Form Terms." *Vanderbilt Law Review* 51(6): 1583–651.

Korobkin, Russell B., and Thomas S. Ulen. 2000. "Law and Behavioral Science: Removing the Rationality Assumption from Law and Economics." *California Law Review* 88(4): 1051–144.

Lane, Robert E. 2000. *The Loss of Happiness in Market Democracies*. New Haven, Conn.: Yale University Press.

Lewis, Alan. 1982. *The Psychology of Taxation*. New York: St. Martin's Press.

Loewenstein, George. 1987. "Anticipation and the Valuation of Delayed Consumption." *Economic Journal* 97(387): 666–84.

———. 1988. "Frames of Mind in Intertemporal Choice." *Management Science* 34(2): 200–14.

———. 1992. "The Fall and Rise of Psychological Explanations in the Economics of Intertemporal Choice." In *Choice Over Time*, edited by George Loewenstein and Jon Elster. New York: Russell Sage Foundation.

———. 2003. "Introduction." In *Time and Decision: Economic and Psychological Perspectives on Intertemporal Choice*, edited by George Loewenstein, Daniel Read, and Roy F. Baumeister. New York: Russell Sage Foundation.

Loewenstein, George, and Jon Elster, eds. 1992. *Choice Over Time*. New York: Russell Sage Foundation.

Loewenstein, George, and Drazen Prelec. 1991. "Negative Time Preferences." *American Economic Review, Papers and Proceedings of the Hundred and Third Annual Meeting of the American Economic Association, May, 1991* 81(2): 347–52.

———. 1993. "Preferences for Sequences of Outcomes." *Psychological Review* 100(1): 91–108.

Loewenstein, George, and Nachum Sicherman. 1991. "Do Workers Prefer Increasing Wage Profiles?" *Journal of Labor Economics* 9(1): 67–84.

McCaffery, Edward J. 1994a. "Cognitive Theory and Tax." *UCLA Law Review* 41(7): 1861–947.

———. 1994b. "Why People Play Lotteries and Why It Matters." *Wisconsin Law Review* 1994(1): 71–122.

McCaffery, Edward J., and Jonathan Baron. 2003. "Heuristics and Biases in Thinking About Tax." USC Law and Econ Research Paper No. 03-22. Los Angeles: University of Southern California. Available at: http://www.ssrn.com/ abstract=467440 (accessed September 21, 2005).

Murphy, Liam, and Thomas Nagel. 2002. *The Myth of Ownership: Taxes and Justice.* Oxford: Oxford University Press.

Neumark, David. 1995. "Are Rising Earnings Profiles a Forced-Saving Mechanism?" *Economic Journal* 105(428): 95–106.

Newport, Frank. 2001. "Americans Suffer from Negative Mental Attitude While Doing Taxes." *Gallup Poll Monthly* 427(April): 43–45.

O'Donoghue, Ted, and Matthew Rabin. 1999a. "Doing It Now or Later." *American Economic Review* 89(1): 103–24.

———. 1999b. "Procrastination in Preparing for Retirement." In *Behavioral Dimensions of Retirement Economics,* edited by Henry J. Aaron. Washington D.C.: Brookings Institution Press.

Okun, Arthur M. 1975. *Equality and Efficiency: The Big Tradeoff.* Washington, D.C.: Brookings Institution Press.

Ostrom, Elinor, Roy Gardner, and James K. Walker. 1994. *Rules, Games, and Common-Pool Resources.* Ann Arbor: University of Michigan Press.

Parfit, Derek. 1984. *Reasons and Persons.* Oxford: Clarendon Press.

Pigou, Arthur C. 1920. *The Economics of Welfare.* London: Macmillan and Co.

Poterba, James M. 2004. "Saving for Retirement: Taxes Matter." *Center for Retirement Research Issue Brief No. 17.* Boston: Boston College. Available at: http://www.ssrn.com/abstract_id=546662 (accessed September 21, 2005).

Prelec, Drazen. 1991. "Values and Principles: Some Limitations on Traditional Economic Analysis." In *Socio-Economics: Toward a New Synthesis,* edited by Amitai Etzioni and Paul R. Lawrence. Armonk, N.Y.: M.E. Sharpe.

Prelec, Drazen, and Ronit Bodner. 2003. "Self-Signaling and Self-Control." In *Time and Decision: Economic and Psychological Perspectives on Intertemporal Choice,* edited by George Loewenstein, Daniel Read, and Roy F. Baumeister. New York: Russell Sage Foundation.

Prelec, Drazen, and George Loewenstein. 1998. "The Red and the Black: Mental Accounting of Savings and Debt." *Marketing Science* 17(1): 4–28.

Read, Daniel. 2001. "Is Time-Discounting Hyperbolic or Subadditive?" *Journal of Risk and Uncertainty* 23(1): 5–32.

Rosenberg, Joshua D. 1996. "The Psychology of Taxes: Why They Drive Us Crazy and How We Can Make Them Sane." *Virginia Tax Review* 16(2): 155–236.

Rubinstein, Ariel. 2003. "Economics and Psychology? The Case of Hyperbolic Discounting." *International Economic Review* 44(4): 1207–216.

Schmedel, Scott. 1997. "IRS's Income-Tax Withholding Game Has Rules That Can Guarantee Defeat." *Wall Street Journal,* May 23, Sec. C, p. 1.

Shafir, Eldar, and Amos Tversky. 1995. "Decision Making." In *An Invitation to Cognitive Science: Thinking,* vol. 3, 2nd ed., edited by Edward E. Smith and Daniel N. Osherson. Cambridge, Mass.: MIT Press.

Shapiro, Matthew D., and Joel Slemrod. 1995. "Consumer Response to the Timing of Income: Evidence from a Change in Tax Withholding." *American Economic Review* 85(1): 274–83.

Shefrin, Hersh, and Richard H. Thaler. 1991. "The Behavioral Life-Cycle Hypothesis." In *Quasi Rational Economics,* edited by Richard H. Thaler. New York: Russell Sage Foundation.

Solnick, Jay V., Catherine H. Kannenberg, David A. Eckerman, and Marcus Waller. 1980. "An Experimental Analysis of Impulsivity and Impulse Control in Humans." *Learning and Motivation* 11(1): 61–77.

Souleles, Nicholas S. 1999. "The Response of Household Consumption to Income Tax Refunds." *American Economic Review* 89(4): 947–58.

Strotz, Robert H. 1955. "Myopia and Inconsistency in Dynamic Utility Maximization." *Review of Economic Studies* 23(3): 165–80.

Sunstein, Cass R. and Richard H. Thaler. 2003. "Libertarian Paternalism Is Not an Oxymoron." *University of Chicago Law Review* 70(4): 1159–202.

Thaler, Richard H. 1985. "Mental Accounting and Consumer Choice." *Marketing Science* 4(3): 199–214.

———. 1992. "Savings, Fungibility, and Mental Accounts." In *The Winner's Curse: Paradoxes and Anomalies of Economic Life*, edited by Richard H. Thaler. New York: Free Press.

Thaler, Richard H., and Shlomo Benartzi. 2004. "Save More Tomorrow™: Using Behavioral Economics to Increase Employee Saving." *Journal of Political Economy* 112(1, part 2): S164–87.

Thaler, Richard H., and Eric J. Johnson. 1990. "Gambling with the House Money and Trying to Break Even: The Effects of Prior Outcomes on Risky Choice." *Management Science* 36(6): 643–60.

Thaler, Richard H., and George Loewenstein. 1992. "Intertemporal Choice." In *The Winner's Curse*, edited by Richard H. Thaler. New York: Free Press.

Tversky, Amos, and Daniel Kahneman. 1981. "The Framing of Decisions and the Psychology of Choice." *Science* 211(4481): 453–58.

U.S. Department of the Treasury. Internal Revenue Service. 2002. *Tax Stats at a Glance*. Washington, D.C.: IRS. Available at: http://www.irs.gov/taxstats/article/0,,id=102886,00.html (accessed September 21, 2005).

———. 2004a. *How Do I Adjust My Tax Withholding?* IRS Publication 919. Washington: U.S. Government Printing Office.

———. 2004b. IRS Withholding Calculator. Washington: U.S. Government Printing Office. http://www.irs.gov./individuals/article/0,,id=96196,00.html.

Weiss, Deborah M. 1991. "Paternalistic Pension Policy: Psychological Evidence and Economic Theory." *University of Chicago Law Review* 58(4): 1275–319.

Wertenbroch, Klaus. 2003. "Self-Rationing: Self-Control in Consumer Choice." In *Time and Decision: Economic and Psychological Perspectives on Intertemporal Choice*, edited by George Loewenstein, Daniel Read, and Roy F. Baumeister. New York: Russell Sage Foundation.

PART III

TAX COMPLIANCE

Chapter 7

Value Added Tax Compliance

PAUL WEBLEY, CAROLINE ADAMS, AND HENK ELFFERS

O VER the last fifteen years there has been a considerable research into tax compliance (Andreoni, Erard, and Feinstein 1998). Many new theoretical models of the compliance process have been devised and a wide range of empirical studies carried out. But the focus of most of this research has been personal income tax compliance. Business tax evasion in general, and VAT compliance in particular, have received very little attention indeed (for a review of research on tax compliance by businesses, see Webley 2004). This is surprising given the economic and social importance of business taxation and the fact that VAT has been introduced in a large number of countries—most recently China (see Yeh 1997) and the ten countries that joined the European Union in May 2004 (see Cnossen 1998). It is difficult to get an accurate picture, but it is clear from the few studies that have been published that VAT evasion is widespread and involves significant revenue losses, though the extent varies considerably across countries. Agha and Haughton (1996) summarize the findings of studies from five countries in Europe and two in Asia: their figures suggest that revenue losses vary from a low of 3 percent (France, United Kingdom) to a high of 40 percent (Italy). Even the low figure represents a huge sum of money ($3 billion for France) and a very high proportion of firms involved in some noncompliance. Duverne (1990), for instance, reports that 66 percent of French VAT taxpayers audited had understated the value of taxable sales (a quarter of them fraudulently) and 40 percent had overstated the value of taxable inputs. Similarly, a study of Dutch businesses found that 34 percent of firms had evaded VAT (Cnossen 1981). All of these studies involve official figures: there have, to our knowledge, been no studies which have studied VAT compliance by asking businesses directly about their actions and no studies that have looked at the role played by psychological and social variables, which makes the studies reported in this chapter unique.

In the absence of theoretical models and empirical studies on the causes of VAT noncompliance, we can draw on general theories of tax compliance and the empirical economic psychological/behavioral economic literature into income tax evasion. There are a very large number of theories from all areas of social science on tax compliance and it would be easy to devote an entire chapter to these theories alone. Here we will only deal very briefly with the most relevant: an excellent general account can be found in James Andreoni, Brian Erard, and Jonathan Feinstein (1998). Economic theories, of which the best known example is probably Michael Allingham and Agnar Sandmo (1972), generally represent the decision to evade as a straightforward matter of maximizing expected utility. In some models the focus is on the taxpayer alone, in others—for example, the game-theoretic approach of Joseph Greenberg (1984)—the analysis is interactive, with the tax authorities being one of the players in the game. Most economic models treat people as rational and amoral though there have been attempts to take a more behavioral approach. Gareth Myles and Robin Naylor (1996), for example, have included group conformity and social customs in their model. These economic models have the merit of being elegant and making clear predictions but to a behavioral economist or economic psychologist there are three major drawbacks to them. First, they ignore how institutions and individuals frame tax compliance decisions (see chapter 8 in this volume). Second, for the most part they treat economic agents as though they have one simple motivation, that of economic self-interest (see chapter 9 in this volume). There is no role for good citizenship, altruism, reputation, and social customs. Third, they assume that the population is homogenous, that all economic agents are alike. These problems suggest that an alternative approach to theorizing may be more successful.

Two theories that bear on this last issue (the heterogeneity of tax payers) will be very briefly considered: Joachim Vogel's (1974) social psychological typology and Henk Elffers (2000) WBAD model. Vogel proposes a persuasive typology of taxpayers using Kelman's (1965) distinction between compliance, identification and internalization. Compliance is doing what an authority requires without believing in it. Identification is behaving in a certain way to be like an admired individual. Internalization involves a real change in beliefs where ideas, values, and behavior are integrated. So a taxpayer who has internalized values pays taxes because he or she believes it is the right thing to do. Vogel combines these distinctions with two kinds of tax behavior (compliance and noncompliance) to provide a six-fold classification of taxpayers. Conforming internalizers pay their taxes because they believe that this is the right thing for good citizens to do whereas deviant internalizers cheat because they believe this is morally right: they are best considered tax protesters rather than tax evaders. Conformist and deviant identifiers will pay (or evade) taxes depending on the social norms of their reference group. Their anxiety is to be different, and they are concerned about social sanctions such as ridicule. Thus, in Britain at least, those working in the building trades would regard cash-in-hand working as normal, and so simply acting as your friends do would lead to evasion. Finally, conformist compliers pay because they fear punishment and deviant compliers evade because they believe the chances of being punished are low. This classification has the merit of recognizing that people may evade or comply for a variety of reasons, though we do not have good empirical evidence for it.

Elffers's (2000) WBAD (willing–being able–daring) or "staircase" model also explicitly deals with different motives. Elffers assumes that most people are at the bottom of the staircase that leads to evasion and are compliant. For these good citizens, penalties and audits are irrelevant. Others will be willing to be noncompliant (they are on the first step of the staircase) but do not have the opportunity or knowledge to evade. Still others (on the second step) are willing and able, but do not dare to evade. These people know how to evade and would be happy to do so but fear the consequences. Research by Paul Webley, Michaela Cole, and Ole-Petter Eidjar (2001) suggests that many British income taxpayers fall in this category. Only for those on the penultimate stair are the costs and benefits relevant. Those who think the risk is acceptable may then "dare to evade" (this is the group of actual evaders on the top stair). This simple model has the advantage of recognizing the existence of different groups with different motivations to comply but does not explain why people fall into these different categories initially.

Empirical studies of income tax evasion (for example, Cowell 1992; Elffers 1991; Lewis 1982; Webley et al. 1991) help us to identify what are likely to be the most important explanatory factors in VAT compliance. Five factors seem likely to be particularly critical: sanctions and punishments (deterrence), equity, personality, satisfaction with the tax authorities, and mental accounting. Each will be considered in turn. Economic models clearly predict that higher penalties and audit probabilities should discourage noncompliance. The evidence suggests that though both have some deterrence effect (Andreoni, Erard, and Feinstein 1998), higher audit probabilities probably have more impact than higher penalties (Hessing, Elffers, Robben, and Webley 1992). The results of several surveys have indicated that self-reported noncompliers are less likely than compliers to believe that such acts would result in apprehension and punishment (Hessing, Elffers, and Weigel 1988). Nothing is known about what people running small businesses believe about the sanctions for VAT noncompliance. It must be remembered that deterrence is not solely a matter of legal sanctions: a belief that one's reputation may suffer as a result of being caught evading is also a deterrent and this may be particularly relevant in a business context.

The perceived fairness of a tax system is important both to its acceptability and smooth functioning. A recent example of how an unacceptable tax system impacts on the public consciousness is the saga of the poll tax in Britain (Cullis, Jones, and Morrisey 1993). A tax can be seen as unfair in a number of ways: if those of similar incomes are taxed differently, for example or if the government is seen as giving little back in return. Frank Cowell (1992) has shown that how a person perceives his own role in influencing the perceived inequity is of central importance and it has been argued that a taxpayer may withdraw from the exchange relationship by evading taxes in order to offset or reduce the disparity. Although such research has looked almost exclusively at the private individual, work by Caroline Adams (1996) showed that perceived inequity in the taxation system was found to be the most important variable predicting noncompliance in those running small businesses in Holland.

Russell Weigel, Dick Hessing, and Henk Elffers (1987) suggest that some individuals may be characterized by egoistic tendencies, and that others may exhibit a strong identification with community responsibilities, and thus be less motivated to avoid taxes owed. In other words, the more egoistic an individual, the less likely he or she will be to comply with rules and laws when compliance conflicts with their interests. There is a good deal of evidence that egoism (Weigel, Hessing, and Elffers 1998) predicts rule-breaking in a number of areas, including income tax evasion (Elffers 1991), social security fraud (Hessing et al. 1993) and parking violations (Adams and Webley 1996).

Dissatisfaction with the tax authorities in other ways has also been suggested by a number of investigators as a motivation to avoid taxation (for example, Elffers 1991; Wallschutzky 1984; Wärneryd and Walerud 1982). What evidence there is suggests that believing the system to be inefficient correlates positively with a propensity to evade (Vogel 1974; Wearing and Headey 1997).

How business people think about the VAT money they collect may also influence their behavior toward it: the notion of mental accounting (see Thaler 1999) may be helpful here. Mental accounting is often described as a psychological mechanism whereby income is framed (Winnett and Lewis 1995). Thaler (1999) proposes, in respect of personal finance, that people have a number of mental accounts that operate independently of one another. What is interesting in the current context is whether business men and women psychologically separate monies owed to the VAT into a separate mental account from that of business turnover. If they do not, they may be more likely to try to evade VAT as a result of seeing it as their money.

The purpose of the studies described in this chapter were first, to provide a natural history of small business people's views on VAT and related issues, second, to see if those psychological factors that play an important causal role in income tax evasion are also relevant to VAT and third, to try to develop an integrated approach to understanding VAT compliance. In the first study, which is reported in more greater detail in Caroline Adams and Paul Webley (2001), three groups of business people were interviewed (restaurant proprietors, flooring/furnishing proprietors, builders). In the second (reported in more detail in Webley, Adams, and Elffers 2002) and third (reported in more detail in Adams 2002), two business sectors (catering; flooring and furnishing retailers) were surveyed as there is some confidential evidence that the first group is generally less compliant with regards to VAT than the second.

Study 1: Equity, Mental Accounting and VAT Compliance Interviews

Method

The businesses were in the catering trade (ten restaurants, cafes, and takeaway proprietors), flooring/furniture trade (eight proprietors, one employed accountant) or builders (eight respondents). All businesses had a turnover of less than one million pounds. All but four of the respondents were male.

A letter was sent to thirty-three flooring proprietors, fifty-five restaurant proprietors, and thirty-five builders requesting an opportunity to speak to them about VAT and Customs and Excise. The letter stressed that their opinion was being sought on these matters and that their views would form part of a report that would be made available to Customs and Excise. Participants were told that the interviews would last approximately thirty minutes.

The interviews were semi-structured and conducted informally and conversationally to encourage spontaneity, raising the issue of compliance indirectly, often with hypothetical questions. The interviews lasted between forty and sixty minutes. After establishing rapports with the participants, the interviewer orally outlined the purpose of the research and guaranteed confidentially.

Twenty-four of the interviews were undertaken at business premises, one at the participant's home (away from his place of business), and two at homes that also served as the business base. The interviews were tape recorded and subsequently transcribed. The data were analyzed using the techniques of grounded theory (Glaser and Strauss 1967).

Analysis and Results

Grounded Theory is a bottom-up approach to qualitative analysis that has developed significantly over the past twenty years (Strauss 1987; Strauss and Corbin 1990, 1994). The primary concept is that issues emerge from the data, rather than are imposed upon it. The analysis uncovered fifteen sub-themes that are likely to influence compliance. From these five primary themes emerged. Four can be found in research from personal income tax compliance: equity; views on the authoritative body; sanctions; and morality. The fifth, mental accounting, is new to tax compliance.

Equity

It is no surprise that this issue produced the most concentrated data, with many people perceiving inequities at some level. A number of different aspects of the tax system were perceived as unfair by some of the participants. Not all participants, however, considered the system as a whole to be inequitable. Some aspects, such as the rigid application of a penalty structure for noncompliance such as late returns, were considered by some to be the only equitable option.

If a business is unable to obtain contracts because their bids are higher than those of nonregistered businesses, the proprietor might perceive the contract award as unfair. Whether this was perceived as a problem was largely due to the location, type, and size of a business. Builders consider it as more of an issue than caterers, for example. This may be due to the fact that VAT on building work is conspicuous to both business and customer, whereas in catering it is largely invisible.

Many builders and some flooring businesses are regularly asked by customers to "knock off VAT." Among builders there is a belief that so-called one-man-band builders regularly do not charge VAT to the customer and thus do not pay it to Customs and Excise.

> A lot of small builders are . . . obviously trying to get around it [VAT] because we're finding that when we're quoting, they are substantial jobs which might be ten or fifteen thousand pounds worth of work and that there are people who have won the job because they're not VAT registered and their prices are obviously 17.5 percent cheaper than what our prices are. . . . If VAT's got to be in and it is because it gets so much revenue then it should be every business with no threshold and have it as a level playing field.

Although a few believe that businesses are generally honest, far more think that people take any opportunity to reduce VAT and that only a lack of opportunity or sanctions prevents them from engaging in wide-scale fraud. Indeed, some believe that there is a permanent state of conflict between Customs and Excise and business people. In their minds a norm exists to minimize VAT by any means. These participants believe that many people are engaging in small-scale fraud as large-scale fraud would be detected.

Among catering businesses and some builders, there is a sense that small businesses bear an unfair burden, in part because they pay a proportionally greater share of VAT and in part because they do not have the financial resources to pay experts to make the most of legal loopholes to reduce their VAT burden.

> Basically, they should do away with VAT as far as I'm concerned because as it stands it's not fair on small businesses and that's why people will try not to pay it.

Business people collect VAT from their customers and pass it on to Customs and Excise, which naturally incurs some cost. The majority of participants have either never given any thought to administrative costs or accept them as part of running a business. Some, however, especially builders, do resent having to do unpaid work for the government.

> I begrudge it of course . . . it's obvious I don't want to be spending thousands to someone, (to undertake VAT administration) you know business is so tight every penny helps.

Sanctions

Most people believe that acts of evasion will generally be detected, but many of these seem to think that though they would get caught, others may get away with it. For many people evasion, except for very small cash deals, would require a good deal of effort. It also invokes a high degree of anxiety, thus anxiety and the effort required act as strong deterrents against fraud.

> Always looking over your shoulder, also it would be burdensome, fiddling takes time, a lot of effort and looking over your shoulder, no thank you.

The general belief is that Customs and Excise wield very strong powers and would use all powers at their disposal to obtain monies owed. The majority believe that these powers are necessary to maximize compliance and act as strong deterrents, but a few believe the powers to be excessive and ineffective.

Most people believe that the severity of any penalty will depend primarily on the amount evaded. Because small businesses tend not to engage in large-scale fraud the main perceived priority on the part of Customs and Excise would be to get the money back, with interest. Those that mentioned imprisonment believed that this was unlikely, but that Customs and Excise would stop at nothing to recover the money even if that meant closing the business down.

Mental Accounting

If people see the money they collect as part of their business turnover rather than merely as money paid by the customer to be passed on to Customs and Excise they may be more likely to engage in fraud.

Only a minority of respondents believe that the money at all times belongs to Customs and Excise. The majority feel that somehow it is theirs and dislike handing it over. Some participants seem to believe at one level the customer is paying the VAT but at a deeper level that it subsequently becomes part of the business funds and so also begrudge paying it.

> VAT takes about twelve thousand a year from my business, so I pay just as much in VAT as what I earn. . . . Don't get me wrong, I accept that VAT is charged and has to be paid, but given stuff I think, you know in my circumstances anyway, I can only speak for myself, it hurts very, very much to pay VAT.

It is clear, on the other hand that this person separates VAT into a separate mental account from business money.

> It's not a cost to the business, we're just looking after the money for the government. There's no point worrying about paying. It's their money.

VAT and Society

Most people agree that taxes are required to maintain our society. However, few spoke of the moral aspects of paying taxes. When the moral aspects of taxation were discussed, most saw the need for taxation and VAT, but agreed that these thoughts were not uppermost when handing over VAT.

> I don't ever feel bothered about paying my share, the system needs everyone to trawl resources up to a point. I'm a capitalist, it's modest we're talking twenty odd percent and that's after tax relief on mortgages and everything else. . . . I suppose really the connection (between paying VAT and the social structure) isn't that strong. . . . Most people including me don't actually think like that.

For this participant, there's clearly a sense that minimizing VAT is good business practice that overshadows good social practice, and though he is aware of the necessity of tax, he speaks of paying his fair share.

Only three people commented on how serious they thought the act of committing VAT evasion was. None of them, however, considered it a serious crime.

Views on the VAT System

A wide range of views were held on Customs and Excise, some positive and some strongly negative. The majority of people find staff helpful and courteous. The main contact business people have with Customs and Excise, however, is through inspections (or audits). When staff were spoken of in negative terms, it was almost always with reference to inspectors. Some people believe that the inspectors are merely bookkeepers who come in open-minded. Others believe they have a strong agenda, that there is a system that gives inspectors the incentive to increase revenue.

> I've heard from a friend that they get commission on top, that's not right is it? They should accept our honesty.

Some people recognize that there are advantages in being VAT registered. These include improved record keeping, the kudos of being a registered company, and the ability to claim VAT back on business assets purchased. There are clearly more financial advantages for some companies than others, depending on factors such as proportion of materials to labor and frequency and amount of assets purchased.

Conclusion

There are strong similarities between the themes that emerged from this study and research on personal income tax compliance. Two factors that seem to play a particularly important role are inequity and mental accounting, which are looked at in more detail in the subsequent studies.

Study 2: Combining Survey and Objective Data to Explore VAT Compliance

Method

The sample consisted of catering, flooring/furnishing business owners with a turnover of less than £1 million, all previously sorted by Customs and Excise into four compliance groups. Group A, all new businesses, had never been visited. Group B had been visited in the last three years.

Group C had been visited in the last three years and assessed for less than £1 thousand (mildly noncompliant). Group D were businesses visited in the last three years and assessed for more than £1 thousand (seriously noncompliant). A random sample of 800 businesses from each category was selected and 3,200 questionnaires were distributed in total. 359 responses were received.

The questionnaire used to gather data was primarily quantitative but had some questions in an open format. It was also color coded according to the Customs and Excise compliance groupings and divided into seven sections.

General Information

Both personal and business related information was requested. The questions asked, among other things, age, gender, main business activity, number of staff employed, the year the business was first registered for VAT and questions about the use of an outside adviser, penalties for late payment of VAT, and the number of times the business had been inspected by the tax authorities.

You, the Tax Authorities, and VAT

This consisted of nine questions, which all focused on the service provided by the authorities and general questions about VAT—about its fairness, about whether VAT money is seen as coming from business funds, and about the prevalence of VAT fraud.

You and Other People

This section comprised twelve questions from the egoism scale. This has an alpha of over .80 (Weigel, Hessing and Elffers 1998).

You and VAT Compliance

This consisted of sixteen questions that dealt with a range of compliance issues from the ease of making unintentional mistakes, through the acceptability of VAT rules and the detectability of VAT fraud by both other businesses and the tax authorities.

Features of VAT

This section included an open question in respect of the purpose of VAT, and two questions about errors in returns: "If you found an error in your returns after you had submitted them, would you bring this to the attention of the tax authorities?" (yes/no) and "If you have ever made an error on a VAT return, why do you think it occurred?"

Declaring VAT

To measure attitude to VAT evasion the question asked: "VAT evasion is . . . ." (five-point scale from wrong to acceptable). Another question asked: "How often over the past five years have you been involved in cash transactions so as to reduce VAT payments?" (very often, often, sometimes, rarely, never). A social norm measure asked: "If my friends knew that I sometimes underdeclared VAT they would say this was . . . ." Answer categories: very wrong, wrong, irresponsible, unwise, normal, a good thing. The final question in this section asked: "If you had the opportunity to pay less VAT than you should do and you believed that there was absolutely no chance of getting caught, would you do so?" Answer categories: certainly, probably, probably not, certainly not.

Hypothetical Situations

Two hypothetical situations were presented, one concerning the introduction of a reward system for paying VAT promptly, the other concerning reactions to a normal supplier offering to deliver some goods or services without charging VAT.

A questionnaire was sent to each sample business with a cover letter stating that we were interested in business people's views about VAT issues and related matters. The letter informed the recipients that their business had been selected as part of a representative sample and that any information given would be anonymous and confidential.

Prior experience with research on compliance suggested that the response rate would be low, which raises the question of how representative the response group would be. Oppenheim (1992) reports that late responders to surveys tend to be similar to nonresponders, so a comparison between late and early responders gives an indication of any likely bias. Replies were date stamped as they arrived in order for this analysis to be carried out.

Results

The main body of results is divided into two main sections. The first section will deal with the descriptive aspect of the data and the second section will deal with the prediction of compliance. No significant differences emerged between the late responders and early responders, so we concluded that the sample could be regarded as representative. The final number of questionnaires received was 359. This equates to a crude response rate of 11 percent. However, annual VAT deregistration rates for newly registered businesses in Britain are 20 percent and for established business 15 percent. Therefore, given that the questionnaire was distributed in January and February, it is likely that approximately 520 of the businesses on the address file are unlikely to be active. The final response rate is more accurately assessed at 13.5 percent. There were no significant differences in self-reported compliance between the two types of businesses. Those in the catering business, however, were more likely to believe fraud was widespread in their line of business (t = 2.08, d.f. = 304, p < .05), were less likely to believe that people were honest (t = 3.36, d.f. = 304, p < .001), and were more likely to believe that underdeclaring VAT could contribute to increased profits (t = 3.25, d.f. = 307, p < .001).

Section 1. Descriptive Data

Two hundred and sixty three (73 percent) of the respondents were male and eighty-seven (24 percent) were female. Ages ranged from under thirty to over sixty, with 83 percent (N = 297) of respondents being between the ages of thirty-one and sixty. As expected, most businesses described themselves as being either in the catering trade (N = 199) or the flooring/furnishing trade (N = 117), but a minority (N = 30) did not fit either of these categories and were coded as other. Some of the other group may well have been in the catering or flooring/furnishing businesses but responses such as company director or all aspects of my business could not be so classified. Some respondents, however, clearly fell outside the expected categories, for example, hairdresser.

The majority of businesses (N = 186, 52 percent) employed between one and five staff members, 86 percent employed between one and twenty. The number of years registered for VAT ranged from 1 to 25 with an average of 11.5 years.

Of the sample, 41 percent (N = 149) employed an outside adviser to do VAT work, 33 percent had been penalized for late payment of VAT monies owed, and 9 percent stated that they regularly received repayments rather than paying VAT monies to the tax authorities. Respondents were asked how many inspections they had had and this information used to construct a code based on the frequency of inspection: for example, infrequent (less than every eight years); normal (every three to seven years); and frequent (every second year or more). If the business had been registered for four years or less and had not had any inspections it was not allocated a code. In sum, 22 percent (N = 80) were coded as infrequent, 53 percent (N = 191) as normal, and 10 percent (N = 35) as frequent.

The majority of respondents (53 percent) did not appear to think that VAT is levied fairly over the whole range of businesses. Only seventy-three (20 percent) of the respondents agreed that it was fair, the remainder took the neutral (middle) option. There was also a strong consensus of 262 of the respondents (73 percent) that small businesses carry an unfair VAT burden. Most people seemed to be unsure of the incidence of fraud in their own line of business with 150 (42 percent) taking the neutral option. As to whether VAT is reasonably straightforward in their line of business, 203 respondents (56 percent) agreed but a significant number, 94 (26 percent), disagreed.

When asked "when I send off my cheque to the tax authorities I think of the money as coming from my business funds" a large proportion agreed (N=236; 66 percent). Only seventy-two (20 percent) disagreed that they thought of the VAT as coming from their business funds.

The vast majority of respondents (N = 262; 73 percent) thought that evasion is wrong with very few (N = 15; 4 percent) viewing evasion as acceptable. Although 188 (52 percent) of the respondents claimed they have never been involved in cash transactions so as to reduce VAT, 159 (44 percent) admitted to having done so at some time in the past though most (N = 102) said that this had happened rarely.

Two hundred and five (57 percent) of the respondents said that if their friends believed they sometimes underdeclared VAT they would believe it was either unwise or normal. Only eighty-seven (24 percent) said that their friends would say it was very wrong or wrong. The remainder said either irresponsible (N = 33, 9 percent) or a good thing (N = 18, 5 percent). If they had the opportunity to pay less VAT and they believed there was absolutely no chance of getting caught, 140 (39 percent) of the respondents said that they would either certainly or probably do so. To the same question, 206 (57 percent) said that they would either probably not or certainly not do so.

Section 2. The Prediction of Noncompliance

Two dependent measures were used. The first is the compliance grouping given by Customs and Excise. The second was a self-reported measure constructed using a variety of questions. Homogeneity analyses using HOMALS (van de Geer 1993a, 1993b) were used to identify which of twelve plausible candidate measures of noncompliance should be used in the main analyses and how information from these should be combined into a single index. HOMALS treats all data as categorical, which is useful as it allows one to check any assumed ordinal relationships. The final one-dimensional solution used the following five measures:

[HQ1] "If you have ever made an error on a VAT-return, why do you think it occurred?" Answer categories: wilful attempt for evasion, other.

[HQ2] "How often in the past five years have you been involved in cash transactions so as to reduce VAT?" Answer categories: (very) often, sometimes, rarely, never.

[HQ3] "If you had the opportunities to pay less VAT than you should do and you believed that there was absolutely no chance of getting caught, would you do so?" Answer categories: certainly, probably, probably not, certainly not.

[HQ4] The second imaginary situation to engage in a questionable trade deal concerning VAT irregularities. Answer categories: won't do it anyway, dependent on circumstances other than C and E-inspection density, (strongly) dependent on C and E-inspection density.

[HQ5] "VAT-fraud is widespread in my line of business." Answer categories: 1 to 5 (strongly disagree to strongly agree).

HOMALS computes a score for the dimension for each individual, but this is not particularly transparent. However, it is straightforward to compute an approximation that makes it easier for the reader to follow what is happening. An index was constructed by assigning the following points: four points for answering "wilful attempt" on HQ1; three points for answering "(very) often" on HQ2; one point for answering sometimes on HQ2; one point for answering "certainly" on HQ3; one point when not answering "won't do it anyway" on HQ4; one point when answering four or five (agree/strongly agree) on HQ5; and then summing.

The resulting compliance score is very highly correlated with the HOMALS score ($r = .91$). After the points had been totaled this produced 171 (48 percent) respondents with a score of zero, 100 (28 percent) with a score of one, and fifty-four (15 percent) with a score of between two and ten. The respondents scoring two or more were placed into a single category making a total of three groups. To further contrast the groups into self-reported noncompliers and self-reported compliers only those with a score of zero (compliers) or two (noncompliers) were used for analysis. By removing the nonconsistent group it is thought that the resulting measure would be better able to contrast compliers and noncompliers. The dependent measure had a final count of 171 compliers and fifty-four noncompliers.

Where possible, a scale of items was constructed as such scales are generally more reliable than single-item measures. Egoism is an established scale. One other scale and one two-item measure emerged from the data. The scale has been named "Quality of service" and the two-item measure has been named "Equity."[1] All the remaining variables are single-item measures. The purpose variable has been recoded into responders who believed that VAT is a general taxation and those who believed it has another (specific) purpose.

Each variable (single item, correlation or scale) was independently analyzed using a t-test or chi-squared and the variables that proved to be significant in explaining differences in self-reported compliance behavior are listed below. We added the qualified effect size of the difference according to Cohen (1977). Cohen deems a difference large if effect size is larger than 0.8, moderate if it is between 0.5 and 0.8, small if it is between 0.2 and 0.5, negligible if it is smaller than 0.2. Table 7.1 presents all the variables on which the two groups differ significantly. This shows that compliers were older than noncompliers. They also wrote their books up more frequently, were more likely to have sought advice, rated quality of service higher than noncompliers, and had stronger beliefs that VAT was equitable. They were more community oriented (less egoistic) than noncompliers, more likely to believe that everybody in their line of business understands how VAT works, less likely to believe that underdeclaration can substantially contribute to profit, and likely to say that business people generally find VAT rules acceptable. They were more likely to believe that a business not paying VAT properly would soon find itself reported to the authorities by other businesses and less likely to believe that if the tax authorities found an error, however small, they would be certain to impose a penalty. They were also more likely to believe that a businessman's reputation would suffer if he was discovered to have underdeclared VAT. Compliers were more likely to believe that VAT is a source of general taxation revenue, that VAT evasion is wrong and that their friends would have a more negative attitude if they underdeclared VAT.

To test the extent to which all of the significant variables taken together can explain compliance behavior the data were analysed by forward-step logistic regression. Results show that the final model of five variables can correctly classify 84 percent of respondents. Each of these variables is also independently significant (see table 7.2). Thus, if we knew that a person believed that underdeclaring profits could substantially contribute to profits, that they believed their friends to be relatively undisapproving if they sometimes underdeclared VAT, that they had an egoistic personality, a positive attitude to evasion and believed that VAT had a specific purpose, we could say, with a very good degree of certainty, that these people are noncompliers.

The data on objective compliance were independently analyzed using ANOVA or Chi-square. Very few significant results were found. People who have never been visited (group A) are younger than the other groups ($F = 5.94$; d.f. = 3, $p < .005$). Group A have been registered for a shorter period ($F = 35.40$; d.f. = 3; $p < .0001$) and have had fewer inspections ($F = 22.37$; d.f. = 3, p<.0001). Group D (seriously noncompliant) have had significantly more penalties for late payment and rate quality of service as lower ($F = 3.20$; d.f. = 3; $p < 0.5$.

Table 7.1 Summary of the Differences Between VAT Compliers and Noncompliers

Variable	t	χ^2	d.f.	p <	Noncompliers		Compliers		Effect Size
					Mean	Standard Deviation	Mean	Standard Deviation	
Underdeclaring contributes to profit	−7.08		221	.001	3.87	1.1	2.47	1.4	1.12
Egoism	−5.94		222	.001	35.91	8.8	28.11	8.3	0.91
What friends say	−5.08		217	.001	4.36	1.2	3.26	1.4	0.85
Attitude to evasion	−5.65		213	.001	2.02	1.2	1.24	.71	0.81
Quality of service	3.87		223	.001	14.31	3.9	16.61	3.8	0.60
Equity	2.98		222	.005	3.69	1.6	4.56	1.9	0.50
VAT rules acceptable	3.05		223	.005	2.83	1.2	3.36	1.1	0.46
Reputation	2.81		221	.01	3.17	1.3	3.71	1.2	0.43
Age	2.48		222	.05	2.42	.81	2.72	.73	0.39
Understand how VAT works	2.46		222	.05	2.94	1.3	3.42	1.2	0.38
Reported by other businesses	2.26		222	.05	2.33	1.1	2.72	1.1	0.35
Penalty for errors	−2.25		223	.05	3.28	1.4	2.83	1.3	0.33
Books written up	−2.05		222	.05	2.53	1.1	2.20	.98	0.31
Purpose		4.67	1	.05					
Advice sought		9.30	1	.005					

Source: Authors' compilation.
Note: Only differences significant at the 0.05 level or more are shown. Variables are ordered by effect size, with those having the largest effect size at the top

Table 7.2   **Results of Logistic Regression Analysis on the Two Compliance Groups**

Variable	Percentage Cases Classified Correctly	Chi Squared		N
		Model	Improvement	
Underdeclaration leads to profit	76.6	34.45***	34.45***	198
What friends say	82.8	50.71***	16.26**	198
Egoism	84.3	60.43***	9.71*	198
Attitude to evasion	83.3	65.50***	5.07*	198
Purpose of VAT	84.3	70.46***	4.61*	198

Source: Authors' compilation.
*$p < .05$; **$p < .001$; ***$p < .0001$

Discussion

Though these results are valuable, there are two obvious threats to the validity and generalizability of the findings. First, the response rate is poor and this raises concerns about the representativeness of the sample. Second, because all of our measures rely on self-report and we are dealing with sensitive issues, one needs to consider how valid the responses are. We believe that the similarity in responses of the late- and early-responders suggests that the sample is reasonably representative of VAT registered catering and flooring/furniture businesses in Britain as a whole. We also believe that the anonymity afforded people in this study means that the responses given are generally valid.

Studies in related areas, such as black labor market participation (Kazemier and van Eck 1992) and welfare and unemployment benefit fraud (van der Heijden et al. 2000), show that though questionnaire surveys do lead to an underestimate of the incidence of illegal behaviors, the extent of this underestimation depends to a considerable extent on the particular method used. Face-to-face questioning leads to much more underestimation than those methods which guarantee the anonymity of the respondent. Recent research into taxation in Australia also suggests that well-designed surveys into tax compliance provide high-quality information (see, for example, Mearns and Braithwaite 2001). Although some of the respondents may well have minimized their participation in VAT evasion and it is clear that the self-report measures are not perfect, we are confident that the noncompliant group is more noncompliant than the compliant group. From a methodological point of view it is encouraging that adding a number of compliance-related (but less sensitive) questions to the single straightforward self-report question produced an index which turns out to be predictable from our independent measures.

A further issue that needs to be borne in mind is the correlational nature of the data used in this and the next study. Whilst we have written about predicting noncompliance, this does not imply that factors such as inequity necessarily cause noncompliance. It is possible that other factors produce noncompliance and that an individual reports that taxation is unfair as a way of justifying their own behavior.

Study 3: Equity and Mental Accounting Survey

The final study had three objectives. First, to replicate the findings of study 2 particularly in respect of equity, second, to improve the measurement of mental accounting, and finally to investigate the role of factors not included in study 2.

Method

The sample was randomly drawn from the same list as in study 2. From this it was noted that Group A (recently set-up businesses, not yet audited) was different from the others, with a lower response rate. Therefore, this group was dropped from the sample. One thousand businesses were randomly selected from Group B (compliant) and another one thousand were randomly selected from Groups C and D to form the noncompliant group.

To increase the response rate, the questionnaire was given the title "Official Bodies and Small Businesses." It was also redesigned to include sections on small business views on official bodies (HM Customs and Excise, Inland Revenue and Health and Safety Executive, the regulatory body responsible for almost all the risks to health and safety arising from work activity in Britain).

General Information

This section covered demographic variables, such as age, gender, business type, turnover, and length of time in business.

Views on Official Bodies

There were five questions in this section requesting information about administration, flexibility of the three official bodies, their approachability, and one question asking to place them in order of their level of negative impact on their business.

HM Customs and Excise

This section had seventeen questions. Some were related to administration and paperwork, and were included so as to disguise the real purpose of the questionnaire. The questions designed to measure mental accounting were:

- "When I send my cheque off to Customs and Excise I think of the money as coming from my business funds."
- "If VAT rates were to increase in the future I would change my prices accordingly."
- "If VAT rates were to decrease in the future I would change my prices accordingly."
- "When I balance my books and bank the income I mentally allow for the 17.5 percent VAT to be deducted."
- "If you ever found yourself in a situation where it was difficult to raise the necessary funds to pay your VAT to Customs and Excise, what do you think your thoughts would be? (Tick one).
  1. I'll ask for some leeway, I'm sure they'll be flexible.
  2. I'm very worried as I'm certain they won't be flexible.
  3. It wouldn't happen as the VAT money I collect does not belong to the business. It's always available to pass on to Customs and Excise.
  4. I'll not send in my return/VAT owed and hope I can gain some extra time.

A number of questions were included to enable us to produce a measure of self-reported compliance. Some had proved useful in study 2. Several new questions were added.

- "If you ever made an error on a VAT return, why do you think it occurred?" Answer categories:
  1. I have never made an error to my knowledge.
  2. Insufficient care due to time pressure.
  3. Desire to reduce liability.
  4. Insufficient knowledge of a particular area.
  5. Other (please state).

- "How often in the past five years have you been involved in cash transactions so as to reduce VAT payments?" Answer categories: often, sometimes, rarely, never.

- "If you had the opportunity to pay less VAT than you should do and you believed that there was absolutely no chance of being caught, would you do so?" Answer categories: certainly, probably, probably not, certainly not.

- "You read in the newspaper that a local businessman has been found guilty of defrauding Customs and Excise of £3,000 VAT monies owed. As a result, he has to repay the money and pay a fine. Which of the following statements most closely reflects your thoughts?

  1. Serves him right, after all, he did commit an illegal act.

  2. Poor thing, everyone does it but he was unfortunate to get caught.

  3. I'll be more careful in the future, I don't want to get caught like he did.

  4. He was very careless, it's easy to underreport and not get caught like he did.

Inland Revenue

These questions mirrored seven of those asked in the VAT section but related to income tax and the Inland Revenue. The general taxation section asked seven questions. Five focused on morality and citizenship and guilt and loss of freedom. The last two were intended for the formulation of the dependent variable:

- "Ben Jones purchased a vehicle which he stated was purely for the use of his business and reclaimed the appropriate tax (100 percent). However, Ben intended to use the vehicle for regular personal use. Do you consider this to be acceptable business practice?" Answer category: yes/no.

- "Bill West, who is self-employed, is completing his VAT return for the previous financial year. His turnover for the quarter was £16,700. £8,125 of this was paid in cash and no invoices were issued. He is debating whether to report all of the cash portion of his income. If he only reports half of the cash amount, he would save himself about £710 VAT for this quarter. If faced with this situation would you underreport your income?" Answer categories: certainly, probably, probably not, certainly not.

The health and safety executive section asked nine questions about the administration required, effectiveness, and flexibility of this organization. A questionnaire was sent to each sample business with a covering letter stating that the Economic Psychology Group at the University of Exeter was interested in business people's views about official bodies. The letter informed them that their business had been selected as part of a representative sample and any information given would be anonymous and confidential. As in study 2, replies were date stamped as they arrived to enable a comparison of early and late responders.

Results

In the representative checks, no significant differences emerged between the late responders and early responders. The final number of questionnaires received was 221, which equates to a crude response rate of 11 percent. However, given the annual deregistration rate, it is probable that approximately 770 of the businesses on the address file are unlikely to be active. The final response rate is more accurately assessed at 18 percent. Catering businesses were less compliant on the Customs and Excise rating variable of objective compliance ($\chi2 = 7.74$; d.f. = 1; $p < .001$), more likely to be run by younger people (t = 2.48, d.f. = 183; $p < .05$), more likely to consider that small businesses carry an unfair VAT burden (t = 2.39; d.f. = 181; $p < .05$); less likely to believe that the VAT system is fair (t = 1.98; d.f. = 182; $p < .05$). Catering businesses would also be less likely to apply any decrease in VAT to their prices (t = 2.32; d.f. = 183; $p < .05$).

Three-quarters of the respondents (N = 166) were male and by far the vast majority of respondents were between the ages of thirty-six and sixty-five (86 percent). Only two respondents (1 percent) were aged less than twenty-five and only sixteen were above the standard retirement age of sixty-five (7 percent). Turnover varied from under £30,000 a year to over £500,000 with 50 percent of respondents falling between £81,000 and £300,000. 70 percent of the respondents had been in operation for at least thirteen years.

With respect to the question "when I send my cheque off to Customs and Excise I think of the money as coming from my business funds," seventy-nine respondents (36 percent) strongly agreed.

To the question "If you have ever made an error on a VAT return, why do you think it occurred?" the following responses were made:

I have never made an error to my knowledge (N = 87; 39 percent)

Insufficient care due to time pressure (N = 84; 38 percent)

Desire to reduce liability (N = 4; 2 percent)

Insufficient knowledge of a particular area (N = 36; 16 percent)

Other (most in this category stated that an accountant completed returns) (N = 9; 4 percent)

On being asked if they had been involved in cash transactions to reduce VAT payments in the past five years, 60 percent reported that they
had not. Most (52 percent) claimed that they would not pay less VAT
than they should even if there was absolutely no chance of getting
caught. Again, in response to the Bill West scenario, most (74 percent)
claimed that if faced with this situation they would probably or certainly
not underreport your income.

Noncompliance Prediction

Two dependent measures were used. The first, the objective measure, is
the compliance grouping given by Customs and Excise, which in this
study has been dichotomized into compliers and noncompliers. The second measure was a self-reported measure and was constructed using a
variety of questions and using the same procedure (homogeneity analysis) as in study 2. The final solution used the variables:

> (HQ1) "How often in the past five years have you been involved in
> cash transactions so as to reduce VAT?" Answer categories: (very) of-
> ten, sometimes, rarely, never.

> (HQ2) "If you had the opportunity to pay less VAT than you should
> do and you believed that there was absolutely no chance of getting
> caught, would you do so?" Answer categories: certainly, probably,
> probably not, certainly not.

> (HQ3) "You read in a newspaper that a local businessman has been
> found guilty of defrauding Customs and Excise of £3000 of VAT monies
> owed. As a result, he has to repay the money and pay a fine. Which of
> the following statements most closely reflects your thoughts?"

> (HQ4) Bill West . . . . is debating whether to report all of the cash por-
> tion of his income. If he only reports half of the cash amount, he
> would save himself about £710 VAT for the quarter.

As in study 2, an index was constructed by points: four points for answering (very) often, two for answering sometimes, and one for answering rarely on HQ1; four points for answering certainly and two for answering probably on HQ2; four points for answering "Poor thing,
everyone does it but he was unfortunate to get caught," two points for
answering "I'll be more careful in future, I don't want to get caught like
he did," and two for "He was very careless, it's easy to underreport and
not get caught like he did" on HQ3; six points for answering certainly and
probably and three points for answering probably not on HQ4 and then
summing. The resulting compliance score is very highly correlated with
the HOMALS score ($r = .90$). To further contrast the groups into self-reported compliers and self-reported noncompliers, only those with a

score of zero (compliers) or more than six (noncompliers) were used for the analysis. The dependent measure had a final count of fifty-three compliers and ninety-two noncompliers.

Self-Reported Compliance Prediction

Each variable (single item, correlation, or scale) was independently analyzed; the variables that proved to be significant in explaining differences in self-reported compliance behavior are listed. Table 7.3 presents all the variables on which the two groups differ significantly.

Compliers are more likely to feel guilty if they underpaid VAT and are less likely to consider the VAT monies they have collected as belonging to the business. They are more likely to believe that the paying of taxes is a moral responsibility of being a good citizen and are less inclined to believe that the VAT system is inequitable and less likely to dread inspections.

Self-Reported Compliance Multivariate Analysis

To test the extent to which all of the significant variables taken together can explain compliance behavior the data were analyzed by forward-step logistic regression. Results show that a model with three variables can correctly classify 74 percent of respondents. Each of these variables is also independently significant (see table 7.4). Thus, if we knew that a person dreaded inspections, felt guilty about not complying and believed that VAT was fair we could say, with a fair degree of certainty, that these people are likely to be compliers.

Objective Compliance

Very few significant results were found between compliers and noncompliers. Noncompliers are younger ($t = -2.63$; d.f = 217; $p < .01$), had been in business for less time ($t = -2.49$; d.f. = 217; $p < .05$), had a higher turnover ($t = 2.78$; d.f. = 210; $p < .01$), and are more likely to be female ($\chi2 = 6.8$; d.f. = 2; $p < .05$). There was no relationship between the objective rating of noncompliance as given by Customs and Excise and the constructed measure of self-reported noncompliance.

General Discussion

Taking all three studies together, it is clear that both mental accounting and equity are important factors in VAT compliance. And, as with income tax compliance, sanctions and punishments (deterrence), personality, and satisfaction with the tax authorities all play a role in VAT compliance.

Does this understanding of how those who comply with VAT regulations differ from those who do not, have any implications for the balance between income and consumption taxes? A number of authors have ar-

Table 7.3 Summary of Differences Between Self-Reported Compliers and Noncompliers

				Noncompliers		Compliers		
Variable	t	d.f.	p <	Mean	Standard Deviation	Mean	Standard Deviation	Effect Size
Guilt	6.40	142	.001	5.11	2.5	7.69	1.8	1.12
Morality	5.10	138	.001	12.46	3.5	15.44	2.9	0.90
Mental accounting	-3.52	142	.001	6.80	2.6	5.15	2.9	0.60
Equity	-3.02	131	.005	14.02	3.9	11.84	3.9	0.60
Dread inspection	-2.50	142	.05	5.64	2.8	4.49	2.4	0.40

Source: Authors' compilation.
Note: Only differences significant at the 0.05 level or more are shown. Variables are ordered by effect size, with those having the largest effect size at the top.

Table 7.4   Results of Logistic Regression Analysis on the Two Compliance Groups

	Percentage Cases Classified	Chi Squared		
Variable	Correctly	Model	Improvement	N
Dread inspections	64.8	16.23***	16.23***	198
Guilt	68.7	28.52***	12.30***	198
Equity	74.2	44.77***	16.25***	198

Source: Authors' compilation.
*p < .05; **p < .001; ***p < .0001

gued (from different perspectives) that a switch toward retail sales taxes might actually increase the amount of tax evasion. Matthew Murray (1997), for example, argues that there might well be increased opportunities for evasion in a high-rate indirect tax system. James Hines (2004), points out that if illegal output is more labor intensive than legitimate activity (as seems plausible), replacing an income tax with a sales tax actually stimulates the growth in criminal and underground economic activity. Our data suggest that VAT systems might be prone to particular compliance problems relative to income tax systems. Taxpayers are very concerned with fairness, and it is certainly harder to achieve horizontal equity with a VAT system. Whether one's income is high or low, the VAT rate is the same. It is possible to operate different bands (and to zero rate certain goods and services) but these adjustments can only be fairly crude. But it is our view what matters is the particular realization of an income or consumption tax and it is not sensible to deal with this issue on an abstract basis. For example, it is possible to evade VAT by paying for a service in cash. This is quite common in the UK and in Italy where plumbers and electricians will often offer a householder the choice of paying in cash (for a lower rate) or paying by cheque (for a higher rate that includes VAT). But in the UK it is only the seller who is breaking the law, whereas in Italy the buyer of the service can also be prosecuted. This sort of operational detail can obviously have a major impact on compliance rates.

We have provided some empirical evidence on what differentiates VAT compliers from noncompliers, but though these kinds of empirical generalities may be useful, we are unlikely to make progress in understanding tax compliance unless we can develop better theories. We therefore conclude with an attempt at combining two recent models, the ATO Compliance model (Braithwaite 2003) and the Willing–Being Able–Daring model [WBAD] (Elffers 2000) described in the introduction. Both, though providing a useful framework for understanding, have limitations. For example, the WBAD is a static model, describing broad categories of taxpayers but saying nothing about how people move from being unwilling to evade to being willing to evade. The ATO model concentrates on the tax authorities and, though it does consider the role of taxpayers, focuses primarily on enforcement. By combining the WBAD and ATO Compliance models and considering the potential dynamics of taxpayer behavior, it is possible to create a hierarchical model that may have some merit (see figure 7.1).

The model in figure 7.1 looks at the classification of taxpayers and the tax authorities, suggesting which strategy the authorities should employ depending on a person's willingness, ability, and daring. It also includes the notion that people can move from one approach to evasion to another.

Level 1: Not Willing or Self-Regulation

Personality is likely to place a person on a particular level. If a person is community focused, he or she is likely to be compliant. For such individuals no action would be necessary. However, others may be unwilling to engage in noncompliance for other reasons. Minimizing noncompliance would involve the authorities in communicating information to taxpayers and educating taxpayers so that they understand that most people think it is wrong to engage in tax evasion, the real extent of tax fraud, and (in the UK at least) that VAT is general purpose tax. If taxpayers have been on a higher level but have since moved down one or more because of the actions of the tax authorities, it is likely that a higher level regulation strategy would be required to keep them from moving up the levels again.

Level 2: Willing but Not Able or Enforced Self-Regulation

It is important that those on the willing but not able level are not given any opportunities to engage in noncompliance. Here the major focus has to be on encouraging them to move down to level 1. This group may benefit from a promotion of good citizenship and being informed of the advantages of being VAT registered. They need to understand that the authorities are making efforts—for example, by closing loopholes that only larger businesses are able to exploit—to make the tax system as fair as possible. The authorities should use record-keeping reviews and real-time business examination so that their monitoring activities are very visible to the taxpayer.

Level 3: Willing and Able but Not Daring or Enforced
Self-Regulation

Members of this group are very clearly potential evaders but do not dare to break the law. So for this group, it is essential to emphasize the risks of

Figure 7.1   Tax Compliance Model of Taxpayer and Tax Regulator

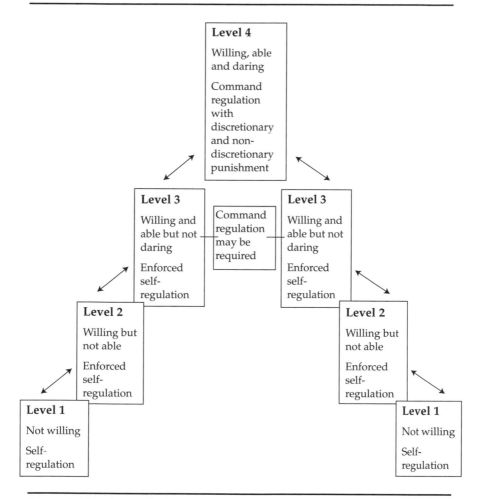

Source: Authors' compilation.

noncompliance. These should include reputational risks as well as financial ones. The authorities will need to use the full range of their repertoire of monitoring activities, which might include unannounced visits or probing inquiries by letter in order to convey the message that they are keeping a close eye on these individuals. This group would also benefit from communicating evidence that evasion is not widespread and that it is generally seen as unacceptable, as this would undermine their willingness to evade.

Level 4: Willing, Able, and Daring or Command
Regulation with Discretionary and Nondiscretionary
Punishment

Because members of this group will take any opportunity to evade taxes, it is necessary to closely monitor them and impose penalties until their behavior changes. Whether long-term evaders can be persuaded by educative and informative measures is doubtful, and so these people should be targeted for command regulation. Punishment should be decided on a case-by-case basis, but they need to be justified, as Brehm and Brehm (1981) found that citizens who feel that the level of punishment is unjustified can display reactance. A study by Williams (2001) suggests that this may have been a factor in his findings that people who had previously been fined for not lodging a tax return had significantly lower lodgement rates in the following few years than those with lower fines.

Although this model is obviously still very descriptive, it is nonetheless able to integrate the roles of the taxpayer and the tax authorities. What is needed to take this area forward is a more formalized dynamic model that does justice to the social, economic, and psychological complexity of VAT compliance, and makes clear predictions. We also need a behavioral economic approach that acknowledges that businesses are organizations rather than individuals and need therefore to be understood and treated differently.

Some of the research reported in this paper was commissioned and funded by HM Customs and Excise. We would like to thank them for all their support and particularly Nigel Froggatt and Alan Lee for their interest and practical help.

Part of the work for this paper was carried out when the first author was a research visitor successively at the Center for Economic Research, University of Tilburg and the International Centre for Economic Research, Turin, and he is very grateful for their hospitality and use of their facilities.

Note

1. The equity variable consisted of two variables: "VAT is levied fairly over the whole range of businesses" and "Small business carry an unfair burden when it comes to VAT" ($r = .26$, $p < .001$).

References

Adams, Caroline J. 1996. "Satisfaction with the Tax Authorities and Propensity to Avoid Taxes." MSc dissertation, University of Exeter.

————. 2002. "The Economic Psychology of VAT Compliance." PhD dissertation, University of Exeter.

Adams, Caroline J., and Paul Webley. 1996. "The Role of Economic and Psychological Variables in Parking Violations." *Psychology, Crime and Law* 3(2): 111–33.

————. 2001. "Small Business Owners' Attitudes on VAT Compliance in the UK." *Journal of Economic Psychology* 22(2): 195–216.

Agha, Ali, and Jonathan Haughton. 1996. "Designing VAT Systems: Some Efficiency Considerations." *Review of Economics and Statistics* 78(2): 303–8.

Allingham, Michael G., and Agnar Sandmo. 1972. "Income Tax Evasion: A Theoretical Analysis." *Journal of Public Economics* 1(3/4): 323–38.

Andreoni, James, Brian Erard, and Jonathan Feinstein. 1998. "Tax Compliance." *Journal of Economic Literature* 36(2): 818–60.

Braithwaite, Valerie. 2003. "A New Approach to Tax Compliance." In *Taxing Democracy: Understanding Tax Avoidance and Evasion*, edited by Valerie Braithwaite. London: Ashgate.

Brehm, Sharon, and Jack W. Brehm. 1981. *Psychological Reactance: A Theory of Freedom and Control*. New York: Academic Press.

Cnossen, Sijbren. 1981. "The Netherlands." In *The Value Added Tax: Lessons from Europe*, edited by Henry J. Aaron. Washington, D.C.: Brookings Institution Press.

————. 1998. "VAT in CEE [Central and Eastern European] Countries: A Survey and Analysis." *De Economist* 146(2): 227–55.

Cohen, Jacob. 1977. *Statistical Power Analysis for the Behavioural Science*. Rev. ed. New York: Academic Press.

Cowell, Frank. 1992. "Tax Evasion and Inequity." *Journal of Economic Psychology* 13(4): 521–43.

Cullis, John, Philip Jones, and Oliver Morrisey. 1993. "The Charge of the Tax Brigade: A Case Study of Government Failure and Tax Reforms." *European Journal of Political Economy* 9(3): 407–25.

Duverne, Denis. 1990. "Coordinate Audits of Income Tax and VAT." Paper presented at the Conference on Administrative Aspects of a Value-Added Tax. Washington, D.C., October.

Elffers, Henk. 1991. *Income Tax Evasion: Theory and Measurement*. Amsterdam: Kluwer.

————. 2000. "But Taxpayers Do Cooperate!" In *Cooperation in Modern Society: Promoting the Welfare of Communities, States, and Organizations*, edited by Mark van Vugt, Anders Biel, Mark Snyder, and Tom Tyler. London: Routledge.

Glaser, Barney, and Anselm Strauss. 1967. *The Discovery of Grounded Theory*. Chicago: Aldine.

Greenberg, Joseph. 1984. "Avoiding Tax Avoidance: A (Repeated) Game Theoretic Approach." *Journal of Economic Theory* 32(1): 1–13.

Hessing, Dick J., Henk Elffers, Henry S. J. Robben, and Paul Webley. 1992. "Does Deterrence Deter? Measuring the Effect of Deterrence on Tax Compliance in Field Studies and Experimental Studies." In *Why People Pay Taxes: Tax Compliance and Enforcement*, edited by Joel Slemrod. Ann Arbor: University of Michigan Press.

————. 1993. "Needy or Greedy? The Social Psychology of Individuals Who

Fraudulently Claim Unemployment Benefits." *Journal of Applied Social Psychology* 23(3): 226–43.

Hessing Dick J., Henk Elffers, and Russell H. Weigel. 1988. "Research in Tax Resistance: An Integrative Theoretical Scheme for Tax Evasion Behavior." In *Applied Behavioral Economics*, vol. 2, edited by Shlomo Maital. New York: New York University Press.

Hines, James R., Jr. 2004. "Might Fundamental Tax Reform Increase Criminal Activity?" *Economica* 71(283): 483–92.

Kazemier, Brugt, and Rob van Eck. 1992. "Survey Investigations of the Hidden Economy: Some Methodological Results." *Journal of Economic Psychology* 13(4): 569–88.

Kelman, Herbert C. 1965. "Manipulation of Human Behaviour: An Ethical Dilemma for the Social Scientist." *Journal of Social Issues* 21(2): 31–46.

Lewis, Alan. 1982. *The Psychology of Taxation*. Oxford: Martin Robertson.

Mearns, Malcolm, and Valerie Braithwaite. 2001. "The Community Hopes, Fears and Actions Survey: Survey Method, Sample Representativeness and Data Quality." Centre for Tax System Integrity Working Paper 4. Canberra: Australian National University.

Murray, Matthew N. 1997. "Would Tax Evasion and Tax Avoidance Undermine a National Retail Sales Tax?" *National Tax Journal* 50(1): 167–82.

Myles, Gareth D., and Robin A. Naylor. 1996. "A Model of Tax Evasion with Group Conformity and Social Customs." *European Journal of Political Economy* 12(1): 49–66.

Oppenheim, Abraham N. 1992. *Questionnaire Design, Interviewing and Attitude Measurement*. London: Pinter.

Strauss, Anselm. 1987. *Qualitative Analysis for Social Scientists*. New York: Cambridge University Press.

Strauss, Anselm, and Juliet Corbin. 1990. *Basics of Qualitative Research: Grounded Theory Procedures and Techniques*. London: Sage Publications.

———. 1994. "Grounded Theory Methodology: An Overview." In *Handbook of Qualitative Research*, edited by Norman K. Denzin and Yvonna S. Lincoln. London: Sage Publications.

Thaler, Richard. 1999. "Mental Accounting Matters." *Journal of Behavioral Decision Making* 12(3): 183–206.

van de Geer, John P. 1993a. *Multivariate Analysis of Categorical Data: Theory*. Newbury Park, Calif.: Sage Publications.

———. 1993b. *Multivariate Analysis of Categorical Data: Applications*. Newbury Park, Calif.: Sage Publications.

van der Heijden, Peter G. M., Ger van Gils, Jan Bouts, and Joop J. Hox. 2000. "A Comparison of Randomized Response, Computer-Assisted Self-Interview, and Face-to-Face Direct Questioning: Eliciting Sensitive Information in the Context of Welfare and Unemployment Benefit." *Sociological Methods and Research* 28(4): 505–37.

Vogel, Joachim. 1974. "Taxation and Public Opinion in Sweden: An Interpretation of Recent Survey Data." *National Tax Journal* 27(4): 499–513.

Wallschutzky, Ian G. 1984. "Possible Causes of Tax Evasion." *Journal of Economic Psychology* 5(4): 371–84.

Wärneryd, Karl Erik, and Bengt Walerud. 1982. "Tax and Economic Behavior:

Some Interview Data on Tax Evasion in Sweden." *Journal of Economic Psychology* 2(3): 187–211.

Wearing, Alexander J., and Bruce A. Headey. 1997. "The Would-Be Tax Evader: A Profile." *Australian Tax Forum* 13(1): 3–17.

Webley, Paul. 2004. "Tax Compliance by Businesses." In *New Perspectives on Economic Crime*, edited by Hans Sjögren and Göran Skogh. Cheltenham: Edward Elgar.

Webley, Paul, Caroline J. Adams, and Henk Elffers. 2002. "VAT Compliance in the United Kingdom." Centre for Tax System Integrity Working Paper 41. Canberra: Australian National University.

Webley, Paul, Michaela Cole, and Ole-Petter Eidjar. 2001. "The Prediction of Self-Reported and Hypothetical Tax-Evasion: Evidence from England, France and Norway." *Journal of Economic Psychology* 22(2): 141–55.

Webley, Paul, Henry S. J. Robben, Henk Elffers, and Dick J. Hessing. 1991. *Tax Evasion: An Experimental Approach*. Cambridge: Cambridge University Press.

Weigel, Russell H., Dick J. Hessing, and Henk Elffers. 1987. "Tax Evasion Research: A Critical Appraisal and Theoretical Model." *Journal of Economic Psychology* 8(2): 215–35.

———. 1998. "Egoism: Concept, Measurement and Implications for Deviance." *Psychology, Crime and Law* 5(4): 449–78.

Williams, Robert. 2001. "Prosecuting Non-Lodgers: To Persuade or Punish?" Centre for Tax System Integrity Working Paper 12. Canberra: Australian National University.

Winnett, Adrian, and Alan Lewis. 1995. "Household Accounts, Mental Accounts, and Savings Behaviour: Some Old Economics Rediscovered?" *Journal of Economic Psychology* 16(3): 431–48.

Yeh, Chang-mei. 1997. "On the Reform of Mainland China's Value Added Tax System." *Issues and Studies* 33(1): 64–86.

Chapter 8

Trust and Taxation

TERRENCE CHORVAT

O NE of the perennial questions in the literature on tax compliance
is what causes people to pay taxes (see Slemrod 1992). This question arises because, if one applies standard game theory or almost any rational choice approach to the problem of tax compliance, the
level of the penalties and enforcement that we see in the United States
would appear to be insufficient to explain the degree of compliance with
the tax laws that we observe.[1] As discussed earlier in this volume, for the
level of compliance that we observe to occur, one or more of the assumptions of these models is likely to be incorrect.[2]

In this chapter I argue that one cannot analyze tax avoidance or evasion as entirely divorced from other activities. Individuals are not merely
taxpayers. They are also citizens who engage in income and wealth producing activities. A variety of psychological influences arising from an
array of sources affect their behavior. People pay taxes for a variety of
reasons including: a sense of honesty, fear, a sense of group membership,
and the like (see Alm, McClelland, and Schulze 1992). These activities
both affect and are affected by decisions about complying with the tax
system. To the extent that honestly paying taxes affects other economic
behavior, an important issue to consider is the role that tax compliance
plays in fostering overall higher levels of trust in society. This chapter
synthesizes the theoretical and empirical evidence and proposes a model
that helps to analyze many of the observed effects of the tax enforcement
system on the economy and how this should be accounted for in designing the optimal tax structure.

Both standard neoclassical models and a fair amount of empirical evidence (Andreoni, Erard, and Feinstein 1998) indicate that higher levels
of fines as well as a greater probability of detection of evasion are associ-

ated with higher levels of compliance (though as discussed earlier, the magnitudes of these responses are less than one might predict based on standard models) (Alm, Jackson, and McKee 1992). However, these results conflict with empirical evidence that in similar situations monitoring the effort exerted in employment contracts and similar agreements may cause compliance with an agreement to decrease. Later we discuss how institutions frame the decision can help explain this difference.

It is difficult to draw firm conclusions from the econometric work on tax compliance. This is in part a function of the fact that it is very difficult to quantify the amount of tax evasion actually occurring. Here I discuss how issues such as self-serving biases of both taxpayers and government agents make the interpretation of much of the econometric evidence opaque. Partially as a result of this opacity, economic experiments to help to understand the underlying decision processes have become standard. I address some of the more prominent findings.

Evidence of the timeliness of this issue—as reported in *Tax Notes Today* on May 10, 2004, in the article "Olson: Increased Enforcement Might Erode Taxpayer Trust"—can be seen in IRS Commissioner Everson's recent attempts to increase the level of IRS enforcement exercised, principally the audit rate. He stated that the attempts of the last few years of reducing enforcement and the creation of a "kinder, gentler" IRS were incorrect. Although it is hard to argue against the idea that people ought to be more honest and pay their taxes, the methods by which this should be accomplished is less clear.

Standard Neoclassical Theory of Compliance

Here we review the standard neoclassical models of tax compliance and discuss some of their limitations. One of the primary predictions of the standard economic models is that increasing the level of audits or penalties should increase compliance.

The Provision of Public Goods

The provision of public goods has been one of the key problems in economics since its inception (Smith 1776/1994, 779). In the *Logic of Collective Action* (1965), Mancur Olson describes the fundamental problem with public goods. Olson discusses how "rational" individuals will not voluntarily contribute to collective goods unless the group is quite small, because only then does the benefit of contributing exceed its cost. This notion has become generalized, and can be viewed as a form of n-person prisoner's dilemma—along the lines of Garrett Hardin's tragedy of the commons (1968). This analysis forms the basis of a utilitarian argument for coercive taxation (Posner 1983). Even if the tax law requires a particular contribution, because such laws are not self-enforcing, the method of enforcing compliance with the law becomes an important element of the structure of tax law.

Tax Compliance Models

To simplify analysis of the standard neoclassical model of tax compliance, we assume that the only purpose of taxes is to provide resources to enable the government to supply public goods. It is important to define the term tax precisely. For this chapter, the term is used to mean amounts collected by a governmental body from individuals to whom there has been no direct transfer of goods or services in connection with these collections and not the result of a criminal penalty (see Shaviro 2004).

Allingham-Sandmo-Yitzhaki Model

The seminal work in the area of tax compliance is a paper by Michael Allingham and Agnar Sandmo (1972) in which they proposed a model of the tax compliance decision based on fairly standard economic assumptions.[3] Given that individuals will have an incentive to retain as much of their wealth as possible, the question then becomes how the decision of whether to cheat will be made. Under the Allingham and Sandmo model, the analysis of how one chooses whether to pay tax or to cheat on one's taxes is based on an expected utility function. Under standard expected utility theory,[4] the form the utility function takes is: $\sum_i p_i u(x_i)$, where x_i's are various states of the world, $u(x_i)$ is the utility in that state of the world and p_i is the probability of that state of the world.[5] In the simple case, the decision of whether to cheat on one's taxes is based on the probability of detection and likely fine if caught. The standard version of the Allingham-Sandmo model examines the payment of income taxes; however, the same framework can be modified for use with the payment of other taxes. Under the Allingham-Sandmo model, the decision can be framed as maximizing expected utility where expected utility (EU) is equal to:

$$(1 - p)U(y(1 - t) + t(y - x)) + pU(y(1 - t) - f(y - x)),$$

where p is the probability of detection, y is pre-tax income, $y(1 - t)$ is true after-tax income, x is the amount of income reported to the government, therefore y-x is unreported income, and U represents a standard utility function. This model states that the individual's expected utility is the utility of the individual if audited multiplied by the probability of being audited plus individual's utility if not audited multiplied by the probability of not being audited (essentially the expected value of the individual's utility).

The predictions of this model will depend on the probability of detection, p, and the amount of the penalty, f. Under standard optimizing assumptions, the taxpayer will chose to report income such that:

$$\frac{U'(y_A)}{U'(y_B)} = \frac{t(1-p)}{pf},$$

where y_A is the amount of income in the state of being audited and y_B is income in the state where the taxpayer successfully evades taxes. Each dollar of understatement then increases the argument of the utility function in state A by t, and decreases it in state B by f. Under this model, and only if $(1-p)t - pf$ is positive, every risk-averse taxpayer will engage in some evasion. In many ways this is analogous to portfolio choice problem.[6]

Shlomo Yitzhaki (1974) introduced a slight modification to this model by pointing out that under most tax systems the penalty is not based on the amount of unreported income, but rather on the amount of tax unpaid. The maximand would become:

$$(1-p)U(y(1-t) + t(y-x)) + pU(y(1-t) - tf(y-x))$$

and the expected payoff per dollar of unreported income becomes:

$$(1-p)t - pft.$$

Under this change, the tax rate has no effect on the terms of the tax evasion gamble, because it appears on both sides of the equation and so drops out. The first order condition then becomes:

$$\frac{U'(y_A)}{U'(y_B)} = \frac{(1-p)}{pf}.$$

In the case of risk neutral taxpayers, they should almost always choose a corner solution of either complete compliance or reporting zero income, depending on the relative probabilities and penalties. Because this rarely happens, it would therefore appear that individuals are risk averse, or that the probability of being audited is dependent on the amount of income reported, or some assumptions of the model is violated, or some combination of these.

*Risk Aversion, Imperfect Information, Ambiguity, and
Other Modifications*

An important feature of the standard economic models is the notion that individuals are averse to penalties. As mentioned, risk aversion would seem to help to explain some of the compliance behavior. However, as

Lars Feld and Bruno Frey (2002) indicate, risk aversion alone does not appear to explain the level of compliance we observe. They argue that the coefficient of risk aversion[7] would have to be many times higher than we observe to explain the high levels of compliance, hence the standard models do not serve us.[8] One possible addition to the model is that unaccounted-for penalties such as prison or social sanctions that follow from being discovered as having cheated on your taxes, are viewed as so undesirable that even a small increase in the risk might prevent one from trying to do so.[9] However, it seems likely that most taxpayers would not seriously fear prison for relatively small acts of evasion, nor do most people even know if those with whom they deal have been found guilty of it. Furthermore, such explanations have a deus ex machina feel to them, because it is difficult to quantify the value of social sanctions, and therefore difficult to test any model based on them.

Another possible addition to the model is the endogenous determination of audit probability. In particular, it seems reasonable to assume that the probability of detection of evasion is monotonically increasing in the amount of unreported income. This can be modeled as increasing the probability either as a function of the amount of income not reported $(p = F(y - x))$ or of tax evaded $p = F(t(y - x))$, or a percentage of income not reported $(p = F((y - x)/y)$. Depending on the shape of this function, it may introduce many of the same considerations as risk aversion. This is to say that it may help to explain why evasion does not reach the predicted levels. Significantly, the Allingham-Sandmo model does seem to give the correct predictions in that cheating appears to be much more prevalent among those who have a greater ability to cheat (see TCMP study in IRS 1996). Furthermore, as Joel Slemrod (2003) notes, a fair amount of income is subject to automatic reporting, and therefore the simple argument about the invalidity of the Allingham-Sandmo is itself incorrect. However, even though approximately 75 percent of individuals' income is subject to automatic reporting, the TCMP report states that over 91.7 percent of these amounts are reported accurately (Andreoni, Erard, and Feinstein 1998). In addition, given that audit rates are so low (approximately 1 to 2 percent), endogenous audit probability likely does not realistically explain the level of compliance we find in areas such as the overstatement of deduction, which nearly all taxpayers could in principle be engaged.[10] Therefore, even based on TCMP estimates, approximately 67 percent of gross receipts not directly reported to the government are reported accurately (see Andreoni, Erard, and Feinstein 1998). Therefore, although the numbers for self-reported income are less dramatic than those often used to argue against the Allingham-Sandmo model, the simpler versions of this model are still inadequate to explain the level of compliance observed. In addition, a key prediction of the simplest forms of the Allingham-Sandmo model would be that as long as the expected value of evasion is positive, all taxpayers should cheat to some degree. However, even using the TCMP numbers, more than two-thirds of taxpayers in fact attempt to pay their taxes honestly (Andreoni, Erard, and Feinstein 1998).

Almost paradoxically, endogenous determination of the probability of audit may actually increase the incentive to cheat on small amounts, because such cheating will almost certainly never be caught, assuming the probability of being audited is even lower for the many (those who cheat for small amounts) than it is for the few (who cheat for large amounts). Therefore, to the extent that audit probability depends on the level of unreported income, social norms enter the equations even for neoclassical models, because if others cheat, then likelihood of detection decreases, which in turn means that the incentive to cheat increases.[11] This is similar to the rational explanations for the otherwise anomalous behavior of players "offering" nontrivial amounts in ultimatum games.[12]

It is possible, even likely, that individuals overweight the probability of being audited. There are a variety of mechanisms by which this could occur. For example, Uzi Siegal and Avia Spivak (1990) discussed models in which the utility function is not differentiable for probabilities near certainty. In this case, one might prefer certainty to almost any gamble, even though the gamble had a very large positive expected utility. Another problem introduced by the complexity of the tax laws is that, to some extent, complying with the tax laws to the best of your ability still leaves you at risk because you may not thoroughly understand those laws. Even if you comply with them as you understand them, you may have misunderstood and thus be subject to a penalty. However, the level of this overweighting seems insufficient to explain the level of compliance observed (Alm, McClelland, and Schulze 1992). Therefore, it is not clear that the discontinuity near certain outcomes applies in a straightforward manner to tax compliance. Experiments indicate that overweighting does not seem to explain the level of compliance we observe (Alm, Jackson, and McKee 1992). Therefore, while the Allingham-Sandmo model is useful, it will need to be modified to explain taxpayer behavior in detail.

"Work or Shirk" and Portfolio Allocation{/B}

As discussed, the standard tax compliance analysis shares much with portfolio analysis and with Becker's crime model.[13] This same basic model of human behavior has also been used to analyze nearly any principal-agent situation. One such example is models of agency problems, in which wages are set at a certain amount unless the employees are caught shirking, in which case they are penalized. One can see the similarity if we try to formally model the objective function as:

$$EU = (1 - p)U(v + (h - e) + pU(v - \theta(h - e)),$$

where p is the probability of detection of shirking, v is the income from the salary and h is the promised level of effort and e is the actual level of effort, θ is the net penalty if caught shirking. The comparative statics of the problem of shirking and the tax compliance problem are almost precisely the same. In a fashion similar to the Allingham-Sandmo-Yitzhaki model, the worker will act so that:

$$\frac{U'(y_A)}{U'(y_B)} = \frac{(1-p)}{p\theta}.$$

One can argue that in the case of workers, they have promised either explicitly or implicitly, to perform a particular function, but in standard neoclassical economics this should not matter (Akerlof 1982; Fehr and Gächter 2000). As I will discuss shortly, the empirical evidence indicates that this model is incomplete in describing human motivation.

The Value of Models

Neither of these models predict certain important aspects of behavior they attempt to explain. If the models are correct in some of their predictions but incorrect in others, what is their value? Merely because a model does not perfectly predict what is occurring in all dimensions does not mean it is wrong. As Milton Friedman(1953) points out in his seminal "Methodology of Positive Economics," the usefulness of model is found in its predictive power concerning the relevant behavior, not whether it is able to predict all aspects of reality. In the case of the Allingham-Sandmo and related models, this usefulness is mixed. Many of the comparative static predictions of the model are correct: fines and audits do appear to increase tax compliance and those who have a greater ability to cheat are more likely to cheat. However, many of the specifics of the empirical predictions are not correct. The total level of compliance does not seem to be well predicted, nor is the behavior in economic experiments. Furthermore, as discussed earlier, one would expect from this model that all taxpayers should engage in some evasion, yet most apparently do not. Therefore, although the Allingham-Sandmo model is quite useful in many ways, it is clearly incomplete.

The Empirical Evidence

To the extent that standard models do give clear predictions, they indicate that, to increase compliance with the tax laws, the government must either increase fines or increase audit rates. Here we discuss the major empirical studies of how taxpayers respond to these incentives, both econometric and economic.

Econometric Evidence

Determining the effects of governmental action on tax compliance behavior is often quite difficult. By definition, it concerns hidden activity, in part because each taxpayer claims that he or she is paying the taxes owed, and in part because it often concerns activity about which reasonable minds disagree.

TCMP Study

The most comprehensive evidence of taxpayer compliance in the United States is that generated by Taxpayer Compliance Measurement Program, or TCMP (IRS, 2002). The most recent version of this study was published in 1996. That report surveyed data from 1985, 1988, and 1992 tax years. It reports the amounts of the so-called tax gap—the difference between reported and actual tax owed the federal government. TCMP members audited approximately 50,000 returns for each of the surveyed years. Because this survey was in fact based on examining actual returns and supporting information, it provided a much closer look at tax compliance behavior than nongovernmental studies have been able to do. This is clearly the most comprehensive survey of tax compliance available. The study found that approximately 83 percent of the taxes owed to the government were in fact voluntarily paid. Furthermore, it found that 91.7 percent of gross receipts were reported accurately.

This study is quite helpful in gauging many of the aspects of the tax compliance problem, and is often used as the basis for many estimates of how much revenue can be raised by increasing tax compliance. There are a number of problems, however, with the way the statistics are calculated that bias the numbers toward showing lower tax compliance, limiting its usefulness in predicting the magnitude of compliance (see Graetz and Wilde1985).

A close examination of the report reveals these problems. The study reports both high and low estimates for the amount of the tax gap in various categories. The high estimate results from findings of TCMP auditors, who audited approximately 50,000 randomly selected returns. Because even these audits might miss some income, the reported amounts are augmented by multiplying the amounts from standard TCMP audits by a factor derived from more strenuous audits of a randomly selected group. They found that for every dollar of unreported income the standard TCMP audit found another $2.28 could have been found with more strenuous audits. Because these more strenuous audits are thought to more accurately report the tax owed, the amounts reported are augmented to reflect these factors.

The report acknowledges that auditors may have self-serving biases, just as taxpayers do, and so therefore this report also includes a low estimate that factors in the probability that the amounts determined would not be sustained by a court. The low estimates are uniformly 97 percent of the high numbers, which the report says is based on the amounts collected in the appeal process and court.[14] For anyone who has practiced in the tax area, this number certainly seems too high, even given the constraints they put on it. Leaving that aside, the discount factor is derived from the percentage collected from all litigated tax cases. The majority of such cases, however, result not from random TCMP audits or even more from the strenuous audits, but instead from the audits conducted on the basis of an item that "flagged" the return for audit.

Hence the success rate is not from a random sample of audits that resulted in the calculation of the tax gap. It could easily be the case that this number is significantly higher than appropriate. In addition, it can also be that the numbers of final tax paid also do not necessarily reflect true tax because of the different incentives and bargaining power of the IRS and individual taxpayers.[15] There is an additional question of how much of the gap is due to evasion and how much to what one might call unsuccessful avoidance. That is, how much of this is as a result of positions taken by taxpayers in good faith, which are simply incorrect, and how much is due to simple negligence or legitimate differences of opinion. This is difficult to measure, as all commentators acknowledge. Although the TCMP study is useful for its intended purpose of helping to ensure consistency of audits, self-serving biases as well as other limitations on estimates make such surveys less useful in estimating the total level of compliance than they might first appear. The TCMP study is therefore likely to be an upper bound on the amount of the true tax gap for the standard, as opposed to the underground, economy, rather than a moderate estimate.

Prominent Empirical Studies

One can find more thorough reviews of econometric studies on tax compliance literature in the reviews of James Andreoni, Brian Erard, and Jonathan Feinstein (1998), and Joel Slemrod and Shlomo Yitzhaki (2002). There have been a number of very interesting studies of tax compliance, including those by Jeffrey Dubin and Louis Wilde (1988), Dubin, Michael Graetz, and Wilde (1987), and a variety by James Alm and Michael McKee, and many others.

An example of both the interesting results and the limitations of these studies, the 1987 study by Dubin, Graetz, and Wilde is worth examining. They studied data from the 1977 to 1986 tax years to estimate the impact of audit rates and tax rates on tax compliance and found that lower audit rates are correlated with lower reported income. Unfortunately, because they were not able to use any sort of random audit of the returns, they had to use proxies for noncompliance. In particular, they used tax collections and returns per capita as inverse measures of noncompliance. The authors noted that there are a number of possible endogeneity problems with these measures such as audit rates may be lower because there is lower income in these areas. In many ways, it is difficult to eliminate these problems because so many factors affect the production of income (see Andreoni, Erard, and Feinstein 1998). It is probably incorrect to treat the audit rate as a variable entirely independent of the factors related to higher or lower income.

An important question for this type of study is whether the public is aware of the audit rates in their local area. If not, we need some other explanation for the data, because some other factor is likely affecting the results. As discussed earlier, much of the population overestimates the probability of audit, indicating that they are not very aware of the audit rate. Most of the other major empirical studies suffer from similar endogeneity problems, but the particular problems of any study are often unique to its particular measure of noncompliance. Therefore, though these studies are quite helpful and suggestive, they unfortunately do not offer definitive proof that audit rates increase compliance or increased fines.

One of the most intriguing studies in this area was conducted by Andrew Cuccia (1994), who found that when tax preparer penalties increased, the CPAs who prepared the returns actually took more aggressive positions. Cuccia argued that this occurred because tax preparers saw these harsher rules as a threat to their autonomy. Unfortunately, the study does not examine other possible explanations, such as changes in compensation of the preparers and similar factors.[16]

Steven Sheffrin and Robert Triest (1992) argue that the attempts to increase audit rates can actually increase the aggressive positions taken.[17] Of course, any such reaction would be in contradiction to standard neoclassical analysis of the Allingham-Sandmo model. There are a variety of psychological models that could explain why this occurs. Feld and Frey (2002) argue that the manner of tax collection might be viewed as part of an implicit contract. Increased enforcement might be viewed as a breach of an implicit contract, because the terms of such a contract are always determined by use. In addition, an increase in enforcement is a one-sided transfer of costs to taxpayers or tax preparers. Whether or not the taxpayer is compliant, he or she now faces the risk of having to pay for an audit and the loss of time associated with an audit, and so forth, at a greater rate than expected. This imposition of costs by the government might give taxpayers an excuse for cheating.

Another interesting finding is the correlation between the receipt of benefits from the government and tax compliance. James Alm (1988) reported empirical evidence that payroll tax compliance in Jamaica for those who received payments from the system is much higher than those who did not receive benefits. Although this finding is not universal (see, for example, Kim 2002), because these are public goods in a large group, receipt of benefits should not matter under the Allingham-Sandmo model to the extent an effect is found in either direction, other factors must affect the tax compliance decision than are considered in the model.[18]

Minnesota State Tax "Field Experiment"

A fundamental problem with many econometric studies is they do not have control groups, though often this can be mitigated to some extent by sophisticated statistical techniques. Because of this, however, we can never be certain that the effects we observe are a function of the independent variables used, or some other variables that may be correlated with the independent variables. Fortunately, a controlled experiment with tax compliance occurred in the state of Minnesota which attempted to increase compliance with tax laws which allowed for a control group. A variety of approaches to increasing compliance were attempted, including appeals to group solidarity, reciprocity, and increases in audit rates, all aimed at different groups. A number of papers rely on or use the data from this experiment, including the official Minnesota Department of Revenue report (Coleman 1996) and a number of papers by Joel Slemrod, Marsha Blumenthal, and Charles Christian (see in particular 2001). Both the report and the papers come to similar conclusions.

Coleman's (1996) report found that increasing the audit rate for low and middle income taxpayers increased reported income. Both studies found that the increase in reported income was larger for those with business income, and other types of self-reported income. For high income taxpayers, Coleman's report found that there was no statistically significant effect on the reporting behavior of those with higher incomes.

Slemrod, Blumenthal, and Christian (2001) also found that the threat of certain audit produced an increase in reported income for low and middle income taxpayers. Under their analysis, for higher income taxpayers, the certainty of audit lowered the amount reported on their tax return. They argued that this might be because if the taxpayer knew there was going to be a conflict, these taxpayers viewed the amount reported on the tax return as an opening bid.[19] These papers are to some degree more convincing than much of the other empirical evidence because of the existence of control groups. However, it is unclear how robust these findings are to different kinds of changes such as what the effects of marginal increases in the audit rate, as opposed to moving the audit rate to 100 percent.

Evidence of Responses to Monitoring in Employment
Contracts

The same mathematical model that describes tax compliance could be altered slightly to describe any potential cheating situation, as discussed earlier. One of these, again, might include the decision to expend labor in an employment contract. Among the most famous investigations of the determinants of the work or shirk decision was made by George Akerlof (1982). In this study, he found that workers routinely gave more effort than required by their employers. This was particularly true if the employees had been paid a high wage relative to the market. Interestingly, the incentives in these contracts resulted in the employees being largely uncompensated for this additional effort. This runs contrary to the basic notions of standard neoclassical economics, under which workers exert the minimum effort necessary to obtain the desired reward. Akerlof argues that this research addresses how humans address concerns of loyalty and norms of how individuals behave in the particular groups. I will now address the issue of why this might apply more in the work setting than in the tax setting.[20] Because this study was limited to a relatively small group of workers, however, it is not clear how applicable these findings are generally.

Experimental Economic Evidence

The problems with the empirical evidence discussed are not unique to tax compliance. Any science that is entirely dependent on observation of uncontrolled situations that involve an enormous number of factors will always be at the mercy of chance observation. In response to problems such as these, beginning at least as far back as L. L. Thurstone in the 1930s and Edward Chamberlin in the 1940s, economists have attempted to create controlled experiments on small groups of individuals (see Ledyard 1995). These experiments are designed to test theoretical propositions of how individuals behave in particular situations.

Public Goods Games

To understand the experiments relating to the provision of public goods, one first needs to understand their basic structure. Public goods experiments are games in which individuals choose how to allocate their individual portfolios between private and public goods.[21] It is fairly standard in these experiments that an amount allocated to the public good will produce more good for the group as a whole than if retained by the individual.[22] On the other hand, from the individual's perspective, allocating to a public good will result in a lower private return holding the contributions of the others constant. Therefore, in these experiments, the optimal standard game theoretic strategy is to allocate the entire amount to the private good and none to the public, though from a group standpoint, everyone would be better off if each player contributed their entire portfolios to the public good. One can view this as an n-person prisoner's dilemma. As it turns out, neither of the corner solutions (full cooperation, zero cooperation) usually occurs.

Many authors have written summaries of the basic findings of public goods games. Examples include works by Charles Holt and Susan Laury (2005), John Ledyard (1995), and many others. In general, these works discuss the factors that are likely to increase investment in public goods experiments. One of the standard results is that there is significant cooperation initially that deteriorates in time, though level of cooperation does not generally ever reach zero. Among the most interesting findings are that face-to-face interactions increase cooperation, and it appears that allowing other players to decide whether to punish defectors seems to increase cooperation. It also seems that allowing the players to allocate public goods and to exclude noncooperators significantly increases cooperation. An intriguing result was found in an experiment (Andreoni, Erard, and Feinstein 1998) in which the experimenters allowed a public goods game to deteriorate to low levels of cooperation, then started a new game almost immediately with the same participants. In this case, they again observed significant contributions to in the first rounds of this second game. This behavior is anomalous under standard economic models.

One condition which significantly increased cooperation was revealed in an experiment by Anna Gunnthorsdottir and colleagues (2001; see also McCabe, Rigdon, and Smith 2004). In that experiment they paired cooperators and noncooperators together (matching cooperators with cooperators and noncooperators with noncooperators). They observed that they were able to maintain cooperation in the high cooperating groups and improve cooperation in the medium cooperating groups, with the result that overall cooperation was increased. Based on this experiment and others like it, one could argue for something like a Tiebout model of local governments catering to the level of cooperation sought by individuals.

In general, the experimental evidence shows that the institution involved can significantly affect the level of contribution to public goods, even if it does not necessarily affect the subgame perfect strategy. Indeed this influence can result in either allowing contributions to drop nearly to zero or to actually increase from their initial level. Another consistent finding in these experiments is that individuals are heterogeneous in their behavior. Conditional cooperators appear to comprise approximately 40 to 60 percent of the population (Ledyard 1995). The rest are divided between high cooperators and noncooperators. A consistent finding in experiments is that high cooperators will often exert resources to punish those who do not cooperate.

Tax Compliance Games

Another group of economic experiments have been framed explicitly as tax compliance experiments. These may result in the subjects bringing into the experiment preconceived notions about taxes and compliance with them and therefore may actually be more accurate indications of how individuals view tax payments. Of course, merely because a frame is given in an experiment does not mean the participants necessarily adopted it. We now look at some of the more prominent results from these experiments.

A number of experiments in the United States have attempted to discover the determinants of tax compliance. James Alm, Mark Cronshaw, and Michael McKee (1993) conducted several studies related to endogenous determination of audit probability. They found that endogenous audit rates generated compliance far better than random audits, even when the random rate was increased to 50 percent. In contradiction to these findings, Jeremy Clark, Laura Freisen, and Andrew Muller (2004) ran an experiment in which they found that random audit rates in fact produced the highest compliance. James Alm, Betty Jackson, and Michael McKee (1992) found that increasing audit rates increased compliance, but increasing fines did not. These studies taken together show that increased audit rates and penalties have at least a moderate positive effect on compliance. The Alm, Jackson, and McKee (1992) study also shows an increase in public goods provision increases tax compliance. Experimental evidence, and empirical evidence indicates that higher tax rates lead to higher amounts of evasion (Alm, McClelland, and Schulze 1992). Most of these studies show that increasing audit rates have more of an effect on tax compliance than does increasing the amount of the penalty.

A set of studies on the cross-cultural determinants of tax compliance was conducted by Ronald Cummings, Jorge Martinez-Vazquez, and Michael McKee (2001). Using individuals from the United States and a few African nations as subjects, they found that risk aversion in the culture did not predict the level of tax compliance. They also found that institutional factors such as political participation played a role in the willingness of individuals to comply with tax laws. It is not clear how these political factors affected the decision. One might explain this as the perception of a reciprocal arrangement, or that the individuals are loyal to the process for a variety of reasons.

James Alm, Isabel Sanchez, and Ana de Juan (1995) conducted a similar study, in which they examined the differences between United States taxpayers and Spanish taxpayers. Their findings included substantial heterogeneity in both populations and benefits to having positive rewards for greater compliance. Rates of elasticity were both fairly low—to fines of .04 and audit rate of .17.[23] They also found that when they introduced a public good to the experiment that was paid for out of the tax revenues, compliance increased, but not statistically significantly.

Trust Games

A related area of experimental work involves research on what are referred to as trust games. In standard two-player games, one party needs to rely on the behavior of the other party to increase the return for both. In most games, the first player extends a benefit to the second, at a cost to the first player. The second player can then reciprocate the first player's trust by sending some amount back to him. If the second player does not reciprocate, the first player is worse off than if he had done nothing. The subgame perfect strategy is for the first player to send nothing to the second. However, studies find that most first players will send something to second players, and most second players send amounts back.

One of the most interesting features of trust games is that, even though voluntary fulfillment of an agreement will yield lower initial levels of compliance than forced compliance, in later runs those who were not forced to comply had higher voluntary compliance than those who had been. There have been a number of experiments that indicate that externally imposed rules tend to "crowd out" endogenous cooperative behavior (Frey 1994). For example, Norman Frohlich and Joe Oppenheimer (1996) conducted an experiment on a variant of a prisoner's dilemma game. One set of subjects played a regular prisoner's dilemma game in which in some rounds players were allowed to communicate and in others they were not. A second set of subjects used an externally imposed, incentive-compatible mechanism designed to enhance cooperative choices. In the first phase of the experiment, the second set gained higher monetary returns than the control groups, as one would expect. In the second phase, both groups played a regular prisoner's dilemma game. The intriguing finding was that in the second round the control groups that played the regular prisoner's dilemma in both phases cooperated at a higher level, especially those who communicated on a face-to-face basis. The greater cooperation that had occurred due to the exogenously created incentive-compatible mechanism disappeared when that incentive was removed. As the authors put it, the removal of the external mechanism "seemed to undermine subsequent cooperation and leave the group worse off than those in the control group who had played a regular Prisoner's dilemma." Bruno Frey and colleagues Bohnet, Eichenberger, and Oberholzer-Gee had conducted an experiment with similar results in 1994 (see Frey 1997, 15). Follow-up studies with larger groups and other situations show similar findings (Frohlich and Oppenheimer 2003).

In a slightly different vein, Ernst Fehr and Simon Gächter (2000) conducted experiments similar to the partial-gift exchange situations Akerlof investigated (1982). In particular, they studied the effects of incentives contracts on actual performance by employees. Effort was not observable socially, and we can therefore abstract away criticisms of Akerlof's work based on this factor. As noted, from a neoclassical perspective, the decision in the tax compliance problem and in the partial gift exchange should be the same in these situations. The results appear sensitive to what would seem to be an innocuous condition, whether there is a specific schedule. It appears the amount contributed drops significantly if there is a specific schedule of benefits.

Two key distinctions between standard public goods experiments and work effort experiments are that in the latter there are both an increased personalization and potential increased social observability of effort. Furthermore, Feld and Frey's notion of implicit contract may play into this as well. If the government is viewed as simply imposing this tax, it might lead to lower compliance than if the taxpayer views compliance with the tax law as part of an implicit contract.

A key question is whether compliance with tax laws or cheating on taxes will spill over to other areas. Although no experiments have yet been conducted on any spill-over effects of the tax compliance decision, the experiments discussed and those similar to them indicate that such effects might occur. Some commentators have discussed this as a concern, that if large numbers of individuals begin to cheat on their taxes, they may begin to violate other laws. A number of experiments indicate that there are spill-over effects of trust and trustworthiness, as well as from one activity to another (Frey and Bohnet 1996). In general, they show that trust and trustworthiness in one area has effects on the trust and trustworthiness in other areas.

The Effect of Enforcement on Taxpayer Behavior

We have discussed the various types of evidence, both theoretical and empirical that address tax compliance problems. We have seen that though many studies indicate increasing audit rates and penalties will increase the rate of tax compliance, these effects are generally fairly small and sensitive to variety of institutional factors (elasticities of .1 for audits and .04 for fines; see Alm, McClelland, and Schulze 1992). As discussed, a fair amount of research in fact gives one reason to believe increasing penalties might actually decrease compliance for many taxpayers, particularly those who currently comply to a high degree (Feld and Frey 2002).

Inclusions of Standard Behavioral Economic Notions

As discussed, the standard neoclassical analysis only seems to allow for audits and fines as tools of compliance. It is clear that one can create models complex enough to explain almost any behavioral phenomenon. Interestingly, the addition of some standard behavioral analysis actually might make it more likely that taxpayers would cheat. For example, if one incorporates the risk preference structure developed from standard behavioral theories such as prospect theory, taxpayers would be more likely to cheat on their taxes than under the neoclassical model. This derives from the fact that under that theory, losses are to be avoided more than gains are to be valued.[24] If tax payments are framed as a loss, then taxpayers should be willing to take risks to avoid this outcome. Of course, if taxes are viewed as neutral (that is, cheating would be framed as a gain, and the penalties would be a loss), the reverse would occur. That is, we should expect taxpayers to be willing to take even greater chances to avoid losses. Although this conclusion depends on framing taxes as losses, it is hard to argue that most taxpayers view taxes as anything other than that (for a discussion, Nagel and Murphy 2002).

Psychological Theories

Lars Feld and Bruno Frey (2002) argue that how taxpayers are treated by the tax authorities can affect compliance decisions. They argue that if the authorities trust taxpayers, taxpayers will in turn behave in a trustworthy manner. Even though much of the evidence indicates that fines and audits might increase compliance, Feld and Frey argue that the manner in which taxpayers are treated seems to have an even greater effect. They discuss the notion that tax rules are a psychological contract between the authorities and the taxpayers. To the extent that this is an accurate depiction of the relationship, it is an implicit contract and therefore difficult to precisely define its terms. One important point about such contracts is that they only can be created by prior conduct. Therefore, large-scale changes in the behavior of one of the parties can be viewed as a violation of the contract. This idea may help to explain the findings of Cuccia as well as those of Slemrod, Christian, and Blumenthal that sometimes enforcement mechanisms may backfire and decrease compliance.

Evidence From Cognitive Neuroscience

A window on economic behavior that has recently opened up is the subdiscipline of neuroeconomics. There have not yet been neuroeconomic experiments directly involving public goods or tax compliance, but many of the experiments already conducted relate to many of the key issues. The research on decision making indicates that we use a reasonably small number of neural mechanisms to solve problems (see Frank 1991). Among the most important areas of the brain involved in decision making are the dorsolateral prefrontal, the ventromedial prefrontal cortex, the insula, and the complex of areas commonly implicated in social behavior.

In most neuroeconomic experiments involving standard trust games, there were basically two types of responders, cooperators (who activated areas such as the paracingulate cortex, superior temporal sulcus, and so on, normally thought of as social areas) and noncooperators (who generally had relatively greater activation in the dorsolateral prefrontal cortex, commonly thought to be involved in executive function and rational decision making) (McCabe et al. 2001). Noncooperators had similar brain activation patterns when interacting with humans as when interacting with computers. This is consistent with the existing neuroeconomic experiments which indicate that, in order to act in a trusting manner, one needs to activate social mechanisms (Chorvat and McCabe 2004).

Another brain mechanism that likely comes into play in connection with tax compliance, particularly to the extent there are violations of perceived social rules, is the insula. That this region may be activated is suggested by the results from studies of the brain activation in ultimatum games (Sanfey et al. 2003). In these games, individuals appear to react to perceived violations of implicit social contracts that require benefits to be shared equally with emotions similar to disgust. Because the behavior in ultimatum games has been commonly associated with the behavior of many subjects in public goods games to punish noncooperating members (Camerer 2003, 103–4), it is likely that the insula may also be activated in perceived violations by others of their duty to contribute, or violations by an institution to the implicit social contract between taxpayers and the government. Understanding that these particular areas are activated may help us to understand the motivation for the compliance behavior observed, and help to predict how taxpayers will react to particular compliance regimes.

The work of Jerome Barkow, Leda Cosmides, and John Tooby (1992) demonstrates a neural mechanism present in nearly all humans that "detects" cheating (and see possible neural mechanism discussion in Goel et al. 2004). The general definition of cheating from these studies is taking a benefit without paying its cost (Gazziniga, Ivry, and Magun 2002, 598–99). The mechanisms appear to be quite general and involved in nearly all social behavior. Furthermore, it appears that our perceptions and judgments of our own actions appear to be related to and involve the same neural mechanisms as our judgments of the actions of others (see Chorvat and McCabe 2004). One can thus argue that we know, because of these mechanisms, whether we are cheating.

To the extent that trust and trustworthiness are the result of neural mechanisms suggests certain likely attributes of these behaviors. In particular, it appears that because behaviors are based on synaptic interactions, and they are likely subject to a process known as long-term potentiation, or LTP (see LeDoux 2002). The effect of LTP is that each time one engages in a behavior, one is slightly more likely to do so again (see discussion of potential short-term exhaustion in Baumeister 2003, 12–14). Although it may be that in the short-term one's capacity for further trusting and trustworthy behavior may be limited, it is likely that because the notion of cheating applies generally, trust and trustworthiness in one area might be carried over into others. This is consistent with the experiments discussed earlier that indicate trustworthy behavior increases after behaving in a trusting manner. In fact, it is likely that this is how we learn to be trustworthy in the first place (Mueller 1986).

If trustworthiness is synaptically based, one can make the argument that, consistent with experimental evidence (see Frohlich and Oppenheimer 1996), the more one behaves in a trustworthy manner, the more likely one is to behave in a trustworthy manner in other situations. To the extent that this is true, paying taxes honestly is likely to recruit such mechanisms, and thus likely to lead to more trustworthy behavior in other circumstances. However, if cheating is the resulting behavior, then the likelihood of cheating would be strengthened, leading to negative social consequences.

To the extent that honest behavior in paying taxes leads to honest behavior in other areas and vice versa, then one has to consider the effects of tax compliance on other areas of society. It is important to note that it might be that forced tax compliance does not have the same effect. The experiments indicate that forced compliance will result in less trustworthy behavior in unforced situations. It may be that such compliance does not utilize trusting mechanisms, but only calculative neural mechanisms. It appears that only voluntary cooperation will have the effect of increasing cooperation in other areas.

Simple Model of Effects of Trust and Taxation

To sharpen the analysis of the effects of the tax system on the economy as a whole, I introduce a mathematical model, which I hope will illustrate some of the key assumptions, as well as suggest some directions for future research. While the initial conclusion one can easily draw from the model may be relatively straightforward, the model will be used to suggest areas for research as well as to illuminate the relationship between trust and taxation. A simple two-period model will suffice to illustrate most of the important considerations. Let us assume that we can somehow denominate intensity of involuntary compliance (that is, fines and audit rates) as p^{25} and specify W as the objective function to maximize (for example, social welfare or some similar value). Let us also assume that $W = F(Y,T)$, that W is a function of Y, income of the society, and T tax revenue. We then maximize a two-period function, $W_0 + dW_1$ where d is a discounting factor, used to illustrate the idea that welfare in the future is discounted relative to current welfare.[26]

If we assume that T_0 is a function of current income and the level of enforcement, which we can denominate p_0, we can refer to period 0 welfare as $W_0 = F(Y_0, T_0(Y_0, p_0))$, that is, that the current level of welfare is a function of current income and current taxes raised, and that current taxes raised are a function of current income and the level of enforcement of the tax laws. If welfare is improved by raising more tax revenue $(\partial W_0/\partial T_0 > 0)$, and tax revenue is increased by increased levels of enforcement $(\partial T_0/\partial p_0 > 0)$, then welfare is improved by increased enforcement of tax laws $(\partial W_0/\partial p_0 > 0)$. To illustrate the long-run effects of enforcement we can represent welfare in period one as: $W1 = F(Y_1(S_1), T_1(Y_1, p_1))$. That is, welfare in the future is a function of income and taxes raised in the future, but income in the future is dependent on the trust inherent in society in the future, where S_n represents the trust level of the society in period n. We assume here that higher levels of trust are associated with higher levels of income and therefore social welfare $(\partial W_n/\partial S_n > 0)$. If we assume that S_n is a function of the level of enforcement in the earlier period as well as S_{n-1}, we can represent this as: $S_n = S_n(p_{n-1}, S_{n-1})$.[27] The optimal level of enforcement for the first period can be found by:

$$\max_{p_0} T_0(Y_0(p_0) - C(p_0) + \delta W_1(Y_1(S_1(S_0, p_0)), T(Y_1, S_1(S_0, p_0))).$$

The crucial element of the model is then the value of $\partial S_n/\partial p_{n-1}$, that is, the effect of current levels of enforcement on trust in later periods. To find the optimal level of enforcement, we will then have to compare $\partial W_0/\partial p_0$ and $\partial W_2/\partial p_1$, which is the effect of enforcement on current welfare, and the effect of it on future welfare. If $\partial S_n/\partial p_{n-} < 0$—the effect of increased levels of enforcement decreases trustworthy behavior in the future—then increased enforcement now can have negative effects on welfare later. The outcome of this model depends on the value of $\partial S_n/\partial p_{n-1}$. The effect of assuming that this term is negative is that an increase in enforcement activities today results in lower trust tomorrow, which then decreases income tomorrow. If the existing level of trust is high, so that most individuals would comply with the laws, then it might be that raising revenue could be suboptimal in the long term, because it would not help to foster more trust in the future. On the other hand, if the level of trustworthy behavior is low (in other words, cheating is high), the sign of this term would likely be either zero or positive.[28] In this case, lower levels of enforcement would likely be to reinforce cheating. Whether society is basically trustworthy or not trustworthy is clearly an empirical question. One way to measure the level of trust is to measure the amounts first players in a trust game are willing to transfer. Several empirical tests have already demonstrated that trust correlates fairly highly with economic growth.

If, contrary to the experimental evidence discussed earlier, $\partial S_n / \partial p_{n-1}$ Q 0, that is, even if the effect of enforcement is negative, we are unlikely to utilize the corner solution of maximum possible enforcement because at the optimum $\partial T_0 / \partial p_0 + \delta \partial W_1 / \partial p_0 = \partial C / \partial p_0$.

From this equation it is easy to see that if $\partial W_1 / \partial p_0 > 0$ and T_0 is concave and C convex, then it is the case than the smaller is $\partial W_1 / \partial p_0$, the lower the optimal level of enforcement. If $\partial W_1 / \partial p_0 < 0$, then the level of enforcement will be below that which would result from optimizing tax revenue for the single period alone.

The optimal amount of enforcement will always be limited to the point where marginal benefits are equal to marginal cost. If we assume that the marginal benefits are concave (that is, decreasing marginal returns), and that marginal cost is either linear or more likely convex (increasing marginal cost per dollar of tax revenue raised), then there will be some point at which these two are equal.

The structure imposed by this model suggests a number of possible directions for future research that are not directly discussed in the model. First, the degree to which trust and trustworthiness spill over from the payment of taxes to other decisions would be an interesting area for research. That is, we have represented trust in society as single variable S. It is entirely possible that we should break trust into different variables, representing trust in the government (S^G), and trust in society in general (S^S). This is important because of the significant impact of trust in society, S^S, on economic growth (Zak and Knack 2001). Even if the effect of increased enforcement efforts on total trust is relatively small, the impact on the economy as a whole may still be large. In addition, experiments on how the intrinsic motivation to pay taxes could be increased is another key area of study. Research on the effect of simple letters appealing to group solidarity and the like seem to have little effect on compliance, although economics experiments seem to indicate that institutional structure can have a large effect on the level of compliance and personal communication. Furthermore, how these behavioral considerations extend to partnerships and corporations and other institutions is another area. Because these behaviors occur when we are making decisions in our individual capacity does not mean they will happen for decisions made in our capacity as agents of an institution. A final area of further research is how to address these questions in the context of a heterogeneous population. It would be important to discover if we can easily segregate those who will comply from those who will not, and if we can, what effect such segregation might have on total compliance.

Conclusion

Any system that relies as heavily as ours does on self-reporting depends heavily on taxpayer cooperation. Therefore, as part of any research on increased tax revenues from compliance efforts, we must also consider the effects on the willingness to cooperate with the system. This chapter argues that econometric and experimental economic evidence indicates that the tax system is able to take advantage of the trustworthiness one finds in society. The most important point we should consider is that while the tax system is very likely affected by the level of trust in society, it also affects it as well. If we have a relatively high-trust society in which we can trust citizens to pay their taxes, then trusting the taxpayer is reinforcing norms. However, if trustworthy behavior is not common, and in particular, individuals are likely to cheat on their taxes, relying on these mechanisms may actually decrease trustworthiness, depending on perceptions of implicit contracts.

The proper question should not be so much whether higher rates of audit or fines can increase compliance, which a significant amount of evidence indicates they do to some degree, but whether they are the best way to increase it. This is particularly true if one accepts the notion that complying with tax laws may lead to greater trustworthiness in other areas of life. If compliance can be increased by other ways, this is likely the optimal way to obtain more tax revenue. However, deciding which mechanism to rely on therefore calls for an understanding of the trustworthy behavior of the members of society.

Professor Chorvat would like to thank: Bruno Frey, David Hasen, Leandra Lederman, Kevin McCabe, Edward McCaffery, Joel Slemrod and the participants in the Behavioral Public Finance Conference, and two anonymous referees for their comments and the Lawrence Cranberg Faculty Research Fellowship and the Law and Economics Center for their financial support.

Notes

1. The so-called tax gap that we observe—which is defined as the difference between what the government ought to collect in tax revenue and what it does collect—is calculated at approximately 17 percent of the total revenue owed the government (IRS 1996). As discussed, there are a number of method-

ological problems with study, which do not make it particularly useful for estimating the total level of noncompliance.

2. It might be the case that individuals overestimate the probability of being caught, the probability of having to pay a penalty, or the probability of going to jail—unless other sanctions such as jail time and social sanctions are so painful to the average taxpayer that the costs are much higher than included in the standard analysis (Frey 1997).

3. This is based on the Becker crime model. In fact Becker himself notes that his model could apply to tax evasion.

4. This form of utility was first discussed in von Neumann and Morgenstern (1948).

5. This can also be written in a continuous version as $\int u(x)p(x)dx$, where $p(x)$ is the derivative of the cumulative density function $P(x)$. Most discussion of this question effectively imposes an inequality constraint of $x \leq y$, but this is not necessary, and relaxing this constraint would result in negative tax. However, see the discussion concerning the possible endogeneity of the audit probability.

6. Cowell (2004) refers to this as the Taxpayer as Gambler Model. If the expected value of an investment is greater than a riskless asset, every risk-averse investor will still have some of the asset in their portfolio.

7. This is calculated under standard Arrow-Pratt calculation. Here the coefficient is the second derivative of the utility function divided by the derivative or U''/U' (Feld and Frey 2002).

8. They calculate that risk aversion rates of greater than 30 would have to have existed in order for the levels of compliance that we observe (Feld and Frey 2002).

9. Actually Allingham and Sandmo mention this possibility. To the extent that this is true, when we double the fines for tax evasion, we do not double the penalty (Holopainen 2003).

10. As discussed infra, there is too little cheating on deductions, Andreoni, Erard, and Feinstein (1998) make this point.

11. This last notion may help to explain the deterioration that one often finds in public goods games.

12. The idea being that first players offer as little as they think they can and still be accepted (Sanfey et al. 2003).

13. In fact, it is explicitly patterned after Becker's model, which itself is based on portfolio models (see Becker 1968).

14. On average, this may be correct but may introduce bias. If the TCMP compliance numbers derive from income that is taxed at different rates (for example, capital versus ordinary income, etc.) than the income from which the 97 percent success rate figure was derived, this may skew the numbers.

15. This could result in either too low a figure (taxpayers may be more motivated than the IRS) or too high a figure (the IRS agent might not internalize the cost of litigation and so the taxpayer might be more willing to settle than the agent). Using this figure then likely biases the number, but it is not clear how.

16. Another possible explanation, which is related to that given by Cuccia, that is explored later that draws off work by Bruno Frey, Ernst Fehr, and others is that taxes are to some extent viewed as an implied contract, and if these changes to the rules are seen as violation of that contract, and as has been

seen in many public goods experiments, individuals are often willing to irrationally punish those who have violated a contract. This would argue that any such changes ought to be done slowly.

17. Steven Sheffrin and Robert Triest (1992) argue that one of the reasons for this might be that after an audit a taxpayer may now realize how easy it is to cheat, and therefore increase his level of cheating.

18. It is possible that those who receive benefits are more highly risk averse than others.

19. They discuss how given a particular version of the Allingham-Sandmo model incorporating endogenous probability of audit this may be rational.

20. One key difference might be that one might gain esteem from one's colleagues for putting in more effort. In this case, effort is observable and this might explain much of the difference.

21. The portfolios generally have been given to them for purposes of the game.

22. In general the payoff function is linear. That is the utility function takes a form something like $u_i = U_i [(E - x_i)] + A \cdot P (\Sigma x_i)$. This is not always the case, and often non-linear forms are used to test various predictions.

23. The audit rates in the study were approximately 30 percent and the fines were two times the taxes owed.

24. Although this is also true under risk-aversion, the utility curve under Prospect Theory is based on gains and losses not wealth, and the utility function has a kink at zero gains, where the individual becomes risk preferring as to losses, but is risk averse as to gains.

25. This variable could be a linear combination of fines and audit probability to maximize compliance (e.g., $c_1 F + c_2 A = p$), of p may be some more complicated function of the two.

26. This can easily be extend an n period problem by using the formula $U = \sum_n \delta^n w_n$, where δ is the discounting factor.

27. We are here representing trust and trustworthiness as a unitary amount, rather than as separate variables for trust and trustworthiness. There is some evidence to indicate that the two are correlated (see Ostrom 2003).

28. There are certain conclusions of this model that are similar to work of Sanchez and Sobel (1993), which discusses how tax authorities may have an incentive to get the highest amount of revenue, but government may not have such an incentive, because it may have an incentive to maximize social welfare, which would include things like Keynesian multipliers (that is, if this income tax is not collected it might increase economic growth). The wisdom of this kind of tax cut would depend on the relative efficiency of how those who cheat on their taxes invest and how the government would invest the money.

References

Akerlof, George A. 1982. "Labor Contracts as Partial Gift Exchange." *Quarterly Journal of Economics* 97(4): 543–69.

Allingham, Michael, and Agnar Sandmo. 1972. "Income Tax Evasion: A Theoretical Analysis." *Journal of Public Economics* 1(3/4): 323–38.

Alm, James. 1988. "Non-Compliance and Payroll Taxation in Jamaica." *Journal of Developing Areas* 22(4): 477–95.

Alm, James, Mark B. Cronshaw, and Michael McKee. 1993. "Tax Compliance with Endogenous Audit Selection Rules." *Kyklos* 46(1): 27–45.

Alm, James, Betty R. Jackson, and Michael McKee. 1992. "Estimating the Determinants of Taxpayer Compliance with Experimental Data." *National Tax Journal* 45(1): 107–14.

Alm, James, Gary H. McClelland, and William D. Schulze. 1992. "Why Do People Pay Taxes?" *Journal of Public Economics* 48(1): 21–38.

Alm, James, Isabel Sanchez, and Ana de Juan. 1995. "Economic and Noneconomic Factors in Tax Compliance." *Kyklos* 48(1): 3–18.

Andreoni, James, Brian Erard, and Jonathan Feinstein. 1998. "Tax Compliance." *Journal of Economic Literature* 36(2): 818–60.

Barkow, Jerome H., Leda Cosmides, and John Tooby, eds. 1992. *The Adapted Mind: Evolutionary Psychology and the Generation of Culture*. New York: Oxford University Press.

Baumeister, Roy F. 2003. "The Psychology of Irrationality: Why People Make Foolish Self-Defeating Choices." In *The Psychology of Economic Decision-Making, Volume 1: Rationality and Well-Being*, edited by Isabelle Brocas and Juan D. Carrillo. Oxford: Oxford University Press.

Becker, Gary. 1968. "Crime and Punishment: An Economic Approach." *Journal of Political Economy* 76(2): 169–217.

Camerer, Colin. 2003. *Behavioral Game Theory*. Princeton, N.J.: Princeton University Press.

Chorvat, Terrence, and Kevin McCabe. 2004. "The Brain and the Law." *Philosophical Transactions of the Royal Society of London* 359(1): 1727–36.

Clark, Jeremy, Laura Freisen, and Andrew Muller. 2004. "The Good, the Bad, and the Regulator: An Experimental Test of Two Conditional Audit Schemes." *Economic Inquiry* 42(1): 69–87.

Coleman, Stephen. 1996. *The Minnesota Income Tax Compliance Experiment: State Tax Results*. St. Paul: Minnesota Department of Revenue.

Cowell, Frank. 2004. "Carrots and Sticks in Enforcement." In *The Crisis in Tax Administration*, edited by Henry J. Aaron and Joel Slemrod. Washington, D.C.: Brookings Institution Press.

Cuccia, Andrew. 1994. "The Effects of Increased Sanctions on Paid Tax Preparers: Integrating Economic and Psychological Factors." *Journal of the American Taxation Association* 16(1): 41–66.

Cummings, Ronald, Jorge Martinez-Vazquez, and Michael McKee. 2001. "Cross Cultural Comparison of Tax Compliance Behavior." Andrew Young School of Public Policy Working Paper No. 01-3. Atlanta: Georgia State University.

Dubin, Jeffrey, Michael Graetz, and Louis Wilde. 1987. "Are We a Nation of Tax Cheaters? New Econometric Evidence on Tax Compliance." *American Economic Review* 77(2): 240–45.

Dubin, Jeffrey, and Louis Wilde. 1988. "An Empirical Analysis of Federal Income Tax Auditing and Compliance." *National Tax Journal* 41(1): 61–74.

Fehr, Ernst, and Simon Gächter. 2000. "Do Incentive Contracts Crowd Out Voluntary Cooperation?" University of Zurich Working Paper No. 34. Zurich, Switzerland: University of Zurich.

Feld, Lars, and Bruno Frey. 2002. "Trust Breeds Trust: How Taxpayers Are Treated." *Economics of Governance* 3(2): 87–100.

Frank, Robert. 1991. *Passions Within Reason*. New York: W. W. Norton.

Frey, Bruno. 1994. "How Intrinsic Motivation Is Crowded Out and In." *Rationality and Society* 6(3): 334–52.

———. 1997. *Not Just for The Money: An Economic Theory of Personal Motivation*. Cheltenham: Edward Elgar.

Frey, Bruno, and Iris Bohnet. 1996. "Cooperation, Communication and Communitarianism: An Experimental Approach." *Journal of Political Philosophy* 4(4): 322–36.

Friedman, Milton. 1953. *Essays in Positive Economics*. Chicago: University of Chicago Press.

Frohlich, Norman, and Joe Oppenheimer. 1996. "Experiencing Impartiality to Invoke Fairness in the n-PD: Some Experimental Results." *Public Choice* 86(1/2): 117–35.

Gazziniga, Michael, Richard Ivry, and George Magun. 2002. *Cognitive Neuroscience*. New York: W. W. Norton.

Goel, Vinod, Jeffrey Shuren, Laura Sheesley, and Jordan Grafman. 2004. "Asymmetrical Involvement of Frontal Lobes in Social Reasoning." *Brain* 127(4): 783–90.

Graetz, Michael, and Louis Wilde. 1985. "The Economics of Tax Compliance: Fact and Fantasy." *National Tax Journal* 38(3): 355–63.

Gunnthorsdottir, Anna, Daniel Houser, Kevin McCabe, and Holley Ameden. 2001. "Disposition, History and Contributions in Public Goods Experiments." Working Paper. St. Louis: Washington University at St. Louis.

Hardin, Garrett. 1968. "The Tragedy of the Commons." *Science* 162(3859): 1243–248.

Holopainen, Ville. 2003. "The Utility Gained by Evading Taxes in Comparison with the Sanctions for Tax Evasion." Working Paper. Joensuu, Finland: University of Joensuu.

Holt, Charles, and Susan Laury. 2005. "Theoretical Explanations for Treatment Effects in Voluntary Contributions Experiments." In *Handbook of Experimental Economic Results*, edited by Charles Plott and Vernon L. Smith. North-Holland: Elsevier.

Kim, Chung Kweon. 2002. "Does Fairness Matter in Tax Reporting Behavior?" *Journal of Economic Psychology* 23(6): 771–86.

LeDoux, Joseph. 2002. *The Synaptic Self*. New York: Viking.

Ledyard, John. 1995. "Public Goods." In *Handbook in Experimental Economics*, edited by John Kagel and Alvin Roth. Princeton, N.J.: Princeton University Press.

McCabe, Kevin, Daniel Houser, Lee Ryan, Vernon Smith, and Theodore Trouard. 2001. "A Functional Imaging Study of Cooperation in Two-person Reciprocal Exchange." *Proceedings of the National Academy of Sciences of the United States of America* 98(20): 11832–835.

McCabe, Kevin, Mary Rigdon, and Vernon Smith. 2004. "Sustaining Cooperation in Trust Games." Working Paper. St. Louis: Washington University at St. Louis.

Mueller, Dennis. 1986. "Rational Egoism Versus Adaptive Egoism as Fundamental Postulate for a Descriptive Theory of Human Behavior." *Public Choice* 51: 3–23.

Nagel, Thomas, and Liam Murphy. 2002. *The Myth of Ownership: Taxes and Justice.* New York: Oxford University Press.

Olson, Mancur. 1965. *Logic of Collective Action: Public Goods and the Theory of Groups.* Cambridge, Mass.: Harvard University Press.

Ostrom, Elinor. 2003. "Toward a Behavioral Theory Linking Trust, Reciprocity, and Reputation." In *Trust and Reciprocity: Interdisciplinary Lessons for Experimental Research,* edited by Elinor Ostrom and James Walker. New York: Russell Sage Foundation.

Posner, Richard. 1983. *The Economics of Justice.* Cambridge, Mass.: Harvard University Press.

Sanchez, Isabel, and Joel Sobel. 1993. "Hierarchical Design and Enforcement of Income Tax Policies." *Journal of Public Economics* 50(3): 345–69.

Sanfey, Alan G., James K. Rilling, Jessica A. Aronson, Leigh E. Nystrom, and Jonathan D. Cohen. 2003. "The Neural Basis for Economic Decision-Making in the Ultimatum Game." *Science* 300(5626): 1755–58.

Shaviro, Daniel. 2004. "Rethinking Tax Expenditures and Fiscal Language." NYU Law School Working Paper. New York: New York University.

Sheffrin, Steven, and Robert Triest. 1992. "Can Brute Deterrence Backfire? Perceptions and Attitudes in Taxpayer Compliance." In *Why People Pay Taxes: Tax Compliance and Enforcement,* edited by Joel Slemrod. Ann Arbor: University of Michigan Press.

Siegal, Uzi, and Avia Spivak. 1990. "First Order Versus Second Order Risk Aversion." *Journal of Economic Theory* 51(1): 111–25.

Slemrod, Joel, ed. 1992. *Why People Pay Taxes.* Ann Arbor: University of Michigan Press.

———. 2003. "Trust in Public Finance." In *Public Finance and Public Policy in the New Century,* edited by Sijbren Cnossen and Hans-Werner Sinn. Cambridge, Mass.: MIT Press.

Slemrod, Joel, Marsha Blumenthal, and Charles Christian. 2001. "Taxpayer Response to an Increased Probability of Audit: Evidence from a Controlled Experiment in Minnesota." *Journal of Public Economics* 79(3): 455-83.

Slemrod, Joel, and Shlomo Yitzhaki. 2002. "Tax Avoidance, Evasion and Administration." In *Handbook of Public Economics,* vol. 3, edited by Alan Auerbach and Martin Feldstein. Amsterdam: Elsevier.

Smith, Adam. 1776/1994. *An Inquiry into the Nature and Causes of the Wealth of Nations.* New York: Modern Library Edition.

U.S. Department of Treasury. Internal Revenue Service. (IRS) 1996. *Federal Tax Compliance Research: Individual Tax Gap Estimates for 1985, 1988 and 1992.* Publication 1415. Washington: U.S. Government Printing Office.

von Neumann, John, and Oskar Morgenstern. 1948. *Theory of Games and Economic Behavior.* Princeton, N.J.: Princeton University Press.

Yitzhaki, Shlomo. 1974. "A Note on 'Income Tax Evasion: A Theoretical Analysis.'" *Journal of Public Economics* 3(2): 201–2.

Zak, Paul, and Stephen Knack. 2001. "Trust and Growth." *Economic Journal* 111(470): 295–321.

Chapter 9

Tax Evasion: Artful or Artless Dodging?

JOHN CULLIS, PHILIP JONES, AND ALAN LEWIS

I F, as Hegel observes, "The rational is the highroad where everyone travels, where no one is conspicuous" (cited in Knox 1952, 230), then that highroad is surely not sign-posted with the axioms of expected utility theory. Rather it is littered with an array of partially analyzed, yet systematic, heuristic responses. The likes of transitivity, strong separability, and the usual rules for combining lotteries have to be replaced by a value function, framing effects, and subjective probabilities that are the product of all sorts of systematic distortions. If these sentences capture the main thrust of behavioral economics, they are relevant when analyzing public finance. When considering activity in stock markets and assessing efficient markets theory, Robert Shiller comments that by the 1990s "The field of behavioral finance developed. Researchers had seen too many anomalies, too little inspiration that our theoretical models captured important fluctuations" (2003, 90–91). Such comments are equally relevant when considering public finance and when assessing neoclassical economic analysis of tax evasion.

A burgeoning empirical literature casts doubt on the proposition that tax evasion reflects the measured decisions of an instrumental calculation of net-expected-utility. Neoclassical economic analysis of tax evasion (the Allingham-Sandmo 1972 model) yields theoretical predictions that often prove at variance with evidence (Torgler 2002). Individuals do not behave exactly as predicted by this theory. But is this because individuals choose a more attractive decision-making rule, or is it because individuals are simply unable to make decisions as instrumentally as assumed in neoclassical analysis?

A behavioral approach to fiscal studies and tax evasion, incorporating input from the softer social sciences, can be traced back to the work of Gunter Schmolders (1970) and Alan Lewis (1982). The perceptions, attitudes, values, and morals of taxpayers are key features of the models. Voluntary compliance is associated with the perception that tax authorities are honest, a positive attitude toward fiscal policy and the belief that tax evasion is morally wrong—a preference to act ethically. This view of the taxpayer replaces the vision of an individual wealth maximizer weighing up the costs and benefits of evasion with a consumer whose continued good behavior must be nurtured.

Behavioral models have been influenced by the disciplines of sociology and law (Kinsey 1986; IRS 1991; Slemrod 1992): contributions from psychology being more social in origin. For social psychologists, people look to others in order to decide what is acceptable, reasonable and expected in a given social context; behavior is not seen as a function of individual choice. So the concepts of norms and conformity need to be added to the list of key features.

Paul Webley and colleagues (1991) have argued that many behavioral models take the form of conceptual maps and are consequently not open to empirical test. Attempts have been made, however, to combine the realism of behavioral models with the characteristic deductive stance of economics (Cullis and Lewis 1997).

Given the asocial nature of economics, it should be no great surprise that the discipline has shown more contemporary interest in cognitive psychology and in particular that branch represented by the work of Daniel Kahneman and Amos Tversky (1979, 2000). Cognitive psychology is more individualistic and is concerned (among other things) with how people make decisions. Cognitive psychologists have always questioned individuals' capacity to engage instrumentally. They question that individuals have the ability to formulate decisions in this way. Psychologists insist that individuals are unable to assimilate and deduce as implied in neoclassical theory. Certainly, there is now a plethora of heuristics that appear to mitigate the problems of decision making. If analysts face a problem, it is that of assessing which heuristic, which rule of thumb is likely to prove apposite. As Elias Khalil notes, "The number of uncovered anomalies is as dizzying as the number of sub-atomic particles discovered by physicists" (2003, 1). Neoclassical economic analysis offers a behavioral assumption for all decisions, but it is premised on axioms that have been called into question and it yields predictions at odds with evidence. Individuals do not appear instrumental, but is this because they choose a different (lower cost) way of making decisions or simply because they are prisoners of their own cognitive constraints?

There is more than one explanation for the failings of the Allingham-Sandmo model. We will consider alternative responses later in the chapter. Although critics prescribe solutions, it is difficult to dismiss the proposition that the Allingham-Sandmo model fails because it is premised on an inaccurate behavioral assumption; individuals are not so instrumental. We then narrow our focus: Is it possible to test whether individuals are able to choose to act more (or less) instrumentally? As the quotations from Shiller and Khalil illustrate, there is now surely ample evidence in behavioral finance of noninstrumental behavior. The questions that remain unresolved are whether individuals choose to rely on a noninstrumental calculus and, if so, how do they make this choice? Are individuals always condemned to repeat the same cognitive errors (errors as defined with reference to correct decisions premised on instrumental maximization of net expected utility), or are they able to change? Are taxpayers capable of being instrumentally artful when responding to tax authorities, or are they simply artless?

The Limits to Instrumental Evasion

In neoclassical microeconomics a self-interested, amoral representative individual is assumed to act instrumentally. In the Allingham-Sandmo (1972) model individuals maximize net expected utility (see also Cowell 1985; Pyle 1989, 1991).

When deciding how much income (Y) to declare (D), the individual might be honest (D = Y), completely dishonest (D = 0) or honest in part (D > 0 < Y). A proportional income tax, t, is levied and punishment for dishonesty depends on the probability of detection p and the fine rate, F. In the Allingham-Sandmo model a fine is levied on all income not declared [Y-D]. The individual must choose D, that is, must select D to maximize expected utility, EU, when:

$$EU = (1 - p) U(Y - tD) + pU(Y - tD - F[Y - D])$$ (1)

An interior optimum (when some income is undeclared) arises for a risk-averse individual if:

$$\frac{dEU}{dD} = t(1 - p)U'(N) - (t - F)p\,U'(C) = 0$$ (2)

and where: $N = Y - tD$ = Not caught income
$C = Y - tD - F[Y - D]$ = Caught income.

Rewriting:

$$-\frac{(1 - p)U'(N)}{pU'(C)} = \frac{t - F}{t}$$ (3)

The solution (equation 3) illustrates the basic tenets of instrumental neo-classical economic theory (Stigler and Becker 1977). With preferences determined exogenously, the individual evades more, or less, depending on changes in constraints, that is, changes in the rate of tax, probability of detection, and level of fine rate.

Results from empirical analysis question the relevance of a model driven solely by instrumental rationality:

- Too much tax is paid voluntarily! It is usually accepted that compliance is far greater than expected by reference to current tax rates, probabilities of detection and fines. James Alm and colleagues note that "a purely economic analysis of the evasion gamble implies that most individuals would evade if they are rational because it is unlikely that cheaters will be caught and penalized" (1992, 22). Andreoni, Erard, and Feinstein (1998) comment that, in 1995 the audit rate in the United States for individual tax returns was 1.7 percent, the civil penalty for underpayment of taxes was 20 percent of the underpayment; very large values for risk aversion would be required to predict tax compliance.[1]

- In the language of mechanism design,[2] the theory contains a truth telling rule. If s is a surcharge rate (such that $F = t + ts$) on detected undeclared income, then the condition to truth-tell about your income is $1 - p/p = s$. The condition is independent of the tax rate and any consideration of risk aversion. If the parameters so dictate, all individuals should either not evade or evade. The theory will never result in a separating equilibrium (where some individuals evade and others do not) because of the rule connecting the probability of detection and surcharge rate that causes tax evasion to be expected utility maximizing for all (that is, a pooled equilibrium).

Of course this prediction is sensitive to the assumption that p and s are common to all individuals. Joel Slemrod (2002) has undermined this assumption for the real world noting for example that the probability of audit may be higher in one geographical region than another. However, in the world of experimentation the condition of a common p and s can be made to hold. In the questionnaire study reported below all participants were given identical p and s values and therefore at this level a separating equilibrium should not be observed.

The Allingham-Sandmo model offers precise analysis of decision making under uncertainty but precision can only be achieved by employing five basic axioms that have been the subject of serious criticism (Schoemaker 1982). In a positive methodology the way to respond to the apparent falsification of a model is to go back to the theorizing stage.

Figure 9.1   Types of Decision Model

| | | Individual Cognitive Capabilities | |
		Faultless Optimization	"Flawed," Bounded Rationality
Objective Function	Narrow Income, Wealth, Value Maximization	1	3
	Wider or Enhanced Utility	2	4

Source: Authors' compilation.

How could the tax evasion model be theoretically revised? As the old (half) joke has it: "There are two types of people in the world, those who believe in types and those who do not." At the risk of oversimplification, consider the four types of individual decision models set out in figure 9.1. The taxonomy relies on what you assume individuals' cognitive capabilities are and the nature of their underlying objective function.

Model 1 typifies the neoclassical Allingham-Sandmo model explored earlier. Model 2 response is to enhance the nature of the objective function to include considerations of equity, efficiency, and elements such as ethical preference—because, after all, the context is crime. Following this response would reconcile prediction and evidence by arguing that representative individuals make decisions with reference to more concerns than those acknowledged in the Allingham-Sandmo model. If anything, such reconciliation suggests that taxpayers are capable of even more instrumental behavior than Allingham and Sandmo (1972) imply. For now individuals appear able to internalize more concerns within an instrumental calculus; now they appear engaged in even more sophisticated (dynamic) games with tax authorities. Such reconciliation would suggest that within the Allingham-Sandmo model individuals are capable of instrumentally assessing a plethora of concerns:

- Considerations of equity are now relevant. Individuals do not simply consider their own circumstances, they also internalize considerations of equity in society generally. Following the lead of Nehemiah Friedland, Shlomo Maital, and Aryeh Rutenberg (1978), Michael Spicer and Lee Becker (1980) considered the relationship between perceived fiscal inequity and tax evasion (see also Spicer and Lundstedt 1976; Song and Yarbrough 1978).[3] Results were consistent with the hypothesis, though the experiment only took horizontal equity into account (all participants at start-up received the same amount of money).[4]

- Perceptions of the return from government expenditure now also matter. Individuals do not simply consider their net pecuniary income but instead look more broadly to social income (influenced by the performance of government). Winifred Becker, Heinz-Jurgen Buchner, and Simon Sleeking (1987) analyzed the effect of transfer payments and found that those received from public sector programs increased compliance.[5] James Alm and his colleagues(1992) report that perceptions of the public good (financed by tax revenue) are important when predicting compliance. Werner Pommerehne, Albert Hart, and Bruno Frey (1994) used a dynamic, recursive analysis of the relationship between government-provided public good, government waste, fairness considerations, and taxpayer compliance, modeling interaction between individuals and institutions as a dynamic process. After each period, the individual has the opportunity to reflect on considerations such as: deviation between the individual's optimal choice of public good provision and the actual level; a higher number of fellow citizens underpaying tax; a higher level of government waste in the previous period. Such considerations eroded willingness to pay taxes. The authors highlight the importance of the principal-agent problem.

In these various responses, the Allingham-Sandmo model would be correct if only its remit were widened. Benno Torgler (2003) illustrates how such concerns can be included. When considering the value of government expenditure over and above personal taxation, the expected value of the gamble is now described as:

$$EV = Y - tD + mh(G + tD) - pF(Y - D) \qquad (4)$$

where: h = the individual share of the group tax fund; G = taxes paid by all other group members; m = the surplus multiplier. In the same vein, the model can be amended to include the concerns of altruists; utility functions can be expanded to include the well-being of others (as in Hochman and Rodgers 1969, for example). Spicer (1986) incorporates the significance of "psychic costs" of evasion by similarly expanding the basic net expected utility function.

Model 3 sees individuals as flawed income maximizers in that they make mistakes with respect to full optimization. Proximate optimizing models fit here as well as models like prospect theory, where individuals are acting to maximize value via hedonic coding but are systematically anomalous in doing so. Decision making here may involve stages as with Thaler's (1985) transaction utility theory approach to consumer theory. This response highlights fundamental behavioral defects in decision making. This set of responses insist that the neoclassical analysis of tax compliance will never be reconciled with behavior because it relies on instrumental rationality (in terms of net expected utility maximization) and ignores the cognitive difficulties that individuals experience. Individuals are more likely to rely (artlessly) on heuristics and social norms; their behavior will never mirror that of homo economicus. In this genre, neoclassical predictions are at variance with evidence because of the following types of arguments.

- Individuals rely on rules of thumb, or heuristics. Spicer and Hero (1985) told twelve participants out of thirty-six that in the previous game participants had paid only 10 percent of taxes due; twelve were told 50 percent, and the rest 90 percent. The amount of taxes evaded was not affected significantly by this information; taxpayers simply appeared to rely on heuristics.

- Individuals' awareness is subject to systematic cognitive bias. Frey and Eichenberger (1989) argue that experience with audit biases estimates of probability of detection. Reliance on rules of thumb and, in particular, on an availability heuristic suggests that probability of detection is overestimated as a consequence of learning from the audit experience of friends and the treatment of detected evaders (see also Alm, McClelland, and Schulze 1992).[6]

- Individuals' decisions are sensitive to framing. If analysis were instrumental, unique decisions would be predicted across different tax frames. It should not matter how information is presented, individuals are able to assess objectives and constraints to maximize net expected utility. However, individuals persist in making decisions according to the way in which identical costs and benefits are presented. For example, White, Harrison, and Harrell discovered that individuals systematically report more income for taxation when claiming back withholding tax (1993).

McCaffery and Baron (2004) draw attention to many instances when decisions prove sensitive to different perceptions of the same costs and benefits. There appears to be no unique (or correct) instrumental response. For example, other things being equal, tax is perceived more negatively than payments; attitudes to progressivity depend on whether progressivity is described in percentage terms or in dollar terms (that is, the metric effect); within tax systems, a child bonus is a childless penalty and a marriage bonus is a singles penalty etc. (penalty aversion); the Schelling effect influences responses (that is, the interaction of penalty aversion and a progressivity illusion equivalent bonus are perceived as too high for rich and too low for poor and an equivalent penalty [surcharge] is seen as too low for rich and too high for poor); individuals are subject to an isolation heuristic—they do not adjust when they are asked about their preferences for progressivity for total taxes, when compared to preferences for payroll tax or personal income tax.

Model 4 is clearly richer but comes at the cost of losing elegance and brevity. Incorporation of a broader objective function serves to exacerbate the problem found in type 3 models by affecting decision-making costs. Here actors are viewed as having an enhanced utility function and as being flawed to some extent in their decision making. A model of tax evasion sketched this way might associate an ethical preference (honest or not) and some recent work on neuroeconomics. Faced with an hypothetical tax evasion decision (as our subjects are) might involve, for those actively engaging with the question, the following questions being answered:

- Do I have an overriding ethical preference for honesty and therefore simply declare honestly?
- Do I have an ethical preference that is not overriding and therefore wish to consider other options and associated outcomes?

Neuroeconomics connects economics to cranial function. Parts of economic theory, it appears, can help explain not only human decision making but indeed also how those decisions are made in the neurological circuits of the brain. In much of this work functional magnetic resonance imaging (fMRI) is used to study the functioning of the brain when economic decisions are made with a view to connecting brain behavior and choices. The version presented here is perhaps made more vivid than the original authors (Gonzalez et al. 2005) would wish to defend. However, following their exploration, assume decisions involve two costs. These are emotional costs that depend on the outcome of the decision and cognitive costs. Emotion and cognition tend to integrate in the prefrontal cortex (PFC) of the brain, and activity in different areas of the brain can be detected by fMRI scans of individuals in the process of making decisions. They postulate that emotional costs are high for what are deemed bad outcomes (say, taxes as opposed to rebates) and induce greater PFC activity, other things being equal. Further risky alternatives require an—albeit simple—expected value calculation producing higher PFC activity, other things being equal.

The scans for the relative costs of a well-known decision problem were consistent with the following schema (table 9.1).

Relative costs suggest:

- Certain gains are preferred to risky gains,
- Risky losses preferred to certain losses,

Table 9.1   Least-Cost Decisions and the Brain

	Emotional Costs	Cognitive Costs
Certain gain	Low	Low
Risky gain	Low	High
Certain loss	High	High
Risky loss	High-ish	High

Source: Authors' compilation.

- Cognitive costs are lower for certain gains as compared to risky gains,
- Cognitive costs for certain losses are equal to cognitive costs for risky losses.

Translated to the world of tax evasion, this suggests that tax evasion will be lower for elements that can be coded as certain gains rather than risky gains; taxation once coded as a risky loss will warrant cognitive evaluation. The predictions for the tax evasion process are that there will be honest declaration if there is an ethical preference override, little evidence of gambling with certain gains (honest claims for rebates should be observed), and evidence of instrumental calculation once losses are deemed to be involved.

This taxonomy of alternative responses, when empirical analysis fails to support theoretical prediction, in effect follows Frey and Eichenberger (1994). It involves amending the objective function, recognizing that paradoxical behavior occurs because individuals face cognitive costs in instrumental action or, in richer model 4, both these elements. Although the first route has been commended, it is difficult (impossible?) to dismiss the argument that individuals simply do not behave so instrumentally. With this assessment of responses to the Allingham-Sandmo model as background, the question pursued here is whether individuals choose not to act instrumentally (for example, chose lower-cost options) or whether individuals are simply unable to act instrumentally.

Exploring the Boundaries of Instrumental Rationality: Do Individuals Prefer to Act Artlessly?

The objective here is to consider the hypothesis that individuals choose to act more (or less) instrumentally. The proposition has been established this way because there is a growing literature that implies that choice is possible. Of course, the competing hypothesis is that individuals are unable to assimilate information and deduce instrumentally. But, for analysis, consider the following arguments that suggest that more (or less) instrumental behavior can be chosen.

One reason for believing that instrumental behavior is not beyond individuals' capability is that both noninstrumental and instrumental responses have been reported. Often students (with no experience) appear vulnerable to behavioral anomalies when, in practice, those with experience act instrumentally. For example, List (2003) reports that more experienced traders are less prone to the endowment effect than students in classroom experiments (see Kahneman, Thaler, and Knetsch 1990). There seems to be evidence that individuals can "get over their psychological 'flaws'" (*The Economist* 2003). It seems that, as the costs of acting instrumentally fall, individuals switch to this approach—that is, cognitive constraints are not binding. Choosing activity in itself may be information generating for an individual and represent a learning process.

In the same vein, Frey and Eichenberger (1994) present an incentives approach. The amount of anomalous behavior is endogenous to the marginal costs and benefits faced by decision makers. The more individuals are punished by anomalous behavior the more they reduce it (a conventionally sloped demand curve for anomalous behavior).

There are also studies that reveal that individuals are competent with instrumental analysis when the task in hand is manageable but that they switch to reliance on heuristics and norms as the task becomes more difficult. Fehr and Gachter note "a sizeable fraction of the people have reciprocal inclinations" (2000, 178) but, in situations where contracts are more or less complete, the self-interested motivation should be retained. Shiller's (2003) study of stock markets identifies a rational expectations conforming minority—smart money—and a majority who are "noise traders" subject to fads and fashions.

A different literature focuses on the intrinsic appeal of noninstrumental behavior. The architects of utility theory (for example, Bentham 1789/1948) emphasized that utility is derived from action, irrespective of the consequences of action. If individuals do not incur all the costs of instrumental assessment of outcomes contingent on action, it might be because they perceive intrinsic merit in adopting norms. Individuals derive self-esteem from action. They self-signal self worth by action; they signal to others by action. For example, if individuals were to choose to be honest (rather than instrumentally deceptive) this may not simply be a least-cost solution; honest behavior might be deemed of intrinsic value.

Neoclassical economic theory has focused on instrumental rationality. In the Allingham-Sandmo model individuals are amoral; honesty is only a solution if the net expected payoff (in terms of income) is maximized by honest declaration of income. Reflecting on Bentham's discussion, Loewenstein comments: "the evolution of the utility concept during our century has been characterized by a progressive stripping away of psychology" (1999, 315). If individuals comply with social norms, rather than with instrumental rational assessments, this might be a least-cost solution but also an action that yields its own intrinsic value. Choice will depend on both the costs of acting instrumentally and the benefits of adopting norms that are deemed intrinsically worthwhile.

Perceptions of the intrinsic value of action depend on the behavior of others. Individuals derive utility from acting as good citizens; empirical work suggests that perceptions of the intrinsic value of such action are important. Policy signals of increased compulsion by tax authorities (for example, as reflected in increased audit and authority) are capable of demeaning perceptions of the intrinsic value of good citizenship (Frey 1997a, 1997b). Such compulsion might itself signal "that others do not, or are not willing to contribute their fair share" (Frey 1997b, 1049).[7] Pooling these arguments yields a literature that suggests (implicitly, or explicitly) that there is choice. As such, we propose the following three tests of that proposition:

> The first relies on a strategy Torgler (2002) recommends. After surveying empirical analysis of tax evasion, he argues that, in behavioral experiments, subjects are often directed to act instrumentally. As, in practice, individuals might choose not to behave as instrumentally this is a shortcoming. Focusing on Nehemiah Friedland, Shlomo Maital, and Aryeh Rutenberg (1978), he notes: "Subjects were instructed as follows 'Your objective is to maximize your net income,'" then argues that such direction could "frame participants to follow behavioral rules which are different from those followed in the actual tax declaration process" and recommends that it would be "useful to tell subjects not to maximize net income but just to complete their tax return" (660).

The first challenge in this chapter is to ask one cohort of subjects in an experiment to address tax questions instrumentally (to maximize net income) but to set no instruction for the other cohort in answering the same questions.

> The second test focuses on the relevance of instrumental action for different groups. When considering collective action, comparisons have been made of the behavior of businessmen and behavior of those employed in caring professions, for example, nurses (Ledyard 1995). In this study the test focuses on a comparison of behavior by students of economics and by students of psychology. Robert Frank, Thomas Gilovich, and Dennis Regan (1993) argue that the study of economics makes individuals more instrumental in their approach (for a different view, see Frey and Meier 2003). Whether this is because they are more adept at instrumental calculus or whether (as Frank and his colleagues suggest) they become more self-interested is moot. Frank and colleagues (1993, 1996) assert that there

is greater instrumental behavior (noncooperative behavior in terms of the prisoner's dilemma) on the part of economics majors. They report, for example, that "the probability of an economics major defecting is almost 0.17 percent higher than the corresponding probability for a non major" (1993, 166).

This result is by no means unusual. Marwell and Ames (1981) found that economics students were far more likely to act instrumentally in terms of opting to free ride when given the chance to contribute to a collective good. They found that economics students contributed, on average, only 20 percent of their initial endowments to the collective goal (significantly less than the 49 percent average for all other subjects). The difference is explained in terms of different perceptions of what was fair. The economics graduate students were about half as likely as other subjects to indicate that they were concerned with fairness.[8]

The test here is also for different responses (more or less instrumental) but is presented with reference to the issue of tax compliance. The question is whether there is evidence of choice to act more (or less) instrumentally and whether choice depends on being part of a self-selecting educational group.

> A third test of the relevance of instrumental rationality is whether different individuals (in this case economists or psychologists) are more vulnerable to framing. Is this cognitive anomaly experienced equally by different individuals or are some individuals able to act more instrumentally?

Prospect theory, developed by Kahneman and Tversky (1979), is an alternative theory of individual decision making under risk. With reference to a value function, the prediction is that individuals are particularly risk averse when they face a gain situation. If they are expecting a tax refund, they are likely to perceive it as a gain. By comparison, if they are faced with declaring income for tax, they are likely to perceive it as a loss. To date, evidence in experiments is consistent with the proposition that individuals will take less risk in a refund situation (a gain) and more when declaring income for tax (a loss). Otto Chang and Joseph Schultz (1990) report that taxpayers in a refund situation are more likely to comply than those in a balance due situation. Henry Robben and colleagues (1990) report that participants in an experiment who recalled making an extra tax payment evade more often than those who recalled receiving a refund. Albert Schepanski and David Kelsey (1990) report that individuals are less likely to claim a dubious deduction when they are in a tax refund situation. Richard White, Paul Harrison, and Adrian Harrell (1993) found that individuals exhibit risk-seeking behavior when tax is due and risk-averse behavior when a refund is pending.

Our objective is to determine whether the influence of framing is less likely if individuals are instructed to act instrumentally or if individuals (economists) are more likely to act instrumentally. Will everyone be equally subject to framing effects, or are those who act more instrumentally less vulnerable?

Empirical Evidence

In this section we describe the development of a questionnaire study before providing a detailed analysis of the results obtained.

Method

The questionnaire was designed to assess the following four questions:

1. Whether audit probability influences the amount of income declared. To this end, the first three questions asked respondents to say how much they would declare where the probability of detection was 1 percent, 5 percent and 25 percent, respectively. This factor has the shorthand PROB. All respondents answered all three questions, analyzed as a repeated measure, within-subject effect.[9] All other effects are between-subject effects necessitating different versions of the questionnaires filled in by different respondents.

2. Whether respondents asked to imagine themselves as an established trader would declare their income differently in cases where taxes had not already been deducted (Questionnaires A and B) compared to respondents where tax had already been deducted based on the previous years income (Questionnaires C and D). This factor has the shorthand FRAMETAX.

3. Whether respondents instructed to behave instrumentally would answer differently from those who were not (Questionnaires B and D compared to Questionnaires A and C). This factor has the shorthand FRAMEINS.

4. Whether respondents taking economics units answer differently to those taking psychology units. The four versions of the questionnaires were distributed evenly across all respondents. This factor is DEGR.

A summary of the design is presented in figure 9.2. The questionnaires are more fully described later.

The final versions were informed by a pilot study of more than one hundred respondents, where it became apparent that it was necessary to simplify both the questions (removing any mention of tax allowances)

Figure 9.2   Design of Questionnaire Study

FRAMETAX	Tax Not Yet Deducted		Tax Deducted Based On Previous Year's Income	
FRAMEINS	Noninstrumental instructions (Be yourself)	Instrumental (Maximize)	Noninstrumental	Instrumental
PROB	Question 1 Three repeated measures common to all versions. Audit probability 1 percent, 5 percent, 25 percent			

◄───►

Versions Evenly Distributed Across All
Respondents Studying Economics Units
or Psychology Units (DEGR)

Source: Authors' compilation.

and the figures. Comments from participants in the pilot study also led us to increase the time available to answer the four questions and to provide more time for respondents to familiarize themselves with the task.

The 307 respondents were second and final year undergraduates from the University of Bath, UK. Of them, 206 were recruited from economics units, 98 from psychology units and three failed to identify their degree program; 173 were male, 131 were female, and three left the relevant box blank.

The questionnaires were administered at the start of economics lectures by Cullis and Jones and at the start of psychology lectures by Lewis. The four versions of the questionnaire (reproduced in appendix A) were evenly distributed among the participants. The administrator thanked participants for their help and then slowly read out the preamble:

> This is a research topic on taxation of the self-employed.
> We are trying to simulate real world decisions and we would like you to fill in your answers in this light.
> You have to identify with the situation of the person described.
> There is no right or wrong way of responding.
> Different tax contexts are described and you are asked to write down your carefully considered answers.
> Typically there are two systems. First, when a self-employed taxpayer declares income and is then taxed. Second, when a self-employed taxpayer is taxed on the basis of last year's income and then reports income, so that changes can be made in tax assessment and appropriate refund can be returned.
> As in all tax systems, the authorities investigate a certain proportion of all income statements made by taxpayers.

Take your time and consider the scenarios carefully.
Thank you for your help.

A printed version of the preamble was then handed out to each respondent along with one copy of a questionnaire. The questionnaires were completed independently, collected in situ, and the data entered on a SPSS for Windows file.

Results

An ANOVA (General Linear Model) was conducted using the SPSS program for the first three questions. There was therefore one within-subject factor, the repeated measures of the three detection rates (PROB), and three between-subject factors: FRAMETAX, whether the tax authorities had already deducted tax; FRAMEINS, whether respondents were instructed to behave instrumentally; DEGR, whether respondents were studying economics or psychology units. Table 9.2 presents the results for the within-group factor. The results reveal that detection rates significantly influence the amount of income declared. The significant interaction effect shows that the amount declared is also influenced by which academic units respondents are studying: table 9.3 makes the relationship clear. The amount declared rises as audit probability increases, an effect that is more pronounced among respondents studying economics units. There are no other statistically significant interactions.

The significance of between-subjects factors is present in table 9.4, which also reveals that the main effects of framing (whether tax has already been deducted) is statistically significant, as is the main effect of the academic unit studied. The main effect of instrumental versus noninstrumental instructions is insignificant as are all the interaction effects. Table 9.5 reveals that respondents who have already had their tax de-

Table 9.2   Within Subjects Effects

	F	SIG (Three Decimal Places)
PROB	100.973	.000
PROB x FRAMETAX	2.847	NS
PROB x DEGR	9.419	.000
PROB x FRAMEINS	2.313	NS
PROB x FRAMETAX x DEGR	0.131	NS
PROB x FRAMETAX x FRAMEINS	0.206	NS
PROG x DEGR x FRAMEINS	0.781	NS
PROG x FRAMETAX x DEGR x FRAMEINS	0.192	NS

Source: Authors' compilation.

Table 9.3   Academic Unit Studied Times Audit Probability

	Income Declared (Mean)	
Audit Probability	Psychology Unit	Economics Unit
1%	£16,830	£13,322
5%	£18,175	£15,820
25%	£19,562	£18,459

Source: Authors' compilation.

ducted declared more in all audit conditions. Furthermore, as table 9.3 shows, respondents studying economics units declare less (and incidentally, in all audit conditions).

Discussion

The significant difference between the three audit rates shows that at least some respondents behave instrumentally. Instrumentality is much more common among economics students who declare less in all three conditions than psychology students. Indeed, the majority of psychology students (53 percent) declare all their income even when the probability of investigation is only 1 percent.

The instruction to behave instrumentally or to be yourself has no statistically significant effect. This suggests that instrumentality is not a choice, not something that can easily be switched on and off. Instrumentality seems to come easily, almost naturally to economists who behave in this way whether they are bidden to or not. Alternatively, psychologists cannot bring themselves to behave in this fashion even when explicitly asked to do so. It seems that even young leopards are unable to change their spots.[10]

This finding is in line with Frank, Gilovich, and Regan (1993), though

Table 9.4   Between Subject Effects

	F	SIG (Three Decimal Places)
FRAMETAX	5.841	.016
DEGR	18.100	.000
FRAMEINS	0.458	NS
FRAMETAX x DEGR	0.736	NS
FRAMETAX x FRAMEINS	0.943	NS
DEGR x FRAMEINS	0.943	NS
FRAMETAX x DEGR x FRAMEINS	0.862	NS

Source: Authors' compilation.

Table 9.5   The Tax Framing Effect

Audit and Frame	Tax Not Yet Deducted	Already Deducted Based on Previous Year's Income
1%	£13,419	£15,516
5%	£15,967	£17,245
25%	£18,368	£19,291

Source: Authors' compilation.

we are unable to say when this differential socialization takes place. The economists are inculcated into instrumental rationality as *the* rational decision-making mechanism; exposed, almost exclusively, to individually motivated forms of analysis (a non-organic view of society); male and therefore apparently more selfish; mathematically trained; and pecuniary orientated (£ signs appear virtually everywhere). The presumption is that in the battle of the pickpockets (tax evasion) the economists can be identified more closely with the artful dodgers.

The framing of taxation, as already withheld or yet to be paid, was statistically significant. In line with Kahneman and Tversky's (1979) paper, when tax is yet to be paid it is perceived as a loss, thus encouraging risk taking. There is also a possible endowment effect when tax yet to be paid is seen as a legitimate part of one's income (a property rights perspective). It is also feasible that participants perceive they have greater opportunities to evade when tax has yet to be deducted (the game is afoot). This framing effect is universal and works whether one studies economics or psychology.

We do not claim that the figures produced here reflect how business people would react to these scenarios or that the figures can be used as a measure of tax evasion. This experiment was set up purely to test the hypotheses by assessing statistical differences. (The absolute figures are of no great importance.) However, we do claim that the findings have a wider applicability and that the study can be viewed as a demonstration, or, if preferred, a metaphor. We have shown that instrumentality is unevenly distributed: some people are instrumental and others are not. Weighing the odds comes naturally to our economists, whereas for most of the psychologists it is just an odd thing to do. Instrumentality is not a choice. For many people the artful dodge is simply not in the frame, which probably accounts for a good deal of voluntary compliance.

Conclusions

The exponential growth of empirical behavioral studies of tax evasion for many leaves little doubt that the neoclassical (Allingham-Sandmo) model is unable to predict tax evasion behavior well enough to be reliable in practical applications. For example, a separating equilibrium (where some evade and others do not) is observed in this experiment where p and s were deliberately chosen to generate a pooled equilibrium (where given the instrumental incentives all should have evaded).

The reader is presented with a literature that offers a confusing (seemingly inconsistent) array of competing explanations for greater than anticipated tax compliance (with reference to heuristics, reciprocity, empathy, intrinsic motivation, stigma costs). The speculative picture drawn here is that individuals:

- differ in their inculcation to act instrumentally, as represented in this experiment by the differences between economists and psychologists (there are tendencies in some individuals to be more narrowly self interested);

- react instrumentally conditional upon their extent of their inculcation (tendencies are modified by incentives albeit from a different base level); and

- are all subject to particular framing effects (all are subject to being fooled to some extent).

These outcomes are not inconsistent with other empirical work. Bjorn Frank and Gunter Schulze (2000) found that economists were more corrupt (especially males) than others and that this was due to self-selection rather than indoctrination. Benno Torgler (2002) observes that despite the fact that the simulated tax experiments are flawed we can conclude with some confidence that higher audit rates lead to more compliance and that taxpayers have a more refined motivational structure than that assumed in traditional economics. Keith Stanovich and Richard West (1998) have shown that respondents with higher cognitive ability are less susceptible to framing. Irwin Levin and colleagues (2002) have suggested that the personality of respondents is related to the strength of framing effects.

Early in the chapter we quoted Shiller to the effect that efficient markets theory has lost the "stock market" battle and "we are all behavioral economists now," but this of course is not the case. In the article that immediately preceded Shiller's in that issue of the *Journal of Economic Perspectives*, the economist Barton Malkiel writes "we will document further apparent departures from efficiency and further patterns in the development of stock returns. But I suspect that the end result will not be an abandonment of the belief of many in the profession that the stock market is remarkably efficient in its utilization of information" (2003, 80). In this context, the chapter perhaps offers two cheers for expected utility maximization and two for behavioral finance and the implication that "we are all eclectics now."

If empiricists have suspected that the neoclassical model fails to encompass all aspects of the decision of how to evade, they have surely been proven correct. However, they have presented a challenge. If comparative analysis of different empirical studies is to prove helpful it is necessary to make sense (impose order) on seemingly rival results and competing motivations. If tax evasion is to be better understood, we must identify the determinants of the domain of instrumental rationality. If anti-evasion policy is to be better designed we must look beyond instrumental responses in isolation and foster an ethical preference.

Appendix: Questionnaires

The questionnaires administered in our study are described in this section.

Questionnaire A

Thank you for helping us with our research. The information you provide is completely confidential and remember there are no right or wrong answers to the questions posed.

Please fill these in first.

Degree Program: ………………..
Year of study: ………………..
Sex: ………………..

Please answer the following questions in terms *of what you would do in these situations*.

Imagine you are an established trader with a taxable income this year of £20,000. It is time to file your tax return and no tax has been deducted so far this year. The tax rate for the whole of the £20,000 is 30 percent.

Q1. In the following three cases you are asked to say what income you would state you earned. Remember the tax authorities conduct investigations of your response and if you are found to be evading, any detected undeclared income will be taxed at 60 percent.

The income I would declare is

Case 1

The probability of investigation is 1 percent (1 in 100)   £…………

Case 2

The probability of investigation is 5 percent (5 in 100)   £…………

Case 3

The probability of investigation is 25 percent (25 in 100) £............

Questionnaire B

Thank you for helping us with our research. The information you provide is completely confidential and remember there are no right or wrong answers to the questions posed.
   Please fill these in first.

   Degree Program: ....
   Year of study: ....
   Sex: ....

   Please answer the following questions with *the objective of maximizing your income.* Imagine you are an established trader with a taxable income this year of £20,000. It is time to file your tax return and no tax has been deducted so far this year. The tax rate for the whole of the £20,000 is 30 percent.
   Q1. In the following three cases you are asked to say what income you would state you earned. Remember the tax authorities conduct investigations of your response and if you are found to be evading, any detected undeclared income will be taxed at 60 percent.
   The income I would declare is

Case 1

The probability of investigation is 1 percent (1 in 100)   £............

Case 2

The probability of investigation is 5 percent (5 in 100)   £............

Case 3

The probability of investigation is 25 percent (25 in 100) £............

Questionnaire C

Thank you for helping us with our research. The information you provide is completely confidential and remember there are no right or wrong answers to the questions posed.
   Please fill these in first.

Degree Program: ....

Year of study: ....

Sex: ....

Please answer the following questions in terms *of what you would do in these situations.* Imagine you are an established trader with a taxable income this year of £20,000. The tax rate for the whole of the £20,000 is 30 percent. Based on your income last year the tax authorities have already deducted the appropriate amount of tax (i.e. £6,000). It is time to file your tax return.

Q1. In the following three cases you are asked to declare your annual income. If you report less than £20,000 you will receive returned tax at a rate of 30 percent. The tax authorities conduct investigations and if you are found to be underdeclaring your income, the undeclared income will be taxed at 60 percent.

The income I would declare is

Case 1

The probability of investigation is 1 percent (1 in 100)   £............

Case 2

The probability of investigation is 5 percent (5 in 100)   £............

Case 3

The probability of investigation is 25 percent (25 in 100) £............

Questionnaire D

Thank you for helping us with our research. The information you provide is completely confidential and remember there are no right or wrong answers to the questions posed.

Please fill these in first.

Degree Program: ....

Year of study: ....

Sex: ....

Please answer the following questions with *the objective of maximizing your income.* Imagine you are an established trader with a taxable income this year of £20,000. The tax rate for the whole of the £20,000 is 30 percent. Based on your income last year the tax authorities have already deducted the appropriate amount of tax (that is, £6,000). It is time to file your tax return.

Q1. In the following three cases you are asked to declare your annual income. If you report less than £20,000 you will receive returned tax at a rate of 30 percent. The tax authorities conduct investigations and if you are found to be underdeclaring your income, the undeclared income will be taxed at 60 percent.

The income I would declare is

Case 1

The probability of investigation is 1 percent (1 in 100)   £.............

Case 2

The probability of investigation is 5 percent (5 in 100)   £.............

Case 3

The probability of investigation is 25 percent (25 in 100) £.............

Notes

1. However, Slemrod (2003) notes: "A wage or salary earner whose employer submits this information electronically to the Internal Revenue Service, but who does not report that income on his own personal return, will be flagged for further scrutiny with a probability much closer to 100 percent than to 2 percent" (9).
2. Mechanism design takes game theory back one step and poses the question as to what would happen if the rules of a game (mechanism) were designed to achieve some objective—here honest tax paying.
3. Fifty-seven students were told that their own tax was based on a tax rate of 40 percent. Nineteen were told that the average tax rate was 65 percent, nineteen others were told that the average tax rate was 15 percent, and the remaining nineteen were told that all participants had the same tax rate. On average, 23.13 percent of total taxes payable were evaded. The group with the high tax evaded 32 percent, the group with the low tax 12.26 percent and the group with the medium taxation 24.5 percent.
4. The instructions may have produced a bias towards a higher noncompliance rate, because participants were asked to maximize their net income.
5. Individuals were informed about their individual share of total transfer payments but not about the amount.
6. The authors report some evidence that compliance is not always caused by overweighting the audit probability or extreme risk aversion. They investigated a case where there was no chance of detection. The average compliance rate was 20 percent, with a variation between 5.3 and 35.8 percent across the groups.

7. Empirical evidence reveals that the perception of avoidance by other persons is important (Klosko 1992). In experiments, cooperation declines if individuals believe that cooperation by others is lower than they anticipated (for example, Brubaker 1975; Taylor 1987).
8. The question of whether action is deemed fair or not also explains different responses by economics students and others in the ultimatum bargaining game. In this game, as John Carter and Michael Irons reported (1991), the allocator has $10 to divide with another player and payoffs depend on agreement by both parties. Assuming the money cannot be divided into units smaller than one cent, the prediction was that an instrumental allocator would propose $9.99 for himself/herself; the receiver will agree (as $0.01 is better than nothing). Economics majors more often behaved in this way.
9. Note that the Allingham and Sandmo model is about how an individual should respond to changes in tax parameters and hence the desire here to ask a given individual a series of questions with changing parameters rather than confront different individuals with the equivalent questions set in isolation from one another. Additionally, although the model is successful, it is essentially a static one. In future work it might be attractive to augment the model by giving respondents a past history of evasion or compliance.
10. Jonathan Baldry (1984) reports two experiments. In the first, involving tax evasion, some participants never evaded tax. In the second experiment, tax evasion was not mentioned, instead it was represented as a pure gamble (with identical payoffs); everyone gambled (and each made the maximum bet). In our study the results are consistent with those of Baldry: it was evident that despite being invited to view tax evasion as a gamble many respondents refused to accept the invitation.

References

Allingham, Michael G., and Agnar Sandmo. 1972. "Income Tax Evasion: A Theoretical Analysis." *Journal of Public Economics* 1(3/4): 323–38.

Alm, James, Gary H. McClelland, and William Schulze. 1992. "Why Do People Pay Taxes?" *Journal of Public Economics* 48(1): 21–38.

Andreoni, James, Brian Erard, and Jonathan Feinstein. 1998. "Tax Compliance." *Journal of Economic Literature* 36(2): 818–60.

Baldry, Jonathan C. 1984. "The Enforcement of Income Tax Laws: Efficiency Implications." *The Economic Record* 60(169): 156–59.

Becker, Winifred, Heinz-Jurgen Buchner, and Simon Sleeking. 1987. "The Impact of Public Transfer Expenditures on Tax Evasion: An Experimental Approach." *Journal of Public Economics* 34(2): 243–63.

Bentham, Jeremy. 1789/1948. *The Principles of Morals and Legislation*. New York: Macmillan.

Brubaker, Earl R. 1975. "Free Ride, Free Revelation or Golden Rule?" *Journal of Law and Economics* 18(1): 147–61.

Carter, John R., and Michael D. Irons. 1991. "Are Economists Different and, If So, Why?" *Journal of Economic Perspectives* 5(2): 171–77.

Chang, Otto H., and Joseph J. Schultz Jr. 1990. "The Income Tax Withholding

Phenomena: Evidence from TCMP Data." *The Journal of the American Taxation Association* 12(1): 88–93.

Cowell, Frank. 1985. "The Economic Analysis of Tax Evasion." *Bulletin of Economic Research* 37(3): 163–93.

Cullis, John, and Alan Lewis. 1997. "Why People Pay Taxes." *Journal of Economic Psychology* 18(2–3): 305–21.

The Economist. 2003. "To Have and to Hold." August 30, 2003, p. 64.

Fehr, Ernst, and Simon Gachter. 2000. "Fairness and Retaliation: The Economics of Reciprocity." *Journal of Economic Perspectives* 14(3): 158–81.

Frank, Bjorn, and Gunter Schulze. 2000. "Does Economics Make Citizens Corrupt?" *Journal of Economic Behavior and Organization* 43(1): 101–13.

Frank, Robert H., Thomas Gilovich, and Dennis T. Regan. 1993. "Does Studying Economics Inhibit Cooperation?" *Journal of Economic Perspectives* 7(2): 159–71.

———. 1996. "Do Economists Make Bad Citizens?" *Journal of Economic Perspectives* 10(1): 187–92.

Frey, Bruno S. 1997a. *Not Just For the Money: An Economic Theory of Personal Motivation.* Cheltenham: Edward Elgar.

———. 1997b. "A Constitution for Knaves Crowds Out Civic Virtues." *Economic Journal* 107(443): 1043–53.

Frey, Bruno S., and Reiner Eichenberger. 1989. "Anomalies and Institution." *Journal of Institutional and Theoretical Economics* 145(3): 423–37.

———. 1994. "Economic Incentives Transform Psychological Anomalies." *Journal of Economic Behavior and Organization* 23(2): 215–34.

Frey, Bruno S., and Stephen Meier. 2003. "Are Political Economists Selfish and Indoctrinated?" *Economic Inquiry* 41(3) 448–62.

Friedland, Nehemiah, Shlomo Maital, and Aryeh Rutenberg. 1978. "A Simulation Study of Income Tax Evasion." *Journal of Public Economics* 10(1): 107–16.

Gonzalez, Cleotilde, Jason Dana, Hideya Koshino, and Marcel Just. 2005. "The Framing Effect and Risky Decisions: Examining Cognitive Functions with fMRI." *Journal of Economic Psychology* 26(1): 1–20.

Hochman, Harold M., and James D. Rodgers. 1969. "Pareto Optimal Redistribution." *American Economic Review* 59(4): 542–57.

Kahneman, Daniel, and Amos Tversky. 1979. "Prospect Theory: An Analysis of Decision Under Risk." *Econometrica* 47(2): 263–91.

———, eds. 2000. *Choices, Values and Frames.* New York: Cambridge University Press.

Kahneman, Daniel, Richard Thaler, and Jack Knetsch. 1990. "Experimental Tests of the Endowment Effect and the Coase Theorem." *Journal of Political Economy* 98(6): 1325–48.

Khalil, Elias L. 2003. "Behavioral Economics and the Transactional View." *Transactional Viewpoints* 11(1): 1–8.

Kinsey, Karyl. 1986. "Theories and Models of Tax Cheating." *Criminal Justice Abstracts* 18(September): 403–25.

Klosko, George. 1992. *The Principle of Fairness and Political Obligation.* Lanham, Md.: Rowman and Littlefield.

Knox, Thomas M. 1952. *Hegel's Philosophy of Right: Translated with Notes.* Oxford: Oxford University Press.

Ledyard, John O. 1995. "Public Goods: A Survey of Experimental Research." In *The Handbook of Experimental Economics,* edited by John H. Kagel and Alvin E. Roth. Princeton, N.J.: Princeton University Press.

Levin, Irwin, Gary Gaeth, Judy Schreiber, and Marco Lauriola. 2002. "A New Look at Framing Effects: Distribution of Effect Sizes, Individual Differences, and Independence of Types of Effects." *Organizational Behaviour and Human Decision Processes* 88(1): 411–28.

Lewis, Alan. 1982. *The Psychology of Taxation.* Oxford: Martin Robertson.

List, John A. 2003. "Does Market Experience Eliminate Market Anomalies?" *Quarterly Journal of Economics* 118(1): 41–71.

Loewenstein, George. 1999. "Because It Is There: The Challenge of Mountaineering for Utility Theory." *Kyklos* 52(3): 315–44.

Malkiel, Barton G. 2003. "The Efficient Market Hypothesis and Its Critics." *Journal of Economic Perspectives* 17(1): 59–82.

Marwell, Gerald, and Ruth E. Ames. 1981. "Economists Free Ride, Does Anyone Else? Experiments on the Provision of Public Goods IV." *Journal of Public Economics* 15(3): 295–310.

McCaffery, Edward, and John Baron. 2004. "Heuristics and Biases in Thinking about Tax." In *Proceedings of the 96th Annual Conference on Taxation (2003).* Washington, D.C.: National Tax Association.

Pommerehne, Werner W., Albert Hart, and Bruno S. Frey. 1994. "Tax Morale, Tax Evasion and the Choice of Policy Instruments in Different Political Systems." *Public Finance/ Finances Publiques* 49(Supp.): 52–69.

Pyle, David J. 1989. *Tax Evasion and the Black Economy.* London: Macmillan.

———. 1991. "The Economics of Taxpayer Compliance." *Journal of Economic Surveys* 5(2): 163–98.

Robben, Henry S. J., Paul Webley, Henk Elffers, and Dick Hessing. 1990. "Decision Frames, Opportunity and Tax Evasion: An Experimental Approach." *Journal of Economic Behavior and Organization* 14(3): 353–61.

Schepanski, Albert, and David Kelsey. 1990. "Testing for Framing Effects in Taxpayer Compliance Decisions." *Journal of the American Taxation Association* 12(1): 60–77.

Schmolders, Gunter. 1970. "Survey Research in Public Finance: A Behavioral Approach to Fiscal Policy." *Public Finance/Finances Publiques* 25(2): 300–6.

Schoemaker, Paul. 1982. "The Expected Utility Model: Its Variants, Purposes and Limitations." *Journal of Economic Literature* 20(2): 529–63.

Shiller, Robert J. 2003. "From Efficient Markets Theory to Behavioral Finance." *Journal of Economic Perspectives* 17(1): 83–104.

Slemrod, Joel, ed. 1992. *Why People Pay Taxes.* Ann Arbor: University of Michigan Press.

———. 2002. "Tax Systems." *NBER Reporter* (June): 8–13.

———. 2003. "Trust in Public Finance." In *Public Finance and Public Policy in the New Century,* edited by Sijbren Cnossen and Hans-Werner Sinn. Cambridge, Mass.: MIT Press.

Song, Young-Dahl, and Tinsley E. Yarbrough. 1978. "Tax Ethics and Taxpayer Attitudes: A Survey." *Public Administration Review* 38(5): 442–57.

Spicer, Michael W. 1986. "Civilization at a Discount: The Problem of Tax Evasion." *National Tax Journal* 39(1): 13–20.

Spicer, Michael W., and Lee A. Becker. 1980. "Fiscal Inequity and Tax Evasion: An Experimental Approach." *National Tax Journal* 33(2): 171–75.

Spicer, Michael W., and Rodney E. Hero. 1985. "Tax Evasion and Heuristics: A Research Note." *Journal of Public Economics* 26(2): 263–67.

Spicer, Michael W., and Sven B. Lundstedt. 1976. "Understanding Tax Evasion." *Public Finance/Finances Publiques* 31(2): 295–304.

Stanovich, Keith, and Richard West. 1998. "Individual Differences in Framing and Conjunction Effects." *Thinking and Reasoning* 4(4): 289–317.

Stigler, George J., and Gary S. Becker. 1977. "De Gustibus Non Est Disputandum." *American Economic Review* 67(2): 76–90.

Taylor, Michael. 1987. *The Possibility of Co-operation*. Cambridge: Cambridge University Press.

Thaler, Richard H. 1985. "Mental Accounting and Consumer Choice." *Marketing Science* 4(3): 199–214.

Torgler, Benno. 2002. "Speaking to Theorists and Searching for Facts: Tax Morale and Tax Compliance in Experiments." *Journal of Economic Surveys* 16(5): 657–83.

———. 2003. "To Evade Taxes or Not to Evade: That Is the Question." *Journal of Socio-Economics* 32(3): 283–302.

U.S. Department of the Treasury. Internal Revenue Service (IRS). 1991. *Closing the Gap: Alternatives to Enforcement*. Conference Report. Washington: U.S. Government Printing Office.

Webley, Paul, Henry Robben, Henk Elffers, and Dick Hessing. 1991. *Tax Evasion: An Experimental Approach*. Cambridge: Cambridge University Press.

White, Richard A., Paul D. Harrison, and Adrian Harrell. 1993. "The Impact of Income Tax Withholding on Taxpayer Compliance: Further Empirical Evidence." *Journal of the American Taxation Association* 15(2): 63–78.

PART IV

RETIREMENT BEHAVIOR

Chapter 10

Accounting for Social Security Benefits

HOWELL E. JACKSON

F OR most working Americans, Social Security benefits represent a significant financial asset, in many cases their principal or sole source of retirement income.[1] According to the Social Security Administration (SSA), the aggregate present value of Social Security benefits promised to those age sixty-two and older was $4.3 trillion dollars in January 2003 (U.S. Social Security Administration 2003). Economists sometimes refer to this figure as the "Social Security wealth" of retirees. Under current statutory formulas, younger workers are also entitled to substantial Social Security benefits with an aggregate present value on the order of $7.4 trillion as of 2003.[2] The total net present value of the Social Security benefits for all American workers and retirees was thus in the range of $ 11.7 trillion at the end of January 1, 2003. By way of comparison, the total market capitalization of the New York Stock Exchange (NYSE) was $12.3 trillion as of year-end 2003. (NYSE 2004). Crudely speaking, then, the Social Security wealth of American workers and retirees is roughly equal to the value of the Big Board.

In this chapter, I address the manner in which the Social Security Administration describes to Social Security participants the nature and value of their entitlements—and particularly their retirement benefits—under the Social Security Act. The critical document is the Social Security Statement, the annual statement that the SSA sends to every worker and retiree over the age of twenty-five. A copy of a sample Social Security Statement is attached in the appendix at the end of this chapter. Given the importance of Social Security benefits to so many Americans, it is surprising how little academic attention has been given to the content and implications of Social Security benefits. Again, a comparison to the stock market is instructive. Financial disclosures for capital market investments are routinely and rigorously analyzed in academic journals, and the regulation of these securities disclosure requirements is amended and supplemented with regularity. Aside from the occasional GAO report (see, for example, U.S. General Accounting Office 1989, 1996a, 1996b, 1997, 1998; U.S. Social Security Administration 2005b), Social Security Statements are almost never subject to public scrutiny or scholarly analysis. This disparity is all the more striking when one considers that the primary users of securities disclosures are institutional investors and other sophisticated parties fully capable of safeguarding their own interests, whereas the recipients of Social Security Statements include the vast majority of U.S. workers and retirees, many of whom have little expertise in financial analysis.

Trust Fund Accounting Versus Disclosures for Social Security Participants

In a recent article, I explored the manner in which the SSA and the federal government account for the Social Security trust funds themselves (Jackson 2004). There I argued that the country and its political leaders would be more likely to come to grips with the financial problems of Social Security if the annual Social Security Trustees Report accounted for the program with a modified system of accrual accounting rather than the cash flow accounting the federal government currently employs. During the course of 2003, the value of Social Security accrued benefits for current workers and retirees increased by approximately $800 billion and equaled roughly $12.7 trillion by year end. As the system's financial resources—principally its investments in special issue government bonds—increased by only $152 billion last year, the Social Security's implicit debt increased by nearly $650 billion in 2003. Had the Social Security Administration reported this $650 billion deficit in 2003 rather than the $152 billion cash-flow surplus it actually reported, the effect on public opinion and our political leadership could have been pronounced. In particular, by locating the source of Social Security's future problems in promises being made today, a modified system of accrual accounting would force both the general public and our political leadership to recognize that with each passing year the system's financial difficulties are worsening significantly. This change in accounting format would, I argue, greatly improve the prospects for meaningful and timely reform of the Social Security system. There, my principal focus was on how changes in the manner in which the government reports the annual financial performance of Social Security could improve public understanding of the problems of the Social Security system and hence the prospects for prompt and much-needed reform. Implicit in my analysis were the propositions that accounting formats matter and that changes in accounting formats could change political outcomes.

Here, I once again consider issues of financial presentation, but emphasize the individualized statements that each Social Security participant receives. For the most part, I am concerned with the usefulness of those statements for helping participants make sensible decisions about their personal financial plans, including both decisions of how much to save for retirement and how long to stay in the work force. My claim is that current Social Security Statements are difficult for most individuals to understand and likely to lead to errors in financial planning and labor market participation. Of course, Social Security participants are also political agents, and the information that they receive in their individual Social Security Statements may also have political consequences, both in terms of their understanding of the value of the current Social Security benefits and the impact and desirability of various reform proposals. Thus, there are political implications both for the current content of Social Security Statements and any changes that might be made to those statements. Thus, at least indirectly, this chapter also touches on the politics of Social Security and its reform.

The Current Social Security Statement

I should preface my analysis by noting that there is much to be admired in the Social Security Administration's existing statement format. Compared to most other government disclosures, the document is clear and well written. The statement, along with companion online resources on the Social Security Administration Web site, undoubtedly provides important and useful retirement planning information for millions of Americans. And even though the Social Security Statements have not received substantial attention in the academic community, one cannot doubt that the Social Security Administration staff has worked diligently to refine the document over time and been conscientious in responding to the concerns of various constituents.

An Overview

Beginning in the late 1980s, the Social Security Administration (SSA) began to experiment with sending out individualized account statements to participants who requested information about their projected benefits. At the time, relatively few participants—less than 2 percent of workers paying payroll taxes—made such requests. Shortly thereafter, Congress mandated that the Social Security Administration initiate a program to distribute annual statements to all eligible workers aged twenty-five or over by 2000. The SSA estimated that this mandate would eventually require the distribution of approximately 123 million statements a year. The initial format of the disclosure statement was a six-page Personal Earnings and Benefit Estimate Statement (PEBES), which was subsequently revised in the late 1990s and replaced with the current four-page Social Security Statement (U.S. General Accounting Office 1996b).

In its current form, the Social Security Statement conveys multiple messages to participants and retirees. Some of the information relates to the program generally. For example, the statement begins with a cover letter from SSA Commissioner Jo Anne B. Barnhart trumpeting the broad scope of Social Security benefits ("Social Security is for people of all ages . . ."), and includes on the fourth page a section titled "Some Facts About Social Security," which explains the different kinds of benefits that Social Security provides and highlights key choices for those near or in retirement. (Participants over fifty-five years also receive a separate, two-page insert discussing retirement options in more detail.) Somewhat in tension with this glowing description of the program, the statement also notes the "serious future financial problems" the system currently faces. In particular, Commissioner Barnhart's cover letter cites SSA estimates that the system's resources will be able to pay only about 73 percent of scheduled benefits in 2042.

Although the Social Security Statement's general information frames the disclosure document in important ways—to which I will return—the heart of the statement lies in pages two and three, where the Social Security Administration reports two kinds of information that are specific to the individual recipient. First and likely of greatest interest to most recipients are estimates of the recipient's projected retirement benefits. For ease of reference, I have reproduced in table 10.1 the relevant information from a sample statement for Wanda Worker (a hypothetical participant formerly known as John Q. Public in earlier versions of the statement) that the Social Security Administration has prepared for illustrative purposes. The statement includes three sets of estimates. The first is for retirement benefits, depending on whether the participant retires at sixty-two, the relevant normal retirement age (sixty-seven for Wanda Worker, who was born in 1963), or seventy. In addition, the form reports the level of disability benefits the recipient would receive if disabled in 2004, and then a range of estimates regarding the survivors' benefits that the recipient's family might be eligible to receive if Wanda were to die in 2004. At the bottom of the page, the statement also includes the participant's name, date of birth, estimated annual earnings in the future, and a truncated Social Security number.

The second category of personalized information comes on page three of the statement and deals with the recipient's earnings history and payroll taxes. The statements report the SSA's records of the recipient's life-

Table 10.1 Your Estimated Benefits

Retirement	You have earned credits to qualify for benefits.
	At your current earnings rate, if you stop working and start receiving benefits
	At age 62, your payment would be about . . . $882 a month
	If you continue working until . . .
	Your full retirement age (67 years), your payment would be about . . . $1,278 a month
	Age 70, your payment would be about . . . $1,594 a month
Disability	You have earned enough credits to qualify for benefits. If you became disabled right now, Your payment would be about . . . $1,169 a month
Family	If you get retirement or disability benefits, your spouse and children also may qualify for benefits.
Survivors	You have earned enough credits for your family to receive survivors benefits. If you die this year, certain members of your family may qualify for the following benefits.
	Your child . . . $911 a month
	Your spouse who is caring for your child . . . $911 a month
	Your spouse, if benefits start at full retirement age . . . $1,215 a month
	Total family benefits cannot be more than . . . $2,233 a month
	Your spouse or minor child may be eligible for a special one-time death benefit of $255.
Medicare	You have enough credits to qualify for Medicare at age 65.
	Even if you do not retire at age 65, be sure to contact Social Security three months before your 65th birthday to enroll in Medicare.

Your estimated benefits are based on current law. Congress has made changes to the law in the past and can do so at any time. The law governing benefit amounts may change because, by 2042, the payroll taxes collected will be enough to pay only about 73 percent of scheduled benefits.

We based your benefit estimates on these facts:

Your name . . .	Wanda Worker
Your date of birth . . .	May 5, 1963
Your estimated taxable earnings per year after 2003 . . .	$35,051
Your Social Security number (only the last four digits are shown to help prevent identity theft) . . .	XXX-XX-2004

Source: Author's compilation from U.S. Social Security Administration (2005b).

time earnings. In the case of Wanda Worker, the earnings go back to 1979, when as a sixteen-year-old she earned $474. (The statements report both Social Security earnings and Medicare earnings, though for Wanda the figures are identical because her earnings have never passed the upper boundary for the imposition of Social Security payroll taxes.) At the bottom of the third page is the final category of personalized information: the level of taxes the recipient has paid to Social Security and Medicare. Both individual and employer taxes are reported, as well as information on the current payroll tax rates for Social Security and Medicare. In Wanda Worker's case, her Social Security taxes "paid over your working career through [2002]" are reported as $24,723, with the same amount reported as being paid by her employers.

The individualized information in the current Social Security Statement serves two distinct purposes (see U.S. General Accounting Office 1989).[3] First, the information about projected benefits is intended to assist recipients in both planning their retirement and in understanding the magnitude of the disability and survivors benefits provided under the program. Second, the statement includes past earnings information to confirm the accuracy and completeness of the Social Security Administration's records. The statement encourages recipients to review this earnings information carefully and report any errors to a toll-free phone number. Because Social Security benefits are directly tied to earnings history, the accuracy of the statement's benefit projections depend on the completeness of the SSA's earnings history for the recipient.

Limitations of Information

Without denigrating the undeniable value of the twin goals of the current Social Security Statement—providing individualized estimates of benefits and inviting correction of SSA earnings records—I now offer a series of comments on the limitations of this disclosure format. I am particularly interested in aspects of the Social Security Statement that might influence (or distort) participants' understanding of true economic value of Social Security benefits and the relationship between Social Security taxes and benefits. As will be clear shortly, the limitations I note do not point ambiguously in one direction. Although on balance I think that the current disclosure format would tend to lead participants to undervalue Social Security benefits, some aspects of the disclosure form likely have the opposite effect.

Benefits Payments Denominated in Monthly Amounts

Consistent with the Social Security Act's benefits formulas, the Social Security Statement reports benefits in terms of monthly payments, presumably because benefit payments are sent out monthly. Generally, however, when people talk about income levels, they speak in terms of annual salaries, which are, of course, twelve times higher than monthly income levels. Although one might resist this point as merely an arithmetic artifact, I would note that the earnings information reported on page three of the Social Security Statement is reported as annual earnings. To the extent that the critical question of retirement planning is projecting and then achieving appropriate levels of income replacement, the Social Security Statement complicates that fact by describing benefits and earnings history in two different currencies. (By way of comparison, if Wanda Worker were informed that her retirement benefit at sixty-seven was projected to be $15,336, she would more easily see that Social Security would replace 43.8 percent of the $35,051 of annual income that she is projected to earn for the rest of her working life.)

Retirement Benefits Based on Projected Earnings

Another important feature of Social Security Statements is that the estimated earnings of participants are based on the assumption that participants will continue to earn income at their current levels.[4] So, in the case of Wanda Worker, she is assumed to continue her current earnings through her retirement, which if she retires at her normal retirement age of sixty-seven means that she is projected to earn $35,051 (in current dollars) a year through 2029. To a degree, this approach to benefits projection is understandable. In planning for retirement, what one needs to know is the projected level of retirement benefits, and it is sensible to include in such projections the benefits attributable to likely future earnings. The approach does, however, have a somewhat peculiar effect on the participant's sense of entitlement to scheduled benefits and on their awareness of the degree to which retirement benefits under the Social Security Act accrue through annual participation in the workforce.

Let me begin with the point about entitlement. By projecting scheduled benefits with hypothetical future earnings, the Social Security Statement is telling participants like Wanda Worker what their retirement benefits are likely to be if they continue working until a particular age. To be sure, the information is prefaced with a warning—"The law governing benefit amounts may change"—and the warning is supplemented with a footnote reiterating Commissioner Barnhart's admonition that, in 2042, system resources will be able to support only 73 percent of benefits.[5] Still, one wonders how most recipients understand these reservations, particularly when projected benefits are so prominently displayed. And, at least for someone Wanda's age, the possibility of benefit reductions in 2042 may seem fairly remote because she will be seventy-nine at that point and twelve years into her retirement, should she retire at sixty-seven.

The manner in which the Social Security Statement disguises the incremental value of work force participation is a bit more complex, but related. By projecting future earnings through retirement, the Social Security Statements make it seem that workers do not get much more in terms of Social Security retirement benefits by working an additional year. Take, for example, Wanda Worker. On her January 2, 2004, Social Security Statement, she was told that she could expect a retirement benefit at sixty-seven of $1,278. An interesting question is what her projected retirement benefit for the same retirement age was when she received her Social Security Statement the previous year—that is, in January 2003. My calculations put it at $1,257—a nominal difference of only $21. (Indeed if one adjusts the two levels of projected benefits to put them in the same current dollars, Wanda Worker's projected real benefits actually declined from 2003 to 2004.)[6] So, at least for this hypothetical worker, a review of successive Social Security Statements would suggest only minimal nominal accretion of benefit value over time.

Opacity with Respect to Social Security Indexing Formulas

Moving to more technical aspects of benefit calculations, the Social Security Statements include a limited amount of information about the indexation of benefits. To begin with, the statements do not purport to project actual benefit levels—that is, the projected retirement benefits are not adjusted for expected inflation but rather are expressed in terms of current dollars. Introductory text does, however, explain that the benefits will be adjusted for cost-of-living increases "after you start receiving benefits." Whether most recipients understand that the starting level of benefits will also be indexed for price increases is not clear, but on balance I think the administration made a sensible choice to express benefit levels in current dollars and not report adjusted levels of benefits.[7] The risk of participants' misconstruing the meaning of benefits denominated in future dollars strikes me as substantial. On the other hand, the current approach does raise the possibility that some readers will undervalue the projections because they do not understand how indexing formulas work.

One of the reasons, I suspect, that the Social Security Statement is artful with respect to the issue of indexing relates to the fact that retirement benefit projections do not include adjustments for projected increases in average real wages. Although Social Security benefits are tied to real wage increases during participants' working lives and the long-term financial projections contained in the Trustees Reports are based on estimated increases in real wages, the Social Security Statements do not assume any increase in real wages in the future.[8] As a result, the aggregate projected retirement benefits in all Social Security Statements (discounted for individual mortality) are a good deal less than the projected benefits reported in the Trustees Annual Reports. Although there may be paternalistic grounds for low-balling projected retirements with respect to average real wage growth that may not in fact occur, this omission—which is nowhere mentioned in the statements themselves—also reduces the perceived value of Social Security retirement benefits as compared with their true value.

The Treatment of Payroll Taxes

The current Social Security Statement has a relatively limited amount of information about individual payroll taxes, just estimates of the amount of taxes paid by both the recipient and employers through the last reported year of earning.[9] So, focusing in on just Social Security taxes, page two of Wanda Worker's statement's estimates through 2002, she and her employers each paid $24,723 of payroll taxes or a total of $49,452. What exactly recipients make of this payroll-tax information is hard to say. Presumably, most readers are not well versed in the standard labor economics view that employer taxes are borne by workers, and it seems plausible that many recipients think only their own share of these taxes counts as an individual's contribution—that is, in the case of Wanda Worker, $24,723. If some, like Wanda Worker, were to compare that figure with the projected monthly retirement benefit of $1,278 at age sixty-seven, Social Security might seem like a very good deal. After all, in less than twenty months of retirement, Wanda Worker would get benefits equal to more than her cumulative payroll taxes. It is, of course, hard to know whether recipients do engage in such ill-informed back-of-the-envelope calculations. If so, this aspect of the Social Security Statement would have the tendency of making the Social Security retirement program seem like an advantageous proposition, undercutting some of the factors discussed elsewhere in this chapter, which generally suggest that statements tend to lead participants to underestimate the true value of the program.[10]

Uncertainty of Benefit Payments

The Social Security Statement's treatment of uncertainty is limited in several respects. In terms of understanding the value of Social Security benefits, participants should in theory consider two different kinds of uncertainty: uncertainty as to the continued provision of benefits as currently structured under the Social Security Act (sometimes described as scheduled benefits) and uncertainty as to the likelihood that a particular individual will actually receive the benefits described.

The current Social Security Statement addresses the first of these uncertainties—the possibility of scheduled benefit changes—in several ways. First, as mentioned, the statement includes two disclosures that in

2042 system resources will cover only 73 percent of scheduled benefits. The statement underscores this solvency concern by elsewhere noting that Congress could reduce benefit levels in the future. While most Social Security experts would agree that reductions in scheduled benefits are a very real possibility—particularly for 40-year-old workers such as Wanda Worker—one limitation of the current formulation of the Social Security Statement is that it offers the same degree of warning to both young and old participants. Most political observers believe that the likelihood of benefit cuts for older workers is lower than the likelihood for younger workers. And should older workers experience some benefit cuts, these will likely be lower than those applied to younger workers. By giving the same level of warning to both workers, the current Social Security Statement may be simultaneously too alarmist and excessively reassuring for different age cohorts of participants.[11]

Another source of uncertainty, not directly disclosed in the statement, is the possibility that participants such as Wanda Worker will not survive to receive retirement benefits or will not live to enjoy those benefits for a substantial period of time. It is unclear what assumptions participants have about their own mortality. Were a participant, such as Wanda Worker, to consult the most recent demographic projections in the 2004 Annual Report of the Social Security Trustees, she would learn that a woman in her birth cohort is projected at sixty-five to have a life expectancy of twenty years, implying that she might reasonably expect benefits payment for eighteen years after turning sixty-seven. But that life expectancy is conditional upon reaching the age of sixty-five, and mortality risk in the intervening twenty-five years is nontrivial.[12]

A related uncertainty concerns the likelihood that participants will receive two other kinds of benefits described in the Social Security Statement: disability benefits and survivor benefits (a form of life insurance). Unlike retirement benefits, these other benefits represent extremely low-probability events. The current Social Security Statement provides no information about the likelihood that these events will occur or any sense of the value of these benefits to participants such as Wanda Worker. Again, it is unclear what participant assumptions would be with respect to the likelihood of receiving these benefits and hence the value of this feature of the Social Security program.

Reprise of Limitations

The implications of these limitations of the Social Security Statement are ambiguous. As I mentioned, the statements are designed to communicate to participants their projected monthly benefits and to corroborate the administration's earnings records. The document is, in my view, reasonably successful on these two dimensions, but at a cost of confusing or misleading recipients on several other dimensions. As explained, some of the confusions would likely lead recipients to underestimate the value of their Social Security benefits: denominating benefits in monthly (as opposed to annual) payments and not more fully describing the system's extremely generous indexing rules are both likely to have this effect.

Other features of the Statement might have an offsetting effect. Most notably, describing payroll taxes in cumulative, nominal terms makes the real cost of Social Security benefits seem much lower than other possible measures of payroll contributions. The fact that benefits are based on total projected benefits has an ambiguous effect on participant perceptions. On the one hand, as explained below, total projected benefits constitute a measure of benefits that is at the upper end of conceivable benefit measures, and accordingly will tend to provide recipients of the statement with a favorable impression of the value of Social Security benefits. On the other hand, by reporting total projected benefits every year, the Social Security Statements disguise the extent to which participation in the labor force increases individual benefits over time and compensates participants, at least in part, for annual payroll tax contributions. The incompleteness of the Social Security Statement's discussion of uncertainty is also, I think, ambiguous. Conceivably, if the statement included a more complete discussion of uncertainties, participants would impose a higher mental discount on their valuations of benefits. However, if the statements dealt with these uncertainties in another, more complete way described in the next section, participants might assign greater values to certain benefits—perhaps just disability and survivors benefits, but perhaps also retirement benefits as well.

The Relevance of Cognitive Biases

I have focused principally on objective limitations in the Social Security Statement—omissions and limitations that would inhibit fully rational individuals in their efforts to comprehend the value of the Social Security benefit and participation in the Social Security program. Now I turn to a range of cognitive biases that may affect participant perceptions of the value of Social Security benefits.[13]

Tendency to Undervalue Retirement Income

I start with the most obvious of biases: the inability of many individuals to balance consumption during their working lives with their need for income in retirement. As Peter Diamond has recently explained, the reason Social Security exists is to correct the distortion caused by the failure of individuals to prepare adequately on their own for retirement income in the absence of a mandated, government program. (Diamond 2004). In part, the case for Social Security rests on a paternalistic notion that many individuals lack the self-discipline or self-awareness to make sensible intertemporal choices about consumption across a lifetime. An alternative justification is that a mandatory governmental program provides a more efficient and effective vehicle for retirement savings than individuals could obtain on their own. Yet another way of understanding Social Security is as a mechanism whereby the government protects itself against opportunistic behavior on the part of individuals who intentionally undersave for retirement with the expectation that they can then rely on government relief in old age.

At least the first of these justifications for Social Security—the inability of individuals to make appropriate intertemporal choices between current consumption and retirement income—has important implications for cognitive biases with respect to the Social Security Statement. It implies that even if the statement gave a perfectly clear and accurate picture of the system's retirement benefits, at least some individuals would value those benefits less than they should. In other words, if we need Social Security because individuals undervalue retirement income, it therefore follows that individuals will tend to undervalue the retirement income that Social Security provides even if those benefits are described accurately and comprehensively.

Tendency to Undervalue Periodic Payments over Time

Aside from the general difficulties that individuals encounter in making intertemporal choices between current consumption and retirement income, a number of more narrow cognitive biases may affect the ability of individuals to value properly Social Security benefits. For one thing, individuals have difficulty in estimating the value of periodic payments, such as monthly benefit checks. As many retailers have discovered, there are advantages of selling products with periodic price-tags ("$9.99 a week" or "only pennies a day") rather opposed to lump-sum payments. In my research, I have uncovered significant differences in the level of compensation that mortgage brokers receive when their compensation is paid through higher monthly payments rather than upfront fees (Jackson and Berry 2002). Additionally, the behavioral economics literature offers ample support for the proposition that individuals have a tendency to overestimate the cost of lump sum amounts as compared with periodic payments. (Lowenstein and Thaler 1989). In other words, there are good reasons to believe that individuals make systematic errors in time value of money calculations, tending to underestimate the present value of periodic payments. This insight has direct implications for the Social Security Statement because all its benefits are expressed in terms of monthly payments. The weight of behavioral economic research suggests that individuals will tend to undervalue the payments presented this way, implying that they will also undervalue the benefit payments described in the Social Security Statement.

Difficulties in Valuing of Annuities and Inflation Protection

Another potential source of bias concerns the particular (and economically valuable) features of Social Security benefits. These are all inflation-indexed, and retirement benefits are structured in the form of lifetime annuities or, in the case of married participants, joint-life annuities. There is an extensive economic literature that explores both annuities and inflation protection. (Brown 2000; Brown, Mitchell, and Poterba 2001). And although some contrary opinions exist, the weight of the evidence in both areas suggest that individuals undervalue both the insurance that ordinary annuities provide against the financial risk of a long life and the protection that inflation-adjusted annuities provide against unexpected increases in price levels. To the extent that one credits the literature on these two points—and I do—they suggest two more sources of cognitive biases that will tend to lead individuals to underestimate the true value of Social Security retirement benefits.

Uncertainty Regarding Benefits Changes and Individual Qualification

Individual responses to uncertainty is another area in which there has been much recent writing on cognitive biases. (Baron 2000). Unfortunately, the literature in the field is ambiguous, as there is evidence that individuals both over- and underestimate the significance of risk in different contexts. Accordingly, the literature does not offer clear insight into how individuals are likely to assess the various risks associated with Social Security benefits: either the overarching uncertainties of whether and how Congress might reduce benefit payments or the individual uncertainties of whether participants will actually receive disability, survivors, or even retirement benefits. Perhaps the best that one can say on this score is that the existence of these uncertainties means that further individual errors in the valuation of Social Security benefits are possible.

The Endowment Effect and Source Dependence

Two other cognitive biases may also bear on participant valuation of Social Security benefits as presented in the current version of the Social Security Statement. First is the endowment effect, as a result of which individuals supposedly value objects more highly when they possess them than when they do not (Thaler 1980). As explained, the current Social Security Statement presents participants with their full projected benefits at retirement under the assuming of continued employment for the remainder of the participant's working life. Arguably, this disclosure format gives participants a kind of constructive possession—or entitlement to—those benefits, thereby increasing the perceived value of the benefits over that of comparable benefits available, for example, by purchase from a private annuity provider but not yet in the participant's constructive possession.[14]

Another potentially relevant phenomenon identified in the behavioral economics literature is source dependence, a tendency of individuals to value objects more highly when the objects are perceived to be awarded in return for the individual's own efforts (Loewenstein and Issacharoff 1994). As explained earlier, the current form of the Social Security Statement obscures the relationship between labor market participation and the accrual of benefits. While the Statements make clear that benefits are generally tied to employment history, the direct relationship between each year's work and benefit accrual is not highlighted in the current statement. The absence of clarity on this point has, as I explain elsewhere, potential implications for labor market efficiencies, but it also could tend to reduce participant's subjective valuation of retirement benefits. If relevant in this context, source dependence might lead individuals to value their Social Security benefits less highly than they would if the benefits were more clearly and directly tied to labor market participation.

Reprise of the Impact of Cognitive Biases

As is often the case in reviews of cognitive biases, there is ambiguity as to the overall effect of the foregoing factors (Posner 1998). Many of these considerations suggest that individuals will tend to underestimate the value of Social Security benefits, in particular, the value of periodic payments, evidence suggesting that individuals undervalue annuities and inflation protection, and source dependence all point towards undervaluation. On the other hand, the endowment effect points towards overvaluation, and the effect of uncertainty in the receipt of benefit payments is ambiguous. On balance, my intuition would be that cognitive biases pointing toward undervaluation likely dominate, but that is only an intuition. An interesting question this analysis raises is how much of the first cognitive bias I identified—the inability of individuals to make appropriate intertemporal choices between current consumption and retirement income—is simply a product of the other more narrow cognitive biases relating to the valuation of periodic payments, annuities, and inflation adjustments. One implication of this analysis is that the failure of individuals to prepare adequately for retirement income may be overdetermined. For current purposes, however, it is enough to note that the behavioral economics literature offers several bases for suspecting that individuals face numerous difficulties in interpreting the benefit descriptions included in the current Social Security Statement.

An Alternative Approach to Presenting Benefits

Here I sketch an alternative approach to presenting Social Security benefits to participants. Rather than emphasizing projected monthly retirement benefits—the focus of the current Social Security Statements—the alternative approach outlined here highlights the expected present value of Social Security benefits over the course of participants' working lives. This approach is generally consistent with the manner in which economists value Social Security benefits when attempting to establish the Social Security wealth of individuals. (Jackson 2004).

As I explain in more detail shortly, the presentation of expected present values has two principal advantages over the current Social Security Statement. First, this alternative may make it easier for participants to understand the economic value of Social Security benefits in comparison to other types of financial assets. Second, it would allow participants to see more clearly the relationship between the annual accrual of Social Security benefits and the amount of payroll taxes that participants and their employers pay into the Social Security trust funds each year.

In presenting this alternative approach to describing Social Security benefits, I am not advocating that it should replace or even necessarily supplement the current Social Security Statement. Nor am I suggesting that it would address all the shortcomings of the current Social Security Statement outlined above. Rather, I am offering it to illustrate the availability of different presentation formats and to explore their implications in terms of financial planning, labor market participation, and ultimately political support for Social Security and its reform. Whether the benefits of alternative format warrant changes in the Social Security disclosures is a matter that requires considerable additional study.

I first consider several ways in which the expected value of Social Security benefits might be defined and then argue in favor of a measure of expected value that represents the accrued value of benefits under current statutory formula. This measure had various advantages in terms of assisting participants in financial planning and understanding the true value of their labor market participation. It is also roughly comparable to the kind of information that the Swedish government provides participants in its public pension program and is similar to the kinds of information that TIAA-CREF participants have received in the past (see boxes 10.1 and 10.2).

Three Approaches to Valuing Retirement Benefits

There are several ways in which one might estimate the present value of a participant's retirement benefits under Social Security.

Total Projected Benefits

First, one could calculate the present value of total projected retirement benefits either at retirement or at the present time. In the case of Wanda Worker, for example, that would mean estimating the value of a lifetime annuity of $1,278 a month or $15,366 a year starting at age sixty-seven. Assuming the eighteen-year life expectancy in retirement that the 2004 Trustees Report projects for a woman of her age and using a 3-percent real discount rate, Wanda Worker's projected benefit has an expected value of $211,116 on the eve of her retirement at sixty-seven in 2030 or $97,893 if discounted back to the end of 2003. (Both amounts are expressed in constant 2003 dollars.) In a sense, these are the values implicit in the Social Security Statement, as they represent the actuarial cost of the projected benefit, using an eighteen-year life expectancy and a 3-percent real discount rate.

Whether this is an appropriate valuation of Social Security retirement benefits is a different question. One obvious problem with this estimate is that it is based on projected benefits, which participants such as Wanda Worker have not yet earned under the Social Security Act. In addition, the valuation does not take into consideration the future taxes that the participant and his or her employers will have to pay over the balance of the participant's working life. In other words, the valuations just described could be considered the value of gross projected benefits without any consideration of future taxes.

Projected Benefits Less Projected Taxes

An obvious refinement would be to adjust the foregoing valuation to account for the cost of future taxes. This approach—valuing projected benefits, less projected taxes—is often employed in economic literature when the task at hand is estimating an individual's Social Security wealth (Jackson 2004). However, the adjustment is complex. One should not deduct all Social Security payroll taxes, because only a portion of them are associated with retirement benefits. For example, disability insurance taxes, which currently constitute 1.8 percent of payroll (or just under 15 percent of combined employee-employer contributions), support another form of benefit: disability insurance. Even the OASI taxes, which on a combined basis constitute 10.6 percent of payroll, are not exclusively dedicated to retirement benefits, as they also support survivors benefits and spousal benefits.

As economists often do, however, one could put aside these complexities and report the net present value of participants' total projected retirement benefits less the present value of future combined OASI combined taxes, and come up with a net valuation of retirement benefits. In the case of Wanda Worker, at the end of 2003, the present value of her projected combined OASI taxes was $66,420, implying a net valuation of her projected retirement benefits equal to $31,474 at that time. To give a better sense of the relationship between net valuations and gross valuations, I have charted in figure 10.1 the gross and net benefit valuations based on Wanda Worker's past and projected earnings record.[15] Note that the two measures converge on the eve of her retirement at sixty-seven, when no more payroll taxes will be paid. The net value of her benefits until she is in her early thirties is negative because the present value of future OASI combined taxes is greater than the present value of her total projected benefits, discounting both measures at a 3-percent real interest rate.

Projected Benefits from Accrued Benefits to Date

Another approach to valuing Social Security benefits is to present their value accrued to date under current statutory formulas. Also occasionally employed in economic analyses of Social Security wealth, this methodology reflects the present value of only that portion of projected

Figure 10.1 Total Projected Benefits and Total Projected Benefits Less Projected OASI Taxes

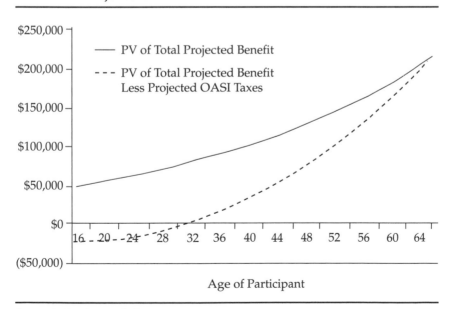

Source: Author's compilation.

benefits based on earnings history-to-date. Because it presents a measure of accrued benefits, it does not factor in the cost of future payroll taxes. As an adjunct to a presentation of this sort, one might also include an estimate of projected retirement benefits if the participant stopped working and made no further payroll tax contributions to the Social Security. For those within the academic community, this presentation style—accrued benefits with projected levels of retirement income based on accumulations to date—is familiar because it is the format the TIAA-CREF annual reports used to follow (see box 10.1).

In the case of Wanda Worker, her Social Security earnings record through the end of 2003 would generate a basic retirement benefit of $799.10 a month ($9,589.20 a year) if she retires at sixty-seven. Just under 63 percent of her total projected benefit at that age is projected in her Social Security Statement. Again assuming an eighteen-year life expectancy and using 3-percent real discount rate, this annuity has an actuarial value of $131,885 on the eve of retirement and $61,154 at the end of 2003. Figures are in constant 2003 dollars. Figure 10.2 reports a time series of this valuation method for Wanda Worker along with the valuation of total projected benefits. Here, too, both time series converge on the same point at the eve of her retirement, because all benefits are fully accrued at that point. Note, however, that the value of Wanda Worker's accrued benefits is always positive because the accruals are not offset by future taxes.[16]

Figure 10.2   Total Projected Benefits and Projected Accrued Benefits

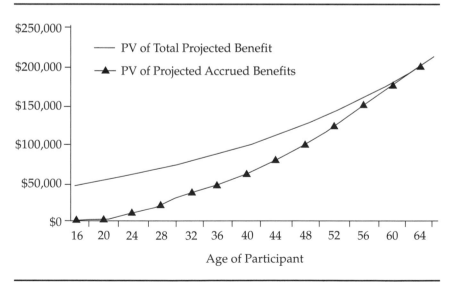

Source: Author's compilation.

**Box 10.1   A Brief History of Disclosure Statements for TIAA-CREF
Participants**

An interesting source of comparison for the Social Security Statement is the annual statement that TIAA-CREF sends to its participants. Originally, the TIAA-CREF statements reported only projected levels of annual retirement income that participants could be expected to receive under the organization's standard annuity option. Over time, however, participants began requesting information on the projected value of their accounts at retirement. Reportedly, participants were interested in comparing the value of other TIAA-CREF accounts to other sorts of savings.

Over the course of the 1990s, the TIAA-CREF statements evolved to include information on current account balances on a quarterly statement and projected annuities based on current account balances on the annual statement, which also contained a second set of projections based on projected account balances assuming a continuation of current contributions and then projected levels of retirement income based on total projected accumulations. Typically, these projections were based on an assumed rate of return along with a higher and lower estimated rates of return.

In the past few years, TIAA-CREF has simplified its statements to report only current accumulations on the quarterly statement and no longer provides an annual statement with written estimates of either projected account balances or projected levels of retirement income. A number of factors apparently contributed to this change, including the expansion of TIAA-CREF's investment options to include mutual funds. NASD regulations also apparently imposed some constraints on reporting projected yields, presumably out of fear of industry abuse. In addition, as TIAA-CREF expanded the range of annuity payout options available to its participants, it became less clear which annuity options were appropriate to use for projecting retirement income. Finally, the availability of web-based software provided an alterative mechanism for allowing participants to make their own projections. This web-based software now provides the principal mechanism through which TIAA-CREF participants can obtain projected account balances and projected levels of retirement income. Participants can also call to request income illustrations.

The TIAA-CREF experience offers an interesting point of comparison. The current Social Security Statement is similar to the original TIAA-CREF statements, which were focused on projected levels of retirement income. In the 1990s, TIAA-CREF moved to a model of annual statements similar to the alternative approach discussed in this chapter: including current balances and also projections of retirement income levels based on both current and projected balances.

Source: Author's communication with TIAA-CREF (2005).

Annual Changes in Benefit Levels

Once Social Security retirement benefits are presented in terms of present values of one sort or another, one might also report changes in valuations from year to year. First differences of this sort offer one perspective on the benefit that individual participants derive in terms of increased Social Security retirement benefits over the course of a single year. In addition, this annual accretion of benefit might plausibly be compared to the participant's annual payroll taxes with potentially important implications for labor market efficiencies.

Let me illustrate how a calculation of this sort might work in the case of Wanda Worker using the accrued benefit valuation techniques described. As mentioned earlier, at the end of 2003, the present value of her accrued Social Security retirement benefits was $61,154. Had a similar calculation been made at end of 2002—that is, a year earlier—the present value of her accrued retirement benefits would have been reported as $56,168. In other words, the value of her accrued benefit would have increased by slightly less than $4,000 in the course of the year.[17] This increase is greater than her combined OASI payroll taxes for the year ($3,715) and a substantial fraction of her total combined OASDI payroll taxes ($4,346). Figure 10.3 presents a time series of the first differences in

Figure 10.3   Components of Annual Increases in Accrued Benefits

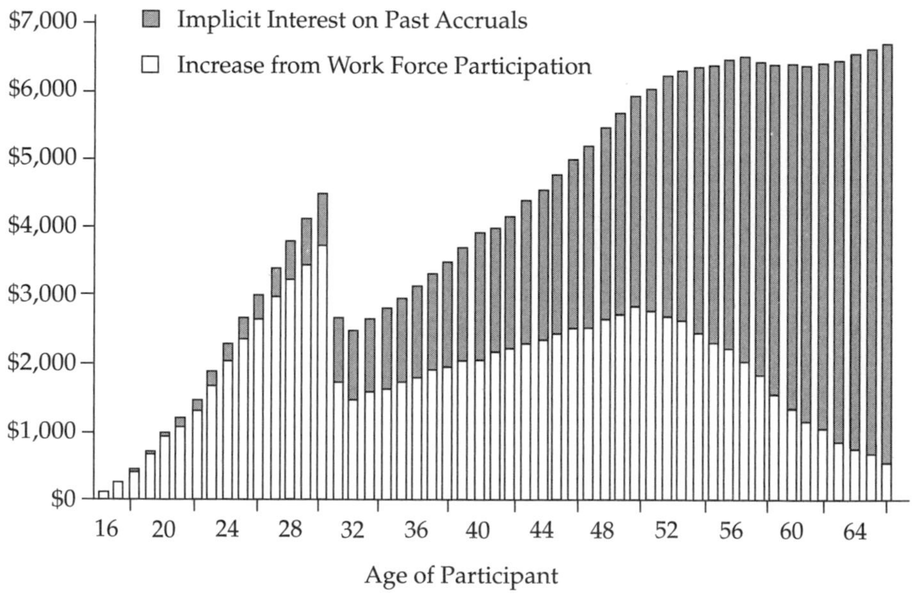

Source: Author's compilation.

accrued benefits values for Wanda Worker over the course of her working life. The figure divides the annual increase in accrued benefits into two components: an implicit interest payment on previously accrued benefits and an estimate of the amount of new benefits that the participant accrued as a result of annual earnings from workforce participation. All entries in this figure are expressed in constant 2003 dollars.[18]

Adjustments for Uncertainty, Individual Characteristics, and Market Values

The valuation estimates reported so far reflect only actuarial values, using projected life expectancies in retirement and a real discount rate of three percent. A number of subtleties are therefore not included. For example, as mentioned, these valuations are contingent upon participants surviving until retirement and the maintenance of Social Security benefits in their current form. Uncertainty exists on both of these dimensions, theoretically requiring a downward adjustment in values to present a more accurate estimate of the expected value of benefits. In addition, the valuations make no adjustment for individual characteristics, aside from the gender of the recipient because the SSA life expectancy estimates are gender-based. Although the administrative burdens of refining estimates based on individual characteristics are considerable, one could, in theory, think of making adjustments in valuation estimates based on health characteristics or information about participants' families (for example, the existence, age, and prior earnings histories of spouses and ex-spouses can substantially increase the value of Social Security retirement benefits because the program offers spousal benefits to many participants).

Even more adjustments would be necessary if the goal were to estimate the market value of Social Security benefits, as opposed to their actuarial value. Although the U.S. insurance market does not provide an annuity product comparable to Social Security benefits, one could estimate the administrative cost and profit margins that private providers would need to recover, and then inflate the actuarial values of Social Security benefits to reflect these costs.[19] Alternatively, one could simply add in a load factor to reflect a reasonable share of the administrative costs of the Social Security Administration.

Valuation Issues for Disability Benefits and Survivors Benefits

The foregoing discussion has focused on Social Security retirement benefits, by far the largest category of Social Security benefits. But the Social Security program also provides a number of important other benefits for participants, most notably disability insurance and survivors' insurance.[20] Unlike retirement benefits, these other benefits are contingent on low-probability events: death or disability during a participant's working life. Although one could value these benefits in a variety of ways, perhaps the simplest approach is to conceptualize the benefits as having an annual value, roughly comparable to the value of purchasing disability insurance or life insurance in the private market. As a first approximation, one could estimate the annual value of these benefits as a participant's pro rata share of the costs of disability and survivor awards that the Social Security program incurs each year.[21]

An Alternative Disclosure Format for Social Security Benefits

To facilitate subsequent discussions, I now sketch out a specific form of supplemental disclosures highlighting both the value of Social Security benefits and changes in those values from year to year. Such a disclosure might appear as supplemental information for the current Social Security Statement, or it might be structured as a separate report available from the Social Security Administration. Or, one might think of this supplemental statement as something that a financial planner or financial planning software might produce for participants, perhaps with information downloaded from the Social Security Administration, which might then allow individuals to compare Social Security benefit values to other financial assets.

The disclosure highlights changes in Wanda Worker's accrued retirement benefits during 2003 (see figure 10.4). After summarizing the amount of payroll taxes that she and her employers paid in 2003—

Figure 10.4   Supplemental Disclosure for Wanda Worker (12/31/03)

Retirement Benefits
In 2003, you and your employer each paid $2,173 in payroll taxes for a combined payroll tax of $4,326. As a result of your participation in the Social Security program last year, the value of your accrued retirement benefits under the Social Security program is estimated to have increased as follows:

Value of Retirement Benefit (as reported for 12/31/02)	$56,158
Implicit Interest on Previously Accrued Benefits	$3,004
New Benefits Accrued in 2003	$1,993
Value of Retirement Benefit (as of 12/31/03)	$61,154

Ancillary Benefits
In addition, as a result of your participation in the Social Security program last year, you received ancillary benefits estimated to have the following values:

Value of Disability Insurance Coverage in 2003:	$631
Value of Survivors Insurance Coverage in 2003:	$300(?)
Total Value of Ancillary Benefits:	$931

Source: Author's compilation.

$4,326—the disclosure restates the accrued value of the participant's re-
tirement benefits at the end of the previous year, which in this case is
$56,158. It then indicates the implicit interest of $3,004 earned in the
course of the year.[22] Next, it adds the value of new benefits accrued in
2003, estimated to be $1,993. Together these adjustments indicate that the
accrued value of Wanda Worker's retirement benefits at the end of 2003
were $61,154.

The other values included in the sample report relate to ancillary benefits: disability insurance and survivors insurance. The value for disability insurance is based on the amount of disability insurance taxes that the
participant and her employer paid in 2003, based on the very rough (and
not entirely accurate) assumption that disability taxes cover costs of disability insurance.[23] My estimate for the value of survivor's insurance is
cut from whole cloth.

Box 10.2   Disclosures Under the Swedish Public Pension System

---

In the 1990s, Sweden reformed its public pension program to include, as its
most prominent component, a notional defined contribution plan, in which
participants receive annual credits equal to 16 percent of earnings. Over the
course of participants' working lives, these account balances grow at the real
rate of increase of per capita earnings in Sweden. Then, at retirement, each
participant's account balances are converted into an annuity reflecting the life
expectancy of the participant's age cohort. The Swedish notional defined contribution plan is conceptually similar to cash balance plans that are increasingly popular in the United States.

The disclosure forms that Swedish officials have developed for their notional defined contribution plan are quite similar to the alternative format
outlined earlier. Like the current Social Security Statement, the Swedish forms
project expected levels of monthly retirement benefits under the assumption
that participants will remain employed until retirement. On top of these projections, the disclosure then includes information about the current value of
account balances, the participant's most recent year's contribution, and an indexation component—akin to an interest payment—reflecting growth in average Swedish wages. Participants also pay an annual administrative charge
for the notional defined contribution plan and receive an annual inheritance
payment, which distributes the account balances of members of participants'
age cohort who die before retirement. The statement also reports adjustments
in account balances for each year's administrative charges and inheritance
gains. The Swedish disclosure forms thus highlight both the current value of
participants' interest in the notional defined contribution program as well as
the manner in which account balances change over the course of a year.

Source: Author's compilation, but for an introduction to the Swedish pension plan, see
Sundén (2000).

In comparison to the current Social Security Statement, a major difference in this supplemental disclosure format is that it attempts to present benefits in the same currency as payroll taxes. In other words, it would invite participants to compare annual payroll taxes to new benefits accrued over the course of the year. So, in this case, Wanda could see that, although her payroll taxes were $4,326 in 2003, she accrued $1,993 in newly accrued retirement benefits plus she enjoyed disability and survivors insurance coverage valued at $931. The sum of these benefits ($2,924) is less than her total payroll taxes ($4,326), but the disclosure statement clearly indicates that she received substantial value for her participation in the Social Security program for 2003. (One potential source of participant confusion with this format is that Wanda might interpret the implicit interest on her previously accrued benefit as a function of her 2003 labor market participation, whereas in fact it reflects a return on prior years' labor.)

The Advantages and Disadvantages of Supplemental Disclosures

Supplemental disclosures along the lines outlined could address a number of the shortcomings of the current Social Security Statement. Here I consider the extent to which they might mitigate both the cognitive biases limiting the ability of individuals to value the lifetime annuities and the difficulties individuals encounter in gauging the incremental value of working in terms of increased Social Security benefits. I also discuss potential drawbacks of supplemental disclosures, including the possibilities that participants might find them confusing and that some workers may respond to more accurate information about the value of their Social Security benefits by reducing other forms of retirement savings.

More Accurate Reflection of the Value of Benefits

Supplemental disclosures based on the actuarial value of Social Security benefits and changes in the actuarial value of benefits offer a measure of valuation that is, in certain respects, easier for participants to understand than the presentation format featured in the current Social Security Statement. Participants would not need to make adjustments for the time value of money or life expectancies in retirement or other uncertainties necessary to value disability or survivors benefit. All of these adjustments are embedded into the valuation estimates, albeit based on population characteristics and not the characteristics of the individual recipient. To the extent that one credits my earlier claims—that a variety of cognitive bases inhibit the ability of participants from accurately valuing their Social Security benefits—there is a benefit in providing participants a more comprehensible summary measure of their entitlements under the Social Security program.

Another advantage of present value calculations of the sort proposed is that they facilitate comparisons between Social Security retirement benefits and other forms of retirement savings. Though it is often said that Social Security is supposed to provide only one leg of a three-legged program of retirement savings, current benefit disclosure provides individuals very little guidance as to the relative size of their Social Security wealth compared with other retirement savings, particularly if that savings takes the form of a defined contribution plan, such as 401(k) plan or an IRA. Getting an annual statement highlighting the value of accrued Social Security benefits would facilitate such comparisons. After all, when one estimates the accrued value of Wanda Worker's Social Security retirement benefits to be $61,154 at the end of 2003, one is roughly equating those benefits to her having $61,154 in an IRA or 401(k).[24]

A larger but related point is that better Social Security disclosures might help educate participants about the magnitude of retirement savings necessary to support adequate retirement income. The relatively low rate of retirement savings for many Americans is a much decried fact of our public economic life, but the government engages in relatively little effort to educate its population on this score. If workers such as Wanda Worker could internalize the fact that even though her accrued Social Security benefit has an estimated value of $61,154 at year-end 2003, this level of Social Security wealth would support only $9,589.20 of annual income—that is, less than 28 percent replacement rate of her projected pre-retirement income of $35,051. Put in that framework, Wanda Worker and other Social Security participants might begin to think more intelligently about the amount of additional retirement savings needed to support a secure retirement. Conceivably—and here perhaps I am being excessively optimistic—individuals might be encouraged to think in terms of accumulating their personal retirement savings at a rate that is equal to, or perhaps even some multiple of, the accrued value of their Social Security benefit throughout the course of their working career.[25] In that way, they would be assured that Social Security benefits would not be the only leg on which their retirement stands.

Beneficial Effects on Labor Market Efficiency

Another potentially valuable benefit of moving to a system of disclosure that includes supplemental information about the actuarial value of Social Security benefits concerns labor market efficiency. A premise of labor economics is that the effect of mandatory benefits, such as Social Security, depends not on the gross costs of these benefits, but on their net impact on workers (see Summers 1989; Jolls 2000; Kaplow 1994). So, if the cost of a mandated benefit equals its value to all workers, the imposition of that mandate will have no labor market effect. Viewed through this lens, the current disclosures regarding Social Security benefits are problematic. After all, if as suggested, limitations of the Social Security Statement itself, coupled with various cognitive biases, cause participants to misapprehend the value of those benefits—and, in particular, the incremental value of working an additional year—then various distortions in the labor market might be expected. If, as much of the foregoing analysis suggests, participants tend to undervalue the amount of the Social Security benefits they accrue or otherwise receive each year, they may be inclined to work less than would otherwise be optimal.

The magnitude of this distortion could be significant. To illustrate this point, consider figure 10.5, on which I have plotted the annual combined OASI taxes for Wanda Worker for each year along with the annual increases in accrued Social Security retirement benefits each year. (I have omitted disability insurance taxes on the assumption that those generate a disability benefit of roughly comparable value.) In terms of labor market efficiency, figure 10.6 is quite interesting. Contrary to the prevailing wisdom that young workers get nothing out of Social Security benefits, this figure suggests that the progressive benefit formula is quite advantageous to workers starting out in this system.[26] The value of annual benefit increases drops precipitously when a worker's average indexed monthly benefits exceed the first bend point (dropping replacement rates from 90 percent to 32 percent), but still constitute a nontrivial percentage of OASI taxes until—at least in the case of this worker—the number of years of significant work exceeds thirty-five and the impact of additional years of earnings diminishes substantially.

I leave it to other, more qualified analysts to decide whether providing this information to the workforce would have a meaningful effect on labor market efficiency. The only point I want to press here is that the picture of annual benefit accruals presented in figure 10.5 is not one that most workers have in their heads today when they think about Social Security benefits. Were they to receive an annual statement highlighting the actuarial value of those benefits and their increase over time, I expect that their perception of the value of those benefits would change.[27]

Complexity of Disclosures

An initial objection to supplemental disclosures based on estimated values of benefits is that this additional information requires additional explanations and could be confusing to many. It is an open question whether estimated values might be explained in a manner that would be intelligible to a wide range of participants. The Social Security Statement, for example, is designed to be accessible to individuals with at least a

Figure 10.5   Taxes to Increases in Accrued Benefits

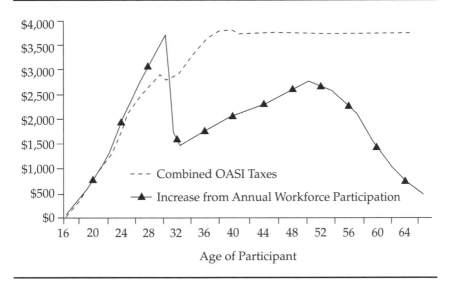

Source: Author's compilation.

seventh-grade education. Arguably, actuarial valuations are inherently more complicated and thus less accessible than projected levels of monthly annual income. So, though actuarial valuations may help some participants understand, they may confuse others.

The aspect of actuarial valuations that is likely to be the most confusing is the apparent loss of wealth that individuals (and their heirs) suffer when participants die shortly before or shortly after retirement and do not have a spouse. Under these circumstances, such participants may seem to have been shortchanged by the system. Apparent losses of this sort are a direct consequence of the fact that actuarial valuations are based on population averages and not individual characteristics, but their effect could be jarring for some and produce unproductive, potentially disruptive public reactions. The current Social Security Statement—reporting only projected monthly payments—does not have this problem, even though participants who die near or shortly after retirement suffer identical losses.

Whether actuarial values of Social Security benefits could be described in a manner that most participants would find intelligible and helpful would require further research and testing. This issue would be of great concern were the supplemental information incorporated directly into the Social Security Statement in that confusion over this new information could diminish the usefulness of information already included in the statement. If, however, the supplemental information were available from the SSA upon request or through third-party vendors, then these concerns would diminish, as participants receiving the information would be limited to those most likely to find the information useful.

Potential Unintended Consequences of Supplemental Disclosures

One of the risks of regulatory reforms is that the consequences of reforms may not conform to the expectations of policy makers. This could also be the case with respect to the outlined supplemental disclosures. Presented with more accurate information about the estimated value of their Social Security benefits and the annual increase in the value of those benefits, participants may react in ways that many would regard as undesirable in terms of financial planning, labor market participation, and even political support for the Social Security program.

Reductions in Other Retirement Savings

Consider, for example, the impact of supplemental disclosures on retirement savings. One of the premises of this analysis is that cognitive biases and other factors likely cause participants to undervalue the economic significance of their Social Security retirement benefits. The supplemental disclosures outlined are intended to help participants correct these cognitive errors and perhaps even encourage them to understand better how much additional retirement savings they will need to achieve appropriate replacement income during retirement. It is, however, possible that participants will react differently. Once they see the true magnitude of their Social Security wealth, some may decide to reduce other forms of retirement savings or even increase their consumer debt. After all, if participants really do underestimate the value of Social Security benefits, it is plausible that they will reduce other forms of savings once they are informed how much Social Security benefits are truly worth. By addressing the cognitive biases that lead participants to undervalue Social Security benefits, supplemental disclosures of the sort proposed above may lead some individuals to conclude that they have accumulated too much retirement savings.

Ambiguous Labor Market Effects

Labor market effects may also work in the opposite direction. The premise of the analysis is that current Social Security Statements obscure the incremental value of additional years of labor market participation. It is further postulated that if workers were given clearer information about the annual accrual of benefits under the Social Security program, their perceived wages would increase, as would their participation in the labor market. It is, however, possible that at least some workers have a different assumption about their payroll taxes—that they currently assume that their annual accrual of benefits under Social Security are roughly equal to their payroll taxes. If so, accurate disclosures of the annual accrual of benefits under the Social Security program could reduce the perceived value of labor, thus tending to reduce labor market participation (albeit not necessarily reducing labor market efficiency). Again, once the veil of ignorance is removed, one cannot be sure how participants will react.

Political Implications of Providing Supplemental Information

For the most part, this chapter addresses Social Security disclosures as a tool for financial planning and as a factor in effecting labor market efficiency. But the Social Security program is a public program, and recipients of the Social Security Statements and any supplemental information are also political actors in both voting and informing public opinion. Here I consider the political implications of supplementing Social Security Statements with estimates of actuarial values. Again, the overall effects are ambiguous and potentially multifaceted.

Public Understanding of the Value of Social Security Benefits

One of the complexities of current public discussions over Social Security is widespread uncertainty about the value of the program, especially for younger workers. Although the lack of public confidence in the continuation of the system is often overstated (Jacobs and Shapiro 1998), there is ample evidence that most members of the public have difficulty understanding the economic value of their Social Security benefits, both because of the cognitive biases outlined and because of the possibility of future benefit cuts. At a minimum, supplemental disclosures of the sort outlined would provide the public an alternative way of understanding the value of their Social Security benefits—putting an annual value on survivors and disability benefits and estimating the actuarial value of their accrued retirement benefits on an annual basis. By making the value of the Social Security more specific and locating the accrual of benefits in specific years, this supplemental information could perhaps increase public support for the program.

Supplemental disclosure would also do a better job of distinguishing the accrued retirement benefits of younger and older workers. In contrast with the current Social Security Statement, which presents total projected retirement benefits for all eligible participants, supplemental disclosures of actuarial values would report much higher actuarial values for older workers than for younger workers. Older workers may find these higher valuation a source of some comfort in the face of general concerns about the long-term solvency of the Social Security program.

Clarity of benefit values could, however, also lead to reduced support for Social Security. As mentioned, it is unclear how program participants currently understand the relationship between the value of their Social Security benefits and the annual payroll taxes paid on behalf of participants. As a matter of economic reality, the annual accrual of benefits for current participants is less than their payroll taxes, and this fact would be revealed in the supplemental disclosures outlined earlier. To the extent that some participants were under the impression that their annual benefit accruals equaled payroll taxes, supplemental information contradicting this understanding could diminish their support for the system. How many participants currently operate under this misapprehension is an empirical question requiring additional research.

Creation of Property Interests and Pressure to Resist Future Changes

A related point concerns the sense of entitlement that participants may develop with respect to retirement benefits expressed in terms of accrued actuarial values. By presenting these benefits in a format that facilitates comparison with bank accounts and other financial assets, the proposed supplemental information may encourage workers to think of those benefits as a form of property. There is no doubt that appropriately crafted disclosures could prevent this view from having legal significance, but, at the same time, a widespread perception that accrued actuarial values are property could make it more difficult for Congress to adjust accrued benefits in the future. Although a case can be made that Congress should be more hesitant to reduce accrued benefits as opposed to benefits to be accrued in the future (Jackson 2004), the legislature needs a wide range of flexibility in this area. This aspect of reporting accrued actuarial valuations may therefore be somewhat problematic.

On this point, however, one must also recognize that the current Social Security Statements are themselves a source of potential public resistence to change. Notwithstanding disclaimers regarding the possibility of future benefit reductions, the current statements project total benefits based on projected earnings of a working life as soon as a participant achieves forty quarters of credits. In other words, the statements report a level of benefits based on both accrued and to-be-accrued benefits. Although many participants may have difficulty converting this projected level of benefits into actuarial values, the current Social Security

Statement invites precisely this calculation. Thus the current statement also potentially generates a fair amount of public resistance to benefit reductions.

Enhancing Transparency of Some of the Redistributive Aspects of Social Security

A further potential consequence of reporting actuarial valuations of Social Security benefits—survivors and disability insurance as well as retirement benefits—is that this form of disclosure will make the redistributive aspects of Social Security benefits more transparent. As indicated, those with much shorter than average life expectancies at retirement will see that they do not enjoy the actuarial value of their retirement benefits. High income workers will see the relatively lower rate at which their benefits accrue, and all workers who participate in the labor force at roughly the same relative earnings level for more than thirty-five years will see how relatively little their payroll taxes generate in additional retirement benefits in their last years of work. Finally—especially if the system is reformed to regain long-term solvency—everyone will see what share of their payroll taxes are being used to service and retire the system's legacy debt.

Whether clarity on all of these points is a genuine drawback is a nice question. To the extent that public support for the Social Security system rests on a misunderstanding of the system's redistributive elements raises some difficult questions of democratic legitimacy. But if we were to move to a system of disclosures that more clearly describe the actuarial value of Social Security benefits to individual participants, then it necessarily follows that it will become clear which participants are getting more value than others and how the overall distribution of benefits compares to payroll taxes and other contributions to the system.

Relationship to Social Security Reform

Finally, the dissemination of supplemental information about the actuarial value of Social Security benefits and the rate of accrual of their retirement benefits might effect the public debate over Social Security reform.

In terms of the reform debate, one potential advantage of highlighting accrued projected benefits is that it provides a new metric for evaluating changes in benefit levels. Currently, proposed benefit changes are typically measured against total projected benefits—not just for current participants, but for future participants as well. Even if the changes are limited solely to benefits that have not yet been earned, experts and politicians often characterize these changes as benefit cuts. Were the general public accustomed to tracking the value of their accrued Social Security benefits, one could imagine that they might be more accepting of changes in benefit formulas related to benefits that accrue in the future. After all, such changes would not reduce accrued benefits, only the rate at which benefits accrue in the future. By expanding the range of ways to restore solvency, an emphasis on accrued projected benefits could increase the likelihood of reforms being enacted.

The development of reports for traditional Social Security benefits based on accrued values would also facilitate public consideration of reform proposals that entail the substitution of individual accounts for a portion of traditional benefits. These choices typically necessitate the comparison of a reduction of monthly annuity payments on traditional benefits on the one hand with new annual contributions to individual accounts on the other. For all of the reasons outlined above, most individuals have considerable difficulty making these comparisons. If, however, traditional benefits were described in terms of accrued values, the comparisons would be much more straightforward.

Finally, the use of accrued values could offer a valuable new perspective on the gradual increase in the overall value of Social Security benefits expected to occur as a result of the increases in life expectancies. Many experts have recommended that the formula for Social Security benefits be adjusted to compensate for increases in life expectancy (see, for example, Diamond and Orszag 2004). Typically, these changes are perceived to be benefit cuts, because the standard way of describing the level of Social Security retirement benefits is as a percent of average indexed monthly earnings. If, however, retirement benefits were expressed in terms of accrued value at normal retirement age, perhaps as a multiple of average indexed annual salary, then the effect of longevity increases would become clearer.

Consider, once more, the case of Wanda Worker. At the eve of her retirement in 2029, the projected value of her retirement benefit (based on an eighteen-year life expectancy in retirement) will be $211,116 or 6.1 times her average indexed annual income of $34,788.[28] However, if a similar worker entered retirement ten years later in 2039 with the same average annual earnings, the actuarial value of that participant's retirement benefit would increase, as a result of projected increases in life expectancies of a half a year, to $215,525.51 or 6.2 times average annual income. Figure 10.5 charts the growth of total projected benefit valuations over four more decades. By 2079, when comparable female workers who retire at sixty-seven can be expected to survive for another two years, the ratio of value to average annual salary will increase to 6.7, reflecting the significant growth in benefit values over the seventy-five-year horizon over which Social Security solvency is typically measured. Cast in this framework, proposals to maintain the ratio of benefit values to average income levels may seem less of a reduction in benefits than an elimination of projected increase.

Figure 10.6   Projected Benefit to Average Indexed Annual Salary

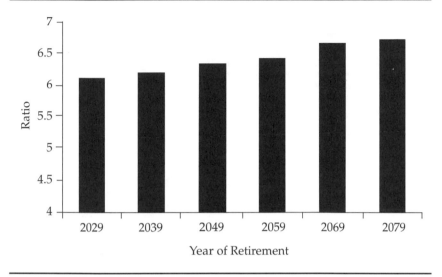

Source: Author's compilation.

Conclusion

For many Americans, Social Security benefits constitute a significant financial asset. Although the current Social Security Statement provides participants useful information about their projected benefits and earnings history, the disclosures are incomplete and subject to misinterpretation. In this chapter, I have explored various ways in which the statements might be supplemented to offer participants a more accurate picture of both the value of their Social Security benefits and the annual increase in the value of those benefits. This information could make it easier for participants to compare Social Security benefits to other forms of savings and to make more informed choices about labor market participants. Without further study, however, one cannot predict with confidence how participants would in fact respond to this supplemental information, either in terms of financial planning or labor market participation. In addition, the political implications of supplemental information are potentially multifaceted and difficult to predict a priori. Accordingly, a fruitful subject for further research would be to conduct market surveys to assess participant reaction to kinds of supplemental information discussed in this chapter and alternative approaches to enhancing disclosures about Social Security benefits.

Appendix

Your Social Security Statement

Prepared especially for Wanda Worker

WANDA WORKER
456 ANYWHERE AVENUE
MAINTOWN, USA 11111-1111

January 2, 2004

See inside for your personal information ➡

▼ *What Social Security Means to You*

This **Social Security Statement** will help you understand what Social Security means to you and your family. This **Statement** can help you better plan for your financial future. It gives you estimates of your Social Security benefits under current law. Each year, we will send you an updated **Statement** including your latest reported earnings.

Be sure to read this **Statement** carefully. If you think there may be a mistake, please let us know. That's important because your benefits will be based on our record of your lifetime earnings. We recommend you keep a copy of this **Statement** with your financial records.

Social Security is for people of all ages...
It can help you whether you're young or old, male or female, single or with a family. It's there for you when you retire, but it's more than a retirement program. Social Security also can provide benefits if you become disabled and help support your family when you die.

Work to build a secure future...
Social Security is the largest source of income for most elderly Americans today. It is very important to remember that Social Security was never intended to be your only source of income when you retire. Social Security can't do it all. You also will need other savings, investments, pensions or retirement accounts to make sure you have enough money to live comfortably when you retire.

About Social Security's future...
Social Security is a compact between generations. For more than 60 years, America has kept the promise of security for its workers and their families. But now, the Social Security system is facing serious future financial problems, and action is needed soon to make sure that the system is sound when today's younger workers are ready for retirement.

Today there are almost 36 million Americans age 65 or older. Their Social Security retirement benefits are funded by today's workers and their employers who jointly pay Social Security taxes—just as the money they paid into Social Security was used to pay benefits to those who retired before them. Unless action is taken soon to strengthen Social Security, in just 15 years we will begin paying more in benefits than we collect in taxes. Without changes, by 2042 the Social Security Trust Fund will be exhausted.* By then, the number of Americans 65 or older is expected to have doubled. There won't be enough younger people working to pay all of the benefits owed to those who are retiring. At that point, there will be enough money to pay only about 73 cents for each dollar of scheduled benefits. We will need to resolve these issues soon to make sure Social Security continues to provide a foundation of protection for future generations as it has done in the past.

Social Security on the Net...
Visit *www.socialsecurity.gov* on the Internet to learn more about Social Security. You can read our publications, use the **Social Security Benefit Calculators** to calculate future benefits, apply for retirement, spouse's or disability benefits, or subscribe to *eNews* for up-to-date information about Social Security.

Jo Anne Barnhart

Jo Anne B. Barnhart
Commissioner

*These estimates of the future financial status of the Social Security program were produced by the actuaries at the Social Security Administration based on the intermediate assumptions from the Social Security Trustees' Annual Report to the Congress.

▼ *Your Estimated Benefits*

To qualify for benefits, you earn "credits" through your work—up to four each year. This year, for example, you earn one credit for each $900 of wages or self-employment income. When you've earned $3,600, you've earned your four credits for the year. Most people need 40 credits, earned over their working lifetime, to receive retirement benefits. For disability and survivors benefits, young people need fewer credits to be eligible.

We checked your records to see whether you have earned enough credits to qualify for benefits. If you haven't earned enough yet to qualify for any type of benefit, we can't give you a benefit estimate now. If you continue to work, we'll give you an estimate when you do qualify.

What we assumed—If you have enough work credits, we estimated your benefit amounts using your average earnings over your working lifetime. For 2004 and later (up to retirement age), we assumed you'll continue to work and make about the same as you did in 2002 or 2003. We also included credits we assumed you earned last year and this year.

We can't provide your actual benefit amount until you apply for benefits. *And that amount may differ from the estimates stated below because:*
(1) Your earnings may increase or decrease in the future.
(2) Your estimated benefits are based on current law. *The law governing benefit amounts may change.**
(3) Your benefit amount may be affected by *military service, railroad employment or pensions earned through work on which you did not pay Social Security tax. Visit www.socialsecurity.gov/mystatement to see whether your Social Security benefit amount will be affected.*

Generally, estimates for older workers are more accurate than those for younger workers because they're based on a longer earnings history with fewer uncertainties such as earnings fluctuations and future law changes.

These estimates are in today's dollars. After you start receiving benefits, they will be adjusted for cost-of-living increases.

▼ **Retirement*	You have earned enough credits to qualify for benefits. At your current earnings rate, if you stop working and start receiving benefits…	
	At age 62, your payment would be about…	$882 a month
	If you continue working until…	
	your full retirement age (67 years), your payment would be about…	$1,278 a month
	age 70, your payment would be about…	$1,594 a month
▼ **Disability*	You have earned enough credits to qualify for benefits. If you became disabled right now,	
	Your payment would be about…	$1,169 a month
▼ **Family*	If you get retirement or disability benefits, your spouse and children also may qualify for benefits.	
▼ **Survivors*	You have earned enough credits for your family to receive survivors benefits. If you die this year, certain members of your family *may* qualify for the following benefits.	
	Your child…	$911 a month
	Your spouse who is caring for your child…	$911 a month
	Your spouse, if benefits start at full retirement age…	$1,215 a month
	Total family benefits cannot be more than…	$2,233 a month
	Your spouse or minor child may be eligible for a special one-time death benefit of $255.	
▼ *Medicare*	You have enough credits to qualify for Medicare at age 65. Even if you do not retire at age 65, be sure to contact Social Security three months before your 65th birthday to enroll in Medicare.	

*Your estimated benefits are based on current law. Congress has made changes to the law in the past and can do so at any time. The law governing benefit amounts may change because, by 2042, the payroll taxes collected will be enough to pay only about 73 percent of scheduled benefits.

We based your benefit estimates on these facts:

Your name…	Wanda Worker
Your date of birth…	May 5, 1963
Your estimated taxable earnings per year after 2003…	$35,051
Your Social Security number (only the last four digits are shown to help prevent identity theft)…	XXX-XX-2004

▼ *Help Us Keep Your Earnings Record Accurate*

You, your employer and Social Security share responsibility for the accuracy of your earnings record. Since you began working, we recorded your reported earnings under your name and Social Security number. We have updated your record each time your employer (or you, if you're self-employed) reported your earnings.

Remember, it's your earnings, not the amount of taxes you paid or the number of credits you've earned, that determine your benefit amount. When we figure that amount, we base it on your average earnings over your lifetime. If our records are wrong, you may not receive all the benefits to which you're entitled.

▼ *Review this chart carefully* using your own records to make sure our information is correct and that we've recorded each year you worked. You are the only person who can look at the earnings chart and know whether it is complete and correct.

Some or all of your earnings from **last year** may not be shown on your **Statement**. It could be that we still were processing last year's earnings reports when your **Statement** was prepared. Your complete earnings for last year will be shown on next year's **Statement. Note:** If you worked for more than one employer during any year, or if you had both earnings and self-employment income, we combined your earnings for the year.

▼ **There's a limit on the amount of earnings on which you pay Social Security taxes each year.** The limit increases yearly. Earnings above the limit will not appear on your earnings chart as Social Security earnings. (For Medicare taxes, the maximum earnings amount began rising in 1991. Since 1994, **all** of your earnings are taxed for Medicare.)

▼ **Call us right away** at **1–800–772–1213** (7 a.m.–7 p.m. your local time) if any earnings for years **before last year** are shown incorrectly. If possible, have your W-2 or tax return for those years available. (If you live outside the U.S., follow the directions at the bottom of page 4.)

Your Earnings Record at a Glance

Years You Worked	Your Taxed Social Security Earnings	Your Taxed Medicare Earnings
1979	474	474
1980	1,123	1,123
1981	1,983	1,983
1982	3,293	3,293
1983	4,461	4,461
1984	5,600	5,600
1985	6,950	6,950
1986	8,813	8,813
1987	10,941	10,941
1988	12,803	12,803
1989	14,520	14,520
1990	16,308	16,308
1991	17,920	17,920
1992	19,655	19,655
1993	20,534	20,534
1994	21,730	21,730
1995	23,155	23,155
1996	24,838	24,838
1997	26,806	26,806
1998	28,720	28,720
1999	30,824	30,824
2000	33,060	33,060
2001	34,237	34,237
2002	35,051	35,051
2003	Not yet recorded	

Did you know... Social Security is more than just a retirement program? It's here to help you when you need it most.

You and your family may be eligible for valuable benefits:

▼ When you die, your family may be eligible to receive survivors benefits.

▼ Social Security may help you if you become disabled—even at a young age.

▼ It is possible for a young person who has worked and paid Social Security taxes in as few as two years to become eligible for disability benefits.

Social Security credits you earn move with you from job to job throughout your career.

Total Social Security and Medicare taxes paid over your working career through the last year reported on the chart above:

Estimated taxes paid for Social Security:		Estimated taxes paid for Medicare:	
You paid:	$24,723	You paid:	$5,820
Your employers paid:	$24,723	Your employers paid:	$5,820

Note: You currently pay 6.2 percent of your salary, up to $87,900, in Social Security taxes and 1.45 percent in Medicare taxes on your entire salary. Your employer also pays 6.2 percent in Social Security taxes and 1.45 percent in Medicare taxes for you. If you are self-employed, you pay the combined employee and employer amount of 12.4 percent in Social Security taxes and 2.9 percent in Medicare taxes on your net earnings.

3

▼ *Some Facts About Social Security*

About Social Security and Medicare...

Social Security pays retirement, disability, family and survivors benefits. Medicare, a separate program run by the Centers for Medicare and Medicaid Services, helps pay for inpatient hospital care, nursing care, doctors' fees, and other medical services and supplies to people age 65 and older, or to people who have been receiving Social Security disability benefits for two years or more. Your Social Security covered earnings qualify you for both programs.

Here are some facts about Social Security's benefits:

▼ *Retirement*—If you were born before 1938, your full retirement age is 65. Because of a 1983 change in the law, the full retirement age will increase gradually to 67 for people born in 1960 and later.

Some people retire before their full retirement age. You can retire as early as age 62 and take your benefits at a reduced rate. If you continue working after your full retirement age, you can receive higher benefits because of additional earnings and special credits for delayed retirement.

▼ *Disability*—If you become disabled before full retirement age, you can receive disability benefits after six months if you have:

— enough credits from earnings (depending on your age, you must have earned six to 20 of your credits in the three to 10 years before you became disabled); and

— a physical or mental impairment that is expected to prevent you from doing "substantial" work for a year or more, *or* result in death.

▼ *Family*—If you're eligible for disability or retirement benefits, your current or divorced spouse, minor children, or adult children disabled before age 22 also may receive benefits. Each may qualify for up to about 50 percent of your benefit amount. The total amount depends on how many family members qualify.

▼ *Survivors*—When you die, certain members of your family may be eligible for benefits:

— your spouse age 60 or older (50 or older if disabled, or any age if caring for your children younger than age 16); and

— your children if unmarried and younger than age 18, still in school and younger than 19 years old, or adult children disabled before age 22.

If you are divorced, your ex-spouse could be eligible for a widow's or widower's benefit on your record when you die.

Receive benefits and still work...

You can continue to work and still get retirement or survivors benefits. If you're younger than your full retirement age, there are limits on how much you can earn without affecting your benefit amount. The limits change each year. When you apply for benefits, we'll tell you what the limits are at that time and whether work would affect your monthly benefits. When you reach full retirement age, the earnings limits no longer apply.

Before you decide to retire...

Think about your benefits for the long term. Everyone's situation is different. For example, be sure to consider the advantages and disadvantages of early retirement. If you choose to receive benefits before you reach full retirement age, your benefits will be permanently reduced. However, you'll receive benefits for a longer period of time.

To help you decide when is the best time for you to retire, we offer a free booklet, *Social Security— Retirement Benefits* (Publication No. 05-10035), that provides specific information about retirement. You can calculate future retirement benefits on our website at *www.socialsecurity.gov* by using the *Social Security Benefit Calculators*. There are other free publications that you may find helpful, including:

▼ *Understanding The Benefits* (No. 05-10024)—a general explanation of all Social Security benefits;

▼ *How Your Retirement Benefit Is Figured* (No. 05-10070)—an explanation of how you can calculate your benefit;

▼ *The Windfall Elimination Provision* (No. 05-10045)— how it affects your retirement or disability benefits;

▼ *Government Pension Offset* (No. 05-10007)— explanation of a law that affects spouse's or widow(er)'s benefits; and

▼ *When Someone Misuses Your Number* (No. 05-10064)— what to do if you're a victim of identity theft.

We also have other leaflets and fact sheets with information about specific topics such as military service, self-employment or foreign employment. You can request Social Security publications at *www.socialsecurity.gov* or by calling us at *1-800-772-1213.*

If you need more information—Visit *www.socialsecurity.gov/mystatement* on the Internet, contact any Social Security office, call *1-800-772-1213* or write to Social Security Administration, Office of Earnings Operations, P.O. Box 33026, Baltimore, MD 21290-3026. If you're deaf or hard of hearing, call TTY 1-800-325-0778. If you have questions about your personal information, you must provide your complete Social Security number. If your address is incorrect on this *Statement*, ask the Internal Revenue Service to send you a Form 8822. We don't keep your address if you're not receiving Social Security benefits.

Para solicitar una Declaración en español, llame al 1-800-772-1213.

This paper benefited from comments and suggestions from Michael Barr, Robert Clark, Peter Diamond, Janet Halley, Daniel Halperin, Christine Jolls, Louis Kaplow, David Laibson, Ed McCaffery, Daniel Meltzer, Martha Minow, Richard Pildes, Todd Rakoff, Michael Sandel, Hal Scott, Daniel Shaviro, Joel Slemrod, Matthew Stephenson, Jeff Strnad, William Stuntz, and participants in the Behavioral Public Finance Conference of April 23–24, 2004, in Ann Arbor, Michigan. I also received valuable research assistance from Laurie Burligame (HLS '06) and financial support from the Olin Center for Law, Economics and Business at Harvard Law School. After this chapter was substantially completed, I became a trustee of the College Retirement Equities Fund (CREF) and its affiliated investment companies.

Notes

1. According to the SSA, Social Security benefits comprise 39 percent of the income of the elderly. For two-thirds of elderly Social Security beneficiaries, the program constitutes 50 percent or more of their income, and for approximately one-fifth of these beneficiaries, Social Security constitutes their sole source of retirement income (see U.S. Social Security Administration 2005a).
2. Id. For current workers under the age of sixty-two, the present value of projected Social Security benefits was $21,015 billion, whereas the present value of projected future taxes to be paid by this cohort of workers (principally through payroll taxes) was $13,576 billion. The difference between these two figures—$7,439 billion—represents an estimate of the net present value of Social Security benefits to workers under the age of sixty-two.
3. SSA officials have also testified that the statements have a third goal to "help educate the public about Social Security and build public confidence."
4. The SSA has online software that allows workers to alter these assumptions and make their own estimates of earnings levels (see U.S. Social Security Administration 2004b).
5. Somewhat inaccurately, the footnote says that payroll taxes will cover only 73 percent of benefits, whereas the actual coverage ratios include both payroll and certain income taxes levied on Social Security retirement benefits.
6. Adjusted with the CPI index, Wanda Worker's 2003 projected monthly retirement benefits would have a value of over $1,285 if expressed in the same constant dollars as appeared in her 2004 statement. The reason for this real decline in benefits is that Wanda Worker's earnings did not increase as fast as the SSA's average wage index in the most recent year, and so her projected earnings through retirement were a little lower in relative terms than they had been a year earlier.
7. The SSA's online software allows participants to project benefits in future dollars as opposed to current dollars.
8. In an April 2004 email response to an online query, an SSA representative explained the administration's policy as follows: "The statement does not reflect 'indexing' because index earnings are based on national average earnings and we cannot predict the national earning level twelve years from now."

9. The previous incarnation of the statement—the Personal Earnings and Benefit Estimate Statement (PEBES), which was discontinued in 1999—was somewhat more complete in that it reported annual employee payroll taxes along with reported earnings, but did not include any estimates of employer taxes.

10. To give readers a sense of the disparity between the level of payroll taxes reported in the Social Security Statement for Wanda Worker—$24,723 for herself and $49,452 combined—and other potentially more complete measures of the value of payroll contributions, I have computed a range of estimates.

    First, as all benefit projections in the Social Security Statement are expressed in terms of current dollars, one might also express payroll taxes in current dollars. This adjustment would raise the level of combined payroll taxes to $61,846 according to my estimates.

    Second, if one were to add in a time value of money element with, for illustrative purposes, a real interest rate of 3 percent, the present value of cumulative payroll taxes paid by Wanda Worker and her employers since 1979 would be approximately $88,255 in current dollars.

    Next, to the extent that the Social Security retirement benefits are being projected based on future payroll tax contributions through retirement, one might be interested in comparing the level of cumulative life-time combined payroll taxes, either simply aggregated in current dollars ($179,196) or adjusted for the time value of money at a 3 percent interest rate ($362,921).

    To be sure, there are good reasons for not amending the Social Security Statement to include any of these cumulative reports of payroll tax contributions. Each could be confusing. The reason I include these alternative estimates here is to suggest how the current statement's reporting of cumulative nominal payroll taxes could give recipients a mistaken view of the true relationship between their payroll taxes and benefits. Although there is much to be said in favor of rallying public support for the Social Security system, including potentially misleading comparisons in the Social Security Statement is not an appropriate mechanism, at least in my view, for accomplishing this end. Under the PEBES, there may have been a justification in reporting annual payroll taxes on the grounds that this information might help recipients corroborate the accuracy of SSA records. It is hard to believe, however, that any appreciable number of recipients keep records of cumulative nominal payroll taxes. If errors are to be detected, recipients seem much more likely to find them from reviewing reported annual earnings records.

11. The manner in which benefit payments are projected—using full scheduled benefits based on a continuation of current earnings until retirement—exacerbates the problem for younger workers because it reports a level of benefits based in substantial part on future earnings.

12. For example, according to the U.S. Social Security Administration (2004a) estimates, the average annual mortality rates for the population under age sixty-five in 2003 was 233.4 deaths per 100,000.

13. Admittedly, the line between what I term objective limitations and cognitive biases is not bright. For example, the limitation of benefits being described in monthly payments—as opposed to an income—rests on assumptions about cognitive biases of a sort.

14. Whereas the endowment effect suggests that participants might value their projected Social Security benefits more than comparable benefits not yet within their possession, participants may still undervalue both forms of benefits for the reasons described earlier.

15. These charts are somewhat stylized as all valuations are based on current benefit formulas and benefits attributed to pre-2003 earnings are adjusted to reflect subsequent wage indexing. Valuations of OASI payroll taxes reflect actual taxes imposed through 2003 and current combined rates projected for the future. Because Wanda's future earnings history and the extent of wage indexation were unknown in years prior to 2003, contemporaneous valuations of her projected benefits would have differed from those shown in these figures.

16. Under current law, participants must pay a minimum amount of payroll taxes spread over forty quarters—that is, over ten years—to be eligible to receive retirement benefits. Accordingly, roughly the first ten years of accruals shown in figure 10.2 represent unvested accrued benefits.

17. This increase reflects a number of factors aside from the accrual of additional benefits from another year of work. Among other things, benefits are adjusted to reflect increases in average real wages in 2003, and there is an implicit accrual of interest on previously accrued benefits. In addition, the change reflects one year's adjustment in the value of current dollars. The year-end 2002 estimate would have expressed in current dollars at the time, one year earlier than the 2003 estimate.

18. Note this figure differs from the nominal differences between reported accrued values each year because the figure adjusts prior year valuations to constant 2003 dollars. In addition, subsequent adjustments for average increases in real wages are attributed to the year in which the wages were earned, not the year in which the adjustment was made.

19. In a voluntary private market, annuity prices also are thought to include an adjustment for adverse selection effects, but these costs would probably not be appropriate for valuing a mandatory annuity program such as Social Security.

20. I do not address SSI benefits in this chapter.

21. Note, the costs of these awards is not the sum of cash payments under the programs each year, but rather the present value of awards claimed during the year plus an allocation of administrative costs and (if the goal is to replicate private market values) a hypothetical profit margin.

22. As the total accrued benefit on her 2002 Statement would have been stated in 2002 dollars, the implicit interest of $3004 in 2003 would include both inflation adjustment on Wanda's total accrued benefit in 2002 ($1280.08) plus a real interest rate of 3.0 percent ($1723.44).

23. As the DI trust fund like the OASI trust fund is increasingly insolvent, the average actuarial value of disability benefits for participants must be greater than the average combined DI payroll taxes.

24. To be sure, the equation is not perfect. If one assumes the 401(k) or IRA account earns more or less than a 3-percent real rate of interest, then that will affect the account's relative value as a source of retirement security. In addition, the very attractive form of annuity that Social Security provides is not

available to private retirement accounts, making direct comparisons between private accounts and the accrued values of Social Security benefits more difficult. Also, the possibility of legislative reductions in benefits levels is a risk that is not typically associated with private retirement savings account. Notwithstanding these and other differences, however, projected accrued benefits do offer individuals a rough handle on comparing Social Security retirement benefits to other forms of retirement savings.

25. More specifically, lower wage workers might be encouraged to accumulate private retirement savings equal to the accrued value of their Social Security benefits; mid-level workers at two times accrued benefits; and workers at the maximum payroll wage perhaps three times accrued benefits.

26. On this dimension, the current Social Security Statement sends exactly the opposite message. Even though workers accrue retirement benefits the minute they enter the workforce, the current Social Security Statement reports no retirement benefits until participants have forty quarters of credit. (Telephone Interview with Rita Bontz, SSA Office of Communication, April 21, 2004.) The justification for this practice is that workers are not eligible for retirement benefits until they have forty quarters of credit, but the effect is to suggest to young workers that their labor market participation has no readily ascertainable value in terms of retirement benefits.

27. There is, I suppose, at least a possibility that my proposed benefit statement might cause some participants to overestimate the value of working. As figure 10.3 indicates, the total annual increase in accrued benefits is greater than the incremental value of an additional year's work. Particularly in later years, the bulk of the annual increase in value comes from implicit interest on past accruals, which occur whether or not the participant continues working (assuming minimum lifetime participation of forty quarters). If participants mistakenly attribute the full increase in accrued benefits to a year's labor, they would be overestimating the value of a year's work.

28. That is twelve times her AIME of $2,899.

References

Baron, Jonathan. 2000. *Thinking and Deciding*. Cambridge: Cambridge University Press.

Brown, Jeffery R. 2000. "How Should We Insure Longevity Risk in Pensions and Social Security." Issue Brief No. 4. Boston, Mass.: Boston College Center for Retirement Research.

Brown, Jeffery R., Olivia S. Mitchell, and James M. Poterba. 2001. "The Role of Real Annuities and Indexed Bonds in an Individual Accounts Retirement Program." In *Risk Aspects of Investment-Based Social Security Reform*, edited by John Campbell and Martin Feldstein. Chicago: University of Chicago Press.

Diamond, Peter A. 2004. "Social Security." *American Economic Review* 94(1): 1–24.

Diamond, Peter A., and Peter R. Orszag. 2004. *Saving Social Security: A Balanced Approach*. Washington, D.C.: Brookings Institution Press.

Jackson, Howell E. 2004. "Accounting for Social Security and Its Reform." *Harvard Journal on Legislation* 41(1): 61–159.

Jackson, Howell E., and Jeremy Berry. 2002. "Kickbacks or Compensation: The Case of Yield Spread Premiums." Mimeo, Harvard University.

Jacobs, Lawrence R., and Robert Y. Shapiro. 1998. "Public Opinion and the Politics of Reforming Social Security: Myths and Misunderstandings about Public Opinion toward Social Security." In *Framing the Social Security Debate: Values, Politics, and Economics*, edited by R. Douglas Arnold, Michael J. Graetz, and Alicia H. Munnell. Washington, D.C.: Brookings Institution Press.

Jolls, Christine. 2000. "Accommodation Mandates." *Stanford Law Review* 53(2): 223–306.

Kaplow, Louis. 1994. "Human Capital under an Ideal Income Tax." *Virginia Law Review* 80(7): 1477–514.

Loewenstein, George, and Samuel Issacharoff. 1994. "Source Dependence in the Valuation of Objects." *Journal of Behavioral Decision Making* 7(3): 157–68.

Loewenstein, George, and Richard H. Thaler. 1989. "Anomalies: Intertemporal Choice." *Journal of Economic Perspectives* 3(4): 181–93.

New York Stock Exchange Fact Book. 2004. New York: New York Stock Exchange.

Posner, Richard A. 1998. "Rational Choice, Behavioral Economics, and the Law." *Stanford Law Review* 50(5): 1551–575.

Summers, Lawrence H. 1989. "Some Simple Economics of Mandated Benefits." *American Economic Review* 79(2): 177–83.

Sundén, Annika. 2000. "How Will Sweden's New Pension System Work?" Issue Brief No. 3. Boston: Boston College Center for Retirement Research.

Thaler, Richard. 1980. "Towards a Positive Theory of Consumer Choice." *Journal of Economic Behavior and Organization* 1(1): 39–60.

U.S. General Accounting Office.. 1989. Statement of Joseph F. Delfico. Testimony Before the Subcommittee on Social Security and Family Policy Committee on Finance, United States Senate. *GAO's Views on an Independent Social Security Administration and The Personal Earnings and Benefit Statement*. GAO/T-HRD-89-23, Washington, June.

———. 1996a. Statement of Diana S. Eisenstat. Testimony Before the Subcommittee on Social Security, Committee on Ways and Means, House of Representatives. *SSA Benefit Statements: Statements Are Well Received by the Public but Difficult to Comprehend*. GAO/T- HEHS-96-210, Washington, September.

———. 1996b. Report to the Chairman, Subcommittee on Social Security, Subcommittee on Ways and Means, House of Representatives. *SSA Benefit Statements: Well Received by the Public but Difficult to Comprehend*. GAO/HEHS-97-19, Washington, December.

———. 1997. Report to the Chairman, Subcommittee on Social Security, Committee on Ways and Means, House of Representatives. *SSA Benefit Estimate Statement: Additional Data Needed to Improve Workload Management*. GAO/HEHS-97-101, Washington, May.

———. 1998. Report to Congressional Requesters. *SSA Benefit Estimate Statement: Adding Rate of Return Information May Not Be Appropriate*. GAO/HEHS-98-228, Washington, September.

U.S. Social Security Administration. 2003. *SSA's FY 2003 Performance and Accountability Report*. Washington: U.S. Government Printing Office. Available at: http://www.ssa.gov/finance/fy03_accountability.html (accessed November 14, 2005).

————. 2004a. *The 2004 Annual Report of the Board of Trustees of the Federal Old-Age and Survivors Insurance and Disability Insurance Trust Funds*. Washington, March.

————. 2004b. *Choose a Benefit Calculator*. Washington: U.S. Government Printing Office. Available at: http://www.ssa.gov/planners/calculators.htm (accessed November 14, 2005).

————. 2005a. *Social Security Basic Facts*. Washington: U.S. Government Printing Office. Available at: http://www.ssa.gov/pressoffice/basicfact.htm (accessed November 14, 2005).

————. 2005b. *Your Social Security Statement (2005)*. Washington: U.S. Government Printing Office. Available at: http://www.socialsecurity.gov/mystatement/ (accessed November 14, 2005).

Chapter 11

Saving for Retirement on the Path of Least Resistance

James J. Choi, David Laibson, Brigitte C. Madrian, and Andrew Metrick

Over the last twenty years, defined contribution pension plans have gradually replaced defined benefit pension plans as the primary privately sponsored vehicle for retirement income. At year-end 2000, employers sponsored over 325,000 401(k) plans with more than forty-two million active participants and $1.8 trillion in assets.[1]

The growth of 401(k)-type savings plans and the associated displacement of defined benefit plans have generated new concerns about the adequacy of employee savings. Defined contribution pension plans place the burden of ensuring adequate retirement savings squarely on the backs of individual employees. However, employers make many decisions about the design of 401(k) plans that can either facilitate or hinder their employees' retirement savings prospects. Although the government places some limits on how companies can structure the plans, employers nonetheless have broad discretion in their design.

Good plan design decisions require understanding the relationship between plan rules and participant choices. Here we analyze a new data set that enables us to carefully assess many such relationships. It is compiled from anonymous administrative records of several large firms that collectively employ almost 400,000 individuals. Many of these companies implemented changes in the design of their 401(k) plans. These plan changes enable us to evaluate the impact on individual savings behavior of institutional variation in 401(k) plan rules. A list of the companies we study, along with the plan changes or other interventions that we analyze, appears in table 11.1.[2]

Table 11.1 Company 401(k) Plan Changes or Other Interventions

Company	Industry	Size[a]	Plan Change or Intervention	Date of Change or Intervention
A	Food	10,000	Savings survey	January 2001
B	Office equipment	30,000	Adopted automatic enrollment	January 1997
			Eliminated automatic enrollment	January 2001
C	Insurance	30,000	Adopted automatic enrollment	April 1998
			Financial education seminars	January to December 2000
			Changed automatic enrollment defaults	May 2001
D	Food	20,000	Adopted automatic enrollment	January 1998
			Increased default contribution rate	January 2001
E	Utility	10,000	Increased match threshold	January 1997
F	Consumer packaged goods	40,000	Changed eligibility	July 1998
			Instituted employer match	October 2000
G	Insurance	50,000	Changed eligibility	January 1997
H	Manufacturing		Adopted automatic enrollment	January 2001
I	Retail	130,000	None	NA
J	Financial Services	50,000	None	NA
K	Pharmaceutical	10,000	Changed eligibility	January 1996

Source: Authors' calculations.

[a] Number of employees (rounded to the nearest 10,000) on December 31, 1998 (company K), December 31, 2000 (Companies A, B, D, E, F, G, I, and J), June 30, 2000 (company C) or December 31, 2001 (company H).

Low employee savings rates have motivated plan administrators to adopt many of the 401(k) plan changes that we discuss throughout the chapter. Using new data from a survey we designed, we find that two-thirds of employees believe that they are saving too little and that one-third of these self-reported under-savers intend to raise their savings rate in the next two months. By matching survey responses to administrative records, we show that employees who report that they save too little actually do have low 401(k) saving rates. However, almost none of the employees who report that they intend to raise their savings rate in the next two months actually subsequently do so.

This finding introduces a theme we return to throughout this chapter: at any point, employees are likely to do whatever requires the least current effort. This phenomenon—which we call passive decision making—implies that employers have a great deal of influence over the savings outcomes of their employees. Employer choices of default savings rates and default investment funds, for example, strongly influence employee savings levels. Even though employees have the opportunity to opt out of such defaults, many never do so.

Employers and policy makers need to recognize that there is no such thing as a neutral menu of options for a 401(k) plan. Framing effects will influence employee choices, and passive employee decision making implies that the default options will often carry the day. Sophisticated employers will choose these defaults carefully, keeping the interests of both employees and shareholders in mind.

Savings Adequacy

In January 2001, we administered a savings adequacy survey to a random sample of employees at a large U.S. food corporation (company A) with approximately 10,000 employees. Of these, 1,202 were sent an email soliciting their participation in a Web-based survey on satisfaction with various aspects of the company-sponsored 401(k) plan.[3] Because participation in the survey was solicited by email and the survey was conducted on the Web, the universe of potential respondents is restricted to those with Internet access at work.[4]

Our survey had two versions. Here we discuss the savings adequacy version sent to 590 of the employees with computers. From this sample we received 195 usable responses. A copy of the complete survey is included at the end of this chapter, though we discuss only a subset of the questions in our analysis. In addition to the survey responses, we also have administrative data on the 401(k) savings choices of survey respondents both before and after the survey. These include participation decisions, contribution rates, and asset allocation choices from January 1996 through April 2001.

Table 11.2   Self-Reported Retirement Savings Adequacy (Company A)

	Distribution of 401(k) Contribution Rates as Fraction of Income		
	0 to 4 percent	5 to 8 percent	9 to 12 percent
Respondents who describe their savings rate as "too low"[a]	36%	36%	27%
Respondents who describe their savings rate as "about right"[a]	12%	15%	73%

Source: Authors' calculations.
[a] See question 11 from the survey reproduced at the end of this chapter. We aggregate the categories "far too low" and "a little too low" into one category ('too low").

We first asked respondents to report how much they should ideally be saving for retirement.[5] The average response is 13.9 percent of income. We then asked respondents to evaluate their actual saving rate. Two-thirds (67.7 percent) report that it is "too low" relative to their ideal.[6] One-third (30.8 percent) report that it is "about right." Only one out of 195 (0.5 percent) reports that it is "too high."

To evaluate how well individual perceptions of savings adequacy correlate with savings behavior, we report in table 11.2 the distribution of actual pre-tax 401(k) savings rates conditional on respondents' answers to the savings adequacy questions discussed above. Because we use the plan's administrative records, our analysis of actual 401(k) savings rates does not suffer from reporting biases. We divide the actual pre-tax 401(k) savings rates into three categories: 0 to 4 percent of income, 5 to 8 percent of income, and 9 to 12 percent of income. Our scale tops out at 12 percent because this is the maximum pre-tax 401(k) contribution rate in company A. Among the respondents who said that their current savings rate is "too low," 36 percent had an actual 401(k) rate of 0 to 4 percent, another 36 percent had one of 5 to 8 percent, and 27 percent had one of 9 to 12 percent. In contrast, among those who said that their current savings rate is "about right," 12 percent had a rate of 0 to 4 percent, 15 percent had one of 5 to 8 percent, and 73 percent had one of 9 to 12 percent. These comparisons reveal that respondents who report that their rate is too low do have lower actual rates than those who report it as about right. In the former group, the average pre-tax 401(k) contribution rate is 5.8 percent of income, in contrast to an average 401(k) savings rate of 9.0 percent in the latter group.

We also asked respondents to describe their plans for the future. None of our respondents expressed an intention to lower their contribution rate. But 35 percent of those who said that their savings rate was too low intended to increase their contribution rate over the next few months. By contrast, 11 percent of those who said their savings rate was about right intended to increase their contribution rate over the next few months. Among those who planned to raise their rate, over half (53 percent) said that they would do so in the next month. Another quarter (23 percent) planned to make the change within two months.

So far our data shows a familiar pattern. Respondents report that they save too little and that they intend to raise their savings rate in the future. Other savings adequacy surveys reach similar conclusions (Bernheim 1995; Farkas and Johnson 1997). Our survey is distinguished by our ability to cross-check responses against actual 401(k) records. We have shown that respondents who say that their savings rate is too low actually do have substantially lower pre-tax 401(k) contribution rates. Their retrospective reports are thus accurate.

We have also checked to see whether their forward-looking plans are consistent with their subsequent behavior. Of those respondents who report that their savings rate is too low and who plan to increase their contribution rate in the next few months, only 14 percent actually do so in the four months after the survey. Hence we find that respondents overwhelmingly do not follow through on their good intentions. In summary, out of every 100 respondents, sixty-eight report that their savings rate is too low; twenty-four of the sixty-eight plan to increase their 401(k) contribution rate in the next few months; but only three of the twenty-four actually do so. Hence, even though most employees describe themselves as undersavers and many report that they plan to rectify this situation in the next few months, few follow through.

These data, of course, are hard to interpret. It's not clear what subjects mean when they say that they save too little. It's also not clear what subjects mean when they say that they intend to raise their contribution rate in the next few months. However, this evidence is at least consistent with the idea that employees have a hard time carrying out the actions that they themselves say they wish to take. Employers seem to be concerned about such failures. Many of the institutional changes we later discuss were initiated by plan administrators in an effort to raise employee savings rates.

Institutional Features of 401(k) Plans

Here we turn to an analysis of how several different 401(k) plan features affect employee 401(k) savings behavior.

Automatic Enrollment

The typical 401(k) plan requires an active election on the part of employees to initiate participation. A growing number of companies, however, have started automatically enrolling employees into the plan unless the employee actively opts out. Although automatic enrollment is still relatively uncommon, a recent survey indicates that its adoption has increased quite rapidly over the past few years.[7]

The interest of many companies in automatic enrollment has stemmed from their persistent failure to pass the IRS nondiscrimination tests that apply to pension plans. As a result, many companies have either had to make ex post 401(k) contribution refunds to highly compensated employees or retroactive company contributions on behalf of the not highly compensated to come into compliance. In addition, many companies have tried to reduce the possibility of nondiscrimination testing problems by ex ante limiting the contributions that highly compensated employees can make. The hope of many companies adopting automatic enrollment has been that participation among the not highly compensated employees at the firm will increase sufficiently such that nondiscrimination testing is no longer a concern.

Although some companies have been concerned about the potential legal repercussions of automatically enrolling employees in the 401(k), the U.S. Treasury Department has issued several opinions that support the practice. The first such opinion on the subject, issued in 1998, sanctioned automatic enrollment for newly hired employees (see revenue ruling 98-30 in IRS 1998). A second ruling, issued in 2000, further validated the practice for previously hired employees not yet participating (see revenue ruling 2000-8 in IRS 2000a and rulings 2000-33 and 2000-35 in IRS 2000b). In addition, during his tenure as Treasury secretary, Lawrence H. Summers publicly advocated that employers adopt automatic enrollment.[8]

A growing body of evidence suggests that automatic enrollment—a simple change from a default of nonparticipation to a default of participation—substantially increases 401(k) participation rates (see Madrian and Shea 2001a; Choi et al. 2004a; Fidelity 2001; Vanguard 2001). To assess the impact of automatic enrollment on savings behavior, we examine the experience of four large companies that implemented automatic enrollment.[9] Company B implemented automatic enrollment in January of 1997 for new hires with a default contribution rate of 2 percent and a stable value fund as the default investment option. Company B subsequently abandoned automatic enrollment in January 2001. Company C implemented automatic enrollment in April 1998 for new hires with a default contribution rate of 3 percent and a money market fund as the default investment option. In May 2001, the company made two changes to its automatic enrollment design. First, it changed the default investment option to a lifestyle fund. And, second, it decided to automatically increase the contribution rate of employees from 3 percent to 6 percent once employees reached one year of tenure if the employees were still contributing at the original default contribution rate of 3 percent.

This change took effect going forward—it did not apply to employees who had obtained one year of tenure prior to May 2001. Company D adopted automatic enrollment in January 1998 for new employees with a default contribution rate of 3 percent and a stable value fund as the default investment option. Company D subsequently applied automatic enrollment to eligible employees who were not participating when automatic enrollment was initially adopted.[10] In addition, in January 2001, company D increased the default contribution rate from 3 percent to 4 percent for all new employees going forward. Company H adopted automatic enrollment in January 2001 for all new employees going forward with a default contribution rate of 6 percent and a balanced fund as the default investment option.

Figure 11.1 illustrates the difference in 401(k) participation rates by tenure before, during, and for—company B—after automatic enrollment.[11] In all four companies, 401(k) participation for employees hired before automatic enrollment starts out low and increases quite substantially with tenure. At six months of tenure, 401(k) participation rates range from 25 to 43 percent at these four companies. Participation rates increase to 50 to 63 percent at 24 months of tenure, and to 57 to 71 percent at 36 months of tenure. The profile of 401(k) participation for employees hired under automatic enrollment is quite different. For these employees, the 401(k) participation rate starts out high and remains high. At six months of tenure, 401(k) participation ranges from 86 to 96 percent at these four companies, an increase of 50 to 67 percentage points relative to 401(k) participation rates prior to automatic enrollment. Because participation increases with tenure in the absence of automatic enrollment, the incremental effect of automatic enrollment declines over time. Nonetheless, at thirty-six months of tenure, 401(k) participation is still a sizable 20 to 34 percentage points higher under automatic enrollment.

Interestingly, it does not appear that the participation rate obtained under automatic enrollment is very strongly influenced by the level of the default contribution rate. Company H has the highest participation rates under automatic enrollment, despite also having the highest initial default contribution rate (6 percent). The participation rate in company C is virtually identical for employees subject only to a 3 percent default and those subject to an initial default contribution rate of 3 percent that increases to 6 percent at one year of tenure. Similarly, the participation rate in company D is virtually identical for employees hired with a 3 percent default contribution rate or a 4 percent default contribution rate.

Although most companies that implement automatic enrollment do so only for newly hired employees, some have applied automatic enrollment to previously hired employees who have not yet opted in to the 401(k) plan. James Choi and colleagues (2004a) show that for previously hired employees at company D, automatic enrollment also substantially

Figure 11.1   401(k) Participation

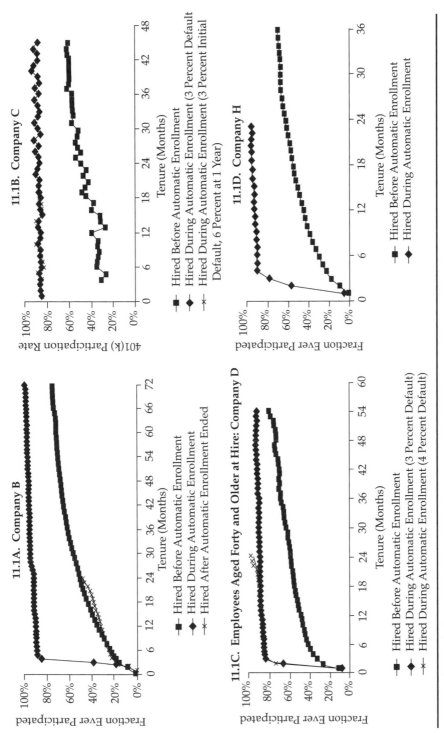

11.1A. Company B

Fraction Ever Participated

Tenure (Months)

- ■- Hired Before Automatic Enrollment
- ◆- Hired During Automatic Enrollment
- ✕- Hired After Automatic Enrollment Ended

11.1B. Company C

401(k) Participation Rate

Tenure (Months)

- ■- Hired Before Automatic Enrollment
- ◆- Hired During Automatic Enrollment (3 Percent Default)
- ✕- Hired During Automatic Enrollment (3 Percent Initial Default, 6 Percent at 1 Year)

11.1C. Employees Aged Forty and Older at Hire: Company D

Fraction Ever Participated

Tenure (Months)

- ■- Hired Before Automatic Enrollment
- ◆- Hired During Automatic Enrollment (3 Percent Default)
- ✕- Hired During Automatic Enrollment (4 Percent Default)

11.1D. Company H

Fraction Ever Participated

Tenure (Months)

- ■- Hired Before Automatic Enrollment
- ◆- Hired During Automatic Enrollment

Source: Authors' calculations.

increases the 401(k) participation rate, though the increase in participation is slightly smaller than that seen for newly hired employees. Both Brigitte Madrian and Dennis Shea (2001a) and Choi and his colleagues (2004a) also discuss how the effects of automatic enrollment vary across various demographic groups. Automatic enrollment increases 401(k) participation for virtually all demographic groups, but its effects are largest for those least likely to participate in the first place: younger employees, lower-paid employees, and blacks and Hispanics.

One might conclude that because 401(k) participation under automatic enrollment is so much higher than under opt-in enrollment, automatic enrollment "coerces" employees into participating in the 401(k) plan. However, if this were the case, we should expect to see participation rates under automatic enrollment declining with tenure as employees veto their "coerced" participation and opt out. But remarkably few 401(k) participants at these companies, whether hired before automatic enrollment or after, reverse their participation. In our four companies, the fraction of 401(k) participants hired before automatic enrollment that drops out in a twelve-month period ranges from 1.9 to 2.6 percent, and the fraction subject to automatic enrollment who drop out is only 0.3 to 0.6 percentage points higher. To us, this evidence suggests that most employees do not object to saving for retirement. In the absence of automatic enrollment, however, many tend to delay taking action. Thus, automatic enrollment appears to be effective in helping employees begin to save for their retirement.

Although automatic enrollment is effective in getting employees to participate in their company-sponsored 401(k) plan, it is less effective at motivating them to make well-planned decisions about how much to save for retirement or how to invest their retirement savings. Because companies cannot ensure that employees will choose a contribution rate or an asset allocation before the automatic enrollment deadline, the company must establish a default contribution rate and a default asset allocation. Most employees follow the path of least resistance and passively accept these defaults.

Figure 11.2 shows the distribution of 401(k) contribution rates at our four companies for employees hired before, during, and—for company B—after automatic enrollment. As noted earlier, the default contribution rate under automatic enrollment varies both across firms at a given point in time, and across time within a given firm. Because contribution rates may change with tenure, it would be preferable to compare the contribution rates of employees with equivalent levels of tenure (as done in figure 11.1). However, because of firm-level changes in the features of automatic enrollment and the timing of the data collection, it is not possible to get employee groups with equivalent levels of tenure for all of the comparison groups of interest. So the tenure composition of the groups

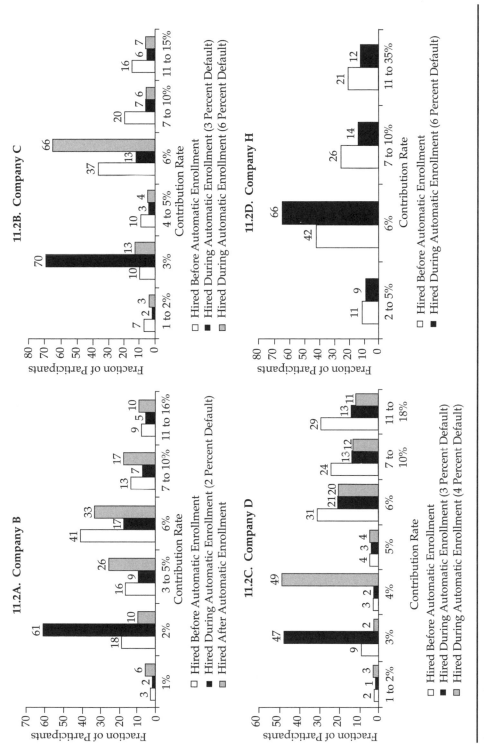

11.2A. Company B

11.2B. Company C

11.2C. Company D

11.2D. Company H

Source: Authors' compilation.

in figure 11.2 do differ somewhat. However, in the previous work we have made more limited comparisons for employee groups with equivalent levels of tenure (for example, Choi et al. 2002, 2004a), and the general patterns of interest hold whether or not tenure is held constant. The impact of the automatic enrollment default on the distribution of contribution rates is readily apparent in figure 11.2. At all four companies, the modal contribution rate of employees hired before automatic enrollment (and during automatic enrollment at company H) is 6 percent, which is the match threshold at all four of these companies. For those employees hired during automatic enrollment at company B (figure 11.2A), the modal contribution shifts to 2 percent, the automatic enrollment default. For those employees hired under automatic enrollment at company C (figure 11.2B) at a 3 percent default, the predominant contribution rate is 3 percent, while for those affected by the automatic increase to 6 percent at one year of tenure, the predominant contribution rate is 6 percent. For those employees hired under automatic enrollment at company D (figure 11.2C) with a 3 percent default, the modal contribution rate is 3 percent, while for those hired after the increase in the default contribution rate to 4 percent, the modal contribution rate is 4 percent. Finally, at company H (figure 11.2D), where the automatic enrollment default equals the match threshold of 6 percent, the fraction of participants at the match threshold is 24 percentage points higher for those hired under automatic enrollment. The default contribution rate clearly has a strong impact on the overall distribution of employee contributions to the 401(k) plan.

Automatic enrollment has similar effects on the asset allocation of plan participants. Table 11.3 shows the fraction of plan participants with any assets allocated to the default investment fund, and the fraction of plan participations with all assets allocated to the default investment fund. In two of the four companies (B and D), the default fund under automatic enrollment is a stable value fund; in company C, the default fund was initially a money market fund, but was later changed to a lifestyle fund; whereas in company H, the default is a balanced fund. As table 11.3 shows, the fraction of 401(k) participants that have all of their assets allocated to the default investment fund is relatively low (less than 15 percent) for those employees hired before (or after) automatic enrollment. In contrast, the vast majority of participants hired under automatic enrollment have their assets entirely invested in the automatic enrollment default fund. Choi and colleagues (2004a) show that this effect is driven both by the conversion of would-be nonparticipants to the defaults and by employees who would have participated in the absence of automatic enrollment but with different elections.

Given the evidence of delay in the election of 401(k) participation before automatic enrollment shown in figure 11.1, one might speculate that there is the same type of delay in the movement away from the default

Table 11.3   Fraction of 401(k) Participants with Balances in Automatic Enrollment Default Fund(s)

	Any Balances	All Balances
Company B		
Hired before automatic enrollment	43.9	12.7
Hired during automatic enrollment	71.6	59.6
Hired after automatic enrollment	27.7	6.8
Company C (partitioned on the basis of differences in the default contribution rate under automatic enrollment)		
Hired before automatic enrollment	17.7	5.2
Hired during automatic enrollment (3 percent default)	88.5	73.5
Hired during automatic enrollment (3 percent initial default, 6 percent at one year)	89.4	73.5
Company C (partitioned on the basis of differences in the default investment fund under automatic enrollment)		
Hired before automatic enrollment	17.7	5.2
Hired during automatic enrollment (money market fund default)	88.7	73.7
Hired during automatic enrollment (lifestyle fund default)	96.5	90.1
Company D		
Hired before automatic enrollment	36.4	14.2
Hired during automatic enrollment (3 percent default)	65.9	53.8
Hired during automatic enrollment (4 percent default)	70.1	61.5
Company H		
Hired before automatic enrollment	3.7	2.5
Hired during automatic enrollment	50.8	45.8

Source: Authors' calculations.
Note: The sample for companies B, C and H is 401(k)-eligible employees. The sample for company D is 401(k)-eligible employees aged forty plus at the time of hire. For company D, the data for those hired before automatic enrollment includes only employees not yet subject to automatic enrollment when it was applied to previously hired nonparticipants.

contribution rate and asset allocation under automatic enrollment. Figure 11.3 suggests that this is indeed the case. At six months of tenure, between 48 and 73 percent of participants contribute at the default and have their assets invested wholly in the default fund. At twenty-four months of tenure, the fraction of participants at the default falls to 37 to 50 percent, and at thirty-six months of tenure to 29 to 48 percent. So, with time, employees do move away from the automatic enrollment defaults. Nonetheless, after three years, between one-third and one-half of participants are still "stuck" at the default.[12]

Taken as a whole, the evidence here indicates that defaults can have a powerful effect on the nature of individual saving for retirement. In terms of promoting overall savings for retirement, automatic enrollment as structured by most employers is a mixed bag. Clearly automatic enrollment is very effective at promoting one important aspect of savings behavior, 401(k) participation. This simple change in the default from nonparticipation to participation results in much higher 401(k) participation rates. But, as with companies B, C (before May 2001), D, and H, most employers that have adopted automatic enrollment have chosen very low default contribution rates and very conservative default funds (PSCA 2001; Vanguard 2001). These default choices are inconsistent with the retirement savings goals of most employees.

This evidence does not argue against automatic enrollment as a tool for promoting retirement savings; rather, it argues against the specific automatic enrollment defaults chosen by most employers. Employers who seek to facilitate the retirement savings of their employees need to respond to the tendency of employees to stick with the default. Employers should choose defaults that foster successful retirement savings when the defaults are passively accepted in their entirety. Automatic enrollment coupled with higher default contribution rates and more aggressive default funds would greatly increase wealth accumulation for retirement (we will discuss another alternative to a higher initial default contribution rate later in the chapter). The results here also suggest an important caveat in thinking about the design of personal accounts in a reformed Social Security system—whatever defaults are chosen will need to be chosen carefully.

Automatic Cash Distributions for Terminated Employees with Low Account Balances

Another aspect of 401(k) plan design that highlights the importance of defaults on 401(k) savings outcomes is the treatment of the balances of former employees. When an employee leaves a firm, the employee may explicitly request a cash distribution, a direct rollover of 401(k) balances to an IRA, or a rollover to another employer's plan. If the terminated em-

Figure 11.3   Participants Hired During Automatic Enrollment at Defaults

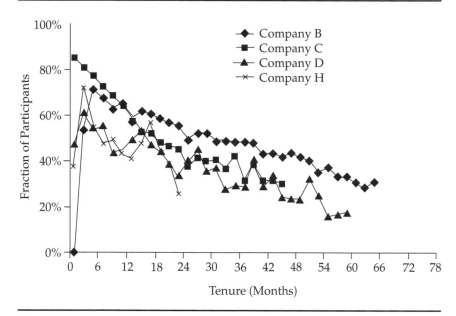

Source: Authors' calculations.

ployee does not make an explicit request, the balances typically remain in the 401(k). Under current law, however, if the plan balances are less than $5,000 and the former employee has not elected some sort of rollover, the employer has the option of compelling a cash distribution.

To document the importance of this mandatory cash distribution threshold, figure 11.4 plots the relationship between the size of 401(k) balances and the likelihood that a terminated employee receives a distribution from the 401(k) plan at companies B, D, I, and J. We consider the experience of 401(k) participants whose employment terminated any time during 1999 or January through August of 2000.[13] We order the employees according to the size of their 401(k) balances and then divide them into groups of 100. We then calculate the average balance size for each group (the x-axis, plotted on a log scale) and the average fraction of employees who receive a distribution from the plan by December 31, 2000 (the y-axis). The measure of 401(k) balances used on the x-axis is the average participant balance as of December 31 of the year prior to the year in which the termination occurred.[14] This measure of balances is likely to understate the actual balances of plan participants at the time of termination because the incremental contributions made to an individual's account between December 31 of the previous year and the date of termination are excluded (as are any capital gains or losses over this period).

Figure 11.4   Balances and the Probability of a Cash Distribution

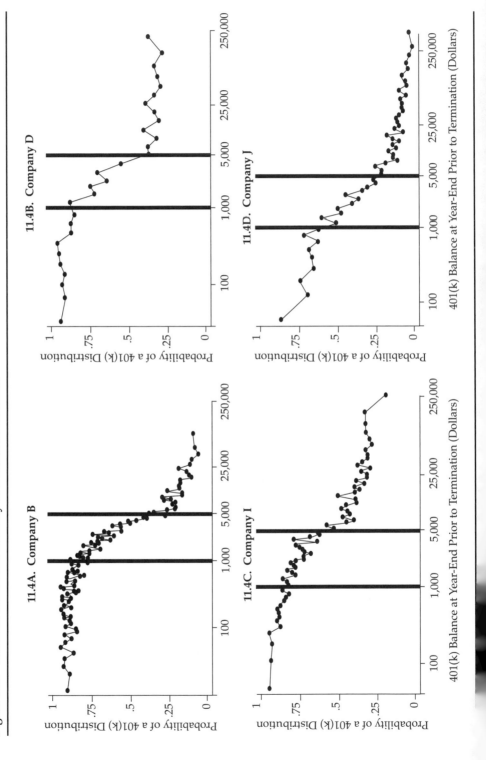

In three of the four companies (B, D and I), 80 to 90 percent of terminated participants with prior year-end balances of less than $1,000 receive a distribution subsequent to termination. In company J, the fraction of terminated participants with a prior year-end balance of less than $1,000 who receive a distribution is somewhat lower at about 65 to 75 percent (interestingly, company J is a financial services firm). In contrast, the fraction of terminated participants with balances in excess of $5,000 prior to termination who receive a cash distribution is much lower. In companies D and I it is rather constant, with about one-third receiving a cash distribution (the exception is former participants in company I with extremely high balances who are even less likely to receive a cash distribution). In companies B and J, the fraction of terminated employees with prior year-end balances exceeding $5,000 who receive a cash distribution is lower still, less than 20 percent, with some additional slight decline as balances increase beyond the $5,000 threshold. Between $1,000 and $5,000 in prior year-end balances, the fraction of terminated participants receiving a distribution falls rather steadily and quite significantly at all four firms. This reflects the decreasing likelihood that terminated participants will have a final balance of less than $5,000 that is subject to an involuntary cash distribution.

For example, consider an employee at company D making $40,000 per year who is contributing 6 percent of pay to the 401(k) plan with a 50-percent employer match that is vested. If this individual leaves his job at the end of August, the additional employer plus employee contributions to the 401(k) plan will amount to $2,400. Assuming no net capital gains or losses, this individual will face a mandatory cash distribution if his prior year-end balances were less than $2,600 (because $2,400 plus anything less than $2,600 will fall under the $5,000 distribution threshold). If his prior year-end balances were higher than $2,600, however, the company would not be able to compel a cash distribution because his total balances subsequent to termination would exceed $5,000. Thus, employees with higher prior year-end balances will be less likely to face an automatic distribution on termination because they are more likely to have had balance increases that bring them above the $5,000 threshold.

Of course, even in the case of an automatic cash distribution, the former employee does have the option to roll the account balance over into an IRA or the 401(k) plan of another employer, regardless of the size of the account balance. But previous research suggests that the probability of receiving a cash distribution and rolling it over into an IRA or another 401(k) plan is very low when the size of the distribution is small. Instead, these small distributions tend to be consumed.[15] When employers compel a cash distribution and employees receive an unexpected check in the mail, it is much easier to consume the distribution than to figure out how to roll it over into an IRA or another employer's 401(k).

This default treatment of the account balances of terminated employees provides another example of how many individuals follow the path of least resistance. When balances exceed $5,000, the vast majority of employees leave their balances with their former employer, the least-effort option. When balances are below $5,000 and subject to a mandatory cash distribution unless the employee elects otherwise, most individuals receive an unsolicited check in the mail and then consume the money rather than rolling it over into another type of saving plan—also the least-effort option.

This analysis suggests that the rollover provisions of the recently passed Economic Growth and Tax Relief Reconciliation Act of 2001 (EGTRRA) will indeed have a positive impact on retirement savings. Under the new law, if the account balance is between $1,000 and $5,000, employers will no longer be able to compel a cash distribution if a former employee does not elect a rollover. Instead, employers will be required to establish an IRA on behalf of participants who choose not to maintain these accounts (Watson Wyatt Worldwide 2001). Although this provision of the law does not take effect until the Department of Labor issues final regulations regarding implementation, firms need not wait until then to voluntarily adopt similar measures.[16] As with automatic enrollment in 401(k) plans, default rollovers have also been sanctioned by the IRS (see rulings 2000-36 in IRS 2000b). Such a change in the default treatment of the small balances of terminated employees is a simple step that would further enhance the retirement savings plans of many individuals.[17]

Automatic Contribution Rate Increases

One 401(k) plan feature designed to capitalize on inertia is the "Save More Tomorrow" (SMT) plan Richard Thaler and Shlomo Benartzi developed (2004). Under this plan, participants commit in advance to saving a portion of future raises. For example, suppose that a worker commits to allocate one-half of future nominal pay raises to increases in his 401(k) contribution rate. If the worker receives 3 percent raises in each of the following three years, then his contribution rate would rise by 1.5 percentage points per year over this period. This plan is carefully constructed to make use of several themes in behavioral economics. By requiring a present commitment for future actions, the SMT plan alleviates problems of self-control and procrastination. And by taking the additional savings out of future salary raises, participants in the SMT plan are not hurt by loss aversion because workers will never see a reduction in their nominal take-home pay. (This presumes that participants are subject to money illusion because the commitment to save is out of nominal salary increases.)

The striking results of the first experiment with the SMT plan are reported in Richard Thaler and Shlomo Benartzi (2004). This first experiment was conducted at a mid-size manufacturing company that was experiencing problems in getting low-salary workers to participate and contribute at high levels to the 401(k) plan. To combat these problems, the company hired an investment consultant to meet with employees and help them plan their retirement savings. After an initial interview with each employee, the consultant would gauge the employee's willingness to increase his or her savings rate. Employees judged to have a high willingness to save more would receive an immediate recommendation for a large increase in their savings rate. Seventy-nine workers fell into this group. Employees judged to be reluctant to save more would be offered the option of enrolling in the SMT plan. Two hundred and seven workers fell into this group. The version of the SMT plan that was implemented set up a schedule of annual contribution rate increases of three percentage points. This is a relatively aggressive implementation, as the annual nominal salary increases at this company were only a little bit higher than 3 percent.

The results of the experiment show that the SMT plan can have an enormous impact on contribution rates. Of the 207 participants offered the SMT plan as an option, 162 chose to enroll. Furthermore, 129 of these 162 (80 percent) stayed with the plan through three consecutive pay raises. At the beginning of the SMT plan, these 162 workers had an average contribution rate of 3.5 percent; by the time of their third pay raise, these workers (including those that eventually dropped out) had an average contribution rate of 11.6 percent. Recall that these original 207 participants were selected from a larger sample based on their relative reluctance to increase their savings rates. In comparison, seventy-nine workers had indicated a willingness to increase their contributions immediately and were never enrolled in the SMT plan; these workers increased their average contribution rate from 4.4 percent to 8.7 percent over the same time period. Because it is reasonable to assume that this second group of workers represents a more highly motivated group of savers than the SMT plan participants, the increases by the SMT plan participants are very striking. As a further comparison, consider that the median 401(k) contribution rate of participants in 401(k) plans in general is approximately 7 percent of pay (Investment Company Institute 2000). Thus the SMT plan participants went from half of this median contribution rate before signing up for the SMT plan to a contribution rate 50 percent higher three years later.

Despite the clear success of the SMT plan in increasing contribution rates, several caveats remain. First, the plan is not guided by any well-specified model of what ideal savings should be. Even if we accept that cleverly designed commitment devices can enable workers to break from suboptimal behavior patterns, these same devices may overshoot the optimal targets. Second, the increases in 401(k) contribution rates may be offset by dissaving elsewhere (for a discussion of asset shifting and its consequences for measuring 401(k) effectiveness, see Engen, Gale, and Scholz 1994, 1996; for evidence that asset shifting effects are not large, see Poterba, Venti, and Wise 1996, 1998b). Although 401(k) saving has many advantages, it may still be inefficient if it leads participants to increase high-interest credit card debt. Also, we do not know how much of the additional contributions were later reduced by plan loans or hardship withdrawals. In a plan that does not have an employer match—unlike the one used in the original SMT experiment—it is not clear that increasing 401(k) contributions is always a good idea. Notwithstanding these caveats, the SMT plan is certainly a provocative attempt to use behavioral economics to increase savings rates, and the early results are highly encouraging and deserve further study.

Our 401(k) survey sheds light on the mechanisms that make the SMT plan work. We generated two versions of our survey. One version (already discussed) asked questions about savings adequacy and intentions regarding planned future investment changes (for example, plans to change the contribution rate and the asset mix). We call this the savings adequacy version. We also generated a pared-down version of the survey that contained no questions about either savings adequacy or intentions. We call this the control version. We randomly assigned the two versions to employees and checked to see whether the savings adequacy questionnaire had had an impact on subsequent 401(k) investment choices. In other words, we looked to see whether the process of thinking about savings adequacy and formulating one's future savings plans actually led to a greater propensity to subsequently increase (or decrease) one's saving rate.

It turns out that this attention manipulation had no impact. In other words, getting someone to think about his or her own savings adequacy did not lead to any differential future behavior. This result sheds some light on the success of the SMT plan. The plan has many different effects. It encourages employees to think about their savings adequacy. It also sets in motion a series of automatic contribution rate increases. Our survey experiment demonstrates that getting employees to think about savings inadequacy is not enough. Employees also need a low-effort mechanism to help them to carry out their plans to increase their contribution rate. The SMT plan provides exactly such a tool.

Matching

Although automatic enrollment and the SMT plan provide food for thought, they are still relatively new 401(k) features that have yet to be adopted on a widespread scale. A more common feature is the employer match. For each dollar contributed by the employee to the plan, the employer contributes a matching amount up to a certain threshold (for example, 50 percent of the employee contribution up to 6 percent of compensation). Although the effects of employer matching on 401(k) participation and contribution rates have been widely studied, the conclusions from this research are decidedly mixed. This derives in part from the inherent difficulties associated with identifying the impact of matching on 401(k) savings behavior.

In theory, introducing an employer match should increase participation in the 401(k) plan. In practice, however, it is difficult to disentangle this effect from the potential correlation between the savings preferences of employees and the employer match. For example, companies that offer a generous match may attract employees who like to save, biasing upward the estimated impact of an employer match on participation.

Using cross-sectional data, a number of studies find a positive correlation between the availability of an employer match and 401(k) participation (Andrews 1992; Bassett, Fleming, and Rodrigues 1998; Papke and Poterba 1995; Papke 1995; Even and Macpherson 1997). The results are more varied, however, in studies that attempt to control for the correlation between the employer match and other unobserved factors that affect 401(k) savings behavior. William Even and David Macpherson (1997) use an instrumental variables approach to account for the endogeneity of the employer match and still find a large positive impact of matching on 401(k) participation. However, it is not clear that the firm characteristics they use as instrumental variables are in fact uncorrelated with unobservable employee savings preferences. Because she uses longitudinal data on firms, Leslie Papke (1995) is able to include employer fixed effects to account for the correlation between the employer match and other factors that affect savings behavior. With the addition of these fixed effects, the relationship between the employer match and 401(k) participation goes away, but these results are difficult to interpret because Papke only observes average match rates, not marginal rates. Andrea Kusko, James Poterba, and David Wilcox (1998) examine several years of individual-level data in a company whose match rate varied from year to year based on the company's prior-year profitability. They also find no relationship between the match rate and 401(k) participation. However, the transient nature of the match rate changes at this company make it difficult to extrapolate these results to the permanent types of match changes that most companies are likely to consider.

The empirical evidence on matching and 401(k) contribution rates is even less decisive than that on 401(k) participation, although in theory the effects here are less straightforward as well. Although introducing an employer match where there wasn't one before should lower the contribution rates of employees who were already contributing in excess of the match threshold (an income effect), its impact on those previously contributing at or below the match threshold is ambiguous (opposing income and substitution effects). The effects would be similar for increasing the match rate while maintaining the same match threshold. Increasing an existing non-zero match threshold while keeping the match rate constant should have no effect on people contributing below the old threshold, increase contributions for people at the old threshold (a substitution effect), have an ambiguous effect for people above the old threshold but at or below the new threshold (opposing income and substitution effects), and decrease contribution rates for people above the new threshold (an income effect).

The empirical research on matching and 401(k) contribution rates has focused largely on the relationship between the match rate and average contribution rates. Emily Andrews (1992) finds that a higher employer match rate reduces the average contribution rate. William Bassett, Michael Fleming, and Anthony Rodrigues (1998) find no effect. Leslie Papke and James Poterba (1995) and Even and Macpherson (1997) find a positive relationship, and Andrea Kusko, James Poterba, and David Wilcox (1998) find a small but positive effect of the match rate on average 401(k) contribution rates. Papke (1995) finds a positive effect of the match rate on total employee contributions at low match rates, but a negative effect on employee contributions at higher match rates. These disparate results are perhaps not so surprising given that theory has little to say about the impact of the match rate per se on the average 401(k) contribution rate. Gary Engelhardt and Anil Kumar (2004) is the only empirical paper in this literature to explicitly recognize the nonlinear saving incentives generated by the employer match. Using a nonlinear budget set methodology, they find that a higher employer match increases both participation in and contribution rates to the 401(k) plan.

In this chapter, we are able to avoid some of the confounds of previous matching studies by examining the individual behavior of participants before and after permanent changes in the 401(k) match structure at two companies. In these natural experiments, participant behavior before the changes serves as a control for behavior after them. We also examine the effect of matching on the distribution of 401(k) contribution rates rather than on the average 401(k) contribution rate and show the importance of considering the match threshold, a facet of employer matching largely ignored in previous research, as well as the match rate.

The first company that we consider, company E, increased its match threshold on January 1, 1997, while keeping its match rate constant. Before that time, union workers received a 50-percent match on the first 5 percent of income contributed to the 401(k) plan, and management employees received the same match on the first 6 percent. On January 1, 1997, the match thresholds for union employees increased to 7 percent and for management employees to 8 percent. Contributions up to the new threshold were still matched at 50 percent, though the match on the incremental 2 percent of the new threshold was invested in employer stock and the match up to the old threshold had been, and continued to be, invested at the discretion of the employee.

To examine the impact of this change in the match structure on 401(k) savings behavior, we use a combination of both longitudinal and cross-sectional data. We have longitudinal data on the 401(k) contribution rate in effect on each day from March 31, 1996, to February 28, 2000, for every worker enrolled in the 401(k) plan during that time. We also have cross-sections of all active employees at company E at year-end 1998, 1999, and 2000 that contain information on participation status, original enrollment date, original hire date, and demographics.

To assess the effect of the threshold change on participation, we estimate a Cox proportional hazard model of time from hire until the date of initial participation in the 401(k) plan. We control for gender and age (with both linear and quadratic terms), and also include a dummy variable that equals 1 after the new threshold took effect (January 1, 1997). We exclude all employees hired before January 1, 1996 because the company eliminated its length-of-service requirement for 401(k) participation on that date. We also exclude employees hired after December 31, 1997, because the company switched from a traditional defined benefit to a cash-balance pension plan at that time for newly hired employees. The first column of table 11.4 presents the estimated hazard ratios associated with each independent variable. As one might expect for a change that does not affect the marginal incentives to participate in the 401(k) plan, we find that this increase in the match threshold has no significant effect on 401(k) participation.

We next look at the impact of the threshold change on 401(k) contribution rates. Figure 11.5 plots the distribution of contribution rates over time for all workers who were contributing to the 401(k) plan on March 31, 1996. As workers leave the firm, they are dropped from the sample. The switch from the old threshold to the new threshold is clear. There is an immediate jump from the old threshold to the new threshold when the change occurred in January 1997, and a continued slower adjustment over the next three years as more and more people shift from the old to the new threshold. This suggests that there is a strong substitution effect for contributors at the old threshold. In contrast, the fraction of participants at the other contribution rates is fairly stable over this entire period, implying only a very small income effect for contributors above the old threshold.

The shift in contribution rates from the old to the new match threshold may also reflect an "anchoring effect" of the match threshold. Specifically, the match threshold serves as a salient starting point in the deci-

Table 11.4   Employer Matching and 401(k) Participation

Independent Variable	Company E (Hazard Ratio)	Company F (Hazard Ratio)
Female	0.8964	0.9890
	(−1.21)	(−0.25)
Age	1.1376**	1.1238**
	(3.54)	(6.53)
Age^2	0.9985**	0.9987**
	(−3.25)	(−5.89)
Threshold change	0.7976	—
	(−1.69)	
Match introduction	—	1.2711**
		(5.12)

Source: Authors' calculations.
Notes: Coefficients estimated from a Cox proportional hazard model of 401(k) participation with time-varying covariates. For company E, the sample is employees hired during 1996 or 1997 and still employed at year-end 1998, 1999 or 2000. For company F, the sample is employees hired on or after January 1, 1998, and still employed at year-end 1998, 1999, 2000 or 2001. In company E, the variable *Threshold change* is a dummy variable that equals 1 after the match threshold was raised in company G (on January 1, 1997). In company F, *Match introduction* is a dummy variable that equals 1 after the company match was announced to employees (on July 1, 2000). The reported coefficients are hazard ratios, with corresponding z-statistics in parentheses.
** indicates that the coefficient is significantly different from unity at the 1 percent level.

sion of which contribution rate to select. Numerous studies have shown that final decisions tend to be anchored by such starting points (Kahneman and Tversky 1974).

The second company that we consider is company F, which introduced a 25-percent match on contributions up to 4 percent of income on October 1, 2000. We suspect that this was adopted as a response to the fact that at year-end 1999, only 34 percent of its active employees had ever participated in its 401(k).[18] Communication about the change started at the beginning of July 2000. Prior to this date, there was no employer match offered in the plan.[19]

Our data include cross-sections of all active employees at company F at year-end 1998, 1999, 2000, and 2001. These data contain information on participation status, original enrollment date, effective year-end contribution rate, original hire date, and demographics. We exclude all employees hired before July 1, 1998, because on that date the company eliminated a one-year length-of-service requirement for 401(k) eligibility.

To assess the impact of the employer match on 401(k) participation, we again estimate a Cox proportional hazard model of time from hire until the date of initial participation in the 401(k) plan. As with com-

Figure 11.5   Evolution of the 401(k) Contribution Rate Distribution: Company E

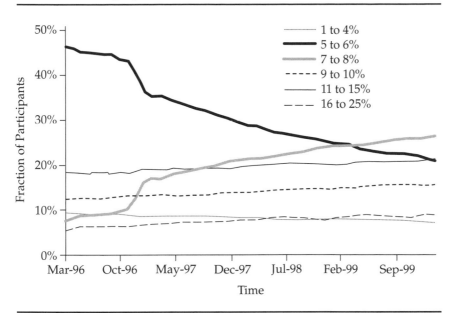

Source: Authors' calculations.

pany E, we control for gender and age, and we include a dummy variable that equals 1 after the match was announced to employees (July 2000). Results are presented in column 2 of table 11.4. We find that introducing the match has a positive and highly significant effect on participation, with a z-statistic of 5.12. To assess the economic significance of the results, we plot in figure 11.6 the predicted participation rate by tenure for a hypothetical population of forty-year-old males. At sixteen months of tenure, the model predicts a 17.8 percent participation rate when there is an employer match, which is 3.6 percentage points higher than would be the case without the match. Results at longer tenure levels are more speculative because we don't observe employees with more than sixteen months of tenure who have had the match in place since hire. Keeping this caveat in mind, we see that the model predicts 20.6 percent participation at two years of tenure (a 4.0 percentage point increase), and 24.5 percent participation at three years of tenure (a 4.7 percentage point increase).

Although these numbers may seem small, note that this company had unusually low participation rates to start with. When compared against the baseline, the employer match appears to have increased participation by about 25 percent. Furthermore, relative to the match structure in other

Figure 11.6   Employer Matching and 401(k) Participation: Company F

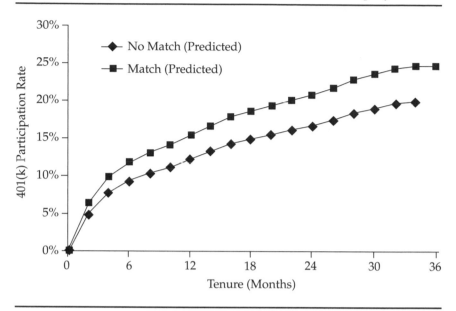

Source: Authors' calculations.

plans, this employer match is not particularly generous.[20] A higher match rate might be expected to have a larger effect on participation.[21]

The introduction of a match seems to have had a meaningful effect on the distribution of contribution rates as well. Figure 11.7 is a histogram of contribution rates by hire cohort at the end of the calendar year after the year in which the cohort was hired.[22] Before the employer match, the most frequently chosen contribution rates of plan participants are 5 percent, 10 percent, and 15 percent. After the match, we see a large increase in the fraction of employees with a 4-percent contribution rate, the new match threshold, relative to previous cohorts with the same level of tenure at the company. This is consistent with our previous observation that the match threshold may serve as a powerful focal point in employees' choice of a contribution rate.

In sum, our limited evidence suggests that employer matching does have a significant impact on both 401(k) participation and contribution rates. Company F demonstrates that implementing an employer match can increase participation. Company E demonstrates that increasing the match threshold can increase contribution rates. Both company E and company F show that the level of the match threshold has an important effect on the distribution of contribution rates, with many participants clustering at the match threshold.

**Figure 11.7   Distribution of Contribution Rates by Date of Initial Hire:
Company F**

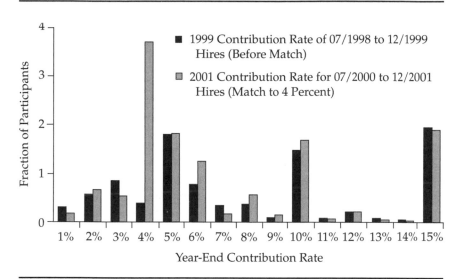

Source: Authors' calculations.

Eligibility

Another common 401(k) plan feature is a waiting period before employees become eligible to participate. Employers adopt eligibility requirements for a variety of reasons, including the fixed costs of administering accounts for newly hired workers with high turnover rates, and because low participation rates of newly hired employees may adversely affect an employer's nondiscrimination testing. This second explanation, however, is less relevant because recent legislative changes have made it easier for companies to institute shorter length-of-service requirements for 401(k) participation without substantially increasing the company's risk of failing nondiscrimination tests.

Earlier eligibility is valuable for employees because a shorter waiting period increases their tax-deferred savings opportunities. The extent of this benefit, however, depends on how waiting periods affect the participation profile, the relationship between 401(k) participation and tenure. For example, waiting periods may merely truncate the participation profile, so that upon eligibility, employee participation quickly catches up to the participation rate that would arise without a waiting period. Alternatively, waiting periods may shift the participation profile, so that employees who face a waiting period have permanently lower participation rates than those who do not.

Here we examine the effect of eligibility requirements on 401(k) participation in three companies that eliminated their eligibility requirements. Both company F and company G went from a one-year eligibility period to immediate eligibility—company F on July 1, 1998, and company G on January 1, 1997.[23] Company K went from a six-month eligibility period to immediate eligibility in January 1996.

To illustrate the impact of waiting periods on 401(k) participation, we plot in figure 11.8 the 401(k) participation profiles of employees who faced either a six-month, one-year, or no eligibility requirement. For company F (figure 11.8A), the two groups are employees hired between July 1, 1996, and July 1, 1997, with a one-year waiting period, and between July 1, 1998, and December 31, 2000, with no waiting period. For company G (figure 11.8B), the two groups are employees hired between January 1, 1995, and January 1, 1996, with a one-year waiting period and between January 1, 1997, and December 31, 1999, with no waiting period. For company K (figure 11.8C), the two groups are employees hired between January 1 and June 30, 1995, with a six-month waiting period, and between January 1, 1996, and December 31, 1996, with no waiting period.

At all three companies, the employees with a waiting period do not immediately attain the 401(k) participation levels achieved at equivalent tenure levels by employees with shorter waiting periods, but this gap closes fairly quickly over time. If we assume that the participation series are drawn independently, the differences between the two groups are no longer statistically significant at eighteen months of tenure in company F, at twenty-two months of tenure in company G, and at nine months of tenure in company K.[24]

Another way to look at these participation profiles is to consider participation rates by the time since 401(k) eligibility. Doing so, we see that conditional on time since becoming eligible, employees with a one-year eligibility requirement actually show a higher participation rate than employees who were immediately eligible. The difference in participation rates is between 2.5 and 4.6 percentage points for company F and is always significant at the 1 percent level for the first twelve months after eligibility. At company G the difference is approximately 7 percentage points and is almost always significant at the 1 percent level for the first twenty-four months. These findings are inconsistent with the notion that eligibility requirements simply shift the 401(k) participation profile without affecting its shape.

Overall, the evidence from these three companies suggests that the 401(k) participation rates of employees who face eligibility requirements catch up fairly quickly (within a matter of months) to levels that would occur without waiting periods. Although this is certainly better for retirement wealth accumulation than if eligibility requirements resulted in permanently lower participation rates, we do not take this as evidence to

Figure 11.8   Waiting Periods and 401(k) Participation

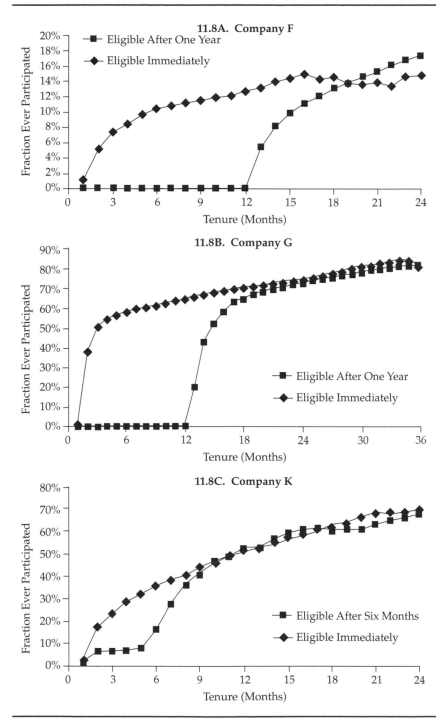

Source: Authors' calculations.

suggest that waiting periods are "not that bad." Nobody seems to lose when shorter waiting periods are adopted, so we see no reason why companies should not be encouraged to allow immediate eligibility for participation in 401(k) savings plans.

Asset Allocation Choices

The bulk of this paper is focused on the 401(k) participation and contribution decisions of employees. If we are concerned about savings adequacy at retirement, we first want to consider participation in a savings program and how much is saved conditional on participation. The next issue is how savings are allocated among different asset classes. A small but growing literature has addressed this third question in recent years; not surprisingly, many of the same behavioral issues present in the participation and contribution decisions also play a role in participants' asset-allocation choices. As discussed earlier, Madrian and Shea (2001a) and Choi et al. (2004a) show that automatic enrollment results in many participants remaining at the employer-specified default for both the contribution rate and asset allocation.

Such passive decision making in asset allocation choices is also present in many other guises. In a series of papers, Shlomo Benartzi and Richard Thaler demonstrate several related behavioral regularities in asset-allocation decisions (2001). Studying the relationship between the menu of investment choices and the eventual pattern of asset holdings across different classes, they suggest that participants use naive diversification strategies that are heavily influenced by the menu offered by their plan—a plan sponsor that offers ten equity options and five non-equity options may be subtly influencing its employees to put two-thirds of their money into equities. Using a database of 170 retirement savings plans, Benartzi and Thaler find that approximately 62 percent of the funds offered in these plans are equity investments; the fraction of total assets held in equities by the participants in these 170 plans is remarkably close to 62 percent as well. Furthermore, they find a positive relationship at the plan level between the fraction of equity funds offered by the plan and the fraction of individual portfolios invested in equities. These findings are further reinforced by experimental data and by evidence on individual decisions made by TWA pilots in their corporate plan.

In another study, Benartzi and Thaler (2002) gave participants a choice between the distribution of retirement outcomes implied by the actual asset allocation in their 401(k) plan and the distribution implied by the average allocation among all participants in the same plan. Most participants preferred the average distribution to the one based on their own allocation. Because most participants have portfolios that are, almost by definition, more extreme than the average allocation, Benartzi and Thaler characterize this result as an example of an aversion to extremeness. Such results call into question whether most participants are choosing an allocation that could be called optimal in an economic framework.

Perhaps the most disturbing aspect of 401(k) participants' asset allocation choices is the large fraction of balances invested in employer stock. About half of all 401(k) plans (by assets) offer participants the opportunity to invest in employer stock. Some plans even require that all matching contributions be held in employer stock, at least for some period. Because this asset class is both volatile (because it consists of only a single stock) and highly correlated with the labor earnings of employees, holding employer stock is certainly a poor diversification strategy for participants. Nevertheless, a significant fraction of plan assets are held in employer stock. For firms that offer employer stock in their 401(k) plans, Holden, VanDerhei, and Quick (2000) find that about 33 percent of plan assets are held in this asset class. Among all firms, including those that do not offer employer stock, this fraction is 18 percent.

This level of holdings itself seems high, but the manner in which participants decide to invest in employer stock is also troubling. Benartzi (2001) finds that current contributions to employer stock are heavily influenced by the returns earned by that stock over the preceding ten years. These findings are corroborated in Choi et al. (2004b). It seems that naive diversification is combined with naive extrapolation of past returns and an apparent lack of concern for the risk consequences of employer stock investment. Indeed, a first-order improvement in diversification could be gained by the simple elimination of employer stock from 401(k) plans.

Interestingly, ERISA restricts the investments of defined benefit pension plans in the stock or real estate of the employer to 10 percent of total assets. 401(k) plans, however, are exempt from this rule. The recent collapse of Enron has publicly highlighted the diversification danger of employer stock in 401(k) plans. With several bills now pending before Congress to address the diversification problems created by 401(k) investments in employer stock, the current policy question has changed from one of whether restrictions on 401(k) investments in employer stock are warranted to what type of restrictions are warranted (and are politically feasible). Although Enron is at the center of the public controversy, class-action lawsuits have been filed by 401(k) participants at several companies in the wake of dramatic declines in the value of employer stock. Even absent legislative reforms, these lawsuits are prompting many other companies to reconsider the emphasis on employer stock in their 401(k) plans. As some companies reevaluate whether they should match in employer stock, others are addressing whether to eliminate employer stock as an investment option altogether.

Financial Education at the Workplace

Recognizing that many employees are ill-equipped to make well-informed retirement savings decisions, particularly with respect to asset allocation, many employers have turned to various forms of financial education provision to help their employees meet the challenges of planning for an economically secure retirement. These efforts, which vary widely across employers, run the gamut and include paycheck stuffers, newsletters, summary plan descriptions, seminars, individual consultations with financial planners, and more recently, access to Internet-based education and planning tools.

The previous literature on the effects of financial education on savings behavior has found rather consistent evidence that financial education positively affects savings behavior, although the inadequacy of the data in many of these studies makes their conclusions somewhat speculative. There are two broad strands in the literature. The first is case studies of the impact of financial education at specific companies or organizations. These studies typically evaluate the effect of a particular financial education initiative, often financial education seminars, on either savings behavior or measures of financial well being (Kratzer and Brunson 1998; HR Focus 2000; DeVaney et al. 1995; McCarthy and McWhirter 2000; Jacobius 2000). Although all of these studies conclude that financial education motivates improvements in savings behavior, the conclusions are often based on dramatic changes in what participants plan to do with respect to retirement saving without actually verifying that the prophesied changes eventually do take place. Unfortunately, a growing body of both theoretical and empirical evidence, including the survey results reported here, suggests that despite the best intentions of employees, retirement saving is one area in which individuals excel at delay (Madrian and Shea 2001a; O'Donoghue and Rabin 1999; Diamond and Köszegi 2003; Laibson, Repetto, and Tobacman 1998). Thus, measures of intended behavior are likely to dramatically overstate the actual effects of financial education.

The second broad category of analyses has used cross-sectional surveys of individuals from across the population, not simply from a single company or organization (Bernheim and Garrett 2003; Bernheim, Garrett, and Maki 2001; Milne, VanDerhei, and Yakaboski 1995), or data from surveys of multiple employers (Bayer, Bernheim, and Scholz 1996; Milne, VanDerhei, and Yakaboski 1996; Murray 1999). This category of studies has the advantages of applying to a general population and utilizing actual savings choices instead of savings intentions.

However, the cross-sectional datasets also pose numerous problems. The greatest drawback to these datasets is that financial education provision and/or utilization may be correlated with other factors that have a strong influence on savings behavior across individuals or organizations (for example, the structure of the 401(k) plan, the availability of other types of savings and/or pension programs, the level and structure of employee compensation, the corporate culture). To the extent that these confounding factors are not completely observed and controlled for, the measured effects of financial education could be quite biased. The definition of what constitutes financial education is also subject to interpretation and likely to vary from one respondent to another.

The household surveys have the additional disadvantage that survey answers to questions about financial education are likely to be subject to recall bias. This could occur, for example, if individuals who participate in and benefit the most from employer-sponsored savings programs find financial education more salient and are thus more likely to remember that such programs were offered. This type of nonrandom measurement error in the availability of financial education will lead to estimates of the effects of financial education that are too large. The employer-based surveys have the additional disadvantage that response rates tend to be quite low, and it is unlikely that the nonresponse is random. Moreover, it is almost impossible to determine how the selection of the firms into the sample is likely to affect the results.

A study by Madrian and Shea (2001b) examines the impact of financial education seminars on savings behavior in company C, which enlisted a financial education provider to give one-hour seminars at its various locations throughout the country during 2000. The curriculum at these seminars was general and covered topics directly related to retirement savings, such as setting savings goals to meet retirement income targets and the fundamentals of investing (asset classes, risk, diversification, and so on), as well as to more general financial issues, such as managing credit and debt and using insurance to minimize exposure to financial risks.

The financial education data from this company are unique in that seminar attendance was tracked in a way that made it possible to match seminar attendance to administrative data on both previous and subsequent savings behavior. We have data on the individuals who attended financial education seminars between January 1 and June 30, 2000, and on the 401(k) savings choices of all employees at this company on December 31, 1999, before any of the seminars were offered, and on June 30, 2000, by which time they had been offered at forty-two locations. One-third of the employees at the company work at these forty-two locations, and about 17 percent of employees at these locations attended the financial education seminars.

Table 11.5 presents basic statistics on the planned changes in savings behavior that attendees of the financial education seminars reported, along with the actual changes in savings behavior that were made subsequent to the seminars. The statistics in table 11.5 paint a somewhat more

Table 11.5   Financial Education and Savings Changes (Company C)

Planned Action	Seminar Attendees		Non-Attendees
	Planned Change	Actual Change	Actual Change
Nonparticipants			
Enroll in 401(k) plan	100%	14%	7%
401(k) participants			
Increase contribution rate	28%	8%	5%
Change fund selection	47%	15%	10%
Change fund allocation	36%	10%	6%

Source: Authors' calculations.
Notes: The sample is active 401(k)-eligible employees at company locations that offered financial education seminars from January–June 2000. Actual changes in savings behavior are measured over the period from December 31, 1999, through June 30, 2000. Planned changes are those reported by seminar attendees in an evaluation of the financial education seminars at the conclusion of the seminar. The planned changes from surveys responses of attendees have been scaled to reflect the 401(k) participation rate of seminar attendees.

muted picture of the impact of financial education on savings behavior than has been estimated in the previous literature. In an evaluation of the financial education seminars given to attendees at the conclusion of the seminar, attendees were asked, "After attending today's presentation, what, if any, action do you plan on taking toward your personal financial affairs?" followed by a list of choices (with multiple responses allowed). 71 percent of those attending the seminars filled out and turned in these evaluation forms.[25]

Of those who filled out the evaluation, 12 percent reported that they intended to start contributing to the 401(k) savings plan. But 88 percent of seminar attendees were already participating, so virtually all of the nonparticipating seminar attendees planned to enroll. By June 30, 2000, however, only 14 percent of the non-participating seminar attendees had actually joined, and some of these individuals would likely have enrolled in the 401(k) without the availability of a financial education seminar (as did 7 percent of the employees who did not attend the seminars).

Of those attendees who were already participating, 28 percent reported plans to increase their contribution rate, 47 percent reported plans to make changes in the selection of their investment choices within the 401(k), and 36 percent reported plans to change the fraction of their money allocated to the various investment choices. By June 30, 2000, however, only 8 percent of 401(k) participants attending the seminars had increased their contribution rate, whereas 15 percent had made changes to their investment choices and 10 percent had changed their fund allocations. Although the fraction of seminar attendees making such changes is slightly higher than that of those who did not attend, it is substantially below what the attendees reported they planned on doing. One could certainly argue that the low rate of actual changes relative to planned changes results from the fact that the data used to observe the plan changes is, for employees at some locations, not long after the actual financial education seminars. However, there is relatively little correlation between the fraction of seminar attendees making changes to their 401(k) savings behavior and the length of time between their seminar and June 30, 2000. It appears that seminar attendees either make changes almost immediately or not at all.

Madrian and Shea (2001b) draw similar conclusions when they try to control for differences in the underlying savings propensities of employees who do and do not attend financial education seminars. Their final assessment is that financial education increases savings plan participation and results in greater portfolio diversification, particularly among employees hired under automatic enrollment, but the estimated magnitudes are not particularly large. Overall, though financial education is important, it does not appear to be a powerful mechanism for encouraging 401(k) retirement savings.

Beyond 401(k)s: Implications for Social Security Reform and Private Retirement Accounts

One of the principles President George W. Bush set forth in the executive order establishing the President's Commission to Strengthen Social Security was that "modernization must include individually controlled, voluntary personal retirement accounts, which will augment the Social Security safety net" (see http://www.csss.gov). The research on 401(k) savings behavior should be used to guide the design of these privatized personal retirement accounts.

Because the U.S. national savings rate continues to be near historic lows, policy makers should consider using the personal retirement accounts envisioned for the Social Security system to encourage new discretionary savings (on top of any contributions from the Social Security system). One key issue is what kind of defaults should be associated with such a system. Individuals could be given a zero discretionary savings rate default, or be automatically enrolled at a positive discretionary savings rate and then given the option to change this default. The 401(k) research implies that the outcomes under these two discretionary defaults would be radically different. If policy makers want to raise the national savings rate, then they should adopt automatic enrollment at a modest discretionary savings rate. For example, all workers could be enrolled with a discretionary contribution of 6 percent of their wages (including wages above the Social Security earnings cap). Employees would be able to opt out or change this discretionary contribution. Naturally, these discretionary contributions should not offset any Social Security benefits.

The 401(k) research also sheds light on asset allocation issues in a system of private accounts. Poor asset allocation choices are common in 401(k) accounts. As discussed earlier, investors use naïve diversification strategies, do not prefer the asset allocation they have actually chosen for themselves (and indeed, often prefer a different asset allocation when asked), naïvely extrapolate past returns as an indicator of future performance (particularly for employer stock), and overwhelmingly stick with the fund(s) chosen as a default by their employer due to inertia and a perception of employer endorsement. In addition, Gordon Alexander, Jonathan Jones, and Peter Nigro (1998) find that the majority of investors do not know the expense ratio of the funds in which they are invested and did not take it into account when making their initial investment decisions.

Henrik Cronqvist and Richard Thaler (2004) study the asset allocation choices of participants in the recently privatized Swedish Social Security system and find that the outcomes there are consistent with the general behaviors observed in 401(k) plans. For example, they find that one-third of investments were directed to the default fund following the initial adoption of the privatized system, despite heavy advertising encouraging participants to select their own asset allocation. After the initial rollout, such advertising was reduced. During this period of diminished advertising, over 90 percent of new participants in the system adopted the default portfolio.[26] Cronqvist and Thaler also find that in portfolios actively selected by investors, management fees were on average 61 basis points higher than management fees in the default portfolio. Finally, Cronqvist and Thaler point to suggestive evidence of returns chasing (naïve extrapolation).

Taken together, this body of work suggests that any privatized system should restrict the set of investment options. For example, a privatized (U.S.) Social Security system might begin by constraining all equity and bond investments to highly diversified mutual funds. Such eligible investments might be index funds (or at least funds with low turnover) that have low expense ratios and small loads. Further constraints could prevent account holders from placing too much of their wealth in one asset class.

Policy makers should also consider adopting a default asset allocation for the system of privatized accounts. The evidence suggests consumers have limited financial sophistication. Hence, defaults for asset allocation are likely to be influential. Of course, picking such default investments is likely to be politically controversial. To mitigate such problems, default investments should be index funds chosen by a government agency using a transparent and competitive bidding process. Mutual funds would compete for such contracts by offering low fees. Participating mutual funds would also need to meet certain criteria for customer support. Such contracts would be subject to ongoing competitive bidding at periodic intervals.

Conclusions

The evidence presented here highlights the importance of passive decision making. For better or for worse, many households appear to passively accept the status quo. For example, in companies without automatic enrollment, the typical employee takes over a year to enroll in his or her company-sponsored 401(k) retirement plan. In companies with automatic enrollment, employees overwhelmingly accept the automatic enrollment defaults, including default savings rates and default funds. For terminated employees, the key determinant of whether they consume or save their 401(k) balances is whether that balance is above or below the automatic cash distribution threshold of $5,000. Many plan participants allow the menu of investment funds to drive their asset allocation decisions. Most employees feel that they save too little, and many plan to raise their contribution rate in the near future, but few act on these good intentions. By contrast, employees do succeed in raising their contribution rates if they are given a low-effort opportunity to sign up for an automatic schedule of increases in their contribution rate.

All of these examples have a common theme: employees often take the path of least resistance. As a result, employers have a large measure of control over the savings choices that their employees make, and employers cannot escape this responsibility. Whatever savings plan an employer creates necessarily advantages certain passive or nearly passive choices over other active choices. Sophisticated employers should choose their plan defaults carefully, since these defaults will strongly influence the retirement preparation of their employees.

Policy makers should also recognize the role of defaults, since policymakers can facilitate, with laws and regulations, the socially optimal use of defaults. For example, defaulting contributions into employer stock may lead to insufficient diversification. Policy makers could legally cap default investments to such problematic asset categories. Likewise, they could facilitate default contributions to more appropriate investments, like the S&P 500, by giving corporations legal protections for picking such risky but highly diversified default funds.

It is easy to identify dozens of ways that thoughtful regulations can influence passive decision makers without encroaching on the freedom of active decision makers to opt out of the defaults and choose in their own (perceived) best interest. However, regulating defaults is a two-edged sword. If one has confidence in the government, such regulations will serve the common good. If one does not have such confidence, regulating defaults will open one more avenue for the misuse of governmental power. Our analysis demonstrates that defaults matter but does address who should control them.

Company Data

- Company A. Cross-sectional survey data from January 2001 for a random sample of employees. Longitudinal 401(k) savings data from January 1996 through April 2001 for all 401(k) participants.

- Company B. Cross-sectional 401(k) savings data from December 31 of 1998 through 2002 for all active employees (both 401(k) participants and nonparticipants) and non-employee 401(k) plan participants.

- Company C. Cross-sectional 401(k) savings data from June 1, 1997; December 31, 1997; June 30, 1998; December 30, 1998; March 31, 1999; June 30, 1999; September 30, 1999; December 31, 1999; March 31, 2000; June 30, 2000, and December 31, 2001, for all active employees. Financial education seminar attendees from January 1, 2000, through June 30, 2000.

- Company D. Cross-sectional 401(k) savings data from December 31 of 1998 through 2002 for all 401(k) plan participants (employee and non-employee), and from December 31 of 2000 through 2002 for all active employees (both 401(k) participants and nonparticipants) and non-employee 401(k) plan participants.

- Company E. Cross-sectional 401(k) savings data from December 31 of 1998, 1999, and 2000 for all active employees (both 401(k) participants and nonparticipants) and non-employee 401(k) plan participants. Longitudinal 401(k) savings data from March 1996 through March 2000.

- Company F. Cross-sectional 401(k) savings data from December 31 of 1998 through 2001 for all active employees (both 401(k) participants and nonparticipants) and non-employee 401(k) plan participants.

- Company G. Cross-sectional 401(k) savings data from December 31, 1999, for all active employees (both 401(k) participants and nonparticipants) and non-employee 401(k) plan participants.

- Company H. Cross-sectional 401(k) savings data from December 31 of 1998, 1999, and 2002 for all active employees (both 401(k) participants and nonparticipants) and non-employee 401(k) plan participants.

- Company I. Cross-sectional 401(k) savings data from December 31 of 1998, 1999, and 2000 for all active employees (both 401(k) participants and nonparticipants) and non-employee 401(k) plan participants.

- Company J. Cross-sectional 401(k) savings data from December 31 of 1998, 1999, and 2000 for all active employees (both 401(k) participants and nonparticipants) and non-employee 401(k) plan participants.

- Company K. Cross-sectional 401(k) savings data from December 31 of 1998, 1999, and 2000 for all active employees (both 401(k) participants and nonparticipants) and non-employee 401(k) plan participants.

The cross-sectional data available for these companies include basic demographic information (age, hire date, gender, income), as well as point-in-time information on 401(k) saving such as participation status, contribution rate, account balances, and asset allocation.

The longitudinal data includes daily information on the 401(k) contribution rate, account balances, and asset allocation of 401(k) plan participants. It does not include demographic information or information on nonparticipating employees.

401(k) Plan Participant Satisfaction Survey Questions

I

1. Which of the following statements describes your current participation in the XXX Company, Inc. 401(k) Plan?

   ☐ I am currently contributing to the plan

   ☐ I am not currently contributing to the plan, but I have previously contributed to the plan

   ☐ I am not currently contributing to the plan, and I have never contributed to the plan

2. For each of the following questions, please indicate how strongly you agree or disagree with respect to the XXX Company, Inc. 401(k) plan. To indicate your level of agreement, please use the following scale (if you have no experience with a given item, please respond with "have no opinion").

   [Strongly agree, Somewhat agree, Neither agree nor disagree, Somewhat disagree, Strongly disagree, Have no opinion]

   a. I have a good understanding of the 401(k) savings plan overall

b. I have a good understanding of the 401(k) savings plan invest-ment fund choices

c. I think the 401(k) plan meets my needs

d. The XXX Company, Inc. 401(k) plan is better than plans offered by other companies

3. For each of the following questions, please indicate how satisfied you are with that aspect of the XXX Company, Inc. 401(k) plan. To in-dicate your level of satisfaction, please use the following scale (if you have no experience with a given item, please respond with "have no opinion").

[Very satisfied, Somewhat satisfied, Neither satisfied nor dissatisfied, Somewhat dissatisfied, Very dissatisfied, Have no opinion]

a. Convenience of payroll deductions for savings

b. Number of investment options

c. Variety of investment options

d. Account statements

e. Internet access to your 401(k) plan

f. Loans

Please use the space provided to fill in your response to the following question:

4. What, if anything, could your company do differently in terms of the XXX Company, Inc. 401(k) plan that would increase your satisfaction level, relating to any of the items listed above?

II

Please check the appropriate box for each of the following questions.

5. How would you describe yourself as an Internet user?

☐ Very experienced

☐ Somewhat experienced

☐ Not too experienced

☐ Not at all experienced

6. Do you have access to the Internet at home?

☐ Yes

☐ No

7. How would you describe your level of financial knowledge?

☐ Very knowledgeable

☐ Somewhat knowledgeable

☐ Not too knowledgeable

☐ Not at all knowledgeable

8. Which of the following best describes your job?

☐ Management

☐ Other salaried position

☐ Hourly

☐ Other

9. Which of the following best describes your level of education?

☐ High school or less

☐ Some college

☐ College graduate

☐ Graduate school

III

These next few questions discuss retirement savings. Please check the appropriate box(es) for each of the following questions, and/or fill in the blanks, as appropriate.

10. First, based on anything you may have heard or read, what percent of your income do you think you should *ideally* be saving for retirement?

☐ 5 percent of income or less

☐ Between 5 percent and 9 percent of income

☐ Between 10 percent and 14 percent of income

☐ Between 15 percent and 19 percent of income

☐ Between 20 percent and 24 percent of income

☐ At least 25 percent of income

11. Think about how much you are *actually* currently saving for retirement. Compare your *actual* saving rate to your *ideal* saving rate. Right now, your *actual* retirement saving rate is:

☐ Far too low

☐ A little too low

☐ About right

☐ A little too high

☐ Far too high

IF YOU ARE CURRENTLY CONTRIBUTING TO YOUR COMPANY 401(K) PLAN, PLEASE ANSWER QUESTIONS 12 THROUGH 17.
IF YOU ARE NOT CURRENTLY CONTRIBUTING TO YOUR COMPANY 401(K) PLAN, PLEASE SKIP TO QUESTION 18.

12.   Are you contributing currently at the maximum 401(k) savings rate?

☐   Yes

☐   No

13.   Which <u>one</u> of the following statements best describes your 401(k) contribution plans over the next few months?

☐   I plan to *raise* my contribution rate.

☐   I plan to *lower* my contribution rate.

☐   I don't plan to make any changes.

IF YOU ARE NOT PLANNING TO MAKE ANY CONTRIBUTION CHANGES, PLEASE SKIP TO QUESTION 15.

14.   What percent of your salary are you planning to contribute?

15.   Which one of the following statements best describes your 401(k) fund allocation plans over the next few months?

☐   I am considering selecting different funds.

☐   I am considering rebalancing among the funds I currently have.

☐   I am not planning to make any changes in regard to my fund allocations.

☐   I am considering both selecting different funds and rebalancing among the funds I currently have

16.   When do you next plan to make changes in your 401(k) plan?

☐   In the next few days

☐   In the next week

☐   In the next two weeks

☐   In the next three weeks

☐   Sometime in the next month

☐   Sometime in the next two months

☐   Other: _____

17.   What company resources will you use to make changes to your 401(k) plan? Check all that apply.

☐   Speak to benefit center representative or use phone-based "Benefits Express"

☐ Use the 401(k) web site: *Your Benefits Resources* (including advice and education resources, for example, mPower and 401Kafe)

☐ Consult the new hire kit (given to all new employees)

☐ Other: Please specify: _____

IF YOU ARE CURRENTLY CONTRIBUTING TO YOUR COMPANY 401(K) PLAN, PLEASE SKIP TO QUESTION 21.
IF YOU ARE NOT CURRENTLY CONTRIBUTING TO YOUR COMPANY 401(K) PLAN, PLEASE ANSWER QUESTIONS 18 TO 20.

18. When you enroll/re-enroll in the XXX Company, Inc. 401(k) plan, what percent of your salary do you expect to contribute to the plan?

☐ Between 0 percent and 3 percent of income

☐ Between 4 percent and 6 percent of income

☐ Between 7 percent and 9 percent of income

☐ Between 10 percent and 12 percent of income

☐ Between 13 percent and 15 percent of income

19. When do you plan to enroll/re-enroll in the 401(k) plan?

☐ In the next few days

☐ In the next week

☐ In the next two weeks

☐ In the next three weeks

☐ Sometime in the next month

☐ Sometime in the next two months

☐ Other: _____

20. What company resources will you use to enroll in the 401(k) plan? Check all that apply.

☐ Speak to benefits center representative

☐ Use the 401(k) web site

☐ Consult the new hire kit (given to all new employees)

☐ Other. Please specify: _____

Thank you for your participation in this survey.
For more information on the XXX Company, Inc. 401(k) plan, click here: URL.

Originally prepared for Tax Policy and the Economy 2001 under the title "Defined Contribution Pensions: Plan Rules, Participant Choices, and the

Path of Least Resistance." Revised in 2004 to include additional data and analysis.

We thank Hewitt Associates for their help in providing the data. We are particularly grateful to Lori Lucas and Yan Xu, two of our many contacts at Hewitt. We also thank James Poterba and Olivia Mitchell for comments, along with seminar participants at the University of Michigan. We appreciate the research assistance of Holly Ming and Laura Serban. Choi acknowledges financial support from a National Science Foundation Graduate Research Fellowship and the Mustard Seed Foundation. Choi, Laibson and Madrian acknowledge individual and collective financial support from the National Institute on Aging (grants R01-AG-16605, R29-AG-013020, R01-AG-021650 and T32-AG00186), which funded the original research. The Social Security Administration (grant 10-P-98363-1 to the NBER as part of the SSA Retirement Research Consortium) funded the empirical extensions of that research as well as the analysis of social security privatization. Laibson also acknowledges financial support from the National Science Foundation and the Sloan Foundation. The opinions and conclusions expressed are solely those of the author(s) and do not represent the opinions or policy of NIA, SSA, NSF, any other agency of the Federal Government, or the NBER.

Notes

1. See *EBRI Databook on Employee Benefits* at http://www.ebri.org/facts/1200fact.htm.
2. To maintain the anonymity of the companies we describe, we refer to each of them with letters.
3. The solicitation included an inducement to actually complete the survey: two respondents were randomly selected to receive gift checks of $250, and one respondent was selected to receive a gift check of $500.
4. Naturally, restricting our sample to Internet users biases our sample toward employees with greater financial sophistication. Our survey reveals that an employee's level of Internet experience correlates with his self-reported financial knowledge. Likewise, home Internet access also correlates with financial knowledge.
5. See question 10 from the survey.
6. See question 11 from the survey. For our empirical analysis we aggregate the categories "far too low" and "a little too low" into one category ("too low"). Likewise, we aggregate the categories "far too high" and "a little too high" into one category ("too high").
7. In a recent survey, Hewitt Associates (2001) reports that 14 percent of companies utilized automatic enrollment in 2001, up from 7 percent in 1999.
8. See "Remarks of Treasury Secretary Lawrence H. Summers at the Department of Labor Retirement Savings Education Campaign Fifth Anniversary Event" at http://www.ustreas.gov/press/releases/ps785.htm, and related supporting documents.
9. The experience of the first three of these companies—B, C, and D—is first

examined in Choi et al. (2004a). We extend the analysis there to account for up to an additional two years of data following the adoption of automatic enrollment.

10. Because of concurrent changes in eligibility for employees under the age of forty at company D, we restrict the sample of employees in the analysis at the company to those aged forty or over at the time of hire. These employees were immediately eligible to participate in the 401(k) plan both before and after the switch to automatic enrollment.

11. Because of differences in the data obtained from these companies, the participation rates across companies are not directly comparable. For company C, we have data on 401(k) participation on the data collection dates, and thus the participation percentages in figure 11.1 for company C represent contemporaneous 401(k) participation rates. For companies B, D, and H we have the date of initial 401(k) participation, and thus the participation percentages in figure 11.1 for these firms represent the fraction of employees who have ever participated in the 401(k) plan.

12. Choi et al. (2004a) show that compensation is the strongest determinant of how quickly employees move away from the automatic enrollment default—highly compensated employees tend to move away from the default more rapidly than those with lower pay.

13. This includes both voluntary and involuntary terminations.

14. That is, employees terminated in 2000 have a balance measure from December 31, 1999, and employees terminated in 1999 have a balance measure from December 31, 1998. We use this measure of balances because it is the only measure that we have in our data.

15. James Poterba, Steven Venti, and Wise (1998a) report that the probability that a cash distribution is rolled over into an IRA or another employer's plan is only 5 to 16 percent for distributions of less than $5,000. The overall probability that a cash distribution is rolled over into an IRA or another employer's plan or invested in some other savings vehicle is slightly higher at 14 to 33 percent.

16. The Department of Labor issued preliminary regulations for public comment in early 2004. Final regulations have not yet been released.

17. We should note, however, that previous research also suggests that although small distributions tend to be consumed rather than rolled over into other retirement savings vehicles, these small distributions represent a relatively small fraction of total retirement savings (Poterba, Venti, and Wise 1998a; Engelhardt 2002). Thus, while automatically rolling such distributions over into an IRA will undoubtedly increase retirement saving, its impact on aggregate retirement saving is likely to be modest.

18. We should note that company F has a primary defined benefit pension plan for its employees.

19. The company did have three acquired divisions that had employer matches previously and were not affected by this change. These divisions, as well as three divisions that were acquired after 1998, are excluded from our analysis.

20. The modal employer match is 50 percent of employee contributions up to 6 percent of compensation (U.S. Department of Labor 1998).

21. However, Bassett, Fleming, and Rodrigues (1998) conclude that the mere

presence of a match increases participation, with no marginal effect from in-creasing the match rate. We cannot test this hypothesis with our data.

22. Although the distribution of employees at the various contribution rates is based on the full sample of employees, not just plan participants, we have excluded the non-contributors from the graph because they constitute over 85 percent of the sample, and including them makes variation in contribu-tion rates across the contributing population difficult to see.

23. Company G also subsequently changed the window in which participants could enroll in the plan. Prior to September 1, 1997, participants could en-roll only once a year. Beginning on November 22, 1997, however, new en-rollments were allowed on a daily basis. To the extent that these deadline changes affect the time path of participation, the results for company G re-sults could be biased.

24. There is a small amount of enrollment before six months of tenure in Com-pany K among the cohort that should not be eligible for enrollment until af-ter six months of tenure. We suspect this is due to some rehires who re-ceived credit for past service.

25. The evaluation responses we have are from all locations offering financial education seminars during 2000, not just those offering the seminars during the January though June 2000 period for which we have savings data. Un-fortunately, we do not have the evaluation responses on an individual basis, only the aggregated responses for all attendees. Thus, we cannot ascertain on an individual basis how many seminar attendees actually followed through on the planned behaviors listed on the evaluation form.

26. Fortunately, the Swedish government selected a well diversified default fund with a low expense ratio. Indeed, Cronqvist and Thaler (2004) suggest that the default fund was better both ex ante and ex post than what in-vestors who opted out of the default fund actually chose on their own.

References

Alexander, Gordon J., Jonathan D. Jones, and Peter J. Nigro. 1998. "Mutual Fund Shareholders: Characteristics, Investor Knowledge and Sources of Informa-tion." *Financial Services Review* 7(4): 301–16.

Andrews, Emily S. 1992. "The Growth and Distribution of 401(k) Plans." In *Trends in Pensions 1992*, edited by John Turner and Daniel Beller. Washington, D.C.: U.S. Department of Labor, Pension and Welfare Benefits Administration.

Bassett, William F., Michael J. Fleming, and Anthony P. Rodrigues. 1998. "How Workers Use 401(k) Plans?: The Participation, Contribution, and Withdrawal Decisions." *National Tax Journal* 51(2): 263–89.

Bayer, Patrick J., B. Douglas Bernheim, and J. Karl Scholz. 1996. "The Effects of Fi-nancial Education in the Workplace: Evidence from a Survey of Employers." NBER Working Paper No. 5655. Cambridge, Mass.: National Bureau of Eco-nomic Research.

Benartzi, Shlomo. 2001. "Excessive Extrapolation and the Allocation of 401(k) Ac-counts to Company Stock." *Journal of Finance* 56(5): 1747–764.

Benartzi, Shlomo, and Richard Thaler. 2001. "Naive Diversification Strategies in Defined Contribution Savings Plans." *American Economic Review* 91(1): 79–98.

————. 2002. "How Much Is Investor Autonomy Worth?" *Journal of Finance* 57(4): 1593–616.

Bernheim, B. Douglas. 1995. "Do Households Appreciate Their Financial Vulnerabilities? An Analysis of Actions, Perceptions, and Public Policy." In *Tax Policy for Economic Growth in the 1990s*. Washington, D.C.: American Council for Capital Formation.

Bernheim, B. Douglas, and Daniel M. Garrett. 2003. "The Effects of Financial Education in the Workplace: Evidence from a Survey of Households." *Journal of Public Economics* 87(7-8): 1487–519.

Bernheim, B. Douglas, Daniel M. Garrett, and Dean M. Maki. 2001. "Education and Saving: The Long-Term Effects of High School Financial Curriculum Mandates." *Journal of Public Economics* 80(3): 435–65.

Choi, James J., David Laibson, Brigitte Madrian, and Andrew Metrick. 2002. "Defined Contribution Pensions: Plan Rules, Participant Choices, and the Path of Least Resistance." In *Tax Policy and the Economy*, Volume 16, edited by James Poterba. Cambridge, Mass.: MIT Press.

————. 2004a. "For Better or For Worse: Default Effects and 401(k) Savings Behavior." In *Perspectives in the Economics of Aging*, edited by David A. Wise. Chicago: University of Chicago Press.

————. 2004b. "Employees Investment Decisions about Company Stock." In *Pension Design and Structure: New Lessons from Behavioral Finance*, edited by Olivia Mitchell and Stephen Utkus. London: Oxford University Press.

Cronqvist, Henrik, and Richard H. Thaler. 2004. "Design Choices in Privatized Social Security Systems: Learning from the Swedish Experience." *American Economic Review* 94(2): 424–28.

DeVaney, Sharon A., Liz Gorham, Janet C. Bechman, and Virginia Haldeman. 1995. "Saving and Investing for Retirement: The Effect of a Financial Education Program." *Family Economics and Resource Management Biennial* 1: 153–58.

Diamond, Peter, and Botond Köszegi. 2003. "Quasi-Hyperbolic Discounting and Retirement." *Journal of Public Economics* 87(9–10): 1839–872.

Engelhardt, Gary V. 2002. "Pre-Retirement Lump-Sum Pension Distributions and Retirement Income Security: Evidence from the Health and Retirement Study." *National Tax Journal* 54(4): 665–86.

Engelhardt, Gary V., and Anil Kumar. 2004. "Employer Matching and 401(k) Savings: Evidence from the Health and Retirement Study." Syracuse University Working Paper. Syracuse, N.Y.: Syracuse University.

Engen, Eric M., William G. Gale, and John Karl Scholz. 1994. "Do Saving Incentives Work?" *Brookings Papers on Economic Activity* 1994(1): 85–180.

————. 1996. "The Illusory Effects of Saving Incentives on Saving." *Journal of Economic Perspectives* 10(4): 113–38.

Even, William E., and David A. Macpherson. 1997. "Factors Influencing Participation and Contribution Levels in 401(k) Plans." Florida State University Working Paper. Tallahassee, Fla.: Florida State University.

Farkas, Steve, and Jean Johnson. 1997. "Miles to Go: A Status Report on Americans' Plans for Retirement." New York: Public Agenda.

Fidelity Investments. 2001. *Building Futures: A Report on Corporate Defined Contribution Plans, Volume II*. Boston: Fidelity Investments.

Hewitt Associates. 2001. *Trends and Experience in 401(k) Plans*. Lincolnshire, Ill.: Hewitt Associates.

Holden, Sarah, Jack VanDerhei, and Carol Quick. 2000. "401(k) Plan Asset Allocation, Account Balances, and Loan Activity in 1998." *ICI Perspective* 6(1) and EBRI Issue Brief No. 218. Washington, D.C.: Investment Company Institute, January, and Employee Benefit Research Institute, February.

HR Focus. 2000. "What is the Value of Financial Education Workshops?" *HR Focus* 2000(February): 15.

Investment Company Institute. 2000. *401(k) Plan Participants: Characteristics, Contributions, and Account Activity.* Washington, D.C.: Investment Company Institute.

Jacobius, Arleen. 2000. "Top-notch Education Campaigns Honored." *Pensions & Investments* 28(3): 29.

Kahneman, Daniel, and Amos Tversky. 1974. "Judgment under Uncertainty: Heuristics and Biases" *Science* 185: 1124–31.

Kratzer, Constance Y., and Bruce H. Brunson. 1998. "Financial Education in the Workplace: Results of a Research Study." *Journal of Compensation and Benefits* 14(3): 24–27.

Kusko, Andrea, James Poterba, and David Wilcox. 1998. "Employee Decisions with Respect to 401(k) Plans." In *Living with Defined Contribution Pensions: Remaking Responsibility for Retirement*, edited by Olivia Mitchell and Sylvester Schieber. Philadelphia: University of Pennsylvania Press.

Laibson, David I., Andrea Repetto, and Jeremy Tobacman. 1998. "Self-Control and Saving for Retirement." *Brookings Papers on Economic Activity* 1998(1): 91–172.

Madrian, Brigitte C., and Dennis F. Shea. 2001a. "The Power of Suggestion: Inertia in 401(k) Participation and Savings Behavior." *Quarterly Journal of Economics* 116(4): 1149–187.

———. 2001b. "Preaching to the Converted and Converting Those Taught: Financial Education in the Workplace." University of Chicago Working Paper. Chicago: University of Chicago.

McCarthy, Mike, and Liz McWhirter. 2000. "Are Employees Missing the Big Picture? Study Shows Need for Ongoing Financial Education." *Benefits Quarterly* 16(1): 25–31.

Milne, Deborah, Jack VanDerhei, and Paul Yakoboski. 1995. "Can We Save Enough to Retire? Participant Education in Defined Contribution Plans." EBRI Issue Brief No. 160. Washington, D.C.: Employee Benefit Research Institute.

———. 1996. "Participant Education: Actions and Outcomes." EBRI Issue Brief No. 169. Washington, D.C.: Employee Benefit Research Institute.

Murray, M. Christian. 1999. "401(k) Plan Sponsors Find Education Pays." *National Underwriter* 103(19): 36–38.

O'Donoghue, Ted, and Matthew Rabin. 1999. "Procrastination in Preparing for Retirement." In *Behavioral Dimensions of Retirement Economics*, edited by Henry Aaron. Washington, D.C.: Brookings Institution Press.

Papke, Leslie E. 1995. "Participation in and Contributions to 401(k) Pension Plans." *Journal of Human Resources* 30(2): 311–25.

Papke, Leslie E., and James M. Poterba. 1995. "Survey Evidence on Employer Match Rates and Employee Saving Behavior in 401(k) Plans." *Economics Letters* 49(3): 313–17.

Poterba, James M., Steven F. Venti, and David A. Wise. 1996. "How Retirement

Saving Programs Increase Saving." *Journal of Economic Perspectives* 10(4): 91–112.

———. 1998a. "Lump Sum Distributions from Retirement Savings Plans: Receipt and Utilization." In *Inquiries in the Economics of Aging*, edited by David A. Wise. Chicago: University of Chicago Press.

———. 1998b. "Personal Retirement Saving Programs and Asset Accumulation." In *Frontiers in the Economics of Aging*, edited by David Wise. Chicago: University of Chicago Press.

Profit Sharing/401(k) Council of America. 2001. "Automatic Enrollment 2001: A Study of Automatic Enrollment Practices in 401(k) Plans." Chicago: PSCA. http://www.psca.org/data/autoenroll2001.asp.

Thaler, Richard, and Shlomo Benartzi. 2004. "Save More Tomorrow™: Using Behavioral Economics to Increase Employee Saving." *Journal of Political Economy* 112(1, part 2): S164-87.

U.S. Department of Labor. 1998. *Employee Benefits in Medium and Large Private Establishments*. Washington, D.C.: Bureau of Labor Statistics.

U.S. Department of the Treasury. Internal Revenue Service. 1998. *Internal Revenue Bulletin 98-25* (June 22, 1998): 8. Available at: http://ftp.fedworld.gov/pub/irs-irbs/irb98-25.pdf (accessed November 14, 2005).

———. 2000a. *Internal Revenue Bulletin 2000-7*. (February 14, 2000): 617. Available at: http://ftp.fedworld.gov/pub/irs-irbs/irb00-07.pdf (accessed November 14, 2005).

———. 2000b. *Internal Revenue Bulletin 2000-31*. (July 31, 2000): 138-42. Available at: http://ftp.fedworld.gov/pub/irs-irbs/irb00-31.pdf (accessed November 14, 2005).

Vanguard Center for Retirement Research. 2001. "Automatic Enrollment: Vanguard Client Experience." Valley Forge, Pa.: The Vanguard Group. Available at: https://institutional4.vanguard.com/iip/pdf/CRR_automatic_enrollment.pdf (accessed November 14, 2005).

Watson Wyatt Worldwide. 2001. "Retirement Plan Provisions: What, When and How Much? Economic Growth and Tax Relief Reconciliation Act of 2001." Washington, D.C.: Watson Wyatt Worldwide. Available at: http://www.watsonwyatt.com/research/resrender.asp?id=W-471&page=1 (accessed November 14, 2005).

PART V

RESERVATIONS

Chapter 12

Second-Order Rationality

RICHARD A. EPSTEIN

FOR much of my academic career I have defended a version of libertarian theory of limited government, a government whose central function is protection of private property and voluntary exchange against force and fraud (see Epstein 1985, 1995, 1998, 2003). This recognizes a role for taxation and eminent domain, not only for the common defense but also for creating infrastructure and controlling and regulating monopoly power. The battle between rational choice theory and behavioral economics—and the common errors shared by both—often calls that classical liberal theory into question on two key issues. The first is the level of rationality, coherence, and stability in the formation of human preferences. The second is the relative strengths of egoism and altruism in human affairs.

In this chapter I confine myself to the first of these two inquiries, which spawns two further lines of investigation. One involves the formation of political order in a state of nature. The other swirls around the contemporary debate over the scope of government regulation of economic activity once that political order is secured, often with the view of placing a minimum safety net under individuals that protects them not only against the bad behavior of other individuals but also against the vicissitudes of nature and, most relevant for this exercise, their own bad judgment and limited capacity. This explicit behavioral rejection of libertarian assumptions has profound consequences for the role of government in social and economic life. Starting from the behavioralist baseline makes it much more plausible to insist on a variety of paternalist regulations whose main purpose is to protect individuals from their own biases and excesses. For example, Oren Bar-Gill has suggested that such legal controls might be appropriate in credit card transactions, on the grounds that individual borrowers suffer from a set of biases that includes "weakness of the will," which leads them to underestimate their level of self-control (Bar-Gill 2004, 1373, 1375), and "optimism bias," which leads them to underestimate the risk of adverse events, such as loss of job, which in turn leads them to borrow more than they ought (1375–76).

Likewise, in dealing with pension plans and retirement, libertarianism generally allows individuals to make their own choices and opposes government mandates to make contributions into plans such as Social Security or Medicare. Yet Social Security has many defenders, some on the grounds that ordinary individuals do not save adequately on their own (see chapter 10 this volume; see also Diamond and Orszag 2004). This point is subject to dispute, and greater difficulties with Social Security arise from a different quarter. The public choice context gives political leaders powerful reasons to engage in massive wealth transfers, which work best when concealed from public view. In this context, the cognitive biases of ordinary people are likely to kick in because they will be exploited by political actors operating in settings where the institutional correctives are likely to be weaker than in private market settings.

First- and Second-Order Rationality

The ongoing debate over human rationality and motivation poses key challenges to libertarian political theory. What assumptions must be made about individual behavior, and to what extent do these assumptions hold true in practice? Libertarian theory is commonly said to rest on the assumption that self-interested individuals make rational choices on matters that affect their welfare.

The common economic account of rationality sets a high bar because it presupposes that, given their own consistent set of preferences, all persons will make the right choices in light of the information available to them under conditions of uncertainty. Gary Becker offers one of the most often quoted summaries of this position: "All human behavior can be viewed as involving participants who [1] maximize their utility [2] from a stable set of preferences and [3] accumulate an optimal amount of information and other inputs in a variety of markets" (Becker 1976: 14; see also 1962).[1] This conclusion presupposes that individuals have a stable set of preferences concerning what they desire not only in the present but also in any future state of the world, and that they can choose those courses of action that will maximize their chances of reaching their chosen goals. I concentrate on the cognitive deficiencies involved.

The libertarian worldview looks promising in a world in which individuals with consistent preferences may act as they please as long as they refrain from the use of force and maximize their well-being as they see it. Such individuals will make only those trades they expect will improve their position. As long as transactions costs are low, the velocity of transactions will hasten the day when individuals will have exhausted all the gains from trade, so that they will reach the best of all positions in the best of all possible worlds. The basic prescription becomes that of Ronald Coase: reduce transactions costs that block the movement to a social maximum (1960).

The implicit cognitive assumptions that underlie this model are vulnerable on the simplest and most powerful of grounds: they are false. A group of behavioral economists believe that the choices individuals make in practice under uncertainty are wrong in systematic and predictable ways. This view holds that individuals are poor calculators of the proper means to chosen ends, and thus rely on heuristics that often lead to systematic error (Tversky and Kahneman 1982; Kahneman and Tversky 1979). "Heuristics and biases" are run together as though they were a single word. Kahneman and Tversky acknowledge that some heuristics help individuals through bad patches, but their empirical investigations do not identify any useful heuristic or explain why it works (see Sunstein 2003). The work of Gerd Gigerenzer, Peter Todd, and the ABC Research Group reveals "simple heuristics that make us smart" (1999)[2] and "fast and frugal" decision making rules that allow complex situations to be stripped down to their essentials (27–28.). For Kahneman and Tversky, the only heuristics are those that lead ordinary individuals astray (see Kahneman, Slovic, and Tversky 1982; Barberis and Thaler 2003). Thus the familiar availability heuristic leads individuals to overestimate the probabilities of events that were most conspicuous in recent experience. Next, it is possible for individuals to fall prey to the so-called anchoring heuristic, whereby they attach too much weight to their initial estimation of the probability of an event, and thus do not make appropriate adjustments to take new information into account. Third, individuals often fall prey to the representativeness heuristic, whereby they overweight the event in front of them and thus ignore the importance of base-rate probabilities. The point here evokes Bayes' Theorem, which suggests that an individual who is 80 percent sure that the bus he has seen is blue will not take the fact that 90 percent of the buses on the route are red into acccount, and will thus overestimate the likelihood that he has seen a blue bus. Finally, strong experimental evidence indicates that individuals are overconfident in the judgments about what they know and in their predictions of what will happen (Dunning et al. 1990, 568, 572).[3]

The question is what impact studies linking heuristics to biases should have on the libertarian view that individuals should have freedom of choice in organizing their own lives and businesses. The first point of concern is how these various biases fit together. In one sense, the heuristics and biases view finds too many sources of cognitive error to know how much weight should be accorded to each. It may well be that the predictions of rational choice theory do not neatly embrace ordinary individuals. Thus one way to read the anchoring bias is that individuals tend to stick to their prior beliefs on probability distributions too long in the face of subsequent information. At the same time, the availability and representativeness heuristics point to the opposite conclusion, that individuals tend to ignore their initial impressions and overreact to subsequent information. It is possible that ordinary folks are irrational in both ways on at least some occasions, but more difficult to imagine that they make both mistakes simultaneously in particular settings. A strong theory of the baleful influence of heuristics would indicate the relative strength of these opposite errors in the various contexts.

But the studies' heavy reliance on decisions college students made in laboratory conditions makes it hard to generate any theory about which of these biases operate most strongly in well-defined social contexts, contexts in which various institutional arrangements may insulate people from the biases. Thus, to return to the credit card situation, individuals are constantly besieged not only by invitations to take out new credit cards, but also by solicitations for loan consolidation programs that reduce the cards' overall carrying costs. And credit card companies, worried about the risk of defaults on debt, typically tie credit limits to income.[4] In dealing with this complex of information, it is hard to predict any uniform response. Some individuals will manage very well, and thus receive substantial benefits from a system that allows them to avoid interest and late fees if they pay off their bills in full at the end of the month. Yet others may career into bankruptcy. In such an environment the effects of cognitive biases are murky at best. Do we assume that individuals will respond strongly to a credit card bankruptcy of a close friend, and choose to borrow too little? Or are they subject to the optimism and self-control biases to which Bar-Gill refers? Rational choice theorists can be forgiven for saying that these behavioral explanations point in all directions at same time and therefore give no guidance as to systematic deviations from the rational choice model as the cognitive bias literature purports to do.

Here is another illustration of the same tension. In a recent study on public attitudes toward taxation and public finance, Edward McCaffery and Jonathan Baron "organize [their] analysis around what we and others term an isolation effect. The effect is similar to, and sometimes perhaps identical with, what others term a focusing effect. In both cases, subjects focus on one especially salient aspect of a choice or evaluation problem and ignore or fail to integrate other less salient items" (2005, n.p.). The isolation effect led to bad results because individuals did not integrate the consequences of the income tax system with Social Security tax in determining the overall incidence of taxation, or understand how to develop an optimal system of taxation for spouses in a world of progressive taxation (1–13). But in many other contexts, it is precisely the ability to ignore lots of irrelevant information that allows for intelligent decisions. The central theme of Malcolm Gladwell's book, *Blink*, for example, is that too much information often kills by distracting people from what really matters, so that rigorous protocols, such as those used in the diagnosis of heart patients, look only to two or three relevant variables (2005).[5] These protocols are systematically designed to stop the use of intuitive judgments, which turn out to be inferior, even for experienced physicians (125–36, stressing why less is more). Once again, the importance of context helps determine whether some psychological tendency will manifest itself, and, if so, with what force.

That objection seems to carry weight against many of the specific claims associated with the cognitive bias literature. It would be a mistake, however, to assume that even large defects in that literature necessarily establish the soundness of the rival rational choice view. Once again, the difficulties in dealing with the pervasive pattern of mistake have long bedeviled rational choice theory: just how is it that people can be described as rational when it is evident that individuals make all sorts of mistakes in their decisions? We did not have to wait until the 1970s to understand that individuals make all sorts of blunders in routine calculations. In its original design, the median score on the Scholastic Aptitude Test (SAT) was 500, with the top score of 800 and the bottom score of 200 having both been set at three standard deviations from the mean. No one can say that these tests were just funny little experiments that test-takers would blow off because they did not count. The payoff of getting a good score on these tests is enormous, as is evident from the hard cash and hours of preparation that college-bound students spend to improve their scores, often with limited success.

By way of example, mathematics teachers have long known that high school and college students can fall into simple traps that arise from their failure to apply mathematical formulas correctly. The average student will often be stumped by such questions as: Smith drives at sixty miles per hour from home to his aunt's house located 180 miles away, and thirty miles per hour on the return trip. What is his average speed? The focal point heuristic, which duly appears as a distractor on every standardized multiple choice test, is forty-five miles per hour. The correct answer is that Smith has gone 360 miles in nine hours for an average speed of forty miles per hour. The perceptual trick: you have to travel a longer time at the slower speed. The large number of college-board takers who tank on this question shows conclusively that many fall for what may be called the centralization bias, taking the midpoint between two extremes by underweighting a concealed time variable. Perhaps this bias is covered by the representativeness bias in the cognitive bias literature, although it seems a poor fit because there is no exemplar overweighed against as background probability. But the classification issue hardly matters: the evidence that many individuals are misled by focal points in the simplest of calculations is conclusive. The strong version of rational choice theory has to make peace with standardized tests and that the median IQ is 100, not 190. Rational choice theory needs to reexamine its definition of rationality.

Rational Responses to Cognitive Deficits

The overall challenges, then, are what it means to talk about rational individuals when ordinary people constantly make mistakes, and what implications these undisputed cognitive weaknesses have for markets. On the first, it is important to be aware of the context of experiments to avoid being overconfident about conclusions. Thus, for example, Dunning and colleagues (1990) asked individuals to predict the behaviors of individuals they knew in certain defined settings, and found that these individuals were more confident in their predictions than their accuracy justified. But, like most such experiments, the study asked isolated individuals about their predictions, but did not try to determine how that behavior might have changed had the individuals been informed of their initial poor performance and then asked to predict a second time. The experiment also sheds little light on how well people would do on other kinds of inquiries, such as those involving the distance between two cities. Here again, it is likely that most people would make mistakes, but less likely that they would do so if they could consult a map or a friend who had one. Nor does the experiment report anything about what would have happened to the error rate had the parties been asked about matters within their expertise. The conclusions therefore have to be qualified because they do not take into account the effects of learning and cooperation. Both are important features of human life precisely because people do know that they are prone to error, especially in dealing with topics unfamiliar to them.

The doubts about this first experiment dovetail into other work that addresses a critical issue: the ability of individuals to be aware of their limitations. The point here has operational significance because the weakest link in many social chains is how is it that we get ordinary people into an environment in which they can be helped by others. Justin Kruger and David Dunning suggest in another well-known study that in many situations ordinary people are not only incompetent, but also unaware that they are, and thus not in a position to do anything about it (1999). Their studies show that individuals overestimate their sense of humor, for example, and their competence relative to their peers. There is no question that these forms of incompetence could have fatal implications if individuals who think that they know about medicine decide to treat themselves.

Once again, however, it is important to note the limits on the responsible inferences that we can draw from these experiments. It may well be that many individuals do suffer from a lack of self-recognition when judged against their peers. But by the same token, few of us who are untrained in medicine think that our knowledge of the field is greater than that of the experts that treat us, or have in those situations any of the issues of ego and pride that seem to play a role in the Kruger and Dunning experiments. There is nothing in those experiments that suggests that large numbers of people systematically think that they have vast skills in areas in which they have no training, and the huge level of specialization in all areas of expertise suggest that most of us will move to experts, who do, in most matters, have a better set of skills than novices or amateurs (Kruger and Dunning 1999; see also Chi 1978, Chi et al. 1982). Indeed, Kruger and Dunning constantly acknowledge, just as we should expect, that different levels of competence produce different levels of performance. Perhaps no one gets medical attention or other forms of help at the optimal time, so that the behavioral impediments have some second-order effect. It is important to put those errors in perspective, however, so that we see how mistakes coexist with rational behavior. It is a safe assumption that in most cases most people at least partly recognize their weaknesses. A second-order form of rationality thus asks the question of whether they take appropriate steps to counter those weaknesses, perhaps by getting help when they need it. Such individuals are rational in the sense that they take steps to limit their mistakes. Even if they do not have a perfect knowledge of their own limitations, they have some, and in general move in directions that minimize the problem, rather than aggravate it. This might be thought of as yet another application of Herbert Simon's principle of bounded rationality (1955). But again the categorical issues are not what is at stake. What matters is that rational people take steps that on average reduce, not increase, the frequency and severity of their errors. The one lesson to learn from Kruger and Dunning is that the real problem often is not with the operations within markets, but with individuals whose limitations keep them from getting help from others before it is too late.

The point, then, is that individuals who are aware of their limited capacity rationally rely on a range of devices to help themselves through the rough patches: they seek advice from friends, hire experts, attend classes, use Mapquest, and adopt rules of thumb or other tricks of the trade, such as lists or acronyms. The behavioralist critique does not deny the role of these decision-making aids, but notes that they are highly imperfect because the error that creeps into individual decision making remains uncorrected (see, for example, Jolls, Sunstein, and Thaler 1998). But there is still a second sort of response, which is that individuals aware of their cognitive limitations enter market transactions with others who have greater skills. The huge volume of voluntary transactions in which individuals seek help—from everyone from financial advisers to lawyers to babysitters—says that often people with sharp limitations do so, even if it takes some prodding from family and friends. The division of labor is alive and well in ways that no psychological experiment can sensibly deny. At this point, the second-order theory of rational choice predicts that many individuals with less competence will typically use various contractual mechanisms to transfer key portions of their decision-making responsibility to others whose skills are superior. The function of markets on this view is in part the transfer of decision-making authority from less to more rational individuals. As long as markets tend to minimize the losses caused by inconsistent preferences, they should be regarded as rational for the way in which they encourage various mechanisms of self-correction. Far from running from the implications of built-in human error, we should acknowledge its central role, because the differential levels of compensation are indispensable to explaining many key features of voluntary markets.

The Necessity of Variation

As the earlier discussion intimates, the key link in the argument requires us to focus on what is meant by competence. In legal settings, it is often used in a dyadic sense: infants and insane persons are incompetent; everyone else has full legal capacity. Most ordinary markets involve individuals deemed fully competent in the sense that they have full capacity to enter into contracts, hold property, make wills, and the like. But this view does not accurately describe actual competence. In some settings, such as end-of-life situations, differences in competence are manifest, and efforts are made to overcome the obvious shortfalls through such devices as living wills and health care powers of attorney. Indeed, some people may easily fall prey to the way in which odds are presented: they may be more willing to undergo an operation if told that they have a 90-percent chance of survival than if they are told that they have a 10-percent chance of death (Jolls, Sunstein, and Thaler 1998, 1161)—at least until they are told that a 10-percent death rate and a 90-percent survival rate give them identical chances, which any competent health care adviser should hasten to do.

Even when we move away from these extremes, however, it is vital to be alert to a common error in traditional rational choice and behavioral economics. Both ignore the high level of variation across individuals in their success with heuristics and rules of thumb, and thus offer no explanation for how a complex social system should take these differences into account. The constant effort is instead to insist that homo economicus, as an archetype, deviates in important ways from real people. Thus, in the Bar-Gill article, it is consumers (as in all consumers) who are subject to the various biases that reduce their effectiveness of credit card transactions.[6] What that article in particular, and behavioral economics in general, fails to address is how homini economici differ conspicuously among themselves in their relative immunity to the intellectual ills that plague humankind. On the matter of cognitive competence, we know that some people are smarter than others. Not every individual gets a 500 on the SATs. Rather there is a bell-shaped curve, in which some individuals do dramatically better than the norm and others dramatically worse.

Here this striking empirical finding is nothing to worry about. The basic principle of population biology is that every trait in any large population is characterized not only by a mean but also by a variance. In the simplest model, we can assume a symmetrical or normal distribution, and then vary the peak (hence the variance) to take the relevant empirical evidence into account. Thus we discover that the average American male is five feet nine inches tall, with a variance of plus or minus three inches. We can discover that the parallel figures for women are five feet five inches, with a variance of +/– two and a half inches. What is true about height is true of every other characteristic from cholesterol levels to intelligence. Numbers wrong? Doesn't matter. Substitute the accurate heights for men and women, and we still observe that the two populations have different means and variances. Put aside any difficulty of measurement, and the only question is the height of the Bell curve, not whether there is a curve. Individual competence, which is some aggregate measure of various key skills, is not a Platonic absolute, but also a variable with a mean and a variance. To the extent that rational choice theory assumes perfect competence on the part of all individuals, it assumes that everyone gets a perfect score on the SAT. It ain't gonna happen.

Yet, by the same token, what should be said of the demonstration of behavioral economics that individuals cannot all do math like Archimedes or play chess like Garry Kasparov? We need to answer two questions: first, what useful purposes can be served by rational choice assumptions on cognition and motivation, and, second, how do ordinary individuals and institutions respond to deviation in abilities in ordinary life. Let's take a quick look at each point in turn.

The Virtues of Perfect Competence

Our initial question concerns the use of models of perfect competence in a world characterized by individuals who differ dramatically in their respective abilities and traits. No one wanting to understand the operation of markets can proceed without a clear understanding of how the world would look *if* all individuals had the supreme competence attributable to them by rational choice theory. To see why this is so, ask if you as a social planner had the choice between perfect monopoly and perfect competition, which mode you would choose. One possible response could begin with an exhaustive account of all the biases and shortfalls of individual behavior. Yet that endless recitation would only reduce the ability to make a sensible social judgment. Dwelling on imperfections of ordinary individuals carries no clear implication as to the appropriate policy choice because there is no directionality to these cognitive errors. Anchoring, availability, and representativeness offer no guidance about the centralized tendencies of human behavior under either competition or monopoly in terms of price, quantity, or consumer and producer surplus.

The only way to gain traction on the question is to start from the opposite pole of perfect rationality and ordinary individual self-interest. At this point we can conclude that the monopolist will set prices above marginal cost and reduce the quantity of goods sold to the point where it maximizes its own profits. That strategy results in the loss of those transactions by individuals who are prepared to pay the competitive but not the monopolistic price for the goods in question. The standard diagram thus shows that monopoly leads to a net gain to the monopolist that is smaller than the net loss to the consumer. The clear implication is that monopoly leads to a reduction in social welfare. One implication of that result is that we could develop an antitrust law to combat the formation of cartels and huge single firms. Another is that we could contemplate rate regulation as a means to control the prices companies charge in natural monopoly situations, that is, where economies of scale are such that a single producer can manufacture the relevant outputs at a lower cost than two or more parties. A third implication is to allow price discrimination so that the monopolist picks up those customers whose demand is below the monopoly price but above the competitive price.

At this point, what do we gain in this analysis by introducing the full range of biases to which both companies and their customers may be subject? Largely nothing. We did not change our views of monopoly and competition when we discovered that the ordinary fallible student got 500 on the SATs. Nor should we change our view of monopoly now that we know that these individuals not only mess up base-rate calculations, but also get misled by the form in which they are asked certain questions.

To be sure, there may be cases at the edges of antitrust law in which some knowledge of cognitive biases proves relevant. One possibility is the question of whether a seller of primary goods, such as copiers, in competitive markets can engage in monopoly pricing in some aftermarket, as with goods and services (Eastman Kodak Co. v. Image Technical Servs., Inc. 504 U.S. 451, 1992). Can, for example, the seller of copy machines raise the prices on repairs after initial sale because optimistic customers underestimate the frequency and severity of those repairs? It is, of course, possible that this happens occasionally, and at least one Supreme Court case has brooked the possibility that such conduct might rise to the level of an antitrust violation. But even on its facts the substantive claim of myopia looks thin. Some customers have historical experience that leads them to temper their initial judgments. Others will actually research the question. Companies will often sell warranties for repair work that obviate the need for a second level of pricing and the like. In addition, the observation overlooks the critical fact that these suits were brought by excluded competitors, not by disgruntled consumers. No recourse was made to any behavioral explanations for these difficulties, and the case in Lexis carries a big red stop sign, indicating that its validity has weakened with time.[7] The cognitive issues do not touch the large questions of state creation of monopoly, cartels, and mergers. A beachhead, perhaps; a dominant position, no way.

The basic point here is simple. The sensible policy prescriptions of the standard neoclassical model are neither upset nor qualified by the onset of behavioral economics. The idealized models of human behavior are just that: they indicate the way in which hypothetical rational and self-interested individuals act. If we understand how the conduct of such individuals might deviate from social optimum or reinforce it, then we can gain a reliable sense of whether certain legal and regulatory initiatives will move us closer to or further from the preferred social state. Indeed, our models should in fact be more reliable than any randomized laboratory tests might suppose, because the individuals selected to make key decisions on price and output are in all likelihood better able to make the requisite calculations than a person chosen at random from the phone book.

The practice should lead to a slow convergence between actual outcomes and those predicted by neoclassical theory. Rational choice theory set our compass on true north. Behavioral economics reminds us that some wobble remains. Even though competitors will make mistakes in product innovation, hiring, pricing, and a thousand other details, we still have no reason to think that these errors, taken singly or in combination, cut in favor of monopoly. Nor does anyone think that the same errors, when made by monopolists, count as an argument for competition. On these large questions of industrial structure, there is no reason to reverse the judgments made by a neoclassical theory that is staunchly oblivious to the shaky nature of its underlying assumptions. Over time, individuals will seek others who have better knowledge than themselves to make critical decisions, at least as long as they have some recourse against fraud and other forms of misappropriation. Markets then are rational to the extent that, on average, the decisions to cede control or to share authority replace worse decision makers with better, leaving both sides to the deal better off than before. Perfection of outcome is simply too strict a condition to have any descriptive or normative relevance.

The same arguments can be extended. In a wide variety of situations, serious coordination difficulties among individuals frustrate reaching some ideal equilibrium. Thus we know that, under the tragedy of the commons, individuals will on average take out too much of a common resource and destroy the value of the pool for all concerned. Similarly, the now-fashionable concern with the anticommons suggests that in some situations the inability of anyone to take or consume a resource without the consent of all leads to a systematic underconsumption of the resource, as when five riparians are each able to impose tolls on the continuous length of a navigable river. In both circumstances, some form of regulation—catch limits in the first case, a toll union in the second—could go a long way to bring the situation back into balance. But neither the acute difficulties of coordination nor the remedies for it depend on the (true) insight that individual bargainers will adopt different strategies and exhibit different levels of skill in negotiating these tricky problems. Those insights might allow us to predict which individuals are likely to do better in dealing with the complex environments, but they cannot undermine the case for regulation or shape the appropriate kind of regulation. The neoclassical model, stripped of all behavioral qualifications, captures the dominant features of the situation and indicates what kinds of midlevel reforms are likely to improve output, whether we deal with oil and gas on the one hand or the fishery on the other. The great danger here is that people will overlook the central difficulties of holdouts and coordination if diverted into a discussion of the individual mistakes in calculation. The same observation that cognitive error creates at most second-order distortions applies to a wide range of regulation that is, in my view, socially destructive. Thus it is easy to denounce any system of price or rent control for the massive distortions it creates in local real estate markets: queues at the gasoline pump, chronic shortages, under-the-table payments, reduced new investment and construction, individuals breaking up large apartments to avoid the regulation, key money paid for transfer, neighborhoods rotting for want of the infusion of new blood. All these follow from the shortages created when prices or rents are set too low, so that demand is high relative to the available supply. It is easy in these situations to believe that inexperienced people will make all sorts of mistakes in working the system, but all these distortions are just second-order problems suggesting that the more skilled are better able to weather the regulatory storm than the less skilled. The moral is the same. Ignore the behavioral complications and you will get a sharper and more sensible critique of the system.

Finally, the same conclusions apply with respect to credit markets and interest rates. There is no doubt, as experiments have shown, that individuals have inordinate discount rates when asked about their time preferences (Frederick, Loewenstein, O'Donoghue 2004).[8] The subjects were asked how much money they would require to be indifferent between a smaller reward today and a larger one payable one month, one year, or ten years later. The results translated into discount rates of 345 percent for the first month, 120 percent for the year, and 19 percent for a ten-year wait. The numbers suggest a real level of impatience in the immediate short run. But it would be a great mistake to assume that any of these numbers explain the interest rates observed in various mortgage markets, in which competitive forces and simple disclosures create circumstances in which short-term borrowers typically receive a lower interest rate than long-term borrowers. A quick trip to the Chase web site revealed a range of mortgages with basic interest rates between 4.875 and 5.250 percent, depending on length and terms.[9] No one can begin to explain these market rates by extrapolation from the experimental data. No one should even try. Rational choice theory looks a lot better here. The forces of arbitrage may not make these financial markets perfectly efficient.[10] But assumptions of pure rationality, even in consumer markets, look a lot closer to the observed interest rates than these experimental figures, which were (for what it is worth) computed based on stated preferences. It is quite unlikely that these numbers would have survived had the experimental subjects been given an effective interest rate next to each of their choices.

Specialization Within the Firm and the Market

The field of economics is not exclusively concerned with explaining large-scale systems of social organization. Recently, the focus of the inquiry has often been the individual workplace, the condominium association, or the religious congregation, in an effort to understand the social dynamics that drive individual decisions in these contexts. At this point, we can no longer take refuge in an application of the law of large numbers. Basic centralizing tendencies need no longer hold, so we should be far less confident of either the decisions that individuals make or the rules used to regulate them. Variations in personality and ability really start to count, which is why the vocabulary used to describe management behavior inside the firm, volunteer organization, or family takes on a much more persistent psychological hue.[11] The way in which a sensible boss gives orders to an able and conscientious worker is quite different from that which he uses for one who is less able or lazy. Anyone who follows the conventional assumptions of uniform competence (or self-interest) for all employees, customers, and suppliers will enjoy only a short career as a manager.

But does it follow that we abandon the use of markets and voluntary arrangements? Not at all. We just have to understand that one key element for success or failure within the voluntary group is an acute awareness of the variations in all critical capacities. No longer is the definition of rationality that individuals get everything right. Now it requires only that the overall organization use the capabilities of its members to the fullest. I put aside matters of motivation (to which a similar analysis applies) and concentrate solely on competence.

Let us suppose that a group of individuals is planning to work together in some kind of association. Assume further that the members of this group have different overall levels of competence and different specialized skills, so that no one within the group meets the exacting specifications of a rational human being with fully consistent preferences. How do these people structure their cooperative arrangements? One possibility is that they assign roles within the organization at random. Another is that they seek to put people in positions so that the overall level of output will increase, given the relative strengths and weaknesses of all the members. To begin this inquiry it is necessary to postulate that enough members are aware of the differences in competence and the way in which those differences may impact the operation of the firm. It is also necessary to postulate that others inside the business, when presented with an argument about differential abilities or specialized skills, are able to understand the situation, even if they are unable to determine the solution. These are not strong conditions, even when all the members of the business arrive on the same day. And when new people are hired into a firm that is already up and running, the condition is trivial.

Within the firm or group, therefore, we should expect that a widespread recognition of differential abilities will drive organizational and staffing decisions. Any naïve model that treats all individuals as pro rata holders in the business will quickly yield to the imperatives created by differential competence and specialized training. On balance people with greater skills will rise to the top of the organization, because others will find it in their interests to follow the lead of someone more knowledgeable than themselves. Likewise, if one individual is skilled at mechanical tasks and another is skilled at artistic ones, we should expect that the job assignments within the firm will on average match people with their demonstrated areas of competence.

The analysis of employment relations has direct and powerful implications on the financial side as well. The individuals who comprise the firm have to decide how to partition the future uncertain income flows within the firm. The division between employer and employee, as opposed to partner and partner, is an implicit statement that the residual value of the firm resides with the employer and the worker is in the position of a creditor—a first priority by contract against firm assets, with equity position, so to speak, to the employer who bears the (leveraged) risks of the business. This arrangement makes sense precisely because the differential knowledge and abilities are such that the employer is the superior risk bearer over the long term. If there were no differential abilities, there would be little or no reason to adopt this form of industrial organization. As with direct matters of control, it is differential competence that makes the implicit long-term capital structure within the employment market so critical.

At this point, then, we have a simple working definition of voluntary transactions within organizations: all parties will benefit from the gains as the organization moves from one configuration of labor, risk, and reward to another. There is no need whatsoever to assume that the movement from state A to state B will be a move from error to perfection. Rather, given the limitations of all individuals in the operation, we should only expect the outputs to be higher than they would have been in the previous state of affairs on average, but never uniformly. It is perfectly consistent with this sensible upward progression that even the leaders within these complicated structures make elementary mistakes, so that they flunk rationality in the strong (but now useless) sense of that term. The right question, however, is whether the organization on balance makes fewer mistakes than it did before the internal sorting. Yet the standard testing models of the cognitive bias literature routinely content themselves with proving that even individuals in high-level positions make mistakes in calculation. It is the right answer to the wrong question. If the firm minimizes the number of errors, then it has indeed made rational second-order decisions.

Where, then, do markets fit in? Quite simply, the decisions made in some organizations are sounder than those made in others. The outsiders to the firm look at quality and price, and don't care why the organization has failed. As my esteemed colleague Bernard Meltzer told me many years ago: "Brother Epstein, you can't publish excuses." Neither, it turns out, can you sell them. By this account, the firms (or other organizations) with the fewest excuses have the highest outputs, and will prevail not because they are perfect but because they are better than what comes in second place. The impersonal judgments from the outside are relentless and persons inside each organization know that the closer they get to ideal decisions on quality and price, the more likely it is that they will succeed. By trial and error an erratic organization will eliminate some mistakes. With time, it could develop sensible protocols to stop them from cropping up in the first place. The gap between what the ideal theory requires and what a particular firm produces will diminish under competitive pressures, even if it is never eliminated. Throw in the ability to learn from past mistakes, to promote, and to fire, and the shakedown period may be shorter than is commonly supposed. If we had perfectly rational individual agents, then, as it were, there would be no place for imperfectly rational firms.

Here is one example of how this process may evolve. The strong rational choice assumption says that ordinary individuals have to play chess like Garry Kasparov, or even like experts. Forget it. But it is a mistake to infer that it is a "false assumption . . . that almost all people, almost all of the time, make choices that are in their best interest or at the very least are better, by their own lights, than the choices that would be made by third parties" (Sunstein amd Thaler 2003, 1163). Clearly it defeats the purpose of the game of chess to have third parties make the moves for the players, when the object is to get some sense of relative skill. System rationality, therefore, in no way depends on whether weak players make the right moves. The issue is instead what sort of institutional arrangements count as second-order rational responses to the obvious fact that chess players differ markedly in ability.

The first point is an obvious one: people who don't care about the game may dabble a bit, but will not be drawn into any organization where performance in chess affects their lives. The initial sorting thus leaves a chess club with individuals who are, no surprise, interested in chess. At this point, the game, with the consent of weak and strong players alike, is organized to take into account the different levels of performance of the various players. Thus it would be a frightful bore to have tournaments in which world-class players waste their time playing against veritable tyros. Hence chess clubs develop a rating system that slots people in at the bottom and then allows them to play their way up through the ranks. This counts as perfect second-order rational response, as ordinary people use the term, to the differential abilities (or, if you must, ordinary rationality) of the players. The structure makes it more likely that games will be contested on relatively even terms, which introduces an element of uncertainty and excitement to the game. The ability to raise one's rating with each victory. or to draw against higher-rated players, preserves parity over time and gives individuals an incentive to improve their games.

In sum, the organization of chess ratings, leagues, and tournaments is a perfectly rational (that is, socially appropriate) response to the differential ability of the players. That structure may itself be modified as circumstances dictate. The economic definitions of perfect rationality are a red herring, irrelevant to the institutional task at hand. Indeed, we could not have any rational institutional structure if all players had perfect ability: all games would either be draws or forced wins. The variation in individual knowledge is a sine qua non for the social organization of chess. The only criticisms that count are those showing that the rules in question do not provide appropriate matching and incentives to the individual players.

Thus far the emphasis has been on the institutional responses to differential levels of competence. But, again, it takes no empirical research to observe that because people do not start with perfect competence, they take steps to improve their skills. In a world of perfect rationality, why would anyone need to go to a tutor to learn chess or math, a teacher to learn to play the violin, or a coach to learn to throw a baseball? But all of these institutions exist, and in rich profusion. Yet we rarely see the expert paying the amateur for the privilege of taking lessons. As with chess ratings, only the perceived differential levels of competence allow for organized processes to convey information. It does not matter whether we talk about the rational choice theorist who believes the assumption of universal omniscience, or the behavioral economist who thinks he has shattered our worldview by reminding us that this assumption is false. In both cases, the social organization of any purposeful activity can only be described as rational, as we commonly use the term, precisely because none of those who participate are rational in the sense that the term is used in the professional literature. From the point of view of the libertarian, as long as there is some reason to believe that imperfect individuals improve their position through voluntary exchange, then a presumptive faith in freedom of contract is justified. The successful adaptations succeed; the others fall by the wayside. The incentive structures help imperfect individuals do better than might otherwise be the case. The pressure on cognitive biases is intense.

Libertarianism: Its Cautious Vindication

Once the second-order sense of rationality is understood, the libertarian institutions of private property and freedom of contract make sense for dealing with a wide range of human interactions. The traditional justification for private property stresses that individuals will take greater care with respect to resources they own relative to those held in common. This was the point of Aristotle when he wrote in his *Politics* that those resources jointly owned by all are tended to by none (1941, II, ch. 3; see also Hardin 1968, 1982). The point here is not that ordinary individuals will always make the right decisions with respect to the management of things they own, but that they have an incentive to improve the care of their property even if they sometimes fail. They will take better care of land if they know that they will be in a position to farm it next year than they will if they know that it will revert to the common. They are less likely to trash an apartment they own than one they rent (from a landlord who does not have a security for expenses, for example).

Similar arguments work for freedom of contract even on this cognitive dimension. People on average will not enter into an exchange unless they hope to gain from it. No stranger has better incentives or better knowledge of their personal tastes and desires. Of course, individuals can go off the rails, but on balance, they tend to learn from their mistakes to avoid a repetition of the bad consequences. Consistent with second-order rationality, their contracts will reflect their knowledge of their personal limits. People uncomfortable with risk will not become professional gamblers. Individuals who can't add will hire a financial adviser or invest in a mutual fund. The full range of contracts is designed to match risk with competence. Although some deals will crater, it doesn't take a wizard to realize that force and fraud are more powerful justifications for government intervention than cognitive error—even when (or at least until) we get to actual pronounced limitations on competence, such as those for infants and insane persons. People take their own differential levels of competence into account in structuring the deals they enter. Often they will enter agreements that leave them subject to legal risk, preferring to rely instead on reputation and informal sanctions to keep the trading partner in line. But that hardly bespeaks cognitive error. It is perfectly consistent with rational risk-taking, given that the high cost of termination acts as an effective form of protection. In a nutshell, the world works tolerably well under the old rules. What might lead us to change our view? Here it is useful to look at some experimental and real-world evidence to see how it squares with this view of how people with limited competence and flawed personalities make their way in the world.

Paternalism Hard and Soft

Against this set of insights, what reasons might be proposed to limit or override the choices that individuals make with their own lives? On this score there are at least two possible positions to take. The first, the traditional form of paternalism, is that people do not know what is in their best interests and that other individuals should therefore make decisions for them. The origin of the word bespeaks volumes about the scope of this doctrine. The state, or someone whom it appoints, should act in the position of guardian with respect to the individuals needing protection, much as a father acts with respect to his minor children. It is therefore important to note the two reasons why all societies routinely accept this power in both fathers and mothers.

The first is that the skills and abilities of parents and children systematically differ. A newborn cannot fend for itself today no matter how intelligent it will become at maturity. As the child grows, its abilities increase, and the case for parental control becomes ever weaker. Ideally, a slow transfer of power seems appropriate, but the legal system cannot implement a system of gradually shifting control. So it opts for a discontinuous break, using a plausible age for emancipation, just as it does for voting, military service, and driver's licenses. Within the family, the transition can be eased as parents can gradually allow their children more autonomy as they age—a wise strategy if they hope to retain some influence over their children once their legal power ceases. The moral is that continuous social adjustments often soften the edge of sharp legal boundaries.

The second reason goes to the parallel interests of parents and their children. No legal system makes a random assignment of adults to children. Rather, it takes advantage of the natural love and affection that parents show their children to the exclusion of others. Again there is always variation in the sample, but the massive dislocations of putting all parents through a test to ensure that these bonds are strong in particular cases are too horrible to contemplate. The state therefore backs up its general rules on parental decision making with a residual power to remove children from the control of their parents in cases of abuse and neglect (where the second is more difficult to define than the first). But in the vast bulk of cases the overlap of interest, subject to inevitable conflicts as children get older, works well enough.

These conditions for paternalism are not remotely satisfied when the state wishes to impose its authority over adults of full age and intelligence, no matter how great their cognitive or emotional flaws. The costs of watching over millions of adults who think themselves capable of running their own lives are considerable. The danger of nullification of the rules is transparent, and the question of who guards the (adult) guardians remains stubbornly unanswered. Typically, therefore, the state does not appoint guardians over adults. Instead, it passes general laws that restrict their freedom to protect them from some supposed advantage-taking by others more sophisticated than themselves. These programs, however, are likely to backfire because any restrictions on liberty are often not to the benefit of those restricted, but to that of other groups in society. Thus legislation that protects women, for example, from arduous labor, is typically a device to introduce economic protectionism for men. Minimum wage laws required for all workers are likely to operate as protectionism for union labor, which can command wages above that level, as compared with unskilled and unorganized labor, which cannot. For these reasons, the libertarian is on strong grounds in opposing such measures. Of course, there are limits to the basic rule that individuals always know their best interests, and the constant struggle over the question of whether suicide and euthanasia should be illegal shows the distance we have to go from ordinary behavior before paternalist arguments might have traction. There are huge numbers of regulations of the employment contract, for example, that should not be justified on paternalist grounds: among them, minimum wage laws, for-cause dismissal laws, and mandatory Social Security laws.

In one effort to dissuade libertarians from their traditional skepticism about paternalism, Cass Sunstein and Richard Thaler advocate libertarian paternalism. This formulation allows the state to set the default provisions of various contracts in ways that provide ordinary workers, for example, the kinds of protections they would demand if they had full knowledge of their best interests (Sunstein and Thaler 2003, 1161n24). This program thus does not always set the default terms in such a way that to mimic the preferences that people would have expressed had they had written what they had wanted. The argument is that default provisions are potent weapons, in that individuals tend to leave them more or less as they are, so that it is possible to have best of both worlds: freedom of choice for those who care enough to exercise it, but limited protection for those who don't, in the form of a default provision (note 9). Supporting this position, Sunstein and Thaler cite a number of studies, particularly those that deal with pension allocations, in which a default term to favor increased savings or increased investments in equity positions turns out in practice to be sticky (1161).[12] The question here whether the behavioralist critiques of individual cognition support these shifts.

The first issue with the proposal is whether it is simply a variation of traditional paternalism. If the position were that the only proper form of state intervention is to set default provisions that either side could reject, all forms of strong paternalism would be consigned to the dustbin of history. But instead Sunstein and Thaler take a discreet pass on the current crop of mandatory provisions—such as those contained in the minimum wage, antidiscrimination laws, and labor statutes. People may "in general" be able to opt out of certain agreements. But it is one thing to favor a regime under which only employees can waive certain protections—not even remotely libertarian position if employers remain duty-bound to offer these protections to prospective employees. The proper understanding of default terms is that either side could insist that the deal be otherwise. The employer who offers a wage that is below the state minimum has therefore not committed a crime: it has only announced in advance that it rejects the state default.

The difference in these two approaches is profound. The Age Discrimination in Employment Act contains a provision whereby only employees are entitled to waive the protection, which typically governs long-term financial packages.[13] The upshot is that employers typically have to purchase retirement at amounts that can equal twice the annual salary of the protected employee. The provision is therefore a far cry from a true default provision, which would allow the employer to require all its workers to waive all ADEA protections as a condition of employment. It is critical therefore to know which form of paternalism is meant.

For the moment, however, let us treat all default terms as subject to reversal by either party at any time. The question remains what terms an employer should offer its prospective employees. In answering, the best approach is to maximize joint benefit. On some points, it seems clear that the welfare of an employee is positively correlated with the welfare of the firm. Thus a firm may choose to offer various kinds of health care or fringe benefits to workers as a way to increase morale or to reduce the level of absenteeism. When the firm insists as a matter of contract that its workers eat certain food while in the company cafeteria, the decision is not a pure case of doing best by those workers who may not do best by themselves (ADEA 1967, 1164). It is also an effort to reduce the employer's health cost by reducing to some degree the dangers associated with overeating unhealthy food. In addition, no firm is likely to run the enormous risk in goodwill by making these choices covertly. Typically, it will seek to secure worker "buy-in" by running a comprehensive campaign that indicates its stake in supplying the information or changing the menu. But whatever the pick, this is not paternalism; it is contractualism. Nor is this firm's power to set a cafeteria menu increased, or decreased, by any assertion that the workers' preferences on this matter are not well formed, or might be changed by imposing a new regime. Workers are free to protest the shifts, and to force the company to back down. Default terms matter, but next to coercion they are small beer. Little is gained by confusing the two notions.

Conflicted and Unconflicted Defaults

One key question is the extent to which employers are likely to embrace or resist state default terms. Here a great deal depends on the content of the provision. One set of examples involves the percentage of earned income workers should put aside in savings plans. There is little reason to doubt the noted empirical finding that this default rule will have an effect on the number of individuals who elect to join the program. But again, why call this paternalism? The obvious explanation for the default term is that the employees think that the employer cares about setting the right total after-tax wage and benefits package it has to pay to each worker. When the employer offers menus and options, the implicit assumption is that these work as they do in restaurants. The firm has committed itself to an indifference curve, and each employee is now free to choose that set of options he or she thinks will maximize his or her utility. The options make each employee better off without making the employer worse off—just the kind of Pareto improvement that drives the libertarian view of contract law.

From the employee side, the initial response is that there is no conflict of interest between the two parties so that the firm (note, not the state) setting the default term to help the worker also indirectly benefits the employer by increasing the worker gains of the package. We should therefore not expect to see the same reaction to default terms if the employer wrote as follows: "Frankly, I don't care how you handle your retirement. I had to pick an allocation as a default, and this is the one that my six-year-old child picked out of the hat. Use it at your own risk." One reason these defaults are sticky is that workers with limited financial sophistication treat the default provision as implicit advice, which they trust enough to avoid the expense and delay of hiring an independent adviser. But the same result does not attach, when the question is whether, for example, the employment contract allows for dismissal at will or only for cause (see Epstein 1984; for a different view, see Sunstein 2001). This default is decidedly not sticky because employers have a huge stake in the outcome, and go to enormous lengths to reverse it. To anyone who runs a business, the for-cause rule, however delicately phrased, creates a civil service–like environment that destroys the adaptability and efficiency of the operation. Firms may in some cases give contracts for particular terms. There are no generalizations here. Some defaults are sticky, and others are not, and the ones that are not sticky are those that are at war with the long-term interests of the side empowered to change them.

Social Security: Its Public Choice and Cognitive Dimensions

As indicated, a second critical area associated with employment relations involves the design of workers' pension funds. The behavioral critique suggests that it often makes good sense for employers to insist that workers set aside some fraction of their income for their old age in light of the familiar cognitive biases (for a summary, see chapter 10). This approach hardly counts as news because many employers, including the University of Chicago, have long required employees to contribute to their pension funds. Employers do not want to be in the position of having a destitute employee begging for a hand-out in his or her retirement. The deal is accepted on the other side because most workers do not of course wish to be destitute. That result here is sensible on both sides, and does not count as a form of state paternalism, either strong or weak. It reflects instead a sensible judgment on risk allocation, done privately.

That system is likely to show more sophistication than any public plan, which by definition cannot take into account the variations across different groups of employees. The University of Chicago, for example, runs two systems. The first is a defined benefit plan for staff, which places the risk of market fluctuations largely on the university. There is also a defined contribution plan for faculty and senior staff, who can choose the mix of debt and equity and then take the risk of good or bad performance. The default recommendation is a fifty-fifty split, which may well be too conservative for younger faculty members even if sensible for older ones. The defined contribution plan is fully funded so that there is no element of cross-subsidy among individuals. Also, because it is instantly vested, it allows for the movement of faculty among universities, thus avoiding the anticompetitive lock-in of defined benefit plans. There is every reason to think that both halves of this program do fairly well. Many people simply follow the university's lead. As pensions get larger with age, more faculty members take advantage of a financial adviser to plan an integrated portfolio. But there are no collective decisions. Employees make their own decisions. I have little doubt that most private employers follow this strategy, in which the center takes into account the strengths and limitations of individual employees, as a sensible theory of firm rationality requires.

In contrast, Social Security offers its own distinctive and highly paternalistic pension system. It is frequently the only source of retirement income available to workers with limited means. Once the government takes its mandatory cut from earnings, it usually does not make sense for low-income workers to put additional funds aside in the face of so many short-term needs. A good libertarian paternalist should have been against the creation of Social Security at the outset. (No one can favor its abolition after it has created so many expectations for nearly seventy years.) It is the design of Social Security that gives rise to so much unease today, now that the question of major reform is on the table. President Bush has proposed scuttling the older system of pay-as-you-go financing in favor of individual Social Security accounts that introduce an increased level of individual responsibility that often approaches that found in employer pension plans or individual retirement accounts.

This portion of the program, which has run into stony resistance from both Republicans and Democrats alike, raises the issue of whether ordinary individuals, if left to their own devices, could make wise savings decisions. On this question, it is instructive to look at the findings from Sweden with respect to its privatization decision. The Swedish system was organized along lines that maximized entry and free choice. As described by Henrik Cronqvist and Richard Thaler, Sweden's default plan operated on a balanced portfolio of stocks and bonds, and domestic and foreign companies (2004). Individuals were, however, allowed to depart from that plan in favor of others offering different mixes. A massive advertisement campaign advised potential plan members of the alternatives. Private firms were allowed to advertise for business, but the default fund was not. As might be expected, about two-thirds of the enrollees fled the default plan to others that offered a higher percentage of equity, with more Swedish and tech stocks. These investment choices were made just before the tech downturn. The default fund declined by about 30 percent and the chosen funds did even worse, declining by close to 40 percent (Cronqvist and Thaler 2004, 427). In the second round of enrollments by young people, the behavior reversed, so that only 8.5 percent of the workers took the personalized options.

This proposal clearly has implications for the Bush proposal to privatize funds, and Cronqvist and Thaler draw two conclusions from the data. The first, with which everyone can heartily agree, is that "the devil is in the details" (2004, 427). The second, which is more debatable, is that "markets can actually increase the biases individuals display in nonmarket settings" (428). In this case, the first item draws the second into question, because it is subject to an alternative interpretation that undercuts the substantive claim. Consider these points.

- Even though entry was free under the program, the system deviated from a market in two important ways. The extensive campaign to urge individuals to exercise their default options is not part of any market system. That subsidy can distort preferences by giving only one side of the case. In addition, the default fund was precluded from advertising, which also counts as a deviation from market principles. The combined effect of these two maneuvers is to increase the rate of shifts, which, ironically, shows how some defaults can become unglued by consistent effort.

- Second, the responses in the period after the tech downturn showed a huge reduction in the number of people shifting out of the default fund, which has to be in part a response to the poor performance of the specialized funds in the original go-round. This suggests that at least some learning takes place in the open market setting, even for the new entrants into the labor force who in all likelihood are somewhat less sophisticated than their elders.

- Third, the Swedish plan did not make use of any professional intermediaries to guide individuals in their investments, which might have slowed the flight from either the default option or similar funds.

The proper understanding of these cases has important consequences. Cronqvist and Thaler, by reading so much into their findings, seem to suggest that investors would make better choices if they were limited to a small number of firms—three, with different levels of risk, or even one fund. If this restriction is imposed by the state, however, it creates a serious monopoly problem at the other end. Nor is there any reason to legislate the point that no consumer can get started by choosing among an incredible array of funds. Charles Schwab has figured it out. Its *Wall Street Journal* advertisement of July 13, 2005, on the editorial page at A15 reads: "There are 17,000 mutual funds out there. How about the 7 that are right for me? Talk to Chuck." Many people invest in retirement through mutual funds right now, and by talking to folks like Chuck they reduce their relevant market in just this fashion. The central lesson from this exercise, however, is that the cognitive difficulties in fund selection are a small part of the problem, assuming it is a problem.

There could be a requirement for an intermediary; or the government could even impose limits on the percentage of assets that could be invested in stocks rather than bonds, and prohibit certain kinds of investments altogether. A suitable form of guidance might be the restrictions that private pension plans impose on their participants. At this point, there is no harm, and perhaps some benefit, from learning from the studies about the mistakes that ordinary individuals make in handling their pensions.

Yet make no mistake about it. The true difficulties with these plans stem not from the cognitive shortfalls of plan participants, but from the basic design of the Social Security program that weaves together so many strands of redistribution that it becomes impossible politically to work out any sensible system of adjustment even in the face of undisputed knowledge of the long-term instability of the program. At a guess, these cognitive errors may account for 5 percent of the problem. The embedded public choice dynamics (which require no experiments to verify) account, alas, for the rest.

To see why, it is useful to back up and give a brief account of the fatal government decisions that gave rise to the justified current anxiety over the long-term soundness of the system. In this regard, recall that Social Security represents not a weak form of default paternalism, but a strong form of mandatory contribution into a government plan called "a social compact between generations." Although the point is not explicitly always mentioned, it is the strong form of paternalism, spurred on by generic beliefs of employee incompetence, that gave rise to the current situation in the first place. As noted earlier, paternalism that overrides voluntary choice is driven in large part by the desire to mask redistribution of wealth by invoking the need to protect individuals against their own weakness of intellect and will. Don't believe a word of it. If the second goal were the only objective of Social Security, then the system could have followed the strategy of many voluntary plans, mentioned earlier, that requires contributions into individual accounts. If it is thought that many cannot be trusted to decide which investments to make, all that is needed is to limit the kinds of investment vehicles that individuals could choose for their accounts: all bonds, some maximum amount of stock, and so on.

Most critically, the creation of separate accounts from day one might have provided an iron barrier against redistribution across individuals. Yet two elements of massive redistribution of wealth were a central part of Social Security from the outset. The first is between generations. The Roosevelt administration thought that it had a Depression-size problem with an ever-larger number of individuals near or over sixty-five years of age. Any system of individual accounts might provide a sound fiscal foundation for those, say, under forty, but would not solve the short-term problem. A political solution might have funded the transfers to the over-sixty-five out of general revenues, requiring everyone else to invest in individual plans with or without mandated benefit structures. In time the initial generation would have died off and the system would have returned to solvency, but not until a huge and explicit transfer system had been on the books for years. The Social Security system as implemented allowed redistribution and paternalism to work arm-and-arm without the transparency that would have rendered it subject to political opposition.

The second form of redistribution is within generations. The designers of Social Security took it as axiomatic that lower-income workers should receive pensions that were a larger fraction of their covered wages than higher-income workers. The upshot was a systematic effort to shift wealth from the top to the bottom of the income scale. The scheme itself is not capable of easy realization if higher-income workers have longer lives, and the position of one worker may tell us little about the next, but that too is part of the overall system. The more complex the system of covert redistribution, the harder it is to root it out by any corrective measures, as the present inconclusive debate over Social Security makes clear.

The die is now cast, however, and for reasons that have nothing to do with the usual behavioral-economics list of cognitive biases. The crux of the difficulty is that the social contract across and within generations has created indefinite rights and duties for all participants within the system. All the profound forces in a public choice universe were unleashed on the system as the current generations of recipients, seniors with prime political influence, pushed to expand the benefits of Social Security so that these exceed the amounts their past contributions to the program could fund. The earlier generations did very well relative to their contributions, but this "compact between generations" will not yield future generations anything like the rate of return their grandparents enjoyed. Unless something is done to alter the balance, the higher benefits, longer life expectancy, and lower birthrates will eventually bring the system down. The most recent report of the Trustees of the Social Security System calculates that the fund will start to draw down its reserves in 2018, and will be unable to meet its obligations by 2042 (U.S. Social Security Administration 2004). Yet any efforts to make across-the-board cuts in the program are met with further objections that they are unfair to one or another cohort, rich or poor, of today's recipients.

Some method has to be found to deal with the accumulated debt to both present and future recipients. In principle, that debt is not binding on anyone and could be cut with a stroke of the pen (Flemming v. Nestor, 363 U.S. 603, 1960). But the want of legal protection does not matter much in this context. As a political matter, these obligations are beyond wholesale repudiation, and it is an open question whether they can be even trimmed without the consent of the current beneficiaries. But because the ownership structure in Social Security is wholly diffuse, the system does not have to make peace between a single lender and borrower, but rather between today's 55 million beneficiaries and the 110 million or so now paying into the system.

The initial, now apparently abandoned, Bush proposal to deal with this situation included privatizing Social Security, so that in the long-term the implicit cross-subsidies of the current plan would be removed. But Bush and everyone else was aware that no system of privatization could remove the accumulated overhang of unfunded obligations generated under the current policy. If all we did was make the contributions private from here on out, the Social Security payments of today's workers would not be available to fund the present political promises. General revenue in the trillions of dollars would be needed to deal with the overhang, which in 2005 terms on best assumptions is about $3.7 trillion (U.S. Social Security Administration 2004, n. 40, at 10). Yet it is also an open question how the basic tax structure should be altered over time and within given years to fund that deficit, especially when there is little agreement on how progressive that system ought to be. It is not cognitive bias or error in some intertemporal dimension that has threatened the system but rather the indefinite nature of the property rights that first created excessive benefits to people who are now dead, and now invites massive political struggle. Accordingly, the relevant set of insights on this question comes from the literatures that deal with public choice in systems of weak property rights, not of behavioral finance. Far more accurate accounts of the order of the battle will come from a naïve view of perfect rationality of the interest group players than any discussion of time horizons, hyperdiscounting, or the other behavioral apparatus.

The initial verdict therefore is that this peculiar system of long-term paternalism has been a profound failure because of its inability to generate a stable long-term equilibrium. The extent to which the system deviates from any system of rational planning is apparent from even the most cursory inspection of the basic terms of the Social Security benefit structure, whose purposive opacity cannot be regarded as user-friendly to ordinary citizens. The benchmarks here are the voluntary pension plans that employers use for their employees and that individuals use for their private accounts. In each of these cases, there is no nominal compact across the generations, which means that one group is not able to take from another. The money can be pooled and the investments diversified without any covert redistribution. Because these property rights are well-defined, they do not set the stage for anything like the protracted struggles over Social Security, which explains why the Bush plan hopes to use them as a model.

Yet the difficulties with Social Security don't stop here. Even if we ignore the long-term debt the system has created, we can see the anomalies that only a political body could devise. The benefits are fully vested after one earns forty credits. Each credit comes from earnings of $920 of wages or self-employment income per calendar quarter. There is a maximum of four quarters per year, such that some benefits for a given year start to kick in at $3,680, a figure that all full-time workers achieve. Presently, the tax base for the plan reaches all wages up to $90,000. The range of benefits, however, does not track the dispersion in compensation. Thus, for workers who have worked thirty years before retirement, the maximum payment is $1,939 per month, and the minimum is somewhat more than half that, at $984.60 (U.S. Social Security Administration 2005). The total amounts are further skewed because it does not matter when these credits are accrued, so that persons who participate in the workforce from age twenty-five to thirty-five are in the same boat as those who work between age fifty-five and sixty-five. Indeed, it seems clear that there is a huge rate of return to all workers for their initial contributions into the plan, which drops precipitately thereafter (for the precise curve, see chapter 10 in this volume). But none of these switches are apparent for the firm. Generally speaking, present value calculations take a back seat to more political concerns. The issue is further complicated by arcane rules that determine whether persons are better off taking their benefits as a primary beneficiary or accepting spousal benefits, when they cannot accumulate both. For persons within the same age cohort there is a crazy-quilt pattern of redistribution that is exceedingly hard to identify, let alone undo, now that it has embedded for seventy years.

The situation gets no clearer on the benefit side. The full age retirement benefit will move from being available at sixty-five for people born in 1937 or earlier to being available at sixty-seven for those born after 1960. But note that there is no increase in the retirement age for those born in the twelve years between 1943 and 1954, which was clearly a sop to a dominant political generation. And the level of benefits available is not transparent. Some of the small oddities are that the schedules in question are given in monthly rather than yearly figures (which may confuse some), that mortality risks are not factored into the situation, and that the projected increases in benefits are not included in the table (see chapter 10). Nor, most critically, does anyone have any idea of the present value of their contributions to the plan, as they would with the ordinary TIAA-CREF program (see chapter 10; the present value of future contributions is not subject to reduction for future tax contributions). Nor is any reference made to the present value of the future tax contributions, which is so critical to people in the early stages of the program. In addition, the forms give little guidance to participants as they approach retirement age. People who can retire with full benefits at age sixty-five can take a 20 percent reduction at age sixty-two; 13.33 percent reduction at age sixty-three, or 6.66 percent reduction at age sixty-four. There is no statement, however, that in present value terms these benefit packages are equal in value to retiring with full benefits, and no effort to break that determination out for subpopulations, such as men and women. The only way, therefore, to make sense of what to do is to get independent advice, even on the simple question of valuation.

Nor is the standard statement any better in providing rates of return. The individual statements prepared for each Social Security recipient dutifully list the years and amounts of contributions but do not indicate any of three figures: what the total contributions would be worth if compounded at various rates of interest, the present value of the various benefit packages under Social Security, or the value of a private plan that could be purchased with the same funds. The best conclusion is that the system of paternalism persists only because the information it supplies is not in usable form for determining the soundness of the program, even if it does give some information as to the amount of money that will be received under various options (see also McCaffery and Baron 2005, 15–18, n. 15). The clear inference is that the original designers built in the ambiguities to make it more difficult to unravel the plan down the road. On this point at least, it seems as if they were right.

What is striking about behavioral financial economics is that it is silent on these questions. In the midst of all the talk about libertarian paternalism, it would be useful to know whether defenders of that approach approve or denounce the hard paternalistic policies that led to the current state of affairs for the high level of covert redistribution that no voluntary plan could tolerate. There is little question, however, that if anyone were given the option to leave the program they should take it to escape the inherited debt that is buried in the plan.

On this view, the question of how to run a privatized system is strictly second order. The first point is that only limited sums can go into that program given the need to fund the accumulated debt. The other points have to do with the transitional issues, and it is here where the imperfect rationality of individual deciders has to leave everyone uneasy about private accounts. The best way to handle this is through employment or expansion of existing IRAs. Neither, however, seems to be part of the current proposal for individual accounts governed by their own rules, many of which are intended to limit the investment choices of ordinary individuals in ways not replicated in private plans—by requiring minimum percentages in fixed-income securities, for example. That effort to limit the options to a manageable number makes some sense, but is typically undertaken by private individuals who deal at most with one or two mutual funds for exactly the same reason. The behavioral economics thus recommends what sensible people would do anyhow, but cannot soften the abrupt transition that might have to be made to accommodate the original structural errors built into the Social Security system. To put matters in perspective, its suggestions deal with the $100 billion problem, relative to the $3.7 trillion deficit that is best explained in public choice terms. But not to worry: it seems as of this writing—referencing Richard W. Stevenson's *New York Times* article "Many Hurdles for Bush Plan" of March 2, 2005—that any such transition will be made in light of the sensible public anxiety that people have over a plan whose complexity they cannot fully understand. The blunt truth is that hard-line paternalism gets us into messes that no set of default rules and plan limitations can solve.

Conclusion

My goal here has been to explore the limitations and uses of both the hard rational choice model and the behavioral alternatives. The former is wrong on descriptive grounds insofar as it postulates relentless forms of self-interest by rational actors that never make any calculation mistakes. But for all its weakness it does suggest a level of aspiration that people have in discharging particular tasks. Hence the rational choice approach will always be indispensable for understanding social institutions, and for individuals who act in many arms-length legal transactions. Unless we know how the perfect models work, we cannot indicate the directions in which flawed people will move as their conduct becomes more rational, either through selection, training, or experience.

These rational choice models, however, are deficient insofar as they overlook the pervasive role that mistakes have in ordinary decision making by individuals of limited capacity. Those errors are, as the experimental literature demonstrates, most likely to lead to mischief when isolated individuals are required to make choices on the strength of their limited abilities. At this point it is possible to explain the importance of voluntary exchange and market institutions as a means to allow individuals with limited competence to acquire at a price education and assistance that reduces the frequency and severity of errors that they make. To understand how these transactions take place when some cognitive errors are the background norm, we need to develop a model of second-order rationality that starts with the natural variation in levels of competence in all populations. Rationality within this context does not assume that individuals never make mistakes, but that these ordinary businesses and social groupings will sort individuals in ways that take advantage of their differential competences and abilities. This account of rationality is not refuted by any demonstration that people make all sorts of cognitive errors: quite the opposite, the model requires that these errors persist, for otherwise there is nothing for people to correct by learning or assistances. All that second-order rationality requires is that people have some understanding of these weaknesses and seek to minimize their consequences.

In this type of setting, freedom of contract works best as a device that leads to incremental improvements. That legal regime cannot be defended on the grounds that it generates instantaneous perfection. It does, however, suggest that we should greet the ambiguous proposals for a libertarian paternalist regime with a healthy dose of caution. Many of its more sensible default proposals are those which savvy employers could initiate on their own by sound management techniques without adding the dramatic element that the oxymoron of libertarian paternalism raises. But whatever we think of these modest interventions, further dangers lurk when these default terms are set in ways that conflict with standard business practices. If libertarian paternalism requires firms to offer for-cause contracts as defaults, it is unwise because it misapprehends how the workplace operates and thus drives people to inefficient arrangements. By refusing to allow an employer to opt out, the position hardly counts as libertarian, but is mischievously paternalist and authoritarian. And as to clear government mandates that neither employer nor employee can negate, of which Social Security counts as one, the hard paternalism that appeals to many cognitive psychologists should be condemned because it breeds opaque and crazy-quilt patterns of redistribution that should make us pine for a regime of free choice on pensions. One hopes that any qualified use of behavioral economics is accompanied by a full-throated attack on the forms of hard paternalism that have worked so much harm in such critical areas as Social Security, where it is far harder to disentangle the mess seventy years into the program than it would have been to stop it dead in its tracks seventy years ago. Cognitive psychology and behavioral economics have much to say about the decision-making processes of individuals, but much less about the proper organization of market institutions.

I should like to thank Ed McCaffery for pushing me to do more work on this paper, and to an anonymous referee who suggested important sources to review, and new lines of argument to examine. My heartfelt thanks to Rachel Kovner, Stanford Law School, Class of 2006, for her rapid and accurate research assistance on the multiple iterations of this project.

Notes

1. "Now everyone more or less agrees that rational behavior simply implies consistent maximization of a well ordered function, such as a utility or a profit function."

2. The Sunstein book review acknowledges the difference: "The second part [of the book], called New Theoretical Directions, discusses the role of emotions and affect, support theory, and alternative perspectives on heuristics. This discussion includes the view, set forth most prominently by Gerd Gigerenzer, that outside the laboratory, our 'fast and frugal' heuristics work very well" (Sunstein 2003, 753–54). But the title of the review, *Hazardous Heuristics*, reveals his emphasis.

3. "Subjects consistently failed to achieve accuracy levels commensurate with their expressed levels of confidence. Mean confidence for predictions based on interviews or on long-standing contact with a roommate ranged from about 75% to 78% across the five studies, whereas mean accuracy rates ranged from 60% to 68%" (citation omitted). All the experiments asked yes/no questions, so that a score of 50 percent is what is expected at random (Dunning et al. 1990, 572).

4. Thus the typical limits for credit cards reach, as of 2001, $35,000 for individuals with income in the top quintile, and about $5,000 for individuals in the bottom quintile (Survey of Consumer Finances, 1970 to 2001).

5. The title—*Blink: The Power of Thinking Without Thinking*—makes it appear that intuition dominates across the board, when in fact the protocols that he reports and endorses are often intended to block the use of intuition.

6. Here is but one example: "Consumers tend to underestimate the likelihood of adverse events that might necessitate borrowing" (Bar-Gill 2004, 1375n2).

7. The same issue is now before the Supreme Court. Independent Ink Co. v. Illinois Tool Works, 396 F.3d 1342 (Fed. Cir. 2005), cert. granted, 2005 U.S. Lexis 4860 (U.S., June 20, 2005) (No. 04-1196). Once again the suit is brought by a rival supplier of ink, and not by any consumer alleging myopia in purchase. Note in this case the market for printers and toners was supplied by five firms, all of whom had patent protection for the printers. The question in the case was whether the patents established a presumption of market power under the law of tie-ins. The proper answer is they do not when the patents compete in the overall market. Here is a case where the losses to the excluded parties do not track the social losses from the marketing practices. Myopia will have little or no role in this case.

8. My thanks to Gregg Bloche for this reference.

9. See Chase Home Finance (2005). Information is not an issue in these markets.

10. Barberis and Thaler note that the key tenets of behavioral financial economics are the inability of arbitrage to work in many markets and the usual list of cognitive biases. The former point is not a behavioral contribution, but is consistent with traditional rational choice analysis. The second plays little role in the overall analysis. Certainly, the arbitrage possibilities for fixed rate paper seem strong indeed, and these rates are so boring in their structure as to make behavioral explanations remotely plausible (2003, note 12). The entire theory suffers an additional weakness in its treatment of so-

called "noise" traders. It does not explain how many of these traders operate in a market dominated by institutional players who seem ill-fitted for the role, and gives no indication as to why these individuals should all deviate from the sound principles in the same direction. Yet if their numbers are small, and their trading patterns random, arbitrageurs should have a better chance in countering noise traders' influence. Magnitudes matter.

11. For one runaway best seller on this point, see Jim Collins (2001).

12. "It is now clear that if an employer requires employees to make an affirmative election in favor of savings, with the default rule devoting 100 percent of wages to current income, the level of savings will be far lower than if the employer adopts an automatic enrollment program from which employees are freely permitted to opt out." See also chapter 11. In addition, to showing the importance of the defaults that the firm sets, the authors note that savings may well be reduced by distributing accumulated savings of less than $5,000 on plan termination. One query here. There is no reason to think that all savings work through tax-free plans. Paying down mortgages is also a form of savings that takes place outside the retirement fund system. When all increments to net worth are taken into account, the conclusion of systematic undersavings is less clear than this literature supposes (see Scholz, Seshadri and Khitatrakun 2004, note 4).

13. The procedural safeguards for the workers were held strict conditions precedent for the settlement in Oubre v. Entergy Operations, Inc., 522 U.S. 422 (1998).

References

Age Discrimination in Employment Act. 1967. *Public Law 90-202, U.S. Statutes at Large* 104: 983, U.S.Code 29 §§ 621–633a.

Aristotle. 1941. *Politics*, Book II. *The Basic Works of Aristotle*, edited by Richard McKeon, translated by Benjamin Jowett. New York: Random House.

Barberis, Nicholas, and Richard Thaler. 2003. *"A Survey of Behavioral Finance."* In *Handbook of the Economics of Finance*, edited by George M. Constantinides, Milton Harris, and Rene Stultz. Amsterdam and Boston: Elsevier/North-Holland.

Bar-Gill, Oren. 2004. "Seduction by Plastic." *Northwestern University Law Review* 98(4): 1373–1434.

Becker, Gary S. 1962. "Irrational Behavior and Economic Theory." *Journal of Political Economy* 70(1): 1–13.

———. 1976. *The Economic Approach to Human Behavior.* Chicago: University of Chicago Press.

Chase Bank. 2005. Chase Home Finance, Home Mortgages. New York: JPMorgan Chase & Co. Available at: http://mortgage02.chase.com/pages/shared/gateway.jsp (accessed September 22, 2005).

Chi, Michelene T. H. 1978. "Knowledge Structures and Memory Development." In *Children's Thinking: What Develops?* edited by Robert Siegler. Hillsdale, N.J.: Erlbaum Associates.

Chi, Michelene T. H., Robert Glaser, and Ernest Rees. 1982. "Expertise in Problem

Solving." In *Advances in the Psychology of Human Intelligence,* vol. 1., edited by Robert J. Sternberg. Hillsdale, N.J.: Erlbaum.

Coase, Ronald H. 1960. "The Problem of Social Cost." *Journal of Law and Economics* 3(October): 1–44.

Collins, Jim. 2001. *Good to Great: Why Some Companies Make the Leap . . . And Others Don't.* New York: Harper Business.

Cronqvist, Henrik, and Richard H. Thaler. 2004. "Design Choices in Privatized Social-Security Systems." *American Economic Review* 94(2): 424–28.

Diamond, Peter A., and Peter R. Orszag. 2004. *Saving Social Security: A Balanced Approach.* Washington, D.C.: Brookings Institution.

Dunning, David, David W. Griffin, James Milojkovic, and Lee Ross. 1990. "The Overconfidence Effect in Social Prediction." *Journal of Personality and Social Psychology* 58(4): 568–92.

Epstein, Richard A. 1984. "In Defense of the Contract at Will." *University of Chicago Law Review* 51: 947–82.

———. 1985. *Takings: Private Property and the Power of Eminent Domain.* Cambridge, Mass.: Harvard University Press.

———. 1995. *Simple Rules for a Complex World.* Cambridge, Mass.: Harvard University Press.

———. 1998. *Principles for a Free Society: Reconciling Individual Liberty with the Common Good.* Reading, Mass.: Perseus Books.

———. 2003. *Skepticism and Freedom: A Modern Case for Classical Liberalism.* Chicago: University of Chicago Press.

Frederick, Shane, George Loewenstein, and Ted O'Donoghue. 2004. "Time Discounting and Time Preference: A Critical Review." In *Advances in Behavioral Economics,* edited by Colin F. Camerer, George Loewenstein, and Matthew Rabin. New York and Princeton, N.J.: Russell Sage Foundation and Princeton University Press.

Gigerenzer, Gerd, Peter M. Todd, and the ABC Research Group. 1999. *Simple Heuristics That Make Us Smart.* Oxford: Oxford University Press.

Gladwell, Malcolm. 2005. *Blink: The Power of Thinking Without Thinking.* New York and Boston: Little, Brown.

Hardin, Garrett. 1968. "The Tragedy of the Commons." *Science* 162(3859): 1243–48.

———. 1982. *Collective Action.* Baltimore: Johns Hopkins University Press.

Jolls, Christine, Cass R. Sunstein, and Richard Thaler. 1998. "A Behavioral Approach to Law and Economics." *Stanford Law Review* 50(5): 1471–1550.

Kahneman, Daniel, Paul Slovic, and Amos Tversky. 1982. *Judgment under Uncertainty.* Cambridge and New York: Cambridge University Press.

Kahneman, Daniel, and Amos Tversky. 1979. "Prospect Theory: An Analysis of Decision Under Risk." *Econometrica* 47(2): 263–92.

Kruger, Justin, and David Dunning. 1999. "Unskilled and Unaware of It: How Difficulties in Recognizing One's Own Incompetence Lead to Inflated Self-Assessments." *Journal of Personality and Social Psychology* 77(6): 1121.

McCaffery, Edward J., and Jonathan Baron. 2005. "Thinking About Tax." Unpublished electronic manuscript. Available at: http://www.psych.upenn.edu/~baron/253/thinking.pdf (accessed November 9, 2005).

Scholz, John Karl, Ananth Seshadri and Surachai Khitatrakun. 2004. Are Americans Saving "Optimally" for Retirement? NBER Working Paper 10260. Cambridge, Mass.: National Bureau of Economic Research.

Simon, Herbert A. 1955. "A Behavioral Model of Rational Choice." *Quarterly Journal of Economics* 69(1): 99–118.

U.S. Social Security Administration. 2004. *Annual Report of the Board of Trustees of the Federal Old-Age and Survivors Insurance and Disability Insurance Trusts Funds.* Washington, D.C.: Government Printing Office.

———. 2005. *Special Minimum Benefits.* Washington, D.C.: Government Printing Office. Available at: http://www.ssa.gov/cgi-bin/smt.cgi (accessed September 22, 2005).

Sunstein, Cass R. 2001. "Human Behavior and the Law of Work." *Virginia Law Review* 87(2): 205–76.

———. 2003. *"Hazardous Heuristics."* A review of *Heuristics and Biases: The Psychology of Intuitive Judgment,* edited by Thomas Gilovich, Dale Griffin, and Daniel Kahneman. *University of Chicago Law Review* 70(2): 751–82.

Sunstein, Cass R., and Richard H. Thaler. 2003. "Libertarian Paternalism Is Not an Oxymoron." *University of Chicago Law Review* 70(4): 1159–1202.

Tversky, Amos, and Daniel Kahneman. 1982. "Judgment Under Uncertainty: Heuristics and Biases." In *Judgment Under Uncertainty,* edited by Daniel Kahneman, Paul Slovic, and Amos Tversky. Cambridge and New York: Cambridge University Press.

Index

Boldface numbers refer to figures and tables.

consumer credit, 128

consumer sovereignty principle, 3, 6, 13

consumption: decoupling from payments, 148, 151, 156; enjoyability of, 148; improving-sequence preference, 142–43, 152–53; and income patterns, 144; in lumps, 143–44, 145, 147, 152; using tax refunds, 79n12, 144, 156–57; when income is not rising, 146

consumption taxes, 127

contracts, 221, 228–29n16, 362, 371–72, 385

cooperation, 27n13, 218, 220, 227, 255n7

corporate income taxes, 11, 39

Cosmides, L., 223

Cowell, F., 27n12, 178, 228n6

credit cards, 322, 355–56, 358, 386n4

Cronqvist, H., 338, 348n25, 377–78

Cronshaw, M., 219

cross-country comparison, of VAT tax compliance, 175

cross-subsidies, 96

crowding out hypothesis, 10

Cuccia, A., 215, 228n16

cultural issues, of tax compliance, 219–20

Cummings, R., 219

Customs and Excise, 181, 182, 183

Deci, E., 114

decision making: behavioral defects in, 238–39; and discussions with others, 126; mistakes in, 154–57, 359, 360–62, 384–85; prospect theory, 244; rationalization in, 117; transfer of responsibility, 362

decoupling: of consumption, 148, 151, 156; of tax payments, 162

deductions, tax, 89–96, 109

default options: employers' resistance to, 375–76; 401(k) plans, 306, 309–10, 312, 314–16, 320, 337, 338, 339–40, 347n12; as intervention for misprediction of utility, 128; and paternalism, 373–75; stickiness of, 376

defense, 99

defined benefit pension plans, 304, 376

defined contribution pension plans, 304, 333, 376–77. *See also* 401(k) savings plans

democracies, 123–24, 125, 131

Dhami, S., 17, 27n11

Diamond, P., 271

dictator game, 34

dictators, omniscient benevolent, 122–23

disability benefits, 264, 270, 281–82, 300n23

disaggregation bias, 8–9, 86, 100, 101, 109

discounted utility (DU), 153

double-loop learning, 120

driving ability, overconfidence in, 53

Dubin, J., 214

Dunning, D., 360, 361

Duverne, D., 175

Earned Income Tax Credit (EITC), 148–49, 156–57

Economic Growth and Tax Relief Reconciliation Act (EGTRRA) (2001), 320

economic models: behavioral assumptions in, 234–35; of cognitive biases, 58–60; of tax compliance, 176, 177, 207–12, 222; of tax evasion, 233, 235–36

economics: education programs for, 110; focus of, 367

economic students, instrumental rationality of, 244, 248

economists: corruption of, 250; incorporation of cognitive biases, 47–48

education, 11, 110

egoism, 178

EGTRRA (Economic Growth and Tax Relief Reconciliation Act) (2001), 320

Eichenberger, R., 239, 241, 242

Eidjar, O., 177

EITC (Earned Income Tax Credit), 148–49, 156–57